FUNDAMENTALS
OF TRIAL TECHNIQUES

Debra E. Werbel
Deputy Public Defender

FUNDAMENTALS
OF TRIAL TECHNIQUES

Second Edition

THOMAS A. MAUET
Director of Trial Advocacy
and Professor of Law
University of Arizona

Little, Brown and Company
Boston   Toronto

LIBRARY OF CONGRESS CATALOG CARD NO. 87-82336

ISBN 0-316-55093-0

Fourth Printing

MV–NY

Published simultaneously in Canada
by Little, Brown & Company (Canada) Limited

PRINTED IN THE UNITED STATES OF AMERICA

SUMMARY OF CONTENTS

CONTENTS

Contents

III.   OPENING STATEMENTS

IV. DIRECT EXAMINATION

Contents

V. EXHIBITS

VI. CROSS-EXAMINATION

Contents

VII. CLOSING ARGUMENTS

Contents

VIII. OBJECTIONS

FEDERAL RULES OF EVIDENCE (as amended through Oct. 1, 1987)

PREFACE TO THE SECOND EDITION

The best compliment an author of an instructional book can receive is that his work is read and used. The reception of the first edition of this book from trial advocacy teachers, law students, and trial lawyers has been most gratifying.

During the past five years, however, much has happened. First, many trial lawyers, judges, and trial advocacy teachers have passed on numerous suggestions and ideas. Most of them have been incorporated throughout this edition. Second, there has been much psychological and linguistics research conducted during the past few years that relates directly, or can be applied, to jury trials. These studies are mentioned generally at various places in this edition, and several parts of the text have been modified to reflect this research. Third, I have revised several sections. These include jury selection, which now reflects new jury selection methods; the exhibits section, which now incorporates additional material on preparing and presenting courtroom exhibits; and the impeachment section, which has been revised and expanded to give a more integrated overview of this subject.

In general, however, I have kept the format and tone of this edition identical to that of the first. As the saying goes: "If it ain't broke, don't fix it." I've kept this in mind and hope you will be pleased with the result.

Thomas A. Mauet

Tucson, Arizona
January 15, 1988

PREFACE TO THE FIRST EDITION

My experiences as a trial lawyer and trial advocacy teacher have made me realize that the effective trial lawyers always seem to have two complementary abilities. First, they have developed a methodology that thoroughly analyzes and prepares each case for trial. Second, they have acquired the technical skills necessary to present their side of a case persuasively in court. It is the synthesis of both qualities — preparation and execution — that produces effective trial advocacy.

This text approaches trial advocacy the same way. It presents a methodology for trial preparation and reviews the thought processes a trial lawyer should utilize before and during each phase of a trial. In addition, it discusses and gives examples of the technical courtroom skills that must be developed to present evidence and arguments in a persuasive way to the trier of fact. This is done in the firm belief that effective trial advocacy is both an art and a skill, and that while a few trial lawyers may be born, most are made. Artistry becomes possible only when basic skills have become mastered.

In trial work, as in many other fields, there is no "right way" to try cases or "authority" on trial techniques. There are just effective, time-tested methods that are as varied as lawyers are numerous. Consequently, while the text presents standard methods of examining witnesses, introducing exhibits, and making arguments, there are different approaches to all of the tasks involved in trial work. Thus, the examples set forth in the text are not the only way of effectively accomplishing the particular task involved. The text makes use of these examples because inexperienced trial lawyers need concrete, specific examples of effective techniques they can learn and utilize in court. Other effective ways of doing things are necessarily a product of experience, and only through experience will you determine what works best for you.

The emphasis of this text is on jury trials, since a lawyer who can effectively try cases to a jury should also be competent during a bench trial. The examples are principally from personal injury and criminal cases, since they involve easily isolated examples of trial techniques, and they constitute the substantial majority of cases tried to juries. If the methodology and techniques applicable to the uncomplicated, recurring situations presented here are mastered, more complex cases can be handled competently as well.

Several persons were instrumental in the development of this text. I gratefully acknowledge the help of Thomas Geraghty, Professor of Law at Northwestern University, whose extensive analysis and review have influenced almost every page of this text; the Honorable Warren D. Wolfson, Judge of the Circuit Court of Cook County, Illinois, whose initial encouragement and continuous advice were largely responsible for my beginning and completing this text; and my wife, Susan Mauet, who patiently supported this undertaking from its inception. Many sources, of course, have contributed to the development of my ideas and approaches to trial work that are expressed in this text. These include many members of the bar and bench with, against, and before whom I have tried cases, as well as several teaching institutions in which I have been active, particularly the National Institute for Trial Advocacy.

I am also indebted to Fred Lane, Attorney at Law, of Chicago, who first taught me the fundamentals of trial techniques, the Honorable Marvin E. Aspen, Judge of the United States District Court for the Northern District of Illinois, the Honorable Benjamin S. Mackoff and the Honorable Robert J. Collins, both Judges of the Circuit Court of Cook County, Illinois, all of whom contributed significantly to my understanding of trial techniques. Finally, I am indebted to Mary Vezina, who tirelessly typed and edited the numerous drafts of the manuscript.

Thomas A. Mauet

Chicago, Illinois
March 1, 1980

FUNDAMENTALS
OF TRIAL TECHNIQUES

I

PREPARATION FOR TRIAL

§1.1. Introduction

You have just been called into the office of a partner of the litigation firm that recently hired you. The partner tells you that he has a case which will be going to trial soon that seems "just right" for you. Witnesses have been interviewed. Discovery has been completed. Pretrial motions have been filed and ruled on. Settlement negotiations have just collapsed. The case now needs to be tried, and you're the person who will try it. With a smile, the partner hands you the file. Apprehensively, you walk out of his office, thinking: "My God. What do I do now?"

What you do, how you do it, and why you do it is what this book is all about, from beginning to end. This chapter will discuss the all-important first steps: how to organize files, prepare a trial notebook, develop a theory of the case, prepare witnesses for direct examinations, structure the order of proof, and prepare cross-examinations of your opponent's witnesses.

§1.2. Organization of files

Ours is an age of records, and the field of law is no exception. Everything is routinely recorded and duplicated. Even a simple case can, and invariably will, by the time it approaches trial, generate an extensive collection of paperwork. Consequently, all files must be organized, divided, and indexed to provide immediate and accurate access to the contents at any time during trial. The lawyer who is organized will appear prepared, confident, and professional to both the court and jury.

1

Files should usually include the following indexed folder categories:

1. *Court papers.* These should normally be bound in the order filed or entered:
   a. pleadings
   b. discovery
   c. motions and responses
   d. orders
   e. subpoenas
2. *Evidence.* Records should be placed in clear plastic document protectors and have evidence labels attached. While records will depend on the specific case, the following are commonly involved:
   a. bills, statements, and receipts
   b. correspondence between parties
   c. photographs, maps, diagrams
   d. business records
3. *Attorney's records.*
   a. running case history (log of attorney's activities in the case)
   b. retainer contract, bills, costs
   c. correspondence
   d. legal research
   e. miscellaneous

There is no magic in organizing files. Most lawyers have developed their own systems for the types of cases they routinely handle. The important point to remember is that your system must be logical, clearly indexed, and bound whenever possible, so that records can be retrieved quickly and accurately.

§1.3. *Trial notebook*

Trial material should be organized in a way that is most efficiently useful at trial. This is different from organizing case files, discussed above. Each part of a trial — jury selection, opening statements, direct and cross-examinations, and closing arguments — requires separate organization and preparation. Accordingly, paperwork necessarily generated during the preparation of each phase of the trial should be organized in a logical, easily retrievable way.

Two methods, the divider method and trial notebook method, are most commonly used. While ordinarily either of the two methods is used, they can also effectively be used in conjunction, especially in large cases. In such instances the notebook can be used as a working trial notebook which keys into a larger divider system. This is frequently done, particularly in large commercial litigation cases.

1. Divider method

Under this method each part of the trial receives a separate, labeled file divider, which has in it all papers pertinent to that phase of the trial. By merely pulling out the appropriate section, the lawyer has immediately at his disposal all necessary materials.

The advantage of the divider method is that it is usually better suited to a long, complex case when the paperwork is so voluminous it cannot physically be organized and contained in a trial notebook.

The disadvantages are primarily logistical. A divider method is only as reliable as the lawyer maintaining it. If a file is misfiled or its contents misplaced, it cannot be readily located and its utility is eliminated. If more than one lawyer represents a party and shares the files, the possibilities of disruption are much greater.

2. Trial notebook method

Under this method all necessary materials for each part of the trial are placed in a 3-ring notebook in appropriately tabbed sections. The advantages are that once placed in the notebook, the materials cannot be lost or misplaced, and are immediately located simply by turning to the appropriate section.

Notes taken during the trial, such as during the cross-examinations of your witnesses or the direct examinations of your opponent's, should be on letter-sized paper, pre-punched for 3-ring notebooks. (Legal pads of this sort are readily available.) The notes can then be placed in the appropriate section of the trial notebook.

While it should be organized to meet individual lawyers' needs, the notebook system works best when it contains enough tabbed sections to make the contents easily accessible. The following sections are commonly incorporated in trial notebooks:

a. Facts

This section should contain all reports, witness statements, diagrams, charts, and other factual materials. It should also contain a summary sheet which recites the parties, attorneys (address and telephone), the counts of the complaint or indictment, and the essential facts and chronology of events involved.

b. Pleadings

This section should contain the complaint or indictment, answer, and other pleadings of each party to the suit. The pleadings should be in chronological order. If amended pleadings have been filed, only the currently operative pleadings should be here. When pleadings are sufficiently complex, a pleading abstract should be included in this section. Where the indictment or complaint is based on a specific statute, a copy of the statute should also be included. Keeping the elements instructions for the claims and defenses in this section is also useful.

c. Discovery

Included should be the following discovery documents:

1. interrogatories and answers to interrogatories
2. deposition abstracts, cross-indexed to tabbed and marked depositions
3. requests to admit and responses
4. requests to produce and responses
5. other discovery

d. Motions

This section should contain all pretrial motions, responses, and orders that have already been made, as well as any that will be presented prior to or during the trial. It should also contain the pretrial memoranda and final pretrial order.

e. Jury selection

This section should contain:

1. A jury chart to record the basic background information about each juror obtained during the voir dire examination, so that you can review it before deciding which jurors you will challenge. The type of chart or diagram you use depends on how jury selection will be conducted. If a "strike system" is used, each prospective juror in the venire will be questioned before any challenges are made. Under this system you can simply use a legal pad to record the basic information about each juror. If a more traditional system is used, jurors will usually be called into the jury box and only those in the box will be questioned. As challenges are made and prospective jurors are excused, others will replace them. Under this system it is obviously necessary to develop a system that keeps track of the jurors in the box. Most lawyers use a jury box diagram to record the jurors' names and backgrounds. When a challenge is exercised, simply put a large "P" (plaintiff), "D" (defendant) or "C" (cause) through the appropriate box to record which party exercised the peremptory challenge or if it was for cause.

Example (jury chart):

The diagram will cover most of a page. Then simply write down the basic background information of each juror in the appropriate box during the voir dire examination, as demonstrated below.

John Doe — 40 — carpenter — self-emp. 10 yrs. — 3C in grade school — W part-time book-keeper 15 yrs. — owns home Chicago, N. side — 2 yrs. army

2. A checklist for questions, if counsel conduct the voir dire examination in whole or in part.

3. A list of questions you want the court to ask, if the court does part or all of the voir dire examination.

4. A list that keeps track of the challenges exercised by each party.

f. Charts

This section should contain the following lists and charts, which can easily be made on standardized forms:

1. Witness list, showing each witness' name, home address and telephone, work address and telephone, a short synopsis of his testimony and other information necessary to locating and scheduling him during the trial. If the list is long, it is useful to put it in alphabetical order.

Example (witness list):

Frank Miller	accountant who
123 North, Chicago — (works at home)	prepared defendant's tax
H (312) 888-1123 W (same)	returns

Mrs. Sharon Jones	bookkeeper at
2300 N. Clark, Chicago, (works 8-12)	defendant's company
H (312) 888-9876 W (312) 726-8231	

H ( )   W ( )

2. An exhibit chart for your party as well as all other parties showing the exhibit number, exhibit description, and boxes to check if exhibit was offered, admitted, refused, reserved, or withdrawn.

Example (exhibit chart — plaintiff):

#	*Exhibits marked for identification*	*Offered*	*Admitted*	*Refused*	*Reserved*	*Withdrawn*
1	Construction contract	x	x			
2	Final payment check	x		x		
3a-g	Monthly progress reports (7)	x	x			

3.   A trial chart showing each element of each claim or defense and the witnesses and exhibits that will prove each required element.

Example (trial chart — plaintiff):

Elements of claim (Count I — Contract)	*Witnesses and exhibits*
1. Contract made	1. Contract (Pl. Ex. #1)

2. Def. executed contract	2. (a) Answer to complaint
	      (b) Def. admission in
	              deposition

3. Pl. performed	3. Pl. testimony
4. Def. breached contract	4. Pl. testimony

5. Pl. damages	5. (a) Pl. testimony
	      (b) Contractor who com-
	              pleted job
	      (c) Checks (Pl. Ex. #4)
	      (d) Records (Pl. Ex. #6)

g.   *Direct examinations (your case in chief)*

Each witness you intend to call in your case should have his direct examination outlined on a separate sheet. The witness sheets should reflect what exhibits the witness will qualify and the location of all prior statements.

When completed, the witness sheets can then be arranged in the same order as the order of proof. In this way putting on your case in chief simply becomes a matter of calling the witnesses according to their witness sheets. Cross-examination notes should be made on paper prepunched for 3-ring binders so that they can then easily be put in the notebook behind the witness sheet for each witness.

Example:

(See example, pp. 14-15.)

h.   *Cross-examinations (opponent's case)*

Each witness that you anticipate your opponent will call should have a witness sheet outlining the cross-examination you plan to conduct. The outline should be placed on one side of the page so you can make brief notes during the direct examination on the other side. The outline should show the location of all prior statements that might be used during the cross-examination.

Example:

(See example, p. 16.)

i. Closing arguments

The closing arguments section should initially contain several blank sheets. Throughout the trial, as certain testimony or other ideas arise that you will want to use in closing arguments, simply note them in this section. At the close of the evidence you will probably have several pages of notes that will be useful when you complete the preparation of your closing argument. Your final closing-argument outline, and notes you take during your opponent's closing, should also be kept here.

j. Jury instructions

This section should contain a copy of all the jury instructions you intend to offer at the instruction conference, which is usually held shortly before the closing arguments. Your instructions, of course, should be drafted *before* trial. In civil cases the court will usually require each side to submit proposed jury instructions as part of the pretrial memoranda. This section will also eventually contain the other side's instructions, which the court will rule on. During the conference you can mark each instruction as being given, refused, or withdrawn.

k. Research

This section should contain a copy of trial memoranda, trial briefs, or other legal research on issues that are likely to arise during the course of the trial. It should also contain photocopies of the principal cases and other authority you are relying on, so that you can quote them or give them to the judge if necessary. This is also a convenient place to keep a copy of the Federal Rules of Evidence.

The trial notebook system enables you to locate any necessary information immediately and present your case in a well-organized, professional manner. All paperwork necessary for the trial will be in the notebook, except transcripts and exhibits.

While not necessary in smaller cases, many lawyers have a file divider for each witness containing a copy of every prior statement this witness has made, such as in a police report or deposition. This folder will then contain all statements useable to refresh recollection on direct and to impeach during cross-examination.

§1.4. Theory of the case

Your trial preparations at this point have included organizing the case files, preparing the trial notebook, drafting jury instructions and reviewing the elements of each count, preparing exhibits, and reviewing the probable testimony of all anticipated witnesses. In conjunction with these preparations, you should complete the development of your theory of the case.

It is essential to develop a theory of the case before trial and act in accordance with it throughout the trial itself. A theory of the case is simply your position and approach to all the undisputed and disputed evidence which will be presented at trial. You must integrate the undisputed facts with your version of the disputed facts to create a cohesive, logical position at trial. That position must remain consistent during each phase of the trial. At the conclusion of the trial your position must be the more plausible explanation of "what really happened" to the jury.

How do you go about developing your theory of the case? This requires several analytical steps. First, review the elements of each claim you have brought in the case. This should already have been outlined in your trial chart and appear in the instructions section of your notebook. Second, analyze how you intend to prove each of the required elements through available witnesses and exhibits. Third, analyze the contradictory facts that your opponent has available to determine what facts will be disputed, and what witnesses and exhibits your opponent will probably present to put those facts in issue. Fourth, research all the possible evidentiary problems that arise, so that you will be able to maximize the admissibility of your proof and minimize your opponent's. Finally, review the admissible evidence you and your opponent have on each element of required proof to determine your and your opponent's greatest weaknesses. After these steps have been completed, you should have a realistic grasp of the areas where the admissible evidence is in dispute. This is where the critical contests during trial will be. You must then marshal as much additional evidence as you can, both direct and circumstantial, to bolster any weaknesses you have, as well as attack your opponent's version of the disputed facts. The evidence you present, particularly in your weak, disputed areas, must be internally consistent and corroborative. In the same vein, your attack on your opponent's versions of the disputed facts must be consistent with the position you have taken on them. This process of developing logical, consistent positions on the disputed facts and harmoniously integrating them with the undisputed facts is what trial lawyers call developing a theory of the case.

Failure to develop and present a theory of the case will be immediately apparent to the jury, which will quickly recognize that your examinations of witnesses, both on direct and cross, have no logical and consistent direction, and will easily spot any inconsistencies between your opening statement, examinations of witnesses, and closing arguments. Your opponent will be quick to point this out, or even argue that you don't have any theory of the case at all.

The theory of the case must be developed before the trial begins, because your approach to each phase of the trial is dependent on the theory. Consider the following:

Example:

In a manslaughter case, the evidence will show that the defendant shot her husband. The defendant's statement to the police is that they argued and struggled over a gun, which the defendant grabbed and then used to shoot her husband.

As prosecutor, is your theory:

a. the defendant's statement is untrue, and the defendant shot her unarmed husband because they had gotten in an argument? (sudden passion)
b. the defendant's statement is true, but the defendant was not entitled to use deadly force against an unarmed person? (unreasonable self-defense)

Example:

In an automobile negligence case, the plaintiff pedestrian is struck by defendant's car at an intersection. Some evidence will place the plaintiff within the crosswalk with the walk-light green. Other testimony will show the plaintiff was outside the crosswalk, jaywalking across the intersection.

As plaintiff, is your theory:

a. plaintiff was on the crosswalk and had the right of way? (ordinary negligence)
b. plaintiff was not on the crosswalk but was injured because the defendant could have stopped his car but didn't? (last clear chance)

Example:

In a murder case, the prosecution's evidence will show that following an altercation, the victim was shot by a man some witnesses will identify as the defendant.

As defendant, is your theory:

a. the defendant did not do the shooting? (identification)
b. the defendant did the shooting, but was justified in defending himself? (self-defense)

As you can see, your position on the facts, both disputed and undisputed, must be developed in advance of trial. Each disputed fact must be analyzed and a position taken that is consistent with your theory of the case. Only then can you intelligently select a jury and prepare your opening statement, direct examinations and cross-examinations of witnesses, and closing arguments.

Once your theory of the case is developed, you should perform the same analysis to determine what your opponent's probable theory and position on the disputed facts will be. This will be important when you prepare for cross-examinations of your witnesses and structure the cross-examinations of your opponent's witnesses.

Most trials, where the issues are close, are usually decided on one or two pivotal points. It may be an admissibility issue on a critical exhibit. It may be the impression a crucial witness makes on the jury. It may involve the permissible scope of cross-examination and impeachment. Whatever the issue, thorough trial preparation must include determining what those issues will be during the trial. In short, you must find out where the contests on crucial issues will be, where you want them to be, and when and how you want these issues raised during the trial. Your job as an advocate is to locate these contests and prepare for the critical issues more thoroughly and convincingly than your opponent, so that the hotly disputed issues will be resolved in your favor. When this is done, the chances that you will be in control, make a better impression on the jury, and ultimately have the jury accept your theory of the case, are necessarily much greater.

§1.5. Preparation of witnesses

Witness preparation for trial purposes is not discovery. This is not the time to learn "what the case is all about" or to obtain interesting information. Witnesses favorable to your side must be prepared for testifying in court to those facts which will support your theory of the case. Preparation involves reviewing those facts which each witness and exhibit can provide, and preparing the witnesses to testify to those facts in a convincing fashion.

Witness preparation, then, involves both evidence selection and testimony preparation. The following steps should be taken to ensure that both purposes are achieved:

1. Witnesses should be prepared for trial individually, since only in this way can you realistically expect each witness to be adequately prepared for his particular role in the trial. In addition, you should personally prepare for trial every witness you will present. Having an associate "prepare" a witness you will present during the trial rarely works satisfactorily. Only where you have personally reviewed the facts the witness can testify to, and know how best to phrase the questions to elicit the desired answers, can you clearly and effectively present the witness at trial.

2. Review with the witness all previous testimony, depositions, answers to interrogatories, written and oral statements, and any other material which could be used for impeachment. Have the witness read these

materials, or read them to the witness. Determine if his present recollection differs in any way with his previous statements. If so, and the witness insists that his present recollection, not the prior statement, is accurate, explain that the opposing lawyer is allowed to impeach him with the prior statement and how this will be done in court.

3. Review with the witness all exhibits he will identify or authenticate. Explain the foundation requirements for each exhibit and how you intend to use them in court.

4. Review the probable testimony of other witnesses to see if any inconsistencies exist. If so, look for explanations for the inconsistencies that can be used to explain them if opposing counsel raises the inconsistencies at trial.

5. Prepare the direct examination of the witness and review it with the witness — repeatedly. Make sure the witness can actually testify to what you anticipate he can. Make sure he can establish the foundation for all necessary exhibits. Once the general outline of the direct examination has been established, go over the actual questions in light of evidentiary requirements. Explain why you can't use leading questions. If possible, review the testimony in an empty courtroom as a dress rehearsal, using the actual questions and answers you intend to present before the jury. Preparation should continue until the witness is thoroughly familiar with your questions and answers them in the clearest, most accurate way. However, preparation should not continue to the point where the testimony sounds memorized or rehearsed.

6. After the direct examination has been prepared, review with the witness the areas that you anticipate the cross-examination will cover. Explain the different rules that apply to cross-examination and the purposes of the examination. Have an associate do a cross-examination of the witness, raising the same points and using the same demeanor the actual cross-examiner is likely to raise and use at trial. Emphasize that the witness should maintain the same demeanor and attitude on cross as he had on direct and answer only the question asked.

7. Prepare the witness for his courtroom appearance. Explain that he should dress neatly and conservatively, with clothes appropriate to his background. Explain how the courtroom is arranged, where the judge, lawyers, court reporter, clerk, bailiff, and spectators sit, how the witness will enter and leave the courtroom, where and how he will take the oath, where he will sit while giving his testimony, and how he should act while there. If the witness is a party that will sit with you at counsel table, remind him that the jury will be watching and assessing him, even when he is not testifying. Instruct him not to whisper to you or interrupt you when court is in session. Instead, have him write on a note pad anything he wants to tell you when you are occupied by witness testimony or other critical matters.

8. Prepare the witness for his courtroom testimony. Explain that following these rules will favorably affect the way the jury will evaluate and weigh his testimony:

a. Listen carefully to every question. Answer only that question. Do not ramble on or volunteer information. Look at the jury when answering questions. Speak clearly and loudly so that the last juror can easily hear you. Don't look at the judge or lawyer for help on difficult questions.

b.   If you do not understand a question, say so and the lawyer will rephrase it. If you cannot remember an answer to a question, say, "I can't recall" or "I can't remember." You will be allowed to review any of your statements to jog your memory. If you don't know an answer, say, "I don't know." If you can only approximate dates, times and distances, give only your best approximation. If you cannot answer a question "yes" or "no," say so and explain your answer. However, give positive, clear and direct answers to every question whenever possible. Answer the questions with the words you normally use and feel comfortable with. Don't use someone else's vocabulary, "police talk," or other stilted speech.

c.   Be serious and polite at all times. Do not exaggerate or understate the facts. Don't give cute or clever answers. Never argue with the lawyers or the judge. Never lose your temper. The lawyer on cross-examination may attempt to confuse you, have you argue with him, or have you lose your temper. Resist these temptations.

d.   You will be allowed to testify only to what you personally saw, heard, and did. You generally cannot testify to what others know, or to conclusions, opinions, and speculations.

e.   If an objection is made by either side to any question or answer, stop. Wait for the judge to rule. If he overrules the objections, answer the question. If he sustains the objection, simply wait for the next question. Never try to squeeze an answer in when an objection has been made.

f.   Explain the purposes of direct, cross, redirect and recross and the forms of questions employed in each type of examination.

g.   Explain trick questions that the other side may ask, such as: "Have you talked to anyone about this case?" "What did your lawyer tell you to say in court?" and "Are you getting paid to testify?" Explain how such questions can be accurately and fairly answered.

h.   Above all, always tell the complete truth according to your best recollection of the facts and events involved.

9.   How should you prepare direct examinations for inclusion in your trial notebook? Two methods are in general use:

a.   *The Q & A method.* Under this method, every question you intend to ask and the witness' anticipated answer are written out. This method is usually employed by inexperienced lawyers during their first few trials. Its advantage is that you can draft your questions in proper form in advance. However, make sure you do not show the actual written questions and answers to the witness, since opposing counsel may ask him if he prepared or saw any outlines of his examination. The disadvantages are that, unless you are a great actor, your questions will sound as if they are being read from a script, creating the impression to the jury that the whole direct examination has been created and choreographed in advance. It also weds you to the script and hinders flexibility.

b. *The witness narrative method.* Under this method you write out in outline form what the witness will say and do on direct. You then simply follow the narrative, posing questions that will elicit the desired answers. The advantages are that your questions will sound fresh and spontaneous and you retain flexibility during the direct examination. Note all exhibits to be qualified at the top of the page, so you can pull them from your files in advance of the examination. In addition, note all places where the witness has made prior statements, so that they can be quickly located if they are not already in a separate file divider. The testimony narrative splits the page in three columns: dates and times, witness narrative, and exhibits to be identified. This makes it visually simple to know where you are and what you should do next at any time during the examination. As the testimony progresses, you simply check off what has been testified to and what exhibits have been identified and offered.

Example (John Doe — direct examination):

Exhibits: 1.   wallet — Pl. exhibit #2
              2.   photos — Pl. exhibits #1 and #6
Prior testimony: grand jury transcript of 6/20/85;
                     police report statements, pp. 6-8

1. Background	— name, age, address how long here work and school family	
2. 8/13/85	— where living describe building describe apt. — doors, layout, lights	*ID* photo (#1)
3. 2:00 A.M.	— in apt. beer, TV lights	
4. What happened	— 2 men burst in describe men guns 1st man held gun to head took wallet searched apt. threats ran out	*ID* defs.
5. Afterwards	— called police, arrived	

6. Lineup	— 9:00 A.M. at station	
	talked to officers	
	saw lineup	
	one of men in it	*ID* lineup photo (#6)
	saw his wallet at station	*ID* wallet (#2)

§1.6. *Preparation of cross-examinations*

Effective cross-examinations of your opponent's witnesses require preparation. Discovery, in both civil and criminal cases, has made it possible to determine what your opponent's witnesses will probably say at trial. Since the direct testimony usually can be determined in advance, your cross-examinations can and should be planned and prepared in advance as well. That preparation should include the following:

1. Review the probable testimony the witness will give on direct examination, including the exhibits he will identify and qualify for admission.

2. Review the pleadings, interrogatories, depositions, and statements the witness made that are relevant to his probable testimony.

3. Have an investigator or associate interview the witness, if possible, to determine what his trial testimony will be and if he can give evidence favorable to your theory of the case or inconsistent with his earlier statements. Try to have the statements put in writing and signed or recorded in some manner. Whenever possible, interview the witness with another witness present. That witness, usually another investigator, may be necessary as an impeachment prove-up witness if the need arises during the trial.

4. Consider what evidence the witness can give that is favorable to your position. What exhibits can he identify or qualify? What testimony must he give that will benefit your position?

5. Consider the areas on which you have a reasonable probability of successfully cross-examining the witness. What testimony is he likely to give that will appear improbable? What testimony is in conflict with what your witnesses will say? What testimony will come in conflict with your exhibits?

6. Consider what possible impeachment you will have of the witness' testimony. Will his testimony be in conflict with his pleadings, interrogatories, depositions, and previous statements? Do any of these materials contain positions and statements the witness must alter or deny at trial? Are any of the materials inconsistent with each other?

7. Once you have evaluated the available materials and have organized the probable cross-examination into three categories — favorable admissions, probably successful cross-examination areas, and impeachment, — you should arrange your cross-examination into specific topics. The fewer topics you have the better. The jury will never remember 10 points you raise on cross. Try to keep your major points to three or less.

8.   When you have decided on the topics your cross will cover, arrange them in an intelligent order. Remember that you should obtain favorable admissions before you attempt to impeach the witness. You should begin your cross-examination on a good point and end on your best point, since the jury is most likely to remember these parts of the cross-examination.

9.   Now that you have determined your topics and arranged them in your best order, it's time to create a witness sheet for each anticipated witness. A common technique is to put a short summary of the witness' probable testimony on direct examination at the top of the page. Also included should be the places where the witness has made previous statements, so that they can be quickly located, even if they are already in a separate file divider. The rest of the page should be split into two sides. One side will contain an outline of your intended cross-examination topics with citations to any impeachment. The other side will have room for notes on the direct examination. This will allow you to make your notes on the direct examination across from the related topics of your intended cross-examination, thereby immediately correlating the useful parts of the direct with your cross. Doing this should allow you time to observe the witness, which is just as important as making accurate, usable notes.

Example (John Smith — cross-examination):

Direct: Witness will probably testify that he was walking down the street late at night, was accosted by the defendant, who claimed he had a gun, was robbed of $35.00, and later identified him as the robber from a lineup.

Prior testimony: grand jury transcript of 6/20/85,
statement to police (pp. 6-8 of reports)

Cross-examination	Direct examination
1. Late at night; lighting poor	
2. Happened suddenly; not expected trouble	
3. Worried about being hurt; kept looking at man's coat pocket for gun	
4. Never saw gun (grand jury transcript, p. 7) (statement, p. 8)	

Effective cross-examinations, then, require a method that systematically analyzes discovery materials, develops fruitful cross-examination areas, and organizes them for effective utilization at trial. The approach reviewed above requires substantial preparation before trial, but then, so does every other aspect of trial work. Cross-examinations should be no exception.

§1.7. Order of proof

1. Selecting witnesses

Having prepared the examinations of witnesses, your next step is to determine which witnesses you will actually call and the order in which you will present them. In determining whether to call certain available witnesses, remember the following considerations:

a. Do not overprove your case. Many lawyers call far too many witnesses, thereby boring the jury or, even worse, conveying the impression that the lawyer doesn't have confidence in his own witnesses. In general, call one witness and no more than one or two corroboration witness on any one point. The jury will legitimately wonder why you called four or five witnesses to establish any one point. It's usually best to make it simple, make it fast, and then quit.

b. You are not required to prove everything, only the elements of your claims or defenses. Call only those witnesses necessary to prove those elements. Avoid calling witnesses merely because they have something interesting to say. Remember that your opponent is trying to destroy your case. Don't give him unnecessary opportunities to do so.

c. On the other hand, do not intentionally fail to call a strong witness with the idea that you will call him in rebuttal. Your opponent may surprise you by resting or presenting evidence only in an area other than that which your witness' testimony relates to, preventing you from calling the witness in rebuttal. In addition, the court may rule that the witness should have been called in your case in chief and is an improper rebuttal witness for any purpose. Finally, psychological research suggests that it is more effective to call the witnesses in your case in chief when the jury is still undecided and more receptive to persuasive testimony.

2. Order of witnesses

The witnesses you decide to call should then be arranged and called in an order that will logically and forcefully present your evidence to the jury. In deciding what order will make the strongest impressions on the jury, remember the following considerations:

a. Start with a strong, important witness to give the jury a favorable initial impression of your case.

b. Finish with a strong witness. Juries generally remember best the beginning and end of your case in chief. These are the principles of primacy and recency. Use them to your advantage.

c. Begin each morning and afternoon session with a strong and interesting witness whenever possible. Juries are freshest at the beginning of court sessions and will retain that testimony better.

d. If you must call your opposing party or an adverse witness during your case in chief, it is usually safer to call him during the middle of your case. If the witness does more damage than he helps, which is always possible, he will not have started your case on a bad note, and you will have the opportunity to follow him with favorable testimony.

On the other hand, some lawyers prefer to take a risk and begin their case in chief by calling the opposing party as an adverse witness, particularly if this will catch the opposition unprepared and the witness will make a bad impression on the jury.

e. An important corroboration witness should normally be called immediately after the primary witness has testified. On the other hand, jurors are easily bored. Routine corroboration witnesses can sometimes be split up with other evidence, so the jury will not repeatedly hear more of the same evidence.

f. Several witnesses are sometimes necessary to establish technical elements of proof that may bore the jury. Unless doing so will disrupt the logical order of your case in chief, these witnesses can sometimes be interspersed with other more interesting witnesses.

However, keep in mind that foundation requirements for exhibits and relevancy requirements for testimony may force you to present your proof in a certain order, unless the court will allow you to call witnesses out of turn on your representation that you will "connect it up."

g. The same rule applies to reading into the record depositions, stipulations, and documentary exhibits. Intersperse these with more interesting aspects of the case, if doing so will not disrupt the overall presentation of your case.

h. Remember that most jurors understand and retain what they see much better than what they hear. Maximize your use of photographs, diagrams, models, and summary charts, particularly if enlarged or projected onto a screen, and recordings, movies, and in-court demonstrations. Jurors respond to and remember dramatic visual presentations.

i. Get your essential exhibits into evidence early in your case and publish them to the jury as soon as possible.

j. Alternate lay and expert witnesses when practical.

k. An expert is often an appropriate final witness, because he can effectively summarize the evidence of your case. This will capsulize your evidence for the jury just before you rest.

l. Present your case in chronological order or in some other logical progression, as viewed from the jury's perspective. Keep in mind that jurors can follow most easily testimony that is ordered chronologically. This is particularly true where occurrence testimony is involved.

Since jurors are familiar with chronological storytelling, use the same approach, unless there is a compelling reason to alter your approach. This is probably the most important consideration in determining your order of proof, and one that will ordinarily override competing and conflicting considerations.

m. Finally, remember that your order of proof must remain flexible. Witnesses, particularly experts, have busy schedules and can be available only at certain times. Last-minute problems inevitably arise, requiring you to adjust your expected order. Remember also that the above considerations can and often will compete with each other, so that there will be no one obvious way in which your proof should be ordered. As usual, there are no simple solutions to this problem. Each case must be completely analyzed, and the advantages and disadvantages of the possible approaches weighed, to arrive at an order that appears to be the most reasonable and logical solution to the strengths and weaknesses of that case. Above all, remember that the primary purpose of the order of proof is to present your case in chief in a logically progressive way that is easy for the jury to follow and understand.

It is obviously difficult to generalize an approach to the usual type of criminal and personal injury cases. The following are simply illustrations of one way the proof could be organized in representative civil and criminal cases.

Examples:

Prosecution (murder case)

1. occurrence witness
2. first officer at scene
3. ambulance driver, to morgue
4. pathologist on cause of death
5. second occurrence witness
6. arresting officer
7. detective on defendant's admissions

Plaintiff (pedestrian-dart-out case)

1. occurrence witness
2. police at scene
3. ambulance driver
4. doctor at emergency room
5. plaintiff
6. treating physician
7. consulting physician
8. former employer

§1.8. *Rebuttal*

Rebuttal evidence is evidence that the plaintiff produces to explain or contradict evidence presented by the defendant. Surrebuttal is evidence that explains or denies rebuttal evidence. Although evidence that could have been presented in a case in chief may also be admissible in rebuttal, courts differ in their approach to this issue. The safer approach is to use rebuttal evidence only to contradict substantial new affirmative evidence presented by your opponent.

Never withhold evidence from your case in chief just so that you will have some for rebuttal. It is dangerous to "sandbag." Your opponent may rest, or present only a limited case and prevent you from presenting the contemplated rebuttal evidence. As a matter of persuasion, such evidence is most effectively presented in the case in chief to corroborate other evidence and make your case appear invincible before your opponent has an opportunity to respond.

When a trial presents a legitimate opportunity to present rebuttal evidence, make sure the witnesses are strong and the testimony is directly contradictory. Calling weak rebuttal witnesses or presenting testimony that is only mildly contradictory only serves to strengthen your opponent's case and suggests to the jury that your case is not as solid as it should be. Rebuttal is hardly the time to suggest a weakness. Use it when it can be decisively employed, or not at all.

§1.9. *Attorney's conduct during trial*

No text on trial techniques can be complete without mentioning some basic rules that govern lawyers' conduct during a trial, rules that are best reflected upon each time you prepare a case for trial.

First, remember that the lawyers, as well as the parties, are on trial; that trial begins when you first enter the courtroom, and ends when the court rules on the last post-trial motion. Remember that your conduct as counsel is constantly being evaluated and compared by everyone in the courtroom.

Respect the judge and jury. Regardless of how familiar you are with the judge, always maintain the proper degree of respect, courtesy, and formality. Jurors treat their obligations seriously and expect courtroom procedure to have a certain degree of formality. This requires that you address the court as "your Honor," stand when necessary, and ask the court's permission at appropriate times. Address other counsel by their last names or as "counsel." The courtroom, in other words, should never be treated like a private club.

Respect the jury's intelligence. The jury, being a collection of minds, always manages to learn and understand everything. Few facts escape its attention. It notices everything you do. Accordingly, make sure your arguments, objections, and examinations have a reasonable basis. Avoid cheap remarks. Doing so will maintain your credibility as an advocate throughout the trial. The lawyer that wins the race for credibility is the one who is a strenuous advocate, fights for his client, yet operates within the bounds of fundamental fairness. Surveys of jurors have shown that the most favorable impressions are created by lawyers who act and look well prepared and knowledgeable, have effective verbal abilities, and demonstrate dedication to their client within the bounds of fairness. The least liked qualities are unnecessary theatrics and lack of preparation, particularly when it wastes time.

Finally, maintain a flexible approach to every trial. Cases, juries, judges, counsel, witnesses, and parties always change. The successful advocate is the one who recognizes that every case is unique and alters his style and approach to adapt to those variables. By your doing so, every case can and should be "your kind of case."

II

JURY SELECTION

§2.1. Introduction

Within the field of trial work, perhaps no area is the subject of more theory and speculation than jury selection. Every trial lawyer develops his own theories. Every trial lawyer has a favorite story that can disprove any theory. Some believe that jury selection is so unpredictable that any twelve jurors will, in a given case, reach the same general conclusion. Others feel that a case is largely won or lost by the time the jury has been selected. Nevertheless, anyone aspiring to be a complete trial lawyer must become familiar with the methods by which juries are selected and the various theories on which their selection can be based.

This chapter will discuss the initial decision to request a jury trial; various methods under which jurors are examined, empaneled, and challenged; basic approaches and theories employed for the selection process; and the ways prospective jurors should be questioned.

§2.2. Do you want a jury?

In most jurisdictions, both parties to a lawsuit, whether civil or criminal, have a right to a jury trial. That right, of course, can be waived. Parties in both civil and criminal cases must therefore make a threshold determination: should you demand a jury trial or take a trial before the court? This decision is based on the following two principal considerations.

1. Who is the judge?

Some jurisdictions, usually in larger cities, use an assignment system for their trial call. Consequently, you will not know who your judge is until shortly before trial. In many jurisdictions, however, your case will be as-

signed to a specific judge well in advance of the trial date. Regardless of
the assignment method used, you can and should make every effort to
determine your judge's track record at the earliest possible time. Is he
plaintiff- or defense-oriented in personal injury cases? What kind of
judgments has he entered in similar civil cases? Do his trial rulings have
any particular bent? In criminal cases, is he prosecution- or defense-
minded? Does he have known attitudes in certain types of cases? What
sentencing disparity does he have between bench and jury trials? Ask attorneys familiar with the judge and other knowledgeable sources what
your reasonable expectations can be in your upcoming trial.

2.   Does your case have jury appeal?

Plaintiff's attorneys in personal injury cases usually demand jury trials on
the theory that most of their cases have emotional appeal, and a jury in
such a case is more likely to find liability and award substantial damages,
while a judge who has heard it all before will have a more detached view
of the evidence and take a harder look at the issues of liability and general damages.

Defense attorneys in criminal cases will usually demand a jury trial if
the client is presentable, the prosecution's case appears strong, the facts
will not shock a jury, and the case has no substantial defense to be raised.
On the other hand, where the prosecution case appears weak or a substantial defense, either legal or factual, can be developed, the defense will
often prefer a bench trial, particularly where a heinous crime or aggra-
vating facts would be shocking to the jury.

Commercial litigation cases usually involve complex issues of law and
fact revolving around substantial quantities of documentary proof. The
suits themselves often involve multiple parties, usually corporations or
other artificial entities. In these types of cases the parties, particularly the
plaintiffs, usually prefer a bench trial, since the facts can be both boring
and confusing to a jury.

This determination, however, can only be intelligently made if done
on a case-by-case basis, considering the facts, witnesses, parties, and lawyers involved. While generalizations are useful guides, they should not
override your evaluation of each individual case.

The final decision to take a bench or jury must also be discussed with
the client, who should be advised of the competing considerations in the
case. This is particularly so in criminal cases, where the defendant's constitutional right to a jury trial can be waived only if the defendant makes
a knowing and intelligent waiver of his right.

§2.3.   *Jury examination and selection methods*

If you have decided on a jury trial, there are several questions that you
must know the answers to before the jury selection process begins:

— Who will question the prospective jurors?
— What kinds of questions will be permitted?
— What jury selection method will be used?
— Will alternate jurors be selected?
— How many peremptory challenges does each party have?
— How will the lawyers exercise peremptory challenges?

The answers to these questions are discussed in this section.

1. Voir dire examinations

There are several methods by which courts conduct the jury voir dire examination. These vary, depending on the jurisdiction, the judge, or even the type of case involved. The only safe procedure, when your case is assigned, is to ask the judge or his court personnel how he intends to conduct the voir dire in this particular case.

There are, nevertheless, three principal methods by which prospective jurors are examined.

a.   The traditional method was for the lawyers to conduct the entire voir dire examination. The judge, following his preliminary remarks to the jury, merely turned the jury over to the lawyers and limited his participation to ruling on objections made during the examination of jurors.

b.   In recent years, the trend has been for the judge to conduct the entire voir dire examination. The lawyer's role in this system is simply restricted to exercising peremptory challenges. Although most trial lawyers have objected to this trend, claiming that their right to examine jurors personally is an inherent right as well as necessary to the intelligent exercise of challenges, many judges favor it, since it keeps the lawyers from "trying their case" during the voir dire examinations, and is more efficient.

If your judge will conduct the examination himself, determine what questions he will ask in your type of case. If there are additional questions you feel should be asked to enable you to exercise challenges intelligently, prepare your proposed supplemental voir dire questions in writing, submit them to the judge, and obtain a ruling. Make sure that your proposed questions and the judge's rulings are made part of the record.

c.   The third method is a hybrid of the first two. The judge asks all preliminary questions of law and determines if any jurors have preconceived attitudes about the case that would result in challenges for cause. Each lawyer is then permitted to ask additional questions. Here, too, you must determine in advance the latitude the judge will give you in questioning the prospective jurors. Many judges, for example, will only permit the lawyers to inquire into jurors' backgrounds and experiences. They will not permit questions of law or questions that test jurors' attitudes on issues and facts related to the case. Where this is the case, you again must submit to the judge in advance questions of law you would like him to ask the jurors.

2. Jury selection methods

How jury panels are examined and selected is controlled by statute, court rules, local practices, and the judge's preferences. Your first step must always be to determine how a jury is selected in your judge's courtroom. When in doubt, ask the judge or his court personnel.

There are many variations in jury selection methods, but most are based on the two principal systems used today. The first is generally known as the "strike system." Under this system every juror in the venire is questioned under one of the methods described earlier. As each juror is questioned, the lawyers simply fill out a sheet, often a printed form, that lists each juror in succession. When the last juror has been questioned, the lawyers for each party designate those jurors against whom they wish to exercise peremptory challenges. The lawyers then give their lists to the judge, who compares them and then simply calls the first 12 names — assuming a 12 person jury — that have not been challenged by any party. These 12 become the jury. Alternate jurors, if necessary, are simply the next unchallenged names on the lists.

The strike system has advantages and disadvantages. Its disadvantage is that it requires questioning every prospective juror in the venire. Its advantages, which probably account for its growing popularity, are that it avoids most of the gamesmanship of the selection process and keeps jurors from knowing which party used a peremptory challenge against them.

The traditional jury selection method, still common today, simply fills the jury box with the necessary number of jurors. Only the prospective jurors in the box are questioned under one of the methods described above. When each has been questioned, plaintiff's lawyer will exercise the peremptory challenges he wishes to use at that time. The challenged jurors are excused and they are replaced by new jurors from the venire, who usually sit in the back of the courtroom. The new jurors in the box are then questioned, and plaintiff's lawyer again can exercise peremptory challenges against them. This process continues until plaintiff's attorney accepts the panel and "tenders the panel" to the defense. The defense lawyer then goes through the same steps, exercising his peremptory challenges, replacing the challenged jurors with new jurors from the venire, and continuing with this process until the defendant's lawyer is satisfied with the panel. He then accepts the panel and tenders it back to the plaintiff. The plaintiff's lawyer can then exercise peremptory challenges against jurors he had not previously accepted. This process goes back and forth until both sides accept the same panel of jurors. Alternate jurors, if necessary, are picked through the same process.

The traditional method also has advantages and disadvantages. Its advantage is that only those jurors in the jury box need to be questioned.

Its disadvantages are that it permits a great deal of gamesmanship during the selection process.

Keep in mind that the two selection methods described above are not the only methods employed. There are numerous variations of these methods. The safest course is always to learn in advance how the jury for your particular case and in front of the particular judge will be selected.

3. Exercising challenges

There are two kinds of challenges that may be exercised against prospective jurors: peremptory and cause. Peremptory challenges are given by statute or court rules, and usually can be exercised for any reason. Cause challenges, usually also enumerated by statute or rules, are granted whenever a juror meets a disqualification basis — most commonly that the juror cannot be fair and impartial in this particular type of case on trial. While the number of cause challenges is always unlimited, each party has a predetermined and limited number of peremptory challenges that can be used during the selection process. Where the strike system is used, challenges are communicated to the judge, so the principal consideration is knowing the number of challenges each party has. Where a traditional method of jury selection is used, however, there are several points that must always be remembered.

First, never run out of challenges. Always keep the remaining jurors in mind when you exercise challenges. A great deal can be learned just by watching the remaining jurors as they sit in the back of the courtroom waiting to be selected. What those jurors look like will have a substantial effect on the rate with which you use your challenges. Always save at least one peremptory challenge. The cases are legion in which one lawyer used all his challenges before the complete jury was picked only to discover that the last juror seated was disastrous for him. Save your last challenge for such an emergency.

Second, make sure you know the number of peremptory challenges you and every other party have. The number of peremptory challenges usually varies according to the kind of case on trial and the number of parties to the lawsuit. Make sure that the numbers are clear to everyone before jury selection begins. In addition, some statutes permit additional peremptory challenges to be allowed in the discretion of the court. Find out if your judge will permit additional challenges in your case. You must also determine, in multiple-plaintiff or multiple-defendant situations, how peremptory challenges will be exercised. Some judges permit all plaintiffs or defendants to pool their challenges and exercise them as a group. Other judges require that challenges be exercised by individual parties. Find out in advance what procedure will be used in your case.

Third, determine if you will be allowed to "reinvade the jury." The right to reinvade refers to your right to challenge jurors you previously accepted when the jury panel is tendered back to you. Some judges allow you to challenge jurors you initially accepted and tendered to the other side. Others do not. Find out in advance what procedure you will be required to follow.

Fourth, find out how peremptory and cause challenges will be exercised in your case. Practices vary greatly. In many courtrooms peremptory challenges are made in open court by the lawyers. In others, however, the judge will call side-bar conferences at the appropriate times to determine which jurors will be challenged. The judge will then excuse the challenged jurors himself. Challenges for cause can also be handled both ways. Where a juror, because of an obvious disqualification, will be excused for cause, the judge will usually excuse the juror himself and let the parties know that he was excused for a cause. Where, however, the questions have elicited a response that you feel entitles you to have the juror excused for cause, but the judge has not excused him, the procedure is somewhat more delicate. Perhaps the safest approach is to ask the judge for a side-bar conference, then argue that the witness' responses justify a challenge for cause.

a. *How do you exercise peremptory challenges?* Here a bit of psychology is crucial. Jurors hate to be excused. Waiting in the jury room to be called for another case is tedious. Jurors want to sit on and hear cases. If possible, therefore, have the court exercise challenges for you, particularly if you anticipate using more challenges than your opponent. If you must exercise your challenges in open court, do it as politely and softly as possible.

Examples:

> *Plaintiff Counsel:* Your Honor, at this time we would ask that Mr. Smith be excused.
>
> *or*
>
> *Plaintiff Counsel:* Your Honor, plaintiff would thank but excuse Mr. Smith.
>
> *Court:* Mr. Smith, thank you, you are excused.

If your decision to excuse a juror is based on unfavorable responses that juror gave you, wait a while and ask questions of other jurors before exercising your challenges, if you wish to disguise the reason you excused him.

b. *How do you exercise challenges for cause?* As mentioned above, ask for a side-bar conference and ask the judge to excuse the juror for cause. Where the judge refuses to hold a side bar, make sure you have clearly demonstrated why you are asking for and are entitled to a challenge for cause.

Example:

Plaintiff is suing a truck driver for injuries arising out of a highway accident.

Plaintiff Counsel: Mr. Smith, what kind of work do you do?

Juror: I'm a truck driver.

Plaintiff Counsel: For how many years?

Juror: Eighteen years.

Plaintiff Counsel: Over those eighteen years, were you ever involved in collisions with automobiles?

Juror: Yes, three of them.

Plaintiff Counsel: Were you ever involved in lawsuits as a result of those incidents?

Juror: Well, on one of those I got sued.

Plaintiff Counsel: Mr. Smith, because you have the same occupation as the defendant, and like him, were also the defendant in a lawsuit, do you think you might start off in this case a little on the defendant's side?

Juror: It's possible.

Plaintiff Counsel: Looking at it from the other side, can you promise us that you have a completely fair and impartial frame of mind and can give my client a fair verdict based solely on the evidence you hear during the trial?

Juror: I'm not sure.

Plaintiff Counsel: Your honor, to be fair to both sides here, we ask that Mr. Smith be excused, for cause.

Court: Mr. Smith, you will be excused. Thank you for your candor in this matter.

If the court refuses to excuse the juror for cause, you must of course exercise one of your peremptory challenges to get this obviously unfavorable and now probably hostile juror off the jury. You have made your reasons clear to the other jurors, and they should not hold your challenge against you.

c.   *How do you accept and tender panels?* Simply tell the judge in open court that you accept the panel and, if appropriate, tender it to the other side.

Examples:

> *Your Honor, plaintiff accepts the panel and tenders it to the defense.*
>   or
> *Your Honor, the defense accepts the tendered panel.*
>   or
> *Your Honor, we accept the panel.*

§2.4. *Purposes of jury selection*

As an advocate your function during the jury selection process is both clear and simple: you want to select a jury that will be fair, is favorably disposed to you, your client, and your case, and will ultimately return a favorable verdict. Your opponent, of course, while also looking for a jury that has an open mind about the case, is also looking for a jury that will react favorably to him, his client and his case. What constitutes a good jury depends on which side of the case you represent and determines how you will exercise your peremptory challenges. When two evenly matched adversaries participate in the jury selection process, injecting their concepts of a good jury into that process, they will ultimately select a jury that will fairly and impartially hear the evidence and reach a just verdict.

With these points in mind, what are your specific aims during the voir dire examination of prospective jurors? There are three:

1. Present yourself and your client in a favorable light to the jury.
2. Learn about the jurors' backgrounds and attitudes, so that you can exercise your challenges intelligently.
3. Familiarize the jury with certain legal and factual concepts, if permitted by the court.

Notice that of these three aims only the second is directly related to voir dire itself. The other two are more concerned with trial advocacy, which begins when the venire first walks into the courtroom and continues until the jury returns the verdict. You and your client as well as the facts are all on trial and affect its final outcome. The successful trial lawyer is the one who recognizes this and conducts himself accordingly.

§2.5. *Theories of jury selection*

One of your purposes in conducting voir dire examinations of prospective jurors, as mentioned earlier, is to learn enough about the jurors' backgrounds so that you can intelligently exercise your peremptory challenges. People's attitudes are inevitably the product of their social background, education, and experiences in life. Jurors are no different. Accordingly, regardless of what approaches you prefer to base your jury selections on, your examinations will necessarily take into consideration the following:

a. age
b. social background
c. marital status
d. family status (children)
e. family history (parents, brothers and sisters, etc.)
f. education (self, wife, children, etc.)
g. occupation (self, wife, children, parents)
h. employment history
i. residence history
j. hobbies and activities
k. relevant life experiences (general and specific)

Remember that jurors usually think and act in ways that are consistent with their backgrounds. On the other hand, they will usually answer questions about their attitudes and understanding of legal concepts in a way they think the questioner would want them answered. Jurors, in other words, want to be selected and will often say what they think you want to hear. Inferring their true attitudes from their backgrounds is usually the lesser risk.

No review of the jury selection process would be complete, however, unless it mentioned some of the time-honored selection criteria lawyers have used over the years. While every trial lawyer ultimately develops his own approach, it is useful to know some of the standard schools of thought. These include the following.

1. Similarity-to-parties method

This method looks at the parties and their principal witnesses and analyzes their characteristics and backgrounds. Each side then picks jurors who have characteristics and backgrounds similar to their side, and dissimilar to the opponent's. This method presumes that jurors will naturally, although subconsciously, give greater weight and credibility to witnesses whose backgrounds are similar to theirs. It has applicability, of course, only where each party and its main witnesses have substantially different backgrounds from the other side's. For example, where in a personal injury case the plaintiff and his main witnesses are blue-collar workers and the defendant is a business executive, plaintiff would probably prefer workers, not executives, on the jury.

2. Ethnic characteristics method

The ethnic characteristics method was the dominant jury selection approach years ago, when substantial numbers of jurors, particularly in large cities, were either immigrants or first-generation Americans. Hence, it was believed that certain ethnic groups had predictable attitudes that they would carry into the jury room. Whether the method is useful today is, of course, subject to question.

The ethnic characteristics method looks at ethnic backgrounds and assumes that attitudes are deep-rooted beliefs that are affected by values acquired early in life from family and social peer groups. Consequently, plaintiff's personal injury lawyers favor Irish, Jewish, Italian, French, and Spanish jurors, under the belief that such jurors are more likely to respond to a sympathetic story and an emotional appeal. Conversely, defendants in such cases look favorably upon English, German, and Scandinavian jurors, Nordic types who are viewed as more responsive to law-and-order arguments and resent windfall damages. Criminal lawyers who subscribe to this theory use the same approach, except that they reverse the conclusions. Prosecutors prefer Nordic types; defense attorneys prefer Mediterraneans.

Closely tied to the ethnic origins approach is the religious beliefs analysis. Catholics and fundamental Protestant sects are viewed as favoring personal injury defendants and the prosecution in criminal cases. Liberal Protestant and most Jewish sects favor the personal injury plaintiffs and the defense in criminal cases.

3. Work and class method

This method presumes that people's attitudes and values are an inevitable product of their work, family status, and socioeconomic class and that these persons will as jurors act consistently with those attitudes. Prosecutors in criminal cases and defense attorneys in personal injury cases look for middle-aged or retired jurors who have average incomes, stable marriages and family lives, work at white- and blue-collar jobs, are businessmen, or hold jobs that demonstrate traditional work ethics. Plaintiff's attorneys in personal injury and defense counsel in criminal cases generally prefer jurors whose backgrounds suggest greater subjectivity and receptivity to emotional appeals, such as single and young persons or young married couples, artists, actors, writers, and other creative individuals, and persons at both extremes of the income and social scales.

4. Body language method

This method has become increasingly popular, due in part to a growing awareness that voir dire examinations can be extremely inaccurate in determining jurors' true attitudes. Since most jurors want to sit on the jury, they will often hide their true feelings and attempt to answer questions about themselves the way they think the questioner wants them answered. In addition, trial lawyers are increasingly realizing that jurors' attitudes toward, and reactions to, the lawyers are important aspects of trial work that can have a significant impact on the outcome of a case.

Consequently, this method looks to a juror's appearance, behavior, and non-verbal responses, since these are viewed as giving a truer picture than verbal answers. It considers the juror's dress. Is he dressed appropriately for his work, age, sex, and class? Are his clothes compensating for a perceived inadequacy? Does his immaculate dress suggest the juror to be meticulous and analytically oriented? Do his clothes suggest what he would like to be, but isn't? The body language method considers physical responses in conjunction with verbal answers. Hands over mouth, licking lips, sighs, swallowing, blushing, and restlessness all suggest that the juror is sensitive or anxious about the subject being discussed. It also considers the juror's attitude toward the lawyer. Leaning back, turning sideways, suddenly crossing arms and legs, hands in pocket, coat buttoned, looking at everything but the lawyer all indicate a negative attitude toward or rejection of the lawyer. It analyzes whether those nonverbal responses are consistent with the verbal answers. Finally, it considers speech patterns. Do his responses have unusual or abnormal pauses? Does he hesitate or look elsewhere before answering? Does his pattern of responses change when certain topics are discussed? Does he hedge his answers?

If, as many trial lawyers believe, a juror's subjective response to you as a lawyer is important, body language may be a significant aspect of the selection process.

5. Strong vs. weak jurors

This approach is based on the general proposition that certain personality types are advantageous to certain parties. Plaintiffs, having the burden of proof and usually requiring a unanimous verdict to prevail, generally prefer jurors who are followers and compromisers, and will eventually go along with the majority. Unless you are convinced that a strong juror is favorably disposed toward your case, having such a juror on the case is dangerous. If such a juror turns out to favor the opposition, he might very well hang the jury or turn it against you.

Defendants in general prefer jurors with strong personalities, since these are seen as more capable of assuming independent positions and more likely to resist the majority. Defendants, in other words, prefer jurors who have strong backgrounds and personalities that label them as "take charge" types, since it often takes only one of these jurors to create a hung jury or force a compromise on damages as the price for a unanimous verdict.

As with any theory involving human nature, the validity of these theories and others is difficult, if not impossible, to confirm or deny, although in recent years numerous studies have analyzed the factors that can help predict how a particular type of juror will react to different cases, and lawyers in major cases have begun to use clinical psychologists and communication specialists to determine what their best and worst jurors will be for the case. The theories simply became part of the ever-increasing folklore surrounding jury selection. The best that any trial lawyer can do is to be familiar with these approaches, use his common sense and experience in determining what his best jurors will be for each case to be tried, and formulate intelligent questions to uncover as much useful information as possible. Jury selection can never be more scientific than that.

§2.6. *Checklist for examinations*

Determine in advance of the voir dire examination what your most and least desirable jurors will likely be in your case. This is best placed on a checklist chart and kept in the jury selection part of the trial notebook. Such a chart is also a convenient place to keep track of each party's exercised challenges, and to outline the special questions you plan to ask during the voir dire in addition to the usual background questions.

Example:

You represent plaintiff pedestrian, a 23-year-old cocktail waitress, struck by truck driver.

(good)	Juror profile	(bad)
Young		Truck, bus, cab, etc. drivers
Service occupation employees		Owners/managers of delivery businesses
Students		Nondrinkers
		Fundamentalist religious sects

Particular areas of inquiry:

1. Social habits — restaurants, nightclubs, taverns
2. Attitudes toward social drinking
3. Ever work as a driver — employ drivers in business
4. Accident and injury history
5. Ever involved in similar lawsuit — result

Challenges: *Pl.*   *Def.*   *Cause*

§2.7. Voir dire examinations

1. Approach

Once you have determined the characteristics of your most and least desirable jurors, outline or draft voir dire questions designed to elicit the information necessary to make intelligent selections. Most of your questions, regardless of the case, will be general background questions. Every case, however, has some particular aspect that will require you to probe into jurors' attitudes on that particular aspect. Sometimes, of course, the topic can be sensitive, yet necessary to probe. If the court will question the jurors, you have no problem. If, on the other hand, the lawyers conduct their own examinations, a high degree of sensitivity is called for.

There is one cardinal rule you cannot forget while questioning jurors: Never embarrass a juror. Make sure you never force a juror to reveal anything about his job, family, home, education, or background that may embarrass him. While it may sometimes be necessary to ask questions about sensitive subjects, don't press a juror if he appears reluctant to talk. There is usually a subtle, indirect way to obtain the information without having that juror and others resent you for prying too much. If you can't find it, don't ask the question.

Remember to ask general, open-ended questions whenever eliciting background information, so that if an answer is embarrassing, the juror will have volunteered the information himself, and no one will blame you for asking a tactless question.

Earlier in this chapter we discussed the principal purposes of jury selection:

1. Present yourself and your client in a favorable light to the jury.
2. Learn about jurors' backgrounds and attitudes, so that you can exercise your challenges intelligently.
3. Familiarize the jury with certain legal and factual concepts, if permitted by the court.

How do you conduct the voir dire examination to achieve these purposes?

The first purpose can be achieved simply by conducting your interviews in a friendly, conversational tone, projecting yourself as a personable, competent trial lawyer.

The second purpose is best achieved by asking open-ended direct-examination type questions that force the jurors to talk. Jurors, like most people, generally don't like to talk about themselves. Your primary task is first to get them talking, then ask about more significant topics. Don't use value-laden terms like "bias" or "prejudice," since these will hardly generate candor.

Example:

Q. What kinds of courses did you take in college?

Q. What kinds of jobs have you done for the XYZ Company?

Q. What does an expediter do?

Q. How do you feel about persons who drink alcoholic beverages?

Q. How do you feel about persons whose occupation requires them to serve alcoholic beverages?

Open-ended questions let jurors answer using their natural vocabulary and manner of expression. How a juror answers, rather than what he says, is often a more reliable indicator of that juror's attitudes on critical issues.

When questioning a juror, follow-up questions are extremely important. Whenever a juror expresses, or you sense, some reservation on a topic, you should explore that topic further using tactful questions.

Example:

Q. How do you feel about persons who drink alcoholic beverages?
A. Well, I guess it's okay.
Q. Why do you say that?
A. Well, it's legal, but I don't approve of it.
Q. Do you disapprove of all alcohol, or do you find drinking beer or wine all right?
A. I don't approve of any of it.

In this situation, a few short follow-up questions uncovered the true attitude, an attitude substantially different from the initial answer the juror thought would be an appropriate response.

On the other hand, some jurors like to talk about their personal achievements, such as successfully raising a family and holding a good job. When this is so, your asking questions in these areas will often make that juror appreciate your interest.

The third purpose, familiarizing the jury with certain legal and factual concepts, requires utilizing cross-examination type questions. Here you want to tell the jurors that certain concepts exist, and determine if the jurors will accept these propositions. Keep in mind, however, that many judges and jurisdictions do not permit the lawyers to ask questions of law, or test concepts on the jury.

Example (defendant in criminal case):

Q. You understand that the prosecution has the burden of proving the defendant guilty beyond a reasonable doubt, don't you?

Q. You'll hold the prosecution to the burden of proof beyond a reasonable doubt, won't you?

Q. We don't have to prove anything or present any evidence at all, do we?

Q. At this point of the trial, if you started deliberating, what would your verdict be?

Example (defendant in civil case):

Q. Merely because a pedestrian was injured on a highway doesn't automatically mean he's entitled to recover money damages, does it?

Q. You agree that the plaintiff has to prove negligence by a preponderance of the evidence before he's entitled to recover damages, don't you?

Q. Could the fact that you might naturally feel sympathetic to one side or another influence your decision in this case?

Q. If the plaintiff received serious injuries but did not prove that the defendant was negligent, what would your verdict be?

The leading questions, suggesting obvious answers, rarely get unexpected answers. However, they serve a valuable purpose by introducing the jurors to legal and factual concepts pertinent to the case. Tactfully phrased, nonleading follow-up questions can then be selectively used to verify the previous responses. It is also important to watch the jurors as they answer these questions, since any hesitancy or other sign of insincerity is obviously as important as the verbal response. Some lawyers leave counsel table and stand before the jury when they ask this type of question to make sure they are looking at the jurors and can detect any non-verbal responses.

2. Topics checklist

The following areas should be considered in deciding what questions to ask the prospective jurors in any case.

a. *Law (usually given by judge):*
  Anything about the case to prevent you from being fair and impartial.
  Set aside sympathy, bias, prejudice in reaching a just verdict.
  Wait until all evidence is in, counsel argues, instructed on law before making up mind.
  Follow the law that the court gives, even if you disagree.
  Consider the evidence in light of your own experiences and observations.

  (civil)
  Plaintiff has burden by preponderance (or greater weight) of evidence.
  If, after all evidence is in, you believe plaintiff has proved case by required burden of proof, you must find for the plaintiff.
  If not, you must find for defendant.
  Award a verdict in a substantial amount if the evidence warrants it.

  (criminal)
  Defendant presumed innocent.
  Prosecution has burden of proof, beyond a reasonable doubt.
  Defendant does not have to prove anything, present any evidence, or testify.

b. *Case on trial (usually given by judge):*
  Know the judge?
  Know the lawyers?
  Know the parties?
  Ever work for any parties?

Friends, relatives work for parties?
c. *Personal background:*
Address and past addresses (general locations by area).
Marital status and family members.
Hobbies and other personal interests (clubs, etc.).
d. *Occupation — self, spouse, children, parents:*
Details of occupations.
Employers — type of company and location.
Past employers.
e. *Education:*
Highest level of school attained (if juror appears to have reached a high level).
Degrees, institutions.
f. *Military service:*
When, where, rank, occupation.
g. *Prior jury duty:*
Where, when.
Civil, criminal.
Type of case.
Experience influence you in this case?
Differing burden of proof between civil and criminal cases.
h. *Court:*
Ever been sued — results.
Ever sue someone else — results.
Ever witness in court — circumstances.
Experience influence you in this case?
i. *Crime:*
Ever victim, witness, accused of crime?
Experience influence you in this case?
Friends, relatives in law enforcement — capacity.
Ever discuss experiences — influence you in this case?
j. *Insurance:*
Friends, relatives work for claims department of any company (if permitted)?
Friends, relatives employed by any insurance carriers (if permitted)?
k. *Volunteer weaknesses and unfavorable facts:*
Client unemployed, felon, alcoholic.
Give client a fair trial, knowing that. . . ?
Potential contributory negligence problems.
Follow the law in problem areas.

Examples:

Background questions applicable to any type of case.

a. Personal background:
Q. Mr. ____, where do you live?
Q. How long have you lived there?

       Q. Before that, where did you live?
       Q. What kind of building do you live in now?
       Q. Are you married or single?
       Q. Do you have any children?
       Q. Are any of them living outside your home?

  b. Work background:
       Q. What is your business or occupation?
       Q. What kind of work does being a ＿＿ involve?
       Q. What company do you work for?
       Q. Where are they located?
       Q. How many years have you worked for ＿＿ company?
       Q. Have you held different jobs for them?
       Q. Before that, whom did you work for?
       Q. Is Mrs. ＿＿ employed outside the house?
       Q. Where is she working?
       Q. What kind of work does she do?
       Q. The eldest son who's no longer at home — where does he live?
       Q. What is his business or occupation?
       Q. The other children still at home — are they all still in school?
       Q. Which schools do they attend?

  c. Education:
       Q. What was the last school you attended?
       Q. Did you receive a degree from ＿＿ college?
       Q. What was your major field of study?

  d. Military service:
       Q. Have you ever served in the armed forces?
       Q. Which years were you in the ＿＿?
       Q. Where were you stationed?
       Q. What assignments did you have?

  e. Prior jury duty:
       Q. Have you ever been called for jury duty?
       Q. Where and when was that?
       Q. Did you actually hear a case and deliberate on a verdict?
       Q. What kind of a case was that?
       Q. Did anything happen during your experience in that case that would affect you in deciding this case?
       Q. Will you set that case aside and decide this case on the evidence you hear and the instructions of the court?
       Q. Will you follow the law the court gives you at the close of the case?
       Q. Would you follow the law even if you might personally disagree with it?
       Q. You agree that this isn't the place to change the law, don't you?

  f. Court:
       Q. Have you ever been a party or witness to a lawsuit?
       Q. What were the circumstances of that case?
       Q. Would you be able to set aside your experiences in that case

and decide this case solely on the evidence you hear in court?

g. Closing routine:

Mr. ____, before selecting you as a juror in this case, is there anything in your background you think we should know about but haven't asked?

or

Mr. ____, as you sit here now, do you have the frame of mind you would want a juror to have if you were either of the parties in this case?

In addition to learning about the jurors' backgrounds, you should, if permitted by the judge, familiarize the jury with certain legal and factual concepts that are applicable to the case. Only in this way can you determine how the jurors feel about the kind of case they will be hearing and the kinds of issues it will involve.

Example (plaintiff in personal injury case):

Q. Do you own or drive an automobile?

Q. Have you or any close friends or relatives ever been involved in a collision?

Q. Did you or anyone else receive any injuries?

Q. Was there a lawsuit arising out of the collision?

Q. What was the outcome of the lawsuit?

Q. Were you satisfied with the outcome? (If juror was a plaintiff and had a small recovery, he'll probably make a bad juror for the plaintiff here.)

Q. Have you ever worked for the claims department of any company, or any casualty company? (If so, the juror will probably favor the defense.)

Q. Will you follow the law that permits compensation for injuries when they were caused by the defendant's negligence?

Q. Will you be willing to award substantial damages if the evidence supports it?

Q. Will you award damages on each proper element according to the court's instructions? (Plaintiff will usually end up discussing damages.)

Example (defendant in personal injury case):

Q. Just because the plaintiff filed a lawsuit against us doesn't mean he's entitled to recover here, does it?

Q. You'll require the plaintiff to prove his case by a preponderance of the evidence, won't you?

Q. If the plaintiff fails to meet his burden of proof, you'll return a verdict in favor of the defendant, won't you?

Q. It's natural to feel sympathetic in a case like this. However, can you set aside those feelings and decide this case on the law and the facts?

Q. If the plaintiff shows he's been seriously injured, but is unable to prove the defendant was negligent, whom would you return a verdict for?

Q. Will you follow the law that says that if the plaintiff was also negligent in causing this accident, he's not entitled to recover damages?

Q. You understand that the plaintiff is required to prove his own due care and caution, don't you?

Q. During the trial the plaintiff goes first and we only have a chance to present evidence afterwards. You'll wait until all the evidence is in before deciding who's right here, won't you?

Q. You understand, don't you, that my client, the XYZ Corporation, is entitled to the same consideration as any other party?

Q. It wouldn't be fair to find in favor of the plaintiff just because my client is a corporation, would it?

Example (prosecution in murder case):

Q. Have you ever been a witness to or victim of a crime?

Q. What happened as a result of that case?

Q. Were you satisfied with the way the case was handled by the police and courts?

Q. Has anyone in your circle of friends, relatives or acquaintances ever been charged with a crime?

Q. What was the outcome of that matter?

Q. Most of us during our lives have, one way or another, come in contact with police officers. Have any of these experiences made you feel one way or another about police officers?

Q. This case is a murder case. Is there anything about the charge that would make you hesitate or feel reluctant to serve on this kind of case?

Q. You wouldn't hold us to a higher burden of proof simply because the charge involved is murder, would you?

Q. Will you use your good judgment, common sense, and experiences in life in deciding what witnesses are believable and which are not?

Q. If we prove the defendant guilty beyond a reasonable doubt, you wouldn't hesitate to sign a verdict of guilty, would you?

Example (defense in murder case):

Q. As my client sits here, he's presumed innocent. You understand that, don't you?

Q. It would be unfair to consider him guilty just because the prosecution charged him with a crime, wouldn't it?

Q. Do you have any difficulty in presuming him to be innocent now?

Q. The prosecution is required to prove any defendant guilty beyond a reasonable doubt. You understand that, don't you?

Q. If they fail to meet their burden, you must find the defendant not guilty. Do you have any difficulty in accepting that proposition?

Q. The defendant has a constitutional right not to present any evidence or testify himself. If my client stands on his rights, you wouldn't hold that against him, would you?

Q. Do you have any relatives or friends who are police officers or work in law enforcement?

Q. A police officer's testimony should be judged by the same standards as any other witness, shouldn't it?

Q. You wouldn't believe a police officer merely because he's a police officer, would you? You'd have to see if his testimony made sense, wouldn't you?

Q. Will you follow the law the judge gives you and base your verdict on the law and the evidence you hear?

Q. If the prosecution fails to prove my client guilty beyond a reasonable doubt, you wouldn't have any reluctance in signing a "not guilty" verdict, would you?

3. Alternative Questions

As plaintiff you have the first opportunity to talk to and question the jurors directly. Accordingly, it may be appropriate to make a short statement to the first juror you question, particularly if the judge has not previously discussed the same points.

Example:

Q. Mrs. _____ , at this time we lawyers have an opportunity to talk to you directly. Please don't feel that any of us are trying to pry into your background. We simply would like to learn as much as possible about you and the other jurors so that we can choose, as the law requires, a completely fair and impartial jury to hear the evidence in this case. You understand that, don't you?

Q. Since you are the first juror, we might take more time with you than some of the later jurors. They will have heard all the questions we have previously asked and will already know how they will answer them if asked. This won't bother you, will it?

Not all of your questions need to be directed to individual jurors. Collective questions to a panel can vary your approach and be more efficient. Follow-up questions can then be directed to individual jurors who respond affirmatively.

Example:

> Q. Do any of you have friends or relatives in the law enforcement field? (Mrs. ____ raises her hand.)
> Q. Mrs. ____ , who would that be?
> A. My nephew is a deputy sheriff.
> Q. Does he ever discuss his cases with you?
> A. Not really.
> Q. Can you set aside whatever you've heard about his cases and decide this case on what you hear in the courtroom?
> A. I think so.

As you and the other lawyers question the jurors, the other jurors are, of course, listening to the questions and answers. Accordingly, sometimes a juror can be asked a series of questions in summary form. This is particularly appropriate if you like the juror and will accept him anyway.

Example:

> Q. Mr. ____ , you heard the questions I asked Mrs. ____ and the other jurors, didn't you?
> A. Yes.
> Q. If I asked you the same questions would you answer them the same way they did?
> A. Yes.
> Q. Would you answer any of those questions in a substantially different way?
> A. No, I feel pretty much the same as they do on those things.

The jury selection process can become tedious, both for the lawyers and the jurors. Endless repetition of the same questions is counter-productive in two ways. First, it bores the jury. Second, later jurors will simply give the same answers that earlier jurors gave. The key to effective jury examinations, therefore, is to vary the questions and vary your style throughout the process, so that the jury will perceive you as the more imaginative and likeable lawyer in the case and be more likely to give truthful answers to your important questions.

§2.8. Summary checklist

The above sections have discussed the various procedures that are utilized during jury selection. Before you participate in that process, always make sure that you have done each of the following:

1. Determine how the jury voir dire examination is conducted in your courtroom.
2. Determine how challenges will be exercised.

3. Determine how many challenges you and the other parties will have.
4. Keep track of the challenges exercised by each party.
5. Submit written voir dire questions to the judge in advance if necessary.
6. Decide what your most and least favorable juror types will be.
7. Set up your jury chart in accordance with how the panels are seated and questioned.
8. Organize the voir dire questions you intend to ask in advance.
9. Phrase your questions properly — open-ended, direct examination questions to elicit information, and leading, cross-examination questions to familiarize jury with legal and factual concepts.
10. Vary your questioning approach to keep the voir dire examination interesting.
11. Keep in mind the limitations of voir dire examinations for determining jurors' real attitudes.

III

OPENING STATEMENTS

§3.1. Introduction

The opening statement will be your first opportunity to tell the jury what the case on trial is all about. As such, it is a critical part of the trial that must be carefully planned, developed, and delivered, yet is probably the most overlooked part of the jury trial process.

Trial lawyers agree that opening statements can and often do make the difference in the outcome of a case. Studies have shown that jury verdicts are, in the substantial majority of cases, consistent with the initial impressions made on the jury during the opening statements. As in life generally, the psychological phenomenon of primacy applies, and initial impressions often become lasting impressions. Accordingly, make sure your case gets off on the right footing. This can only be achieved when you forcefully deliver a logical opening statement that clearly demonstrates the facts that entitle your party to a favorable verdict.

This chapter will discuss the elements and structure of effective opening statements and will present illustrative opening statements in representative civil and criminal cases.

§3.2. Elements

Effective opening statements invariably have the same recurring components. They are delivered forcefully, state the facts of the case simply, and are organized in a manner that communicates clearly to the jury. Opening statements, therefore, must meet several practical as well as legal requirements. Chief among them are the following.

1. State the facts

Perhaps the most common mistake inexperienced trial lawyers make during opening statements is that they fail to state what the facts will be. Instead, they merely allude to them in conclusory fashion. An effective opening statement must state the facts that you expect to produce during the trial that, you will later argue, entitle your client to a favorable judgment. Failure to state the facts is a lost opportunity to persuade the jury.

Example:

Mary Smith will also testify. She was standing right on the corner of North and Clark when the collision occurred. She will tell you that my client, Bob Jones, was driving north on North Avenue through the intersection. He had the green light. At the same time, the defendant, driving east on Clark Street, drove right through the red light, never slowed down, and crashed into the side of Bob Jones' car.
vs.
Mary Smith will testify how my client was driving carefully and just how the defendant caused the accident.

2. Be clear, forceful, and positive

An opening statement, to be convincing, must be clear. This means that your sentence structure must be simple and direct and your choice of vocabulary basic. Your organization must be progressive and logical. This is not the place to demonstrate your linguistic capabilities. Remember that you cannot persuade a jury that does not clearly understand what you are talking about. The opening statement can and should be forceful and positive, without being argumentative. Your word selection should emphasize a strong yet basic vocabulary.

Example:

On April 25, 1985, at 4:00 P.M., John Smith was walking along Spring Street. Suddenly, a car came from behind, struck John in the back and threw him into a ditch.
vs.
We believe the evidence will show that on the day in question the plaintiff was injured in an accident that was caused solely and entirely by the defendant.

While both examples cover the same ground, the former is preferable. Why? It uses active language. It is explicit and forceful. In short, it is convincing because it discloses the facts, not just the conclusion. The same elements that make good writing also make effective speech.

3. Do not be argumentative or state personal opinions

Arguments are reserved for closings. They are improper in opening statements. An easy way to keep the distinction in mind is to remember that opening statements state facts. Closing arguments, in addition to stating evidence, also can argue conclusions, inferences, credibility of witnesses, common sense, and other matters beyond the evidence itself. A rule of thumb is to ask yourself: do I have a witness that will state the facts I'm telling the jury in my opening statement? If so, it is proper.

Stating the rule against arguments is quite easy. Determining where the line is, or when you have crossed it, is not easy, since judges differ widely in their interpretation of what constitutes impermissible argument. Some give considerable leeway, while others give the prohibition a strict interpretation. In addition, practices vary between jurisdictions. The only solution is to learn what your particular judge's attitude is and adjust to it if necessary. Learn it before trial, so you can modify your opening statement accordingly. If your judge runs a very tight ship, you have simply got to eliminate anything potentially objectionable, so your opening will still flow smoothly, without interruption.

Example:

In this example, the first version is proper; the second will usually be considered argumentative.

He was going 50 mph in a 30-mph zone.	vs.	*He was racing his car, scaring and endangering children.*
He drove off the road on a clear, dry day on a straight stretch.	vs.	*He negligently drove off the road.*
She will say that she took a handgun away from a 250-lb. football player.	vs.	*Her testimony about how she got the handgun will be neither convincing nor credible.*

It is improper to state directly your personal opinions about the facts or credibility of witnesses. Phrases like "I believe," "I think that," or "we believe that" state personal opinions and are objectionable. In addition, they are not persuasive statements. These phrases should be eliminated from your trial vocabulary.

4. Do not overstate

Nothing is more damaging than to overstate the facts in your opening statement. The jury will remember it and resent your misrepresentations. Worse yet, your opponent during closing arguments will in all likelihood point out each representation that you failed to deliver on. Accordingly, if you err, do so on the side of caution. When in doubt, understatement is the better part of wisdom. The jury will be pleasantly surprised to learn that your case is even better than they expected.

5. Personalize your client

One of your objectives in any trial is to personalize your party so that the jury sees him as a person and can identify with him. If the jurors like your client and identify with him, they will necessarily be more likely to find in his favor. That's simply human nature. Accordingly, refer to your client by name whenever possible. The other side of the coin is just as applicable. Refer to your opponent in a depersonalized way to keep the psychological distance between your opponent and the jury at a maximum. Call your opponent the "plaintiff," "defendant," "they," "the other side," "the corporation" or other similar suitable terms.

Example:

On April 25, 1974, Mary Smith, the victim, was sleeping in her bedroom. About 10:00 A.M. she was startled by a noise. Ms. Smith looked up and saw a large man standing in the doorway of her bedroom. That man was the defendant. The defendant then. . . . The defendant next. . . .

6. Use exhibits

A chart or diagram can often be an effective demonstrative aid in an opening statement. However, since such exhibits will not be in evidence, determine from your opponent if he intends to oppose the admission of those exhibits. Where there is no objection, or it appears extremely probable that the exhibits will be admitted in evidence, many courts will permit their use during opening statements. Obtain a ruling from the court in advance. For example, an aerial photograph or diagram in a case involving occurrence testimony and a complex scene can be an effective way to present your evidence to the jury.

§3.3. *Strategic and evidentiary considerations*

Strategic and evidentiary considerations also play a significant role regarding the opening statement.

1. What is your theory of the case?
2. How complex is the case?
3. How many witnesses will be called? Are any of them critical? Do any of them corroborate each other?
4. Are there substantial weaknesses that must be volunteered?
5. Should you waive or reserve the opening statement?
6. How should you deliver the opening statement?

These kinds of assessments are significant, since there are a variety of techniques that can be selectively employed in certain types of cases. Among them are the following.

1. Develop your theory of the case

The first chapter has already discussed how critical it is to develop a theory of the case, which should incorporate all uncontested facts as well as your party's version of the disputed facts. Your opening statement is your first opportunity to tell the jury what your theory of the case is. Take advantage of the opportunity. Give the jury a logical, coherent, integrated overview of your evidence. If you fail to do so, you can expect the other side to argue during closing arguments that you never had a theory at all, but were merely waiting to hear the evidence before committing yourself to one.

2. How extensive should the opening statement be?

While every opening statement should adequately and positively state what your evidence will be, there are obviously different levels of completeness that the statement can reach. An exhaustively thorough review of all your evidence is simply not the most effective approach in every case.

What is best will depend in large part on the character of your witness testimony. Does your case consist principally of one critical witness, or does it have several witnesses that corroborate each other? Where your case consists of one principal witness, you should ordinarily give a full, detailed opening statement that will parallel the witness' testimony. When the witness testifies, he will repeat what the jury already heard. This should enhance the credibility of the witness as well as of the lawyer.

Where, however, your case has several witnesses, all of whom corroborate each other, none of whom is critical, it does little good to tell the jury in detail what each witness will say. You will succeed only in boring the jurors, not informing them. Hearing the repetitious testimony during your case in chief may be tedious enough. Under these circumstances, it may be more effective to tell "what happened" once and simply mention that several witnesses will corroborate it.

3. Narrative vs. witness testimony

The description of your evidence can take two basic forms. In the narrative form, you present a summary of the events as seen through the eyes of an outside observer. In the witness testimony form, you describe the events through your witness' eyes.

You must, of course, decide in advance which method of picturing your evidence will more effectively present your particular case. In general, your choice will parallel the choice on the extensiveness of the opening statement. The witness testimony form is usually preferable when your case hinges on one principal, largely uncorroborated witness, because this form will most closely parallel that witness' subsequent testimony. This, as mentioned previously, enhances the credibility of the testimony. On the other hand, the narrative form is usually preferable where you have several witnesses who corroborate each other. The narrative form can effectively summarize their collective testimony, and present it in a way that can be refreshingly different from the repetitive testimony that will necessarily follow.

Example (narrative form):

Several witnesses observed a robbery:

On April 25, 1985, there was a tavern called Otto's which was located at 1875 N. Bissell Street. In the tavern around 7:00 P.M. were the owner, a waitress, and several patrons. Everything was normal. Suddenly, two men armed with shotguns burst through the front door and announced a stickup. The patrons were told to place their money and wallets on the bar. One of the robbers came behind the bar, collected the money and wallets, and placed them in a cloth bag. Etc.

Example (witness testimony):

The only eyewitness to the robbery was the bartender:

On April 25, 1985, Frank Smith went to work at Otto's Tavern, where he worked as the bartender. At 4:00 P.M. the place was still empty. He sat down on a bar stool furthest from the front door. From that location he could see down the length of the bar, the front door, the picture window facing the street and waited for the after-work crowd. Suddenly, around 4:15 P.M., while the tavern was still empty, Frank Smith saw a man, armed with a shotgun, burst in the tavern and point the shotgun at him. The man was white, about 25, 6 feet tall, and weighed around 170 pounds. He wore jeans, a plaid shirt and western boots. His hair was brown and shoulder length. That man, the defendant, walked up to Frank Smith until he was face to face, within three feet, and put the shotgun barrel in Frank's neck. Etc.

4.   How and when to volunteer weaknesses

Often a difficult decision in opening statements is whether, and if so how, to volunteer weaknesses. This involves determining your weaknesses and predicting whether your opponent intends to use them at trial. There is obviously no point in volunteering a weakness that would never be raised at trial. Where, however, that weakness is apparent and known to the opponent, you should volunteer it as soon as possible. If you don't, your opponent will, with twice the impact. How do you volunteer the weaknesses? The key is to mention the weakness without emphasis, and present it in its least damaging light, when it will blend easily into the story.

Example:

Your client is the plaintiff in a personal injury action. He was involved in a collision with another automobile at an intersection. The defense is contributory negligence, based in part on the fact that your client had been drinking.

On April 25, 1985, John Smith went to work as usual. At 4:00 P.M., when his shift got out, he and several of his fellow employees went to Frank's Tavern, as they often did, and he had a couple of beers and talked with the other men there. After about one hour, John left to drive home for dinner. It was on the way home that he was struck by the defendant's car.

5. Waiving or reserving opening statements

The right to make an opening statement is a right you can waive. Moreover, some jurisdictions permit the defendant to reserve an opening statement until he begins the defense's case in chief.

It is difficult to imagine a situation where a party, either plaintiff or defendant, would find it advantageous to waive making an opening statement. Remember that trials are conducted to see which viewpoint of a disputed set of facts the jury will accept as true. Making an effective opening statement gives you a head start over your opponent. Take advantage of the opportunity.

The defendant, however, has a more realistic decision to make: if permissible, should he make an opening statement immediately after the plaintiff or should he reserve it for the defense case in chief? Most defendants open immediately after the plaintiff. Reserving the opening statement means that plaintiff's version of the facts will go unchallenged. Coupled with a strong case in chief, the plaintiff may well have convinced the jury before you get a chance to tell your side of the case. Some defense lawyers prefer to reserve opening statements because they will have the benefit of hearing the plaintiff's evidence before deciding exactly what to say. However, reserving the defendant's opening statement necessarily creates the impression that you did not have a defense, so you waited to see what the plaintiff's case looked like before devising one.

Nonetheless, the defendant should at least consider reserving his opening statement where he has a strong case and there are significant strategic advantages in that approach. This situation exists most commonly in criminal cases where a strong affirmative defense exists and, because of limited discovery, the prosecution does not know what the defense will be. Reserving the opening statement in such a situation will prevent the prosecution from altering its case in chief to blunt the anticipated defense. The defendant might also reserve his opening statement when he has more than one defense to raise, and cannot make up his mind which one to raise until he has heard the prosecution's case in chief. For example, in a murder case, where the prosecution's evidence is weak on identification, the defense could be based on that issue. If the identification evidence is strong, the defense of self-defense could be asserted.

6. Lawyer's position and delivery

During opening statements, unless required to use a fixed lectern, you should position yourself in the courtroom to maximize your presence before the jury. Although this is a matter of personal style, the most advantageous position is usually directly in front of the jury, a few feet away, where you can comfortably maintain eye contact with each of the jurors. Standing at either end of the jury box gives the impression of favoring some jurors and ignoring others. Standing too far away reduces your presence, while too close makes jurors uncomfortable by invading their personal zone.

Example:

In this schematic diagram of a courtroom, the lawyer should usually stand near the position "X."

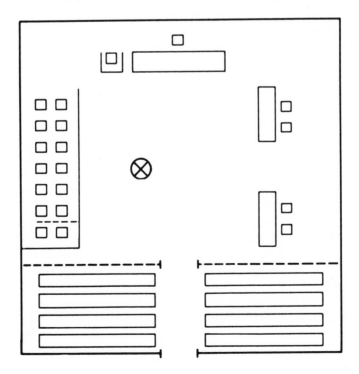

Regardless of where you make your opening statement, guard against mannerisms that detract from your delivery. Keep your hands out of pants or coat pockets, avoid playing with coins, pencils, or papers, and restrict constant or aimless wandering about the courtroom. Use upper body gestures, those involving your hands, arms, shoulders, head, and face, since these usually strengthen your speech. Remember that your physical and verbal mannerisms should always reinforce your speech.

A trial lawyer should know his case well enough and have prepared his opening so that extensive notes are unnecessary. If possible, avoid notes altogether. This permits you to exude confidence, use your hands and arms for effective gestures and maintain continuous eye contact with each of the jurors. Lawyers who can give an opening statement without notes have a decided advantage over their opponents.

§3.4. Structure

The following outline should be useful in organizing your opening statements. While no outline should be religiously adhered to under all circumstances, following an outline will force you to prepare, organize, and deliver an opening statement that will present your evidence in a logical and clear progression that the jury can follow and remember.

1. Introduction
2. Parties
3. Scene
4. Instrumentalities
5. Date, time, and weather
6. Issue
7. What happened
8. Basis of liability/nonliability or guilt/nonguilt
9. Anticipating and refuting defenses (plaintiff only)
10. Damages (civil cases only)
11. Conclusions

While this type of outline should be useful, it is by no means the only way an opening statement can be organized. Like most aspects of trial work, nothing is etched in stone. It can and should be modified to meet the unique facts of each case, your personality and style as well as that of your opponent. Only time and experience will determine what approaches work best for you.

Although the outline is advisory, the requirement of preparation and organization is not. Like any other phase of the trial, the opening must be carefully organized, planned, and delivered. Giving an opening statement "off the top" usually leads to disaster.

1. Introduction

The beginning of your opening statement is your first opportunity to speak directly with the jury. It is your first chance to impress them with the merits of your case and your abilities as an advocate. First impressions are usually lasting impressions. In a short period of time you should be able to achieve several purposes:

    a. Present a one-sentence capsule of the case.
    b. Explain the purpose of the opening statement.
    c. Explain how a trial is conducted, if the judge has not already done so.
    d. Demonstrate your abilities, confidence, and integrity through your delivery and demeanor.

Example (plaintiff):

May it please the Court, counsel, members of the jury, my name is John Doe. I represent the plaintiff, John Smith. On April 25, 1985, Mr. Smith had his leg broken when, at the intersection of North and Clark Streets in Chicago, he was walking across North Street with the light and he was struck on his hip by a car which was being driven by the defendant, and thrown down on the pavement. Mr. Smith has brought this lawsuit to recover damages for his broken leg and other injuries which, we will show, were caused by the defendant.

If the judge has not told the jury how a trial is conducted, you may want to provide an explanation of trial procedure. Some lawyers feel this is an opportunity to build up your image as a knowledgeable and experienced trial lawyer. This is often done along the lines of the following.

Example (plaintiff):

After the opening statements are concluded, the parties will present their cases. As the plaintiff, we will present our witnesses first, and the defendant's lawyer will have an opportunity to cross-examine them. After we have finished, the defendant may present witnesses and we will have a chance to question them. After all the evidence has been presented to you, both of us will make closing arguments, when we are allowed to argue what the evidence has proved. Afterwards, the Court will instruct you on the law that applies to this kind of case. Finally, you as jurors will return to the jury room and decide among yourselves on a verdict.

Example (defendant):

May it please the Court, counsel for the plaintiff, members of the jury: My name is John Burns, and I represent Frank Jones, the defendant in this case.
    As you know, there are always two sides to every question, and this case is no exception. The evidence will show that there are two sides to this case as well.

Indeed, we are confident it will show that the plaintiff was injured because he tried to cross the intersection when the "don't walk" light was still on. We only ask that you wait until all the evidence is in before you decide whether the plaintiff has met his burden of proof in this case.

Many trial lawyers, however, today avoid these standard introductory routines and immediately get to the facts of the case. Others skip the introductory routines if the judge has adequately told the jury what the purpose of an opening statement is and how the trial will be conducted. This is because they feel the standard routine detracts from your credibility as an advocate and is demeaning to the jury's intelligence and experience.

Example (plaintiff):

May it please the Court, counsel, members of the jury: This case involves Sharon Jones, who on June 18, 1985, while crossing the street at the intersection of Maple and Oak Streets, was struck by a pickup truck driven by the defendant, thrown down on the pavement, and killed. How did Sharon Jones come to die that day?

Example (defendant):

May it please the Court, Mr. Singer, members of the jury: Mr. Singer told you part of the story and he told it well. However, if it were as clear as Mr. Singer tells you, there would be no reason for any of us to be here. It's pretty much like the summary of a book on the inside jacket of the cover. Often the summary is incomplete and tells only half the story. I'd like to tell you the other half of this case.

2. Parties

The next section should introduce the essential characters, both parties and critical witnesses, to the extent appropriate. Your description of the plaintiff in a personal injury case should include his activities at work, home, and play. Tell a story about your client. Build him up and make him a human being the jury can relate to and sympathize with. In addition, remember that the credibility of your important witnesses is determined not only by what they say and how they say it, but by who the witnesses are.

Accordingly, show the jury that your important witnesses are the kind of people who can responsibly and accurately relate a past event. As defendant, discuss the important parties and witnesses the plaintiff did not mention or glossed over. Make sure, however, that you build up only those witnesses that have credible backgrounds since, by talking about that witness, you arguably are putting his character in issue. This can be a delicate decision. Safety is the better part of wisdom. Discuss only those witnesses you know have solid backgrounds that cannot easily be attacked.

As always, make sure that whatever you do bring out about any parties or witnesses will be supported by testimony at trial. Since a witness' background will usually only be brought out through that witness' testimony, discussing the background in the opening statement may commit you to calling the witness at trial. For this reason, defense lawyers in criminal cases will rarely discuss the defendant's or other defense witnesses' backgrounds in their opening statements, unless they are certain these persons will testify. In this way they remain flexible in deciding to present a defense at all.

Example (plaintiff):

There are a number of persons whose names will be frequently mentioned in this case, and I would like to tell you a little about them.

First, there is the plaintiff himself, John Smith, who is an accountant. Mr. Smith, before April 25, 1985, was a completely healthy young man. He had worked steadily as an accountant at the XYZ Company for 15 years, supporting his wife and three children. He enjoyed tennis, jogging, camping, and a number of other athletic activities. Never during the course of any of these activities did he have any problems with his back.

Example (defendant):

Counsel for the plaintiff has covered the history and background of the plaintiff. He also told you that my client, Mr. Jones, is a truck driver. Counsel failed to tell you, however, that Mr. Jones has worked for the ABC Construction Company for eight years. Over the past two years he was promoted to the position of head driver, a responsibility that involves hiring, firing, training, and scheduling all the other drivers of the company.

Example:

My client, ABC Hospital, has been located at North and Clark Streets for over 60 years. It provides basic health care and emergency services for the surrounding community and is the only hospital within a two-mile radius.

3. Scene

In most personal injury and criminal cases, the scene of an occurrence is usually important. In these cases you must meticulously describe the scene so that the jury can visualize it. Remember that the key to describing scenes is to develop verbal pictures such that if you close your eyes and listen to the description you should actually be able to form a mental picture of the scene described. Here clarity is critical. If the jury cannot visualize what you are describing, the rest of your opening will make little sense.

Juries, like lay people, often have difficulty in understanding compass directions. Instead, it is usually more effective to ask the jury to assume that they are facing a given direction, then "walk" the jury through the scene involved. Give one fact at a time, slowly enough to be absorbed and make a mental picture of it. It's generally best to give the jury the minimum amount of detail necessary to accurately picture the scene. Too much detail at this time runs the danger of confusing the jury.

Example (plaintiff):

This collision occurred at the intersection of Clark Street and Division Street. Picture yourself in a car traveling south on Clark Street toward the intersection of Division Street. Clark Street is a two-lane street. There are parking lanes on both sides, which are always filled. Both sides of Clark Street near the intersection have commercial buildings approximately three stories high. Division Street is a four-lane street which intersects at right angles with Clark Street. It has no parking lanes and is also lined with commercial buildings. Consequently, as you drive down Clark Street you can't see the traffic coming down Division Street until you are in the intersection itself.

Defendant, speaking after the plaintiff, should describe those details of the scene plaintiff left out, or with which you disagree.

Examples (defendant):

Counsel has described part of the scene to you but he failed to mention that. . . .

It is important for a complete understanding of this case to keep in mind that. . . .

A diagram, enlarged photograph, or other exhibit can be an effective aid in your opening statement, but several considerations must be kept in mind in deciding whether to use them. First, find out if the judge will allow you to use the exhibit during your opening statement. If you represent to the court that you can establish a foundation for the exhibit, or your opponent has no objection to its admission, the judge will ordinarily permit use of the exhibit during your opening statement. Second, keep in mind that the exhibit can be both an attraction and a distraction. It is attractive because the exhibit, in an appropriate case, can help the jury understand the case. On the other hand, the exhibit is distracting, because jurors will find it much more interesting than listening to you talk. The standard way of dealing with this problem is to use the exhibit only when necessary, then move it out of sight when done. Third, using the exhibit during opening statements will mean that the exhibit is no longer new when it is formally introduced in evidence later. Where the exhibit will help spice up a tedious but necessary examination, you might consider saving it to use for the first time during that examination.

4. Instrumentality

In many cases, particularly personal injury and products liability, the instrumentality is an important part of the case. These would commonly involve vehicles, machinery, equipment and other products. In such cases the instrumentality should be described fully. Use the same picturization technique used to describe scenes.

Example:

This bus was 40 feet long and had front and rear exits on its right side. Each exit had three steps. There were handrails on both sides of the exits.

Example:

The scaffolding used on this construction site consisted of a platform 20 feet long and two feet wide, which was suspended from the roof by two steel cables. An electric winch was attached to each cable.

Example:

These life insurance policies had a face value of $50,000. They also had a double indemnity clause, a clause which said that in the event of an accidental death, the insurance company would pay twice as much.

5. Date, time, and weather

In cases where the date and precise time of an event are important, or the weather conditions are significant, describe these in detail.

Example:

This collision occurred on April 25, 1985, just before 3:00 P.M. It had been a sunny day. Although showers were expected, the streets were still clear and dry.

Example:

This robbery occurred at 11:30 P.M. on April 25, 1985. Although it was nighttime, this intersection was well lighted. There was a streetlight directly over the spot where Mr. Smith was robbed. There were other streetlights further down the street in each direction, on both sides of the street. There was additional light-ing from the storefronts that lined the street on both sides.

6. Issue

As defendant, your picture of what happened should be preceded by a denial of the plaintiff's version of the disputed facts of the case that the jury has just heard. How you make your denial is critical. It must be done directly and with conviction. You must force the jury to get away from plaintiff's version of the facts and keep an open mind about your evidence.

Plaintiff, of course, can also state what the issues in the case will be. However, it is usually preferable for him to proceed directly into the "how it happened" phase, since plaintiff will not usually want to tell the jury that the defense disagrees with his version immediately before he tells it.

Example (defendant):

Counsel for the plaintiff has told you that he expects to prove that this acci-dent was caused by Mr. Johnson's negligence. But that's not what the evidence will show here!

What really happened on that day? We will show through the witnesses that we were not negligent, and that if anyone caused this accident, it was the plaintiff himself who was negligent and at fault.

7. What happened

Up to this point you have established the necessary foundations for your picture of the occurrence involved. You have set the stage: the parties, scene, instrumentality, weather, date and time have all been described. A complete background has been created. The jury has a mental picture against which you can describe the action. You are now able to make an uninterrupted description of the actual event involved, with the kind of force and pace that will recreate the event and make it come alive. Action can only come alive if you present it in an uninterrupted way.

Remember that you are competing with your opponent to create the more plausible description of how the event actually occurred. If you can make the jury visualize the event *your* way, you are well on the road to a favorable verdict. To do this successfully, your description must be a logi-cal progression, simply yet forcefully stated; it must be paced so that the jury can follow easily; and it must be given from the perspective most advantageous to you.

As defendant, your primary problem is to persuade the jury to see the event *your* way, the way your evidence shows it really happened. You should directly deny that the event occurred in the way plaintiff has claimed, if you have evidence that will contradict the other side's version. If you have such evidence, you can in good faith deny their version and tell the jury what your side's proof is. However, what do you do if you have no contradictory evidence? Ethical considerations may keep you from directly denying your opponent's version or stating it's not true. You can, however, state that your opponent's evidence will be unpersuasive, will fail to convince, or will not meet his burden of proof. There is nothing improper in challenging your opponent's ability to prove what he is required to prove.

Example (plaintiff — civil):

Ladies and gentlemen, what happened the day this tragedy occurred? John Smith was driving south on Clark Street. He was driving at about 25 mph, and was looking out for other cars and pedestrians. He could see the intersection of North Avenue ahead. The light was green for the Clark Street traffic. There were no cars in the intersection. Mr. Smith slowed down as he approached the intersection and could see no traffic or pedestrians. When he was halfway through in the intersection, without warning another car came from his left, ran the red light, and rammed Mr. Smith's car in the left rear.

Example (defendant — civil):

What really happened at the intersection of Clark and North? Frank Jones was driving westbound on North Avenue. As he approached the intersection of Clark and North, the light was red. Mr. Jones let his foot off the accelerator and began to slow down. Just before he reached the intersection, the light turned green. Mr. Jones accelerated and entered the intersection. Suddenly, another car shot through the intersection late, directly in front of Mr. Jones' car. Mr. Jones, although he had the green light, slammed on his brakes, but it was too late. The front of his car struck the other car on the rear driver's side.

Example (plaintiff — criminal):

Suddenly, at 9:05 A.M., three men with guns and masks burst through the front door of the bank. One man, armed with a shotgun, stood by the front door. The other two men ran to the tellers' area. One leaped over the counter and herded the tellers into a corner. The man standing before the counter announced, "This is a stickup. Don't do anything stupid."

Example (defendant — criminal):

At 11:30 P.M., while somebody else was robbing the unfortunate victim, my client, Frank Jones, was three blocks away, walking home from a movie. Suddenly, a police car with lights flashing came around the corner and pulled up next to Frank. Both officers, with guns drawn, ordered Frank to stand against a wall; Frank kept asking, "What's this all about?" One of the officers said, "You are under arrest for robbery." That, ladies and gentlemen, was the first time Frank Jones ever knew that a robbery had occurred.

8. Basis of liability/nonliability or guilt/nonguilt

As plaintiff, this should be the emotional peak of your opening statement. You want to make a summary of the facts and conclude that your client is entitled to win. This should be done in a suitably indignant and forceful manner. State the basis of liability immediately after your narration of your version of the facts.

As defendant, it is usually safer not to directly challenge the plaintiff's ability to prove certain facts. Assume that plaintiff will introduce some evidence to support his version. The safer approach is to suggest that plaintiff's picture of the disputed events will not be persuasive or convincing, then emphasize your *own* picture and conclusion.

Example (plaintiff — civil):

Members of the jury, this evidence will show that the defendant did not keep a proper lookout for other cars, did not look out for pedestrians, did not sound his horn, did not slow down, and did not stop at the red light.

Example (defendant — civil):

The evidence will show that Mr. Jones was at all times driving carefully, and obeyed all the traffic signals on the streets. This accident was caused because the plaintiff improperly drove his car into that intersection.

Example (plaintiff — criminal):

The evidence, in short, will prove that on April 25, 1985, this defendant, while armed with a loaded revolver, took $60.00 in United States currency and personal papers from the victim, Robert Smith.

Example (defendant — criminal):

We will prove, then, that Robert Smith, far from robbing anyone on April 25, 1985, was, at the time this robbery occurred, working as usual at his job as a dockworker at ABC Trucking Co.

Example (defendant in criminal case not intending to present a defense):

This evidence, which the state is required to present, will prove one thing. It will show that the state failed to prove, beyond a reasonable doubt, that my client was the robber. If it convinces you of anything, it is that the police arrested the wrong man.

Of course, there are situations where you may want to challenge the other side's facts with a direct denial. Where you do, however, make sure that you can prevail on the disputed facts. Nothing will damage your credibility faster than to directly claim that the other side's version is incorrect, then fail to prove it. Save such denials for safe situations.

9. Anticipating and refuting defenses (plaintiff only)

As plaintiff, you should consider a short statement that will anticipate the probable defense and deny it. Remember that the plaintiff has no right of rebuttal in opening statements. Hence, anything resembling rebuttal must be contained in your opening.

However, keep in mind that anticipating defenses can be tricky, particularly in criminal cases. The defendant, not having the burden of proof, is not required to present evidence. In criminal cases this right reaches constitutional dimensions. Accordingly, you cannot directly allude to evidence you expect the defense to produce. (Doing this in a criminal case might well create reversible error.) You can, however, refer to the evidence *you* will produce and state indirectly yet positively that it will not show that a defense to your case exists.

Example (plaintiff — civil):

Mr. Smith was driving his car at a speed of 20 mph in a 25-mph zone. He did everything the ordinarily prudent man would have done under the circumstances.

This rebuts the anticipated defense of contributory negligence.

Example (plaintiff — criminal):

This evidence will show that at no time was the victim, Mr. Smith, armed in any way, nor did he do anything to provoke the defendant's assault.

This rebuts the anticipated defense of self-defense.

10. Damages (civil cases only)

As plaintiff, you should describe damages in detail, particularly where they are extensive. In some injury cases, liability will not be seriously contested, so the only remaining issue is the extent of damages. Your organization of damages should therefore include symptoms, diagnosis, immediate treatment, prognosis, and conclusion. You should refer to the properly recoverable damages elements such as out-of-pocket expenses, earnings losses, and intangible losses. Your approach to damages should be in a resigned, somber fashion. Many plaintiffs' lawyers do not tell the jury the precise dollar amount plaintiff will request, allowing flexibility in modifying the request based on how well the evidence was received.

As defendant, you should express your regret that the plaintiff was injured, but firmly state that it was the plaintiff's fault, or certainly not your client's, particularly if you are defending solely on the issue of liability.

Example (plaintiff):

    a. Symptoms.
    What happened to Mr. Smith? The truck struck his hip and Mr. Smith fell to the pavement. He felt a sharp, stabbing pain in his hip. (Demonstrate on your own body where these injuries were.)

    b. Diagnosis.
    Several persons came to Mr. Smith's help and they tried to make him comfortable. Finally, an ambulance came, attendants put Mr. Smith on a stretcher, placed him in an ambulance, and drove him to the Mercy Hospital Emergency room. Shortly afterwards, Dr. Franklin arrived, examined him and ordered X rays and other tests. The examination, X rays, and lab tests all showed that Mr. Smith had sustained multiple fractures of his left leg and hip.

    c. Immediate treatment.
    Mr. Smith's leg was placed in traction. He was given shots to relieve the radiating pain in his leg. After one week, his leg and pelvis were placed in a cast. The cast extended from his waist to his ankle.

    d. Further treatment.
    Several weeks later it became apparent that the leg and hip were not healing properly. Dr. Franklin performed another operation to correct this problem.

    e. Prognosis.
    What is Mr. Smith's condition today? He was examined as recently as last week. The examination revealed that his left leg was almost one inch shorter than the right. His left thigh and calf were substantially smaller and weaker.

    f. Conclusion.
    Mr. Smith was in the hospital for four weeks. He incurred substantial hospital and medical bills. He was out of work for four months. Even today he is no longer able to work a full day, play with his children, or do ordinary household chores. To this date, he has a continuous shooting pain which radiates from his left hip to his foot.

Example (defendant — where the defense is primarily on liability):

It is, of course, unfortunate that the plaintiff was injured. In this case, however, plaintiff's injuries were simply not our fault. The evidence will show that he was in a hurry, crossed the street without a walk light, and, without looking, stepped directly in front of a car that had no chance to stop. Because of this, the plaintiff must be responsible for the results of his own negligence.

11. Conclusion

Both plaintiff and defendant should conclude the opening statement by simply and directly telling the jury that the facts of the case will support his side, and ask for a verdict. As plaintiff in a personal injury case, you should make a request for damages a part of your conclusion. Many lawyers generally advise against mentioning the specific monetary amount of damages you are seeking. Simply state that you are going to ask for adequate, lawful compensation and a verdict in the plaintiff's favor. After the jury has seen the plaintiff and understands how seriously he was injured, a large specific damage request will appear reasonable and realistic. On the other hand, other lawyers think it is better to begin conditioning the jury on damages by requesting a certain sum.

Example (plaintiff — civil):

Members of the jury, at the close of all the evidence, and under the instructions of the Court, we will ask you to award lawful compensation and damages to Mr. Smith for the losses and injuries he has sustained as a result of this collision. We will ask compensation for his medical expenses, compensation for his past and future loss of earnings, and compensation for his continuing pain and suffering, mental anguish, and inability to enjoy a healthy, normal life.

Example (defendant — civil):

And so at the close of all the evidence and under the instructions of the Court, we will request that you return a verdict in our favor, a verdict finding in favor of Mr. Jones and against the plaintiff.

Example (plaintiff — criminal):

After you have heard the evidence, we are confident that you will find the defendant guilty of each and every count in this indictment.

Example (defendant — criminal):

At the conclusion of this case, you will have grave doubts that my client, Frank Jones, was anywhere near the robbery when it occurred. If anything, you will be convinced that someone else did it. Consequently, Frank Jones is simply not guilty of anything.

§3.5. *Examples of opening statements*

1. Criminal case (murder): *People v. Sylvester Strong*

(The defendant, Sylvester Strong, has been charged with murdering Shelley Williams on April 25, 1985. The prosecution claims that the shooting was in retaliation for a prior incident. The defense claims the shooting was justifiable self-defense.)

Opening statement — prosecution

May it please the Court, counsel, and members of the jury. My name is Barbara Berry and my partner is Charles Sklarsky. We are both Deputy County Attorneys and represent the State of Illinois in this case. You are here because the defendant, Sylvester Strong, is charged with intentionally shooting and killing an unarmed man, Shelley Williams, on April 25, 1985.

(Introduction)

This is a traditional opening routine. Today many lawyers skip this routine and go directly to the evidence.

As the court has told you, this part of the trial is called the opening statements. Often the evidence in a case is presented in little bits and pieces and it's sometimes difficult to understand how each piece fits into the case. For that reason we are permitted to tell you what the overall picture will be now, so that each piece of evidence you hear will make sense when you hear it.

Don't tell the jury directly that what you say is not evidence. Why diminish your credibility before the jury?

If the court has not done so, you might explain how the rest of the trial will be conducted.

There are several persons whose names will be mentioned frequently throughout the trial. First, there is the victim, Shelley Williams, who was 23 years old when he was shot to death. His mother, Rosie Garrett, and brother, Clarence Williams, both lifelong residents of Chicago, were both present when the shooting occurred. Of course there is the defendant, Sylvester Strong, who, as we will learn, shot and killed the victim with a handgun. He obtained that gun from George Howard, his brother-in-law. These are some of the names you will constantly hear about during the course of the trial.

(Parties)

In this case the names and backgrounds of the principal witnesses are not significant, so they are mentioned in a cursory way.

This shooting happened on April 25, 1985, at approximately 3:30 P.M. It was a clear and bright day.

(Date, time, weather and lighting)

These issues are not in dispute.

The shooting itself happened in the 2300 block of Bloomingdale Street in Chicago. Bloomingdale is a two-lane residential street that runs east and west. At one end of the block is Western Avenue, which, as you know, is a main thoroughfare. At the other end is Winnebago Avenue. One side of this block of Bloomingdale Street has an elevated railroad track, so the entire block on that side consists of a cement wall about ten feet high. The other side of the street, the north side, has a typical sidewalk and a mixture of residential buildings and small businesses. Most of what happened that afternoon occurred on the sidewalk near the middle of the 2300 block of Bloomingdale Avenue.

(Scene)

The location of the crime is, as is the case in most criminal cases, an important point. Consequently, it should be described in sufficient detail to give the jury a solid mental impression of the scene, so that the action will make sense to them. In short, set the stage before describing the action.

What, then, happened on Bloomingdale around 3:30 during the afternoon of April 25? The evidence you will hear during this trial, we believe, will show the following:

Earlier that afternoon Rosie Garrett and Shelley Williams had decided to drive to the home of Rosie's sister. They drove in two cars. Rosie had about seven people in her car, while Shelley had his brother and two friends in his. On the way back they decided to drive over to another sister who lived on the 2300 block of Bloomingdale. Shelley drove first, followed by Rosie. They drove down Winnebago until they reached the corner of Bloomingdale.

(What happened)

It is usually advantageous to tell the jury up front that "you believe" the evidence will show certain things. Do this once, then go into the narrative of the events. This allows you to tell what happened without constantly repeating that phrase "we believe the evidence will show that. . . ."

After turning the corner, the first car, driven by Shelley Williams, stopped a short distance down Bloomingdale when he saw the defendant, Sylvester Strong, riding a bicycle down the street. He stopped his bicycle a few feet from the car. Shelley got out of his car, walked up to the defendant and exchanged some words with him. This quickly escalated into an argument. The argument was based upon an argument the defendant had gotten into with Shelley's mother the previous day.

Note how the action is described in an active, immediate way, which gives the jury a "feel" of how it really happened.

While this argument was going on, Rosie Garrett, Shelley's mother, arrived at the corner in her car and parked the car a short distance from Shelley's. She saw her son and the defendant having words. Her son motioned to her, so she got out of her car and walked to where Shelley and the defendant were standing. Shelley asked her, pointing to the defendant: "Is this the one who cursed you out?" She said: "Yes, it is." Shelley demanded an apology.

At this time George Howard, the defendant's brother-in-law, came to the corner and asked Shelley's brother, Clarence, and one of his friends what was going on. Both said they didn't know what the argument was all about. George Howard then took a gun out of his pocket and fired the gun twice into the air. Nobody was hurt. The defendant walked up to his brother-in-law and said: "You're not trying to hit him, give me the gun." He then took the gun from his brother-in-law.

The defendant immediately aimed that gun at Shelley Williams and shot him once through the arm. When Shelley turned to get away, the defendant fired a second shot in his back. Shelley then fell to the ground, face down. The defendant then walked up to him and fired a third shot into his back.

> The heart of the case can be acted out. Here the prosecutor can act out how the defendant held the gun and fired it.

Immediately after firing the third shot, the defendant ran down the sidewalk and attempted to escape. The victim's brother, Clarence, having just seen the defendant shoot his brother, jumped into his brother's car, drove it a short distance down Bloomingdale and cut off the defendant as he tried to run away. The defendant ran into the car and knocked himself down to the ground. Clarence got out of the car and kicked the defendant in the head, trying to keep him on the ground and hold him for the police.

> A weakness in the prosecution case is that the defendant was, in fact, severely beaten by the victim's friends and family following the shooting. This problem is usually best handled by volunteering the unfavorable evidence now, so that its impact will be blunted before the defense can discuss the weakness the way it wants to.

The defendant repeatedly tried to get up and Clarence kept trying to subdue him. A relative of the defendant brought a baseball bat from her house and came to the scene, but Rosie took the baseball bat from her. Rosie then took that baseball bat and hit the defendant over his head to keep him down until the police came.

When the police arrived at the scene, they found the defendant being held right by the car. He had been beaten up, but was being held for the police. They also recovered the gun, which had been taken to Rosie's house for safekeeping. An ambulance was called, but by the time he could be taken to a nearby hospital, the victim, Shelley Williams, was dead. A later autopsy showed the fatal bullet to be one that entered the victim's back, piercing his lungs and heart.

That, ladies and gentlemen of the jury, is what we expect the evidence to show. It will prove that on April 25, 1985, the defendant, Sylvester Strong, committed the crime of murder when he intentionally took a handgun and fired three shots into an unarmed victim, Shelley Williams. The third shot, the fatal shot, entered the victim's back as he lay helpless on the sidewalk, face down. The evidence will show that the defendant was in no way justified in shooting Shelley Williams.

(Basis of guilt)

This summary should be stated emphatically.

Since the defense need not present evidence, the prosecutor cannot comment on the anticipated defense directly.

At the close of all the evidence, we will ask that you find the defendant, Sylvester Strong, guilty of the crime of murder as charged in this indictment.

(Conclusion)

Opening statement — defense

May it please the Court, counsel, ladies and gentlemen of the jury, good morning. My name is Steven Cole and this is my partner, Sharon Hill. We are here on behalf of the defendant, Sylvester Strong.

(Introduction)

The purpose of the opening statements, of course, is to give you a preview of what we expect the evidence in the case to show. Immediately after the opening statements, the prosecutors will start with their witnesses. After each witness completes his testimony, we, as defense counsel, have an opportunity to cross-examine those witnesses. It is important that you recognize that the testimony you hear

Since most of the defense will be based on the cross-examinations of the prosecution's

during the cross-examinations is as significant as the direct examinations.

I ask you to listen very carefully to these witnesses. Observe their demeanor. Make a determination as to their truthfulness and their credibility. Draw upon your own life experiences as you hear this testimony to determine what is fact and what is fiction.

Only after the prosecutors have presented their case will Sylvester Strong have an opportunity to present his case. We ask that each of you keep an open mind about who is right here until you have heard all the evidence, ours as well as theirs. However, before I talk to you about what we believe the evidence will show, I want to make one fact perfectly clear to each of you. We do not contest the fact that Sylvester Strong did in fact shoot and kill the deceased, Shelley Williams, on April 25, 1985, on Bloomingdale Avenue in Chicago. That fact, however, is not the issue in the case.

The *only* issue in this case is whether or not Sylvester Strong was defending himself when the shooting happened. In other words, ladies and gentlemen, was Sylvester Strong justified in defending himself under the facts and circumstances that unfolded during the afternoon of April 25th? Please remember that we, as the defense, don't have to prove anything. It's the *prosecution* that has to prove, beyond a reasonable doubt, that Sylvester Strong was *not* justified in defending himself. The evidence will show that Sylvester Strong was in fact justified in doing what he did and thus is not guilty of any crime.

What really happened before and during the incident? On April 24th, the day before, there was an argument involving the family of Shelley Williams with Sylvester Strong. On April 25th, the very next day, Sylvester Strong was riding a bicycle on Bloomingdale when he was confronted on the street by Shelley Williams,

witnesses, stressing the cross-examinations now is an effective approach.

(Issue)

Framing the issue in a way most advantageous to your position is extremely important.

After stating the issue, you must then emphatically answer it, then move directly into a review of the facts that support your position on that issue.

(What happened)

Note that the narrative of this action is done this time from the defendant's perspective.

his family, and other friends of the Williams family.

The evidence will show that Sylvester Strong was first struck in the face by Shelley Williams. Immediately thereafter Williams and his family attacked Sylvester with baseball bats and two-by-fours. Sylvester was unarmed and tried to protect himself from the people who were attacking him, but to no avail. He was repeatedly struck on his head and body. In desperation, he grabbed a gun from George Howard, who had arrived at the scene. With blood streaming down his face, he repeatedly fired the weapon, striking Shelley Williams.

There's nothing wrong with giving the defendant a sympathetic portrayal.

The only reason he fired that gun was to get that crowd off of him, a crowd that was attacking him with two-by-fours and baseball bats.

When this group of individuals who had been assaulting Sylvester realized that the gun was empty, they continued their assault with baseball bats and two-by-fours. Sylvester's head and face were a mass of blood.

Knowing that his life was in danger, he attempted to flee by running across the street, but was chased and caught by the mob, knocked to the ground, and again beaten until he lost consciousness. The only reason his life was spared was that the police arrived moments later.

In short, ladies and gentlemen, we expect the evidence to show that under these circumstances Sylvester did nothing more than what any other reasonable person would have done under those circumstances. He simply defended himself from an armed mob. Therefore, he is simply not guilty of murder or any other crime.

(Basis of nonguilt)
As with the plaintiff, this is the high point of the opening, and must be stated with emotion and conviction.

I ask you, ladies and gentlemen, at this time to withhold any thoughts you may have about this case. Please withhold your judgment until you have heard all of the evidence from all of the witnesses, and I am confident that upon hearing all of the evidence you are going to render

(Conclusion)
The jury must be reminded that the prosecution has the burden on the issue of reasonable self-

a verdict in this case that will be fair. We believe that the prosecution will not be able to prove, beyond a reasonable doubt, that Sylvester was *not* justified in defending himself. We expect that after you deliberate and carefully weigh the evidence in this case you will return the only possible verdict, a verdict of not guilty. I thank you.

defense, since it's entirely likely that some of the jurors will assume that the defense should have to prove any defense it chooses to raise.

2. Civil Case (products liability): *Hi-Temp, Inc. v. Lindberg Furnace Company*

(Hi-Temp, a company that treats metal products in furnaces, purchased an industrial vacuum furnace in September, 1983, from the defendant manufacturer. On December 31, 1984, the furnace exploded. Hi-Temp had the furnace repaired. Hi-Temp claims that a design defect in the furnace, particularly in a valve, was the cause of the explosion. Lindberg maintains that the furnace was safely designed and manufactured.)

Opening statement — plaintiff

Good afternoon, ladies and gentlemen. As Judge Aspen told you, my name is Larry Kaplan, and I represent the plaintiff in this case, Hi-Temp, Inc.

(Introduction)

This is our opportunity to tell you what we expect the evidence in this case to show. We expect it to prove the following.

Many lawyers now use this type of simple, quick introduction.

Hi-Temp is a company in business in Northlake, Illinois. Hi-Temp treats various metal products using high-temperature vacuum furnaces. The defendant, Lindberg Furnace Company, designs, manufactures, and sells such furnaces. In 1983 Hi-Temp entered into negotiations with the defendant for the purpose of purchasing a vacuum furnace.

(Parties)

Vacuum furnaces come in all shapes and sizes, but they all have the same basic components. The central part is a lined vacuum chamber. A large hatch allows materials to be placed in the chamber. The furnace works through a series of pumps, valves and heating elements. After the materials are placed inside, all the air is removed from the furnace, using the pumps and valves.

(Instrumentality)

Since this case centers on a mechanical device, it should be described with appropriate detail.

The heating elements then go on and heat whatever is in the furnace to the required temperature. This process tempers the metals, making them stronger and harder.

This would be a good place to use a diagram in the opening statement.

When Hi-Temp negotiated with Lindberg for the vacuum furnace, they told Lindberg the necessary requirements for the furnace. They told Lindberg the kind of heat that would be needed. They told Lindberg the temperatures which they would be heating at. They told Lindberg all the specifications and requirements that the furnace would have to meet.

Lindberg adjusted their design and manufactured a vacuum furnace for Hi-Temp at a cost of $103,000. This purchase was made with the understanding that the furnace would do what it had been manufactured to do, that is, to heat the materials that Hi-Temp needed.

The furnace went into operation some time in September, 1983. The whole time the furnace was in operation, the maintenance, care and concern shown by Hi-Temp for this furnace was meticulous. If there were any maintenance problems, repair problems, or anything of that sort, they were immediately dealt with. Often Lindberg itself was called in to consult on how to fix a problem.

(Anticipating defenses)

The expected defense is that the explosion was somehow caused by faulty maintenance, operation, or misuse. This statement helps rebut the expected defense.

On December 31, 1984, the furnace was in operation. During the afternoon this furnace was heating turbine blades and other aircraft parts. The heat was cycled to a temperature of 2,000 degrees and then cooled, and then heated again to a temperature of 1800 degrees and then cooled. This went on in a series of stages. Everything was routine.

(Scene)

That evening the furnace was loaded with more turbine parts and was set in operation again. All the instruments were set properly. The loading was done properly. There is nothing to indicate that Hi-Temp could have contributed to the explosion.

The anticipated defense is again rebutted forcefully.

Around 8:30 that evening there was an explosion that tore off the sides of the furnace and damaged other parts. Immediately after the explosion an investigation was started to try to determine the cause of the explosion. Based upon all the evidence here, you will conclude that there was a defect in the design of the vacuum furnace which was directly responsible for the explosion.

(What happened)

This furnace was designed in such a way that it would pump down from atmospheric pressure to a vacuum. The pressurized portion of the furnace was separated from the vacuum portion by a valve attached to the main vacuum pump, called a foreline valve. The furnace was manufactured and designed in such a way that this foreline valve could open between the atmospheric portion and the vacuum portion without first shutting down the furnace and without being coordinated with other valves on the unit. If the foreline valve somehow opened, atmospheric pressure would rush right into the vacuum portion, under incredible speed and pressure, creating shock waves in the furnace.

In this case the plaintiff's major problem is explaining causation — how the alleged design defect actually caused the explosion that occurred. Hence, this part of the opening is very carefully stated, so that there is no direct claim that the plaintiff, through its experts, will precisely be able to explain why the explosion occurred.

That, ladies and gentlemen, is what happened on December 31, 1984. After the foreline valve improperly opened, atmospheric pressure rushed into the vacuum portion, creating gigantic shock waves, which knocked off the sides of the furnace and did other damage.

(Basis of liability)

Plaintiff's theory of the case is simply stated — if the valve had a safety lock, there would have been no explosion.

You will learn that this explosion was directly caused by Lindberg's design and manufacture of this foreline valve, and that the explosion could have been prevented if Lindberg had simply built a foreline valve that had a locking safety device on it.

After the explosion, Hi-Temp had the vacuum furnace rebuilt. This took several weeks, during which time they could not process any of their customers' orders. The loss to Hi-Temp for the repairs, as well as for the business interruption, was $55,000.

(Damages)

The real issue in this case is liability, so damages are only mentioned briefly.

At the end of all the evidence, I will be asking you to return a verdict in favor of Hi-Temp, Inc. and against Lindberg for the sum of $55,000.

(Conclusion)

Opening Statement — defendant

May it please the Court, counsel, members of the jury: My name is Mary Jones and I represent the defendant, the Lindberg Furnace Company.

(Introduction)

Lindberg's business is devoted to designing and building what are called vacuum furnaces for purchasers throughout the world. We have been in this business since 1947, and build furnaces based on the individual customer's requirements.

(Parties)

We believe the evidence will show that the design of the Hi-Temp furnace was a standard one with proven performance and safety over 20 years, and that whatever caused the furnace to explode, it had nothing to do with its design or manufacture. If anything caused the explosion, it must have been Hi-Temp's maintenance, operation, or use of the furnace.

(Basis of nonliability)

Furthermore, the evidence will show that the furnace could have been repaired in about two weeks at a cost far less than $55,000, and that it could have been put back into service after that time.

(Damages)
While the defense is on liability, it is usually desirable to at least touch on damages.

Simply put, the plaintiff will not be able to show, by a preponderance of the evidence, that we did anything wrong here in designing and manufacturing this furnace that produced this so-called explosion. Accordingly, at the close of all the evidence we will ask that you return a verdict against the plaintiff and in favor of the Lindberg Furnace Company.

(Conclusion)

This unusually short opening has the advantage of sounding extremely confident. It forcefully states that the plaintiff will be unable to prove either a design defect or causation. In openings, brevity can sometimes be an effective technique.

IV

DIRECT EXAMINATION

§4.1. Introduction

Experienced trial lawyers recognize that most trials are won on the strengths of their case in chief, not on the weaknesses of their opponent's case. Consequently, effective direct examinations that clearly, logically, and forcefully present the facts of the case will usually have a decisive effect on the outcome of the trial.

The purpose of a direct examination must be kept in mind. It should elicit from the witness, in a clear and logical progression, the observations and activities of the witness so that each of the jurors understands, accepts, and remembers his testimony.

Consequently, direct examinations should let the witness be the center of attention. The lawyer should conduct the examination so that he does not detract from his witness. After all, a witness will be believed and remembered because of the manner and content of his testimony, not because the questions asked were so brilliant. Witness credibility is determined by who the witness is (background), what he says (content), and how he says it (demeanor). If the jurors remember one of your witnesses as being particularly convincing, but are not sure who conducted the direct examination, you have done your job well.

This chapter will discuss the components of effective examinations and review the kinds of direct examinations that are repeatedly encountered in civil and criminal trials.

§4.2. Elements

A good direct examiner is like the director of a film crew. Although limited by the script, the director can inject his own approach and perspective into the production. He has many variables to work with in portraying a scene. He can choose the locations of his cameras, the angles of the shots, and the types of lenses. He can use panoramic shots, close-ups, stop action frames, and slow motion. When the shooting is complete, he has the luxury of editing. The final product, while still a film of a recognizable scene, is a unique product of the director.

A good trial lawyer approaches witness testimony the same way. He does much more than simply "get the story out." He decides how he wants to portray a certain event or scene, then makes the technical decisions necessary to achieve the desired result. Unimportant matters are avoided or glossed over. Important ones are stressed, details are zoomed in on, and action is slowed down. Critical matters can be shown in stop-action sequences.

The important point is that trial lawyers view trials, and particularly direct examinations, as a creative art, one which allows you to tell a story to the jury in a way that is most advantageous to your party. The tools for this creative approach are analyzed in this section.

Effective direct examinations exhibit recurring characteristics that should be remembered each time you plan any direct examination. These include the following.

1. Keep it simple

Inexperienced trial lawyers often make two interrelated mistakes. On the one hand, they elicit too much unimportant testimony. On the other, they spend too little time on the critical part of what the witness has to offer. The former results in the jury being bored or, even worse, becoming confused about what is important. It also permits opposing counsel to develop additional points for cross-examination. The latter, by rushing through the critical facts, fails to fully develop them so that the jury understands and appreciates them.

Remember that the jury is laboring under two handicaps: It has never heard the testimony before, and it is receiving the information aurally. Any person's ability to absorb and retain aural information is limited. Therefore, don't make the jurors' difficulties greater by injecting into the direct examination unnecessary information and details. Determine in advance what the critical part of the witness' testimony is, get to it quickly, develop it sufficiently, then stop. In short, keep your direct examinations simple. In direct examinations, as in your case in chief, brevity is the better part of wisdom.

2. Organize logically

Once you have determined what the key elements of the direct examination will be, you must organize those points in a logical order. Usually, but not always, this will result in a chronological presentation of the testimony. Experience has shown that jurors, like other people, are best able to comprehend a series of events or other information if they are presented in the same chronological order as they really occurred. Jurors are used to hearing stories presented chronologically, so they will be more likely to grasp and retain evidence at trial if a story is presented in this way. The basic logical sequence is witness background, scene description, then action description. Exhibits are usually best used at the end of the examination to highlight the principal facts.

Example:

The witness, the plaintiff in an automobile collision case, should usually present testimony in the following order:

a. his background
b. description of collision location
c. what occurred just before the collision
d. how the collision actually occurred
e. what happened immediately after the collision
f. emergency room and initial treatment
g. continued medical treatment
h. present physical limitations and handicaps
i. financial losses to date
j. exhibits that highlight the main points

On the other hand, a straight chronological narrative, while the usual way of organizing direct examinations, particularly of occurrence witnesses, is not invariably the only way testimony can be presented.

Presenting the most dramatic or important testimony early in the direct examination, when the jury is most alert and its retentive power is greatest, can sometimes be the better approach. Thereafter, earlier events or substantiation of conclusions can be brought out. For instance, where expert testimony is involved, it may sometimes be preferable to have the expert give his conclusions and opinions before he discusses the various examinations and tests he based them on. In this way the expert will give his opinions early in the examination, when the jury is still attentive. The supporting examinations and tests, while important, may be lengthy, tedious, and difficult to comprehend. These could then be brought out after the opinions.

As in most areas of trial work, there are no easy rules available. The trial lawyer must exercise his best judgment and decide, with each witness, the order that will most effectively present his testimony.

3.   Use orientation and transition questions

Since jurors know nothing about the witness when he first gets on the stand, orienting questions are useful because they let the jurors know what to expect.

Example:

> Q. Officer Rich, you were the first police officer at the Johnson house?
> A. Yes.
> Q. You arrested the defendant?
> A. Yes.
> Q. And you ran a lineup?
> A. Yes.
> Q. I'm going to ask you questions first about arriving at the Johnson house. When did you get there?

With these orienting questions, jurors know what to expect, and not to expect. Since the questions are preliminary, the fact that they are leading does not matter.

Transition questions are also useful devices; they operate like sign posts during direct examination. When the witness will testify on several topics, transition questions let the jurors know when the questioning on one topic is finished and the testimony on the next topic is to begin. They operate like chapter headings in a book, making the direct examination much easier to follow, and serving to periodically renew the jury's interest in the testimony.

Example:

> Q. Mrs. Smith, I'm going to ask you first about your professional background.

> Q. Let's turn now to the day you bought the machinery from the ABC Manufacturing Company.

> Q. Mrs. Smith, I'm going to ask you questions now about what happened during the afternoon of June 15.

4. Develop witness background

Whenever a witness takes the stand, several questions will go through the jurors' minds. "Who is she?" "Why is she here?" "Why should I believe her?" Hence, your first order of business on direct examination is to let the jury know why the witness is here, and why the witness should be believed.

The first purpose, showing why the witness is here, can be quickly disclosed.

Example:

> Q. Mrs. Smith, tell us your full name.
> A. Jennifer R. Smith.
> Q. Mrs. Smith, you were standing near the collision when it happened, weren't you?
> A. Yes.

This simple question orients the jury to the general nature of the testimony.

The second purpose, showing why the witness should be believed, involves several considerations. First, the jurors want to know a little bit about the witness so that they have an initial basis for assessing credibility. Hence, you should quickly develop some general background with a few short questions.

Example:

> Q. Mrs. Jackson, where do you live?
> A. At 3742 Tulip Street.
> Q. For how long?
> A. About 15 years.
> Q. Does anyone live there with you?
> A. Yes, my husband and two teen-aged boys.
> Q. Do you work outside the home?
> A. Yes, I'm an accountant for the order department at Jewel Foods.
> Q. How long have you worked there?
> A. Almost eight years.

With a few simple questions you have shown that the witness is married, has children, is a long-time resident of the community, and holds a responsible job; all facts that show the witness is a mature, responsible person.

These simple background questions should be asked of all witnesses, because credibility is always an issue. Whether the background should be developed further depends on who the witness is and how important the witness testimony is. The plaintiff in a personal injury case, the defendant in a criminal case, and experts such as police officers or medical doctors should have appropriate additional background facts developed. These types of witnesses are discussed in detail later in this chapter.

5. Elicit scene description first, then action

The chapter on opening statements stressed the importance of organizing openings so that the description of parties, the scene, and other significant information precedes the description of the occurrence. The jury should have a complete description of the scene before hearing about the action. The stage must be set before the action can begin.

The same approach should normally be used in direct examinations, particularly of occurrence witnesses. All necessary preliminary descriptions and information should be elicited before reaching the action. Why? Action testimony is most effectively and dramatically presented if presented in an uninterrupted manner. Once into the action part of the direct examination, you should never have to interrupt to provide additional background. This is disruptive, and reduces the impact of the action testimony.

It is usually best *not* to use exhibits such as photographs or diagrams during the action testimony. The exhibits also interrupt the action. Save the exhibits for use after the witness has described what happened. The exhibits will then highlight the important points.

6. Elicit general, flowing descriptions

Direct examinations, particularly where occurrence testimony is involved, should elicit descriptive narratives. The witness' responses should paint a picture that the jury can actually visualize. This should be your goal, even if you have photographs, diagrams, and charts to supplement the testimony. The direct examination should provide enough information so the jury will fully understand what happened. However, avoid excessive detail. Too much technical information clutters up the direct examination, detracts from your central points, and bores the jury. Exact distances, times, and other details are things the cross-examiner will usually stress in his search for inconsistencies. When you elicit such detail during the direct, you succeed only in giving the cross-examiner additional facts to use during the cross.

How do you find the line between too little and too much detail? It may be useful to look at your proposed direct examination through your opponent's eyes. Are there sections of the direct examination, which you, as opponent, would not seriously challenge? If so, these can safely be discussed in some detail. Are there sections of the direct which you would probe in detail? If so, those are the areas where you will want the direct examination to avoid any unnecessary details.

Example:

Q. Where did this crash happen?
A. At the corner of Elm and Maple.
Q. What directions do these streets go?
A. Elm is a north-south street; Maple is an east-west street.
Q. What kind of streets are they?
A. They're both commercial streets with small shops. Both Elm and Maple have two lanes of traffic, with meter parking on both sides of the street.
Q. What were the lighting conditions like at the time?
A. It was dark outside, but that corner had two street lights on it, and there was more light coming from the stores. You could see without any trouble.
Q. Where were you when the crash happened?
A. I was standing on the southwest corner, waiting to cross Elm Street.
Q. Where did the crash happen?
A. Right in front of me, in the middle of the intersection.

Here you have painted a general description of the location of the robbery and of the lighting conditions that existed at the time. More detailed elaboration is unnecessary. Let the cross-examiner ask exactly how wide Maple Street was, exactly how far the witness was from the location of the accident, and how far each streetlight was from the accident.

These details will not substantially add to your direct examination. Prepare your witness for those detail questions, of course, but committing your witness to those details on direct adds nothing except grist for the cross-examiner's mill.

7. Use pace in describing action

Pace involves controlling the speed of the examination. This is particularly important where occurrence testimony is concerned. Pace, fortunately, can be easily controlled by the examiner, simply by eliciting the witness' testimony in small segments at the most advantageous rate.

Remember that the jury, unlike you and the witness, has never heard the testimony before. Its ability to receive, digest, and comprehend is limited. The critical part of most automobile collisions, for instance, will take place in a few seconds. In such a situation pace can be controlled to *slow down* the action. You may want to present the occurrence frame-by-frame, much like a slow-motion or stop-action movie. Only by slowing down the action will the jury be able to picture how the collision actually happened.

Example:

Plaintiff in most collision cases will want to slow down the action to demonstrate that he was exercising due care under the circumstances.

Q. As you approached the intersection of Elm and Maple, did you observe any traffic?
A. No, not at that time.
Q. What was your speed at that time?
A. About 20 mph.
Q. As you approached the intersection, what did you do?
A. I slowed down and looked left and right.
Q. Where was your car when you first saw the other car?
A. I was entering the intersection.
Q. How fast were you driving then?
A. About 15 mph.
Q. Where was the other car then?
A. It was approaching the intersection from my left.
Q. How fast was he going?
A. I couldn't tell.
Q. What did you do next?
A. I kept going through the intersection.
Q. Did you see the other car again?
A. Yes.
Q. When?
A. When I was in the middle of the intersection.
Q. How fast were you going then?
A. About 15 mph.
Q. At that time, could you estimate the other car's speed?
A. Yes.
Q. What was it?
A. Around 20 to 25 mph.
Q. Where was the car?
A. It was coming right at me, in the intersection.
Q. How far from your car was his?
A. Around 15 feet.
Q. What did you do?
A. I stepped on my brakes and turned my wheel.
Q. What happened next?
A. His car rammed mine.
Q. What part of the intersection was the collision in?
A. Almost exactly in the middle of it.
Q. What part of his car struck what part of yours?
A. His left front bumper struck the left rear side of my car.
Q. Where did the cars end up?
A. My car stopped near the southeast corner of the intersection. His car was still stuck to the rear left side of my car, perpendicular to it.

In the above example, you have slowed down the action by having the witness describe four separate segments of the occurrence: (a) approaching the intersection, (b) just before the collision, (c) the collision itself, and (d) where the cars stopped. By having the witness describe each sequence in some detail, you have created a slow-motion word picture of what actually took very few seconds. The jury is able to follow the testimony, understand it completely, and form a picture of the collision. In addition, you have created an impression that the driver was totally alert as he drove to the intersection and could not possibly have caused the collision.

In some situations you will want to convey the impression that an event happened very quickly, unexpectedly, without time to deliberate or react. In those situations you will want the pace *speeded up.*

Example (defendant, in the above example):

Q. Mr. Jones, as you entered the intersection of Elm and Maple, did you see any other traffic?
A. No.
Q. How fast were you going?
A. Around 15 mph.
Q. What's the next thing you did?
A. I kept going straight ahead through the intersection.
Q. What happened next?
A. Well, I was about in the middle of the intersection when suddenly another car flashed in front of me, coming from my right. Before I even had a chance to hit my brakes, the other car collided with mine.

By delivering the critical testimony quickly, you create a sense of how unexpectedly and quickly the accident occurred. The impression the jury gets from this examination, the one you want to convey, is that the accident was inevitable.

In every witness' testimony, therefore, you must decide if you want to expand, shorten, or leave alone the pace of your witness' description of the occurrence in the way you want the jury to view it, and frame your direct examination questions accordingly.

8. Use simple language

Keeping the direct examinations simple also involves choosing simple words and phrases for your questions. Psychological studies have repeatedly demonstrated that how a question is phrased has a significant impact on how it is answered. Word choice, that is, affects the answer. Asking a witness "how fast" a car was traveling, rather than "how slowly," will invariably get a greater speed from the witness. Terms such as "smash" and "collided" convey different impressions than "struck" or "hit." In each case, therefore, you must decide in advance what words and phrases you want to employ to create advantageous impressions, then use them consistently during your examinations of witnesses and the other phases of the trial.

Eliminate "police talk" and other jargon from your vocabulary, as well as your witnesses'. Consider the following:

Example:

When did you exit from your vehicle?	vs.	*When did you get out of your car?*
Did you have an occasion to converse with him?	vs.	*Did you ever talk to him?*
How long have you been so employed?	vs.	*How many years have you been a bricklayer?*
Subsequent to your arrest, what, if anything, happened?	vs.	*What happened after they arrested you?*

The latter phrasing is obviously preferable. It is a clear, simple and understandable way of asking a question. Eliminating the stilted language will be appreciated by the witness as well as the jury.

9.   Use nonleading, open-ended questions

Basic to the rules surrounding direct examinations is the general prohibition against leading witnesses. Inexperienced lawyers usually lead too much on direct. Although it is a rule of evidence with, of course, certain exceptions, it is also a rule of persuasion. By suggesting the answer in your question, you diminish the impact of having the witness volunteer the facts himself. Jurors will wonder if the witness would have given that answer if the lawyer had not practically put it in the witness' mouth. If the witness gives only "yes" and "no" answers, the jury has no adequate way of assessing his credibility. A cardinal rule on direct examination is that the lawyer should never do anything that will detract from his witness or diminish the impact of his witness' testimony. Leading, suggestive questions do exactly that.

Example:

What kind of streets are at the intersection?	vs.	*The streets at the intersection are both two lanes, aren't they?*
Please describe what the man looked like.	vs.	*Was the man six feet tall and about 25 years old?*

What happened after he an-   vs.   *Did the man take the wallet*
nounced a robbery?   *from your purse after announc-*
                                             ing a robbery?

The examples in the left column are obviously the nonleading ones. These don't put words in the witness' mouth, and are much more effective before the jury. On the other hand, preliminary matters that are not in dispute can often be brought out more smoothly and effectively by leading. This will get you to the important testimony more quickly, before the jury gets bored.

Effective direct examinations are best achieved by using open-ended questions that elicit descriptive responses. This serves two functions. First, such questions let the witness tell the story and reveal the important evidence himself. Second, they minimize the presence of the lawyer. Remember that during direct examinations the witness should be the center of attention. Your questions should merely guide the witness from one area to another as he testifies, and break up the testimony into digestible capsules. In the preceding example, the first questions are all open-ended.

Once you have directed the witness to a certain area, the questions below can be effectively and repeatedly used to break up the testimony and to control its pace. They are short, broad, open-ended, and nonleading and do not detract from the witness.

Example:

    Q. What did you see (next)?

    Q. What did you hear (next)?

    Q. What did you (he, they) do (next)?

    Q. Did anything happen?

    Q. What happened (next)?

    Q. Then what happened?

On the other hand, using only short, open-ended questions can become monotonous, running the risk that the jury will, in ignoring your questions, ignore the answers as well. Accordingly, vary your form periodically. Ask specific explanatory and follow-up questions where appropriate. Where a witness gave a particularly good answer, use the answer as part of your next question. Remember, however, that this is effective only when sparingly used.

Example:

    Q. After the defendant said, "Give me the money," what happened?

10.   Have the witness explain

Many times a witness will say something that makes no sense, or uses a technical term or phrase. Since your overall purpose is to give the jury a clear understanding of the events involved, any confusion should be clarified immediately. Put yourself in the jury's shoes. If the jury looks confused or wants an explanation, you must get it for them. This, however, must be done without embarrassing or demeaning the jury. When seeking additional details or explanations, use narrowly phrased questions that go directly to the problem area.

Examples:

> *Q.* I'm sorry, Mr. Doe, I didn't follow you there. Where were you standing when you actually saw the collision?

> *Q.* Dr. Jones, exactly what is a herniated disc?

The jury will appreciate your immediately having something important clarified or explained, without having suggested that they didn't understand it the first time.

11.   Volunteer weaknesses

Conventional wisdom has it that you should volunteer weaknesses during the direct examination. In this way, it is believed, you will take the sting out of the weakness by voluntarily disclosing it before the cross-examiner can effectively use it.

While this conventional wisdom is useful as a general proposition, its intelligent application to any given witness is often difficult. How damaging is the weakness? Does your opponent know about it? Will this weakness become apparent during the course of the direct examination? Can you gracefully volunteer the weakness? Does your opponent have trial skills that can effectively expose the weakness during the cross-examination? These are the kinds of considerations that must be evaluated and weighed before deciding whether to volunteer the weakness during the direct examination. Remember, however, that direct examinations should be positive and forceful. Volunteering weaknesses necessarily works against this goal. Consequently, unless the weakness is significant, and other considerations point to volunteering it, the weakness might better remain undisclosed.

When you do decide to volunteer a weakness, it is usually best to bury it in the middle of the direct examination. Remember that jurors, like people in general, remember best what they hear first and last. (These are the general principles of "primacy" and "recency.") Accordingly, it is usually best to start the examination on a positive note, disclose the unfavorable information afterwards, and end on another positive point.

The weakness will have less impact when volunteered after the witness has made an initial good impression. Studies have shown that people are reluctant to change their initial impressions when confronted by unfavorable facts.

12. Use exhibits to highlight facts

Exhibits should be used during the direct examination to highlight the central facts of your case and explain important details to the jury. The preferable time to use exhibits is after the witness has substantially completed his oral testimony. In this way the exhibit will not interrupt or detract from the oral testimony. Using exhibits at the end of the direct examination is usually an effective way to repeat and emphasize the important facts brought out by the witness. The effective use of exhibits at trial is discussed in §5.4.

13. Listen to the answers

While attentiveness is usually thought of as applying to cross-examinations, it has equal application to direct examinations. Although your position during direct examinations should be behind the jury if possible, jurors will from time to time look at you, as well as everyone else in the courtroom. Accordingly, appear interested in the witness' answers. Maintain eye contact with him. You can hardly expect the jury to hang on the witness' words if you look and sound bored. Appearing interested has other consequences. It carries over to and infects the witness. It eliminates any suggestion that the direct has been choreographed and rehearsed in advance. Finally, it helps you avoid making mistakes and makes you alert to the unexpected answers that inevitably appear.

14. Lawyer's position

In many jurisdictions, lawyers are permitted to walk around the courtroom and place themselves in the most strategic locations during examinations. In others, the lawyers are required to conduct their examinations from a lectern or counsel table. Where court rules permit, however, you should use the available arena to the fullest possible extent. This means, during direct examinations, that the witness' contact with the jury is maximized while yours is minimized. This is best achieved by conducting your examination near the far end of the jury box.

Example:

In the following schematic diagram of a courtroom, you can effectively conduct the direct examinations near the position marked "X."

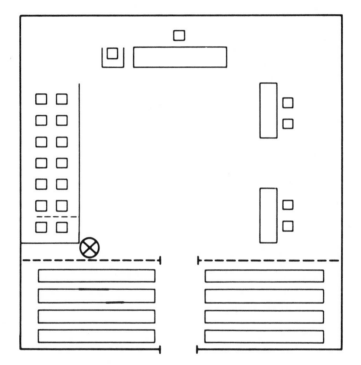

Doing this has several immediate benefits:

a. It removes you from the jury's line of sight to the witness, thereby eliminating a visual distraction.
b. It allows you to use written notes for the examination without the jury being actively aware of it.
c. It forces the witness to speak up, since he will subconsciously talk loudly enough for you to hear him, thereby ensuring that every juror will easily hear his testimony.
d. It forces the witness to look at the jurors, thereby maintaining critical eye contact with them.

§4.3. Occurrence witnesses

The most common type of witness in trials is the occurrence witness. An occurrence witness is simply any witness who saw, heard, or did anything pertinent to the case. Most jury trials involve either personal injury or criminal cases in which one event, usually an accident or a crime, forms the core of the case. Since these cases involve events, the eyewitnesses will be the critical witnesses at trial. How these occurrence witnesses testify will in large measure determine the outcome of the trial. Accordingly, the ability to forcefully and clearly present an occurrence witness at trial is an essential component of every trial lawyer's arsenal.

Presenting occurrence witnesses effectively requires utilizing the elements discussed in the previous section. The direct examination should be simply and logically organized; it should develop what is important and only mention what is peripheral. The questioning should elicit witness background and scene description first, so that the action can be presented in an uninterrupted way. Both the background facts and action should be elicited with short, open-ended questions that allow the witness to present flowing descriptions the jury can picture. Finally, the direct examination should have a pace that makes the testimony come alive.

When well done, the direct examination should recreate for the jury not just what the witness saw, heard and did, but also the atmosphere and intensity of feelings that existed during the event. A direct examination that achieves these objectives, that clearly recreates the event for the jury, is one of the most difficult and rewarding achievements a trial lawyer can attain.

Types of occurrence witnesses are numerous, and it would achieve little to attempt to illustrate all representative types. Instead, this section will present the direct examinations of a few common types of occurrence witnesses in question-and-answer form, with an accompanying explanation showing why the questions were asked and framed as they were. When the reasoning underlying these direct examinations is understood, that knowledge can be applied equally well to any type of occurrence witness.

1.   Example — direct examinations in a civil case

In the following civil case, plaintiff James Smith has filed suit against defendant Frank Jones, alleging that he was injured when Jones negligently drove into him as he was walking across the street at the intersection at Elm and Maple Streets on December 13, 1984. Jones has denied liability, claiming that he had the right of way and that Smith walked against the light. Hence, at trial the central issues are whether the defendant was negligent and whether the plaintiff was contributorily negligent.

Following are the direct examinations of the plaintiff and an eyewitness to the collision, two common types of witnesses in personal injury cases.

Example (victim in an automobile collision case):

Plaintiff James Smith — direct examination

Q. Mr. Smith, what is your full name?

A. James P. Smith.

Q. Where do you live?

A. At 1650 N. Maple.

Q. How long have you lived there?

A. For seven years.

Q. Where are you from originally?

A. I've lived in Chicago all my life, 36 years.

Q. Who lives with you?

A. My wife and two daughters.

Q. How old are your children?

A. Well, Betsy's five and Becky is three.

Q. Is your wife employed outside your home?

A. Not right now, but she used to be a school teacher before the kids came.

Q. What is your occupation?

A. I'm also a school teacher.

Q. What school do you teach at?

A. At Central School, part of the Chicago Public Schools.

Q. How long have you been at Central?

A. Eight years.

Q. What grades do you teach?

A. I've always taught 8th- and 9th-grade math.

Q. Do you have any other employment?

A. During the school year I've coached the junior high boys' basketball team. During the summer I'm a counselor at Camp Thather, a co-ed day camp for children.

Q. How long have you held these positions?

A. Ever since I started teaching.

Q. Mr. Smith, where did you receive your basic schooling?

A. I attended Chicago public schools.

Q. After that, where did you continue your education?

A. First I attended the University of Illinois and received a bachelor's degree in 1976. I

(Background)

These are the easy background questions, sometimes called the "love and affection" questions. They enhance his credibility as a witness by showing him to be a normal man, and allow him to relax and get used to testifying in the courtroom environment.

Notice that the witness gives short, factual answers to the background questions. Answers that are too flowery and obviously self-serving can backfire before a jury.

then continued my studies in mathematics at Northwestern and received a master's degree in 1977.

Q. Do you have hobbies and other interests you pursue in your free time?

A. Yes, I do.

Q. What are those?

A. Well, my main hobby was hiking and camping, usually with the family. We'd do that on weekends and summer vacations. In addition, I used to play basketball with a church league once a week during the school year. I also did the usual kind of gardening, lawn mowing, and repairs around the house.

Q. Mr. Smith, let's turn now to where the collision happened. Are you familiar with the intersection of Elm and Maple Streets?

A. Yes, I am.

Q. How many times have you been there?

A. I've been there thousands of times. It's just down the street from my house.

Q. Which directions do Elm and Maple go?

A. Elm is an east-west street. Maple runs north and south.

Q. How many lanes do they have?

A. Elm has four traffic lanes as well as parking lanes on both sides of the street. Maple has two lanes of traffic and parking on both sides.

Q. Does the intersection have any traffic controls?

A. Yes, it has traffic lights.

Q. Where are those located?

A. There are lights on poles on each corner. These include traffic signals and pedestrian lights.

Q. Does the intersection have other markings or controls?

A. Yes, sir.

Q. How are they marked?

A. The traffic lanes are marked with white dotted lines. There are four pedestrian crosswalks marked with solid white lines, and white stop lines in front of the crosswalks.

Q. Mr. Smith, let's turn now to when this collision happened. What was the date and time when you were struck?

The extracurricular activities should be demonstrated because they bear significantly on the issue of damages. The response paints a picture of the plaintiff that shows he is a likable, normal man who could be anyone's neighbor.

(Scene)

The description of the intersection is important in this case, so it should be described clearly, even if you have photographs and charts to supplement the intersection testimony. The witness' ability to describe the intersection accurately will enhance his credibility.

The description should include:

  a. direction of streets
  b. size of streets
  c. lane markers
  d. traffic lights
  e. pedestrian lights and crosswalks
  f. stop lines

Note the transition question.

A. It was December 13, 1984, at approximately 12:30 P.M.

Q. What was the weather like at that time?

A. It was clear, partly cloudy.

Q. What were the traffic conditions like?

A. It was fairly busy. There were lots of cars as well as pedestrians.

Q. What was the condition of the streets and sidewalks?

A. They were dry and clear.

Q. What were you doing at that time?

A. I was walking on the sidewalk, northbound, on the east side of Maple, going toward Elm.

Q. Did you reach Elm?

A. Yes, I did.

Q. As you reached Elm, for which streets were the lights green?

A. They were green for Elm Street traffic.

Q. What did you do?

A. I waited for the lights to change.

Q. Were there any other pedestrians waiting for lights?

A. Not at my corner. I think there were people waiting on the others.

Q. Were there any cars waiting for the light?

A. There were cars on Maple Street.

Q. What happened next?

A. I stood at the corner, looking north at the traffic lights on the northeast corner. The lights began to turn.

Q. What did you do next?

A. I looked up and down Elm Street. There weren't any cars coming.

Q. What happened next?

A. The light for Maple turned green and the walk-light for pedestrian traffic across Elm turned to "walk."

Q. What did you do?

A. I stepped off the curb and started walking on the crosswalk across Elm.

Q. What happened next?

A. I took three or four steps off the curb and was walking in the cross-walk when I was hit from behind by a car. I remember the car crashing into my left leg, and being thrown into the street. I remember hearing brakes screeching after I was hit.

The description should also include:
  a. weather
  b. road surface conditions
  c. traffic conditions

The background description is now completed. It is time to begin the action part of the testimony.

(Action)

The action can now begin without the interruption of further description. This makes the action flow with sufficient pace.

Show due care and caution, and absence of contributory negligence.

Notice how short the questions have become. They don't detract from the witness, particularly during the critical part of the testimony.
Notice also that the pace of the testimony has quickened. Good pace makes the testimony come alive. This is the worst place to bore the jury with testimony that drags on.

Q. Mr. Smith, what is the first thing you noticed about yourself?

A. All I can remember is a stinging, burning kind of pain coming from my left knee. I remember I couldn't move my leg.

Q. Where were you at this time?

A. I was more or less facedown in the street.

Q. What happened next?

A. Several people ran to me and told me not to move.

Q. Then what happened?

A. I stayed on the street for I don't know how long, and finally an ambulance came. They put a stretcher next to me and they slowly eased me on the stretcher. They then put me in the ambulance and took me to the Memorial Hospital emergency room.

Q. On the way to the hospital, how did you feel?

A. Not very well. I kept having these shooting, stinging pains going up and down my left leg and began feeling very dizzy and nauseated.

Q. What happened when you reached the Memorial Hospital emergency room?

A. The ambulance attendants took me out of the ambulance and wheeled me into one of the emergency rooms.

Q. What happened there?

A. Some nurses cut off my trouser leg, others were attaching a tube to my arm and drawing blood.

Q. What happened next?

A. They moved a portable X-ray unit to my table and started taking X rays.

Q. What happened after that?

A. A doctor came over and talked to me.

Q. What happened next?

A. They gave me a shot of anesthesia and that's the last thing I remember.

Q. Mr. Smith, what is the next thing you can remember happening?

A. Next thing I remember is waking up in a hospital room.

Q. What is the first thing you noticed about yourself?

A. Well, I remember feeling very groggy and heavy. I had this dull throbbing, pulsating

Developing the victim's condition immediately after the collision is important to the issue of damages.

The testimony should review the medical treatment and recovery in a step-by-step way, since pain and suffering will be a substantial part of any verdict in this case.

   a. immediate treatment in hospital

   b. postoperative period in hospital

kind of pain in my left leg. I looked down at my leg and saw that they had applied a cast from my left toe that reached up to my crotch.

Q. How long did you remain at Memorial Hospital?

A. About five days.

Q. What did you do during those five days?

A. Nothing, really. I just lay on my back, and they had my left leg up on a pile of pillows to reduce the swelling.

Q. During those five days, how did you feel?

A. Well, I started getting very stiff and sore because I was always lying on my back. I had trouble sleeping in that position. I could not get up for anything. I had to use a bedpan for bowel movements. The pain in my leg changed to a dull throbbing ache.

Q. Mr. Smith, let's talk now about your condition after you left the hospital. First, how did you get home?

A. The attendants wheeled me outside in a wheelchair with my foot elevated. They helped me get into my car, on the back seat, and helped me put my leg on the seat. My wife drove me home. When I got home I was carried into the house, and put to bed, and again put my left leg as high as I could.

Q. How long did you remain in bed at home?

A. About two more weeks.

Q. After that two-week period were you able to do anything else?

A. I started to get up for a few minutes at a time, using metal crutches. Usually I went to the bathroom or got up to stretch for a few minutes.

Q. Did you notice anything about your leg during those times?

A. Yes. Every time I would get up and use the crutches the throbbing in my leg would get a lot worse. The leg would start swelling and feel very warm.

Q. What did you do when that happened?

A. I would have to lie down and raise my leg again.

Q. After going home, did you see the doctor again?

Notice that the pace has slowed down, since the immediate trauma of the collision and emergency-room treatment has passed.

Another transition question.

c. initial recovery period at home

A. Well, I saw Dr. Bartells at the hospital about six weeks later. He removed the cast and put on another one.

Q. What kind of cast was this one?

A. It was like the first one. It was from my ankle up to my crotch.

Q. How long did you have that second cast on?

A. About eight more weeks.

Q. During that period of time, what was the condition of your leg?

A. The pain and throbbing were getting better, except if I kept my leg down for any period of time. Then I would have to put the leg up again.

Q. When was the next time you saw Dr. Bartells?

A. About eight weeks later I went back to his office. Dr. Bartells removed the second cast and took more X rays. He then wrapped my knee and calf with an elastic bandage.

Q. What did you notice about your leg after the cast was removed?

A. The first thing I noticed was how skinny it was. My left thigh was maybe half the size of the right one. In addition, I could only move my knee maybe three or four inches in either direction.

Q. What happened when you tried to bend your knee?

A. It just wouldn't bend much and hurt when I tried to bend it.

Q. Could you walk without crutches at that time?

A. No, I didn't start putting weight on the leg for another month.

Q. During that month, what were you doing?

A. I was still at home. I had to apply as much heat to the knee and leg as I could and attempt to bend the knee joint. I had to do this several times each day.

Q. How did you feel during this therapy?

A. It was mainly very painful. You had to stretch the ligaments in the knee to get the motion back.

Q. How long did you do this treatment?

d. continued medical treatment

e. continued therapy

It is important to show that plaintiff, at considerable pain and effort, tried to rehabilitate the leg to its former condition.

A. I did it continuously for about five weeks. After that I did it a couple of times a day for maybe three more months.

Q. Did you ever get full motion back in your knee?

A. Not completely. I could straighten my leg all the way, but I could never bend it the other way as far as it used to go.

Q. Mr. Smith, let's talk for a moment about the effect all this had on your teaching job. When was the first time you returned to work?

A. I went back to work after spring vacation, which would have been the middle of April.

Q. From the day of the accident until you returned to work, were you able to do any kind of work at all?

A. No.

Q. After returning to work, were you able to do all the things you used to?

A. No, by that time I was walking without crutches, but still limping a great deal. I couldn't coach basketball or do anything like sports.

Q. After returning to work, did you have further therapy on your leg?

A. Yes, sir. I still continued the heat treatment, the bending exercises, every day. I also did weight exercises to build up the muscles in that leg.

Q. Finally, Mr. Smith, let's talk about how you feel and what you can do now. What is the condition of your leg today?

A. Well, the leg is still smaller than the other one. The pain is gone as long as I take it easy on the leg.

Q. Is there anything you cannot do today that you could do before the collision?

A. Yes, sir. I cannot play basketball or go hiking like I used to.

Q. What happens when you attempt these activities?

A. My knee swells up. It starts aching and throbbing.

Q. Have you ever played or coached basketball since the collision?

A. No, sir. I tried it once or twice, but it just doesn't work. It just hurts too much.

Also important is any permanent disability from the injury. (You might have the plaintiff demonstrate the degree of movement and appearance of the leg to the jury, although some lawyers feel this can backfire.)

This testimony is necessary to establish the lost wages element of damages.

Continuing present pain is also important on the issue of damages.

Permanent limitation of activities should be demonstrated.

Notice that the witness is testifying in a very factual way, avoiding the danger that too emotional a presentation will cause a jury reaction.

Q. Mr. Smith, before this collision occurred, what was your health like?

A. I was in perfect health; I didn't have any problems.

Prior good health should be shown.

Q. As a result of this collision, how have your injuries affected your life?

A. As I said, I can't do things like basketball and hiking that I used to do. I can't play with my wife and daughters as I used to. I pretty much have to take it easy and not do anything that strains the leg, or else the swelling and pain always come back.

This last question and answer sum up the changed circumstances of the plaintiff's life and relate it to his family. After such a high point, stop.

Q. Thank you, Mr. Smith. Your Honor, we have no further questions on direct.

Example (eyewitness to an automobile collision case):

The following witness, an eyewitness to the same collision, will be called after the plaintiff has testified. Because of this, certain areas the plaintiff already covered need not be duplicated. Instead, the witness will be used to corroborate certain critical facts and sequences that establish that the defendant was negligent and the plaintiff was not.

Witness John Doe — direct examination

Q. Mr. Doe, please state your full name.

A. John J. Doe.

Q. Where do you live?

A. I live at 1550 N. Maple.

Q. How long have you lived there?

A. About 1½ years.

Q. Whom do you live there with?

A. I'm single. I live by myself.

Q. What kind of work do you do?

A. I'm the custodian of the 1500 N. Aster Street condominium.

Q. How long have you been working for that building?

A. About two years.

Q. Have you always been employed in the building maintenance field?

A. Yes, sir, for about 20 years.

Q. Mr. Doe, are you familiar with the intersection of Elm and Maple Streets?

A. I sure am.

Q. How often do you go there?

A. I go by there two times a day, on my way to work and coming back.

Notice that, since this is an occurrence witness, not the plaintiff, only those aspects of his background that bear directly on his credibility as a witness are brought out. Notice that the witness is only asked to estab-

Q. Were you at the intersection of Maple and Elm Streets on December 13, 1984, around 12:30 P.M.?

A. Yes, I was.

Q. Where at that intersection were you?

A. I was on the northeast corner of the intersection waiting on the light.

Q. When you say waiting "on the light" exactly what do you mean?

A. I was standing on the corner, waiting for the green walk-light so I could walk south across Elm Street.

Q. When you first got to that corner, what color were the lights?

A. The lights were green for the Elm traffic. The crosswalk light for crossing Elm was on "don't walk."

Q. When that crosswalk light changed to "walk," where were you?

A. I was still on the northeast corner facing south.

Q. After the walk-light changed, what did you do?

A. I started to step off the sidewalk into the street.

Q. At that time did anything happen?

A. It sure did.

Q. What was that?

A. As I was stepping into the street, another man was also stepping into the street from the other corner, walking directly toward me.

Q. Which corner was the man on?

A. That would have been the southeast corner.

Q. What happened next?

A. Suddenly, a car made a right-hand turn from Maple going eastbound on Elm.

Q. What happened next?

A. As the car was completing the turn, it struck the man right in the side.

Q. What part of the car struck what part of the man?

A. The right front bumper of the car struck the man's left leg.

Q. Where was the man when he was hit?

A. He was on the crosswalk around ⅓ of the way across the street.

Q. What happened after that?

lish his familiarity with the intersection. He should not describe it again. This has already been done by the plaintiff. Moreover, he might contradict the plaintiff's description in some respects.

When the witness says something that is not clear, have him explain the term.

Since the walk-lights are an important issue, this witness should corroborate the plaintiff's version of the facts (that he had the green walk-light when he stepped off the curb).

At this point the pace should pick up to help recreate the occurrence.

Notice that no unnecessary detail is elicited here. The witness testifies to the important facts efficiently. Exact times and distances are avoided. (These are the kinds of details the cross-examiner will probe. Why

A. The car screeched to a halt and the man was knocked down on the ground.

Q. After you saw all this happen, what is the first thing you did?

A. I ran over to where the man was lying on the street and told him not to move and not to try to get up.

Q. What did you notice about the man?

A. His face was all contorted and he was sort of squirming on the ground. He kept trying to grab his left knee.

Q. What happened next?

A. I and some other people tried to make him comfortable and keep him quiet until an ambulance could come.

Q. Did an ambulance come?

A. Yes, five or ten minutes later.

Q. What happened then?

A. The ambulance people put the man on a stretcher, very slowly, put him in the ambulance, and drove off.

Q. What is the next thing you did?

A. By that time some policemen were there directing traffic and talking to people, so I talked to one of them and told them what I had seen when all this happened.

Q. Thank you. I have no further questions.

make it easier for him by committing the witness to the details in advance?)

The evidence of the victim's pain and suffering should be brought out.

Notice that this witness' direct examination is short. He contributes a few corroborative details on important points, then stops.

2. Example — direct examinations in a criminal case

In the following criminal case, John Smith is charged with raping Sharon Jones in the bedroom of her apartment on April 10, 1985. The defendant, while denying he committed the rape, does not contest that a rape occurred. Hence, the central issue in the case is the identification of the offender.

Following are the direct examinations of the victim and the first police officer who arrived at the scene of the crime, probably the two most common witness types in criminal cases.

Example (victim in a rape case):

Victim Sharon Jones — direct examination

Q. Please state your full name.

A. Sharon Jones.

Q. How old are you, Ms. Jones?

A. I am 23.

The victim's age is a necessary element in a rape case under state statutes.

Q. Are you single or married?

A. I'm single. I've never been married.

Q. Do you live here?

A. Yes, I live on the north side.

Q. How long have you lived there?

A. About five years.

Q. Where are you from originally?

A. I was raised in Rockford and lived there until I finished high school.

Q. Did you ever attend any schools after high school?

A. Yes, I went to college at the University of Illinois.

Q. Did you receive a degree?

A. I received a bachelor of arts degree with a specialty in education.

Q. What did you do after graduating from college?

A. For the last year I have been working as a 7th-grade teacher in the Public School System.

Q. Which school do you teach at?

A. I teach at Hawthorne School on the south side.

Up to this point the questions have elicited the victim's background. By this time she should feel more at ease.

Q. Ms. Jones, on April 10, 1985, where were you living?

A. I was living at 2501 North Halsted Street.

Q. Did you live there with anyone?

A. No, I lived there by myself.

Q. What kind of building is that?

A. It is a two-flat building. I lived in the second-floor apartment.

The scene of the crime is important. Hence, the witness is asked to describe it in some detail. This must be done in a logical, progressive fashion.

Q. Describe the entrances to your second-floor apartment.

A. There is a front door that serves both apartments. There is an inside stairwell which leads up to my apartment. There is also a rear porch with a stairwell leading to the second floor. The rear entrance from the porch goes to my kitchen.

Q. Do the doors at the top of the stairs and in the kitchen have locks?

A. Yes, they do.

Q. Were those doors locked when you last entered your house the evening before?

A. Yes, they were. Both doors have deadbolt locks. I always keep them locked.

Q. Describe the rooms in your second-floor apartment.

A. The apartment has four rooms. When you go up the front steps, you enter into the living room. Behind the living room toward the rear of the apartment, a kitchen is in one corner and my bedroom is in the other corner. The bathroom is between the living room and the kitchen.

The description has progressed from the building, to the apartment, and finally to the bedroom, where the rape actually took place.

Q. Describe your bedroom as it looked on April 10.

A. As you stand in the doorway there is the far wall which has two windows. Against the right-hand wall there is my bed. Against the left-hand wall there are two dressers. On top of a dresser is a lamp.

Q. What are the approximate sizes of the windows?

Since the primary trial issue is identification, the lighting conditions must be described and explained in detail.

A. Each of the two windows is about two feet wide and four feet tall.

Q. Did those windows have curtains?

A. Yes, they did.

Q. Were the curtains open or closed that morning?

A. The curtains were open.

Q. What was the weather like that morning?

A. It was a bright, sunny day.

Q. What were the lighting conditions like in the bedroom that morning?

A. It had good lighting. I had no trouble seeing things in the room.

Q. Ms. Jones, where were you during the morning hours of April 10, 1985?

A. I was dozing in bed.

Q. How long had you been in bed?

A. Since about 2:00 A.M. that morning.

Q. What kind of clothing were you wearing?

A. I was wearing a nightgown.

Q. Had you woken up at any time that morning?

The description of the setting is now complete. The action portion of her testimony can now safely begin.

A. Yes, I did.

Q. When was that?

A. I woke up around 10:00, drank a glass of water and went back to bed.

Q. Did you fall back to sleep?

A. Well, I was dozing on and off.

Q. Ms. Jones, at approximately 12:30 P.M., did anything happen?

A. Yes.

Q. What was that?

A. I heard a noise that startled me. I looked up and saw a man standing in the doorway to my bedroom.

Q. What was that man doing?

A. He just stood there.

Q. What did that man look like?

A. Well, he was white, 25 to 30 years old, around 6 feet tall, and weighed 180 to 200 lbs.

Q. Did you notice anything about his face?

A. I noticed that he had dark hair and a mustache.

Q. What kind of clothing was he wearing?

A. I remember he had on a dark blue V-neck sweater and dark-colored, casual-type slacks. I didn't notice his shoes.

Q. Ms. Jones, the man you saw standing in your doorway on April 10, 1985, at approximately 12:30 P.M., do you see him in court today?

A. Yes, I do.

Q. Would you please point to him and describe what he is wearing in court today?

A. He is the man right over there (pointing). He is wearing a blue suit with a light blue paisley shirt.

Q. Your Honor, may the record reflect that the witness has pointed to and identified the defendant, John Smith?

Court: The record will so reflect.

Q. When you saw the defendant standing in your doorway, what did you do?

A. I screamed.

Q. What happened next?

A. He walked from the doorway, leaped on my bed, and grabbed my throat.

Q. What happened next?

A. We were struggling on the bed. He kept on grabbing my throat, and I was screaming and trying to get his hands off me.

Q. Which direction was he facing?

A. He was looking down at me.

Q. Which direction were you facing?

A. I was looking up at him.

Q. How far was your face from his face?

A. No more than two feet apart.

Q. During this time did the defendant say anything?

Since the issue is identification, the victim's description of the offender, particularly when it is very accurate, should be brought out in detail.

Here the witness is asked to identify the offender as the defendant as early in the testimony as is possible. Thereafter, you can refer to him as the "defendant," which depersonalizes him and gets the jury to look at him each time he is mentioned.

The testimony, now being in the action part, should have pace. It should move to recreate the horror of the event. The questions are short, and merely help break up the narrative into digestible segments.

The face-to-face confrontation is important to the identification.

A. He kept saying he would kill me if I didn't do what he said.

Q. What happened next?

A. He pulled the blankets off the bed and pulled my nightgown up.

Q. What happened after that?

A. While he was holding me by the throat he kept telling me to shut up and he was undoing his belt and trousers with his left hand.

Q. While he was doing that, what were you doing?

A. I was just trying to breathe and push him off.

Q. What happened next?

A. He started to have intercourse with me.

Q. Exactly what did he do?

A. Well, you know, he forced his penis in my vagina.

Q. How long did that go on?

A. Maybe a couple of minutes, I'm not sure.

Q. What happened after that?

A. He just lay there for a few minutes, then got up, pulled up his trousers and ran out of the bedroom.

Q. From the time you first saw the defendant in the doorway to the time he ran out of the bedroom, how much time had passed?

A. Maybe 10 minutes.

Q. What happened after the defendant left?

A. I lay there for a couple of minutes, trying to get my breath back. Then I called the police. Then I just cried.

Q. Did any police arrive?

A. Yes.

Q. Who were they?

A. Two policemen in uniforms came up to the apartment. I don't remember their names.

Q. Did you talk with them?

A. I did, but I don't remember what I told them.

Q. How long were the policemen in your apartment?

A. Maybe 10 minutes.

Q. What happened next?

A. They took me downstairs to their squad car and drove me to Memorial Hospital.

Q. Where at the hospital did you go?

> Since penetration is a required element in a rape case, this fact must clearly be established.

> At this point the pace can begin to slow down again.

A. They took me to the emergency room.

Q. What happened there?

A. Some nurses and doctors examined me. They examined my neck and they gave me a pelvic exam. They also gave me some medication.

Q. How long were you in the emergency room at Memorial Hospital?

A. About one hour.

Q. What happened after that?

A. The same two policemen drove me to my friend's home.

Q. How long did you remain there?

A. I stayed there for several days.   This question again reminds the jury how

Q. Did you ever go back to your apartment?   terrifying the event

A. No, I never went back there.   was for the witness.

Q. Other than seeing the defendant in your bedroom on April 10, 1985, had you ever seen him before?

A. No.

Q. Is there any question in your mind today as to the man who attacked you on April 10, 1985?

A. No.

Q. Who was it?

A. The defendant, the man right over there.   This is a good way to

Q. Your Honor, we have no further questions.   stop. Have the witness re-identify the defendant as the last question of the direct examination.

Example (police officer at scene of rape):

Just like the eyewitness in the automobile collision case, the police officer is being called to corroborate certain important facts — that a rape did in fact occur, and that the lighting conditions were sufficient for the victim to observe the offender and subsequently identify him.

Witness Officer McCarthy — direct examination

Q. Please tell us your full name.

A. Jane J. McCarthy.

Q. What is your occupation?

A. I'm a police officer with the City Police Department.

Q. For how many years?

A. Five.

Q. ·Where are you presently assigned?

A.   Third District.

Q.   How long have you been in that district?

A.   All five years.

Q.   What have your assignments been over those five years?

A.   I've been a patrol officer doing regular patrol duty.

Q.   Officer McCarthy, were you working as a police officer on April 10, 1985?

A.   Yes, I was.

Q.   What shift were you working that day?

A.   I was on the day, the 8 to 4 shift.

Q.   Were you working with anyone?

A.   Yes, sir, my partner, Officer Byrne.

Q.   What was your assignment that day?

A.   We were on routine patrol duty in our squad car.

Q.   What area were you patrolling?

A.   Our beat was between North and Fullerton Avenues along the lakefront.

Q.   At approximately 12:45 P.M., did anything happen?

A.   Yes.

Q.   What happened?

A.   We received a message over our police radio.

Q.   After receiving the message, what did you do?

A.   We went to 2501 N. Halsted St., to the second-floor apartment.

Q.   How did you enter the apartment?

A.   We walked up the front stairs and walked into the front room.

Q.   Was anyone in the apartment?

A.   Yes. We met a young woman, a Sharon Jones, in the front room.

Q.   When you first saw her, what did Sharon Jones look like?

A.   She was dressed in a nightgown. Her hair was messed up. She was crying and shaking.

Q.   Did you talk to her?

A.   Yes.

Q.   Other than yourself, your partner, and Ms. Jones, was anyone else in the apartment?

A.   No.

Q.   What's the first thing she said to you?

Since the witness has described herself as a patrol officer, no further description is really necessary.

The actual content of the message will usually be hearsay.

This is the first important fact elicited on direct. This circumstantially corroborates the fact that the victim had just experienced something traumatic.

A. As we walked in, she said: "I've just been raped. The man that did it ran out a couple of minutes ago."

Q. What happened next?

A. She sat down and started to cry.

Q. What is the next thing you did?

A. I sat down next to her and tried to comfort her. My partner got her a pair of shoes and overcoat. She put on the shoes and overcoat.

Q. What happened next?

A. I went over to the bedroom.

Q. What did the bedroom look like?

A. Well, the sheets on the bed were all crumpled. There was a blanket half on the floor, and a pillow on the floor next to the bed.

Q. What was the lighting in the bedroom like?

A. It was pretty light in there.

Q. What happened next?

A. We put Ms. Jones in the squad car and drove her to the Memorial Hospital.

Q. What happened at the hospital?

A. We walked her into the emergency room and took her to one of the examining rooms. Some nurses and a doctor came to the room. We stayed outside in the waiting area.

Q. About how long was Ms. Jones in the examining room?

A. Perhaps an hour.

Q. After that hour, what happened?

A. We went into the examining room and talked with Ms. Jones for awhile.

Q. What was her condition at this time?

A. She had calmed down quite a bit. She had no difficulty talking to us about what had happened.

Q. How long did you talk to her?

A. About 15 minutes.

Q. What happened next?

A. We drove her in our squad car to a friend's house that Ms. Jones wanted to go to.

Q. What did you do next?

A. We went back to the station and prepared a written report summarizing what we had done in this case.

The prompt outcry of a rape victim is usually admissible as an exception to the hearsay rule.

The condition of the bedroom and the lighting conditions are important facts which must be corroborated, since they support the victim's testimony that she was violently attacked.

Notice how quickly this direct examination went. The witness corroborated the victim on a few important facts — that she was raped, that it occurred in the bedroom, and that the lighting conditions there were good — then stopped. Nothing unnecessary was asked.

§4.4. Conversations and statements

Conversations are frequently introduced as evidence in trials. However, since these conversations are out-of-court statements, they are usually hearsay and are inadmissible unless an exception to the hearsay rule applies. Accordingly, whenever you intend to introduce a conversation or statement in evidence, review the evidentiary basis for its admission. First, is the statement being offered for the truth of the matters asserted in the statement? If so, the statement is heresay. Second, if it is hearsay, is there any exception to the hearsay rule that applies? If so, the statement is admissible. You should always review FRE 801, 803, and 804 to determine if any exception is applicable.

The most common exception is admissions by party opponents. Whenever one party makes a statement and an opposing party wishes to introduce it, the statement is ordinarily admissible. If the statement made by a party opponent is part of a conversation, the conversation between the party opponent and another person is admissible, since the entire conversation is necessary to put the party opponent's statements in context.

Statements by agents and employees of party opponents are also admissible. These statements are admissible against the principal, the party opponent, if there is independent evidence that the agency relationship existed, that the agent's statements were made during the course of the agency relationship, and that the statements were about matters within the scope of the agent's employment. The same basic rules also apply to statements made by co-conspirators in criminal cases.

There are, of course, many hearsay exceptions to out-of-court statements. The most common ones are present sense impressions, excited utterances, statements against interest, statements of then-existing mental or physical conditions, and statements made for the purpose of diagnosis and treatment. As always, you must think expansively whenever you are trying to introduce out-of-court statements. Where necessary, research the problem and have supporting authority available when you introduce the statement in evidence.

Introducing conversations into evidence is a common, everyday occurrence during trials, one that can and should be handled routinely and smoothly. Conversations need proper foundations to be admissible. The basic requirement is authentication, that is, the witness must reasonably identify the participants to the conversation. (See FRE 901(b)(5).) The foundation should be established for every conversation, even if the opposing side may not object to its absence. First, opposing counsel can always decide to object, thereby breaking up the flow of your direct examination. Second, the foundation enhances your witness' credibility by demonstrating his ability to remember details.

Elements:

The following foundation elements must be established to properly admit in evidence a conversation between two or more persons:

1. When the conversation occurred.
2. Where the conversation occurred.
3. Who was present during the conversation.
4. Who said what to whom.

It is not necessary that the witness actually participated in the conversation. He may properly testify to a conversation he witnessed between two or more other persons as long as the conversation is otherwise admissible under hearsay rules.

Example (admission by party-opponent):

Q. Did you personally talk with Frank Jones?
A. Yes, I did.
Q. When did that conversation with the defendant take place?
A. I talked to him on April 25, 1985.
Q. What time of day was that?
A. That was about 3:00 in the afternoon.
Q. Where did that conversation take place?
A. We talked in his office.
Q. What's the address of his office?
A. It's at 150 North Clark Street, Suite 100.
Q. Who was present during that conversation?
A. There was just myself and Mr. Jones.
Q. What did you and Mr. Jones say at that time?
A. I said: "Mr. Jones, you still owe me $2500 for the roofing job on your house." He said: "I know I do. I just don't have the money to pay you right now."

Example (excited utterance):

Q. What happened right after you heard the shot?
A. Well, people came running to the scene.
Q. Did you know any of them?
A. Other than my wife, no.
Q. What happened next?
A. Well, there was a middle-aged man standing just a few feet from me, and he suddenly screamed: "Look out! He's got a gun!"

§4.5. Telephone conversations

Telephone conversations, also commonly admitted in trials, are introduced in much the same way as face-to-face conversations, but have an additional element. The witness must be able to identify the speaker on the other end of the line. (See FRE 901(b)(5),(6).) There are four basic factual situations under which the foundation for the identity of the other speaker can be established.

1. Witness knows other person

Elements:

The following elements must be established for a telephone conversation between two persons, where the witness knows and recognizes the other person's voice.

1. When the conversation occurred.
2. Where the conversation occurred (where witness was).
3. Witness recognized the other voice.
4. How witness knows the other voice.
5. Whose the other voice was.
6. What other persons participated.
7. Who said what to whom.

It is not necessary to show who placed the call. Where this is known, of course you should show it, since it adds to the credibility of the witness and the reliability of the voice identification, but that knowledge is not a necessary element of the foundation. As in face-to-face conversations, it is also not necessary that the witness have personally participated in the conversation, just that he heard it.

Example:

Q. At approximately 4:00 P.M. on April 25, 1985, where were you?
A. I was in my house.
Q. Did anything happen at that time?
A. Yes.
Q. What happened?
A. The telephone rang.
Q. What did you do?
A. I picked up the phone and said "hello."
Q. Where were you when the telephone rang?
A. I was in the kitchen right next to the phone.
Q. What happened next?
A. A voice answered.
Q. Did you recognize that voice on the other end of the line?
A. Yes, I did.
Q. How did you recognize that voice?
A. I have talked to the same person numerous times over the past several years, in person and over the telephone.
Q. Whose voice was it?
A. It was Frank Jones'.

Q. Did anyone else take part in that telephone conversation?
A. No.
Q. Tell us what you said and what he said during that conversation.
A. He said: "Hi, this is Frank Jones." I said: "Hi." He said: "You still owe me $2500 for the roofing job on your house." I said: "No, I don't. Your job was defective. I won't pay it."

Note that it is not necessary to show that the voice on the other end can be recognized because of previous telephone conversations. Face-to-face conversations are a sufficient basis for the identification. Of course, where the previous conversations were on the telephone, this enhances the reliability of the identification.

It would be improper to bring out that the caller identified himself before establishing the foundation. The concept behind the foundation requirement is voice recognition, which should eliminate imposters posing as someone else. The identification of the caller can properly be brought out in the conversation itself. (But see, FRE 901(b)(6)(A), allowing "self-identification.")

2. Witness does not know other person, but later learns identity through subsequent conversations

Elements:

The following elements must be established for a telephone conversation between two persons, where the witness learns the identity of the other person through later face-to-face conversations.

1. When the conversation occurred.
2. Where the conversation occurred (where speaker was).
3. Witness did not recognize the other voice at the time.
4. At later dates, witness talked to the other voice personally.
5. Witness now recognizes other voice during the call.
6. Who other voice was.
7. What other persons participated.
8. Who said what to whom.

Example:

Q. On April 25, 1985, at approximately 4:00 P.M., where were you?
A. I was in the kitchen of my house.
Q. What happened at that time?
A. The phone rang.
Q. What did you do?
A. I picked up the phone and said "hello."
Q. Did you recognize the voice on the other end?
A. Not at that time.

Q.   Mr. Smith, directing your attention to April 30, at approximately 4:00 P.M., where were you?

A.   I was in Frank Jones' office at 150 North Clark St., Suite 100.

Q.   Did you have a conversation with him?

A.   Yes, I did.

Q.   Since that day, have you had any other conversations with Frank Jones?

A.   Yes.

Q.   About how many?

A.   Maybe 10 or 12.

Q.   Mr. Smith, now directing your attention back to the telephone call you received on April 25, 1985, are you now able to recognize whose voice was on the other end?

A.   Yes, I am.

Q.   Whose voice do you now recognize it to be?

A.   Frank Jones'.

Q.   Were any other persons present during that conversation?

A.   No.

Q.   What did you say and he say at that time?

A.   He said: "You still owe me $2500 for the roofing job on your house." I said: "No, I don't. The job is defective."

3.   Witness does not know the person, but later learns identity through some transaction

Elements:

The following elements must be established for a telephone conversation between two persons, where the witness learns the identity of the other person through either a prior or subsequent transaction (other than a conversation).

1.   When the conversation occurred.
2.   Where the conversation occurred.
3.   Witness did not recognize the other voice at that time.
4.   Witness was engaged in a prior or subsequent transaction which identified the voice for him. (In some jurisdictions the subsequent act that identifies the voice must have occurred prior to the beginning of litigation.)
5.   Witness now knows the other voice.
6.   What other persons participated.
7.   Who said what to whom.

Example:

Q.   On April 25, 1985, at approximately 4:00 P.M., where were you?

A.   I was in the kitchen of my house.

Q. Did anything happen at that time?
A. Yes, the phone rang.
Q. What did you do?
A. I picked up the phone and said "hello."
Q. Did you recognize the other voice at that time?
A. No.
Q. Mr. Smith, I show you Plaintiff's Exhibit #1 for identification. Do you recognize it?
A. Yes, I do.
Q. When did you receive this letter?
A. I got it around April 30, 1985.
Q. Is that letter in the same condition now as it was on the date you received it?
A. Yes, it is.
Q. Do you recognize the signature at the bottom of the letter?
A. Yes.
Q. Whose signature appears at the bottom?
A. Frank Jones.
    (Offer the exhibit in evidence. After it has been admitted, proceed as follows:)
Q. Please read the first line of that letter to the jury.
A. "Dear Mr. Smith, I am writing to confirm the substance of the telephone call I made to you the afternoon of April 25, 1985."
Q. Do you now know who the voice on the telephone was on April 25, 1985 at approximately 4:00 P.M.?
A. Yes, I do.
Q. Whose voice was it?
A. It was Frank Jones'.
Q. Did anyone else take part in the telephone conversation?
A. No.
Q. What was said during the conversation?
A. He said: "Mr. Smith, I am calling you about your roofing problem. We can resurface your roof for $2500." I said: "That looks pretty good to me."

What have you established? There was only one person speaking on the telephone. Hence, only that person, in addition to yourself, could reasonably know the nature of the conversation. When the subsequent letter arrives, you know from its contents who the previous caller was. The letter, an admission, identifies the caller. While not as reliable as voice recognition, it is sufficient to qualify the conversation for admission.

4. Witness does not know the person, but has dialed a listed business telephone number and spoken with the person there

Many jurisdictions hold that dialing a business number listed in a telephone directory is prima facie proof that you have called the listed party or his agent. (See FRE 901(b)(6)(B).)

Elements:

1. When the conversation occurred.
2. Where the conversation occurred.
3. Witness obtained business number from the current telephone directory.
4. Witness dialed the number listed in the directory.
5. Voice on the other end acknowledged it was the business entity.
6. What other persons participated.
7. Who said what to whom.

Example:

Q. On April 25, 1985, at 4:00 P.M., where were you?
A. I was in the kitchen of my house.
Q. What did you do at that time?
A. I got out the telephone directory and looked up the number of the ABC Company.
Q. Was the ABC Company listed in the directory?
A. Yes, it was.
Q. What did you do next?
A. I dialed the number for the ABC Company listed in the directory.
Q. After you dialed that number, what happened?
A. Someone picked up the phone at the other end and a voice said, "ABC Company; can I help you?"
Q. Did anyone else take part in the conversation?
A. No.
Q. What was the conversation you had at that time?
A. I said: "I want to order some roofing tar paper." The other person said: "That's no problem at all. What kind of tar paper do you need?"

§4.6. *Refreshing a witness' recollection*

Witnesses often find testifying in court a frightening experience. They are in strange surroundings and must follow unfamiliar rules. They are expected to testify from memory. Hence, it is not surprising that many times a witness will simply forget an important part of his anticipated testimony. When that happens, the lawyer must refresh the witness' recollection, that is, jog the witness' memory. Although anything can be used to refresh recollection, this is most commonly done through writings such as statements, documents, reports, and depositions.

A certain litany must be followed to establish the foundation for refreshing recollection. Explain the litany to your witness before he testifies. Explain that there is nothing wrong with failing to remember and reading a document to refresh recollection while on the witness stand.

Explain that the cue words, "Do you recall, or remember, anything else," indicate that the witness forgot something important and that you are about to begin the refreshing recollection litany.

Elements:

The following elements must be demonstrated to establish a foundation for refreshing the recollection of a witness who is on the witness stand:

1. Witness knows the facts, but has a memory lapse on the stand.
2. Witness knows his report or other writing will jog his memory.
3. Witness is given and reads the pertinent part of his report or other writing.
4. Witness states his memory has now been refreshed.
5. Witness now testifies to what he knows, without further aid of the report or other writing.

Example:

A police officer recovered a coat, shoes, and gun from the defendant's house. These facts are all contained in his police report.

Q. Did you remove anything from the defendant's house?
A. Yes, I did.
Q. What items did you remove?
A. Let's see.... I got a coat from a closet and his shoes from a hallway.
Q. *Do you recall removing anything else?* (The cue words.)
A. No, that's all I can remember.
Q. Officer, would anything refresh your recollection?
A. Yes.
Q. What is that?
A. I'm sure my report would.
Q. Mr. Reporter, please mark this two-page report State Exhibit #1 for identification. (Reporter marks report.)
Q. I am now showing State Exhibit #1 for identification to opposing counsel. (Shows report to defendant's lawyer.)
Q. Officer, I am handing you what has been marked State Exhibit #1 for identification. Do you recognize it?
A. Yes, that's my report.
Q. Please read it to yourself. (Witness reads report.)
Q. Do you now remember the items you removed from the defendant's house?
A. Yes, I do.
Q. May I have the report back, please. (Officer returns report.) Please tell us what those items were.

A. Yes, sir. In addition to the coat and shoes, I recovered a revolver from a bedroom.

Inexperienced lawyers commonly make three mistakes when attempting to refresh recollection. First, they fail to have the document marked as an exhibit and show it to opposing counsel. The document should be marked for identification purposes even though you will not offer it in evidence. Second, they fail to retrieve the document after the witness has read it. This will often cause the opposing lawyer to object that the witness does not really have a present recollection but is merely reading from the report. Eliminate this problem by getting the report back before asking the final questions. Third, lawyers fail to use the *do you recall* or *do you remember* language. Instead, they will ask: "Did you remove any other items?" and the witness will answer: "No." When you then attempt to refresh the witness' recollection, the opposing lawyer may object on the ground that the witness has answered the question, and there is no need to refresh recollection.

Finally, remember that under FRE 612 anything used to refresh recollection, both while or before testifying, must be made available to opposing counsel for use during cross-examination. If what you used to refresh recollection has not previously been made available to the other side, this could affect your decision to use it at all, since the documents may contain other facts that can be effectively used during cross-examination. In most instances, of course, a witness' prior statements will be in the other side's possession through pretrial discovery. Even more important, FRE 612 permits the cross-examiner to introduce into evidence the relevant portions of the document used to refresh recollection.

When a witness has made a previous record of an event, and the record does *not* refresh his recollection, it may be admissible as past recollection recorded. The foundation requirements for this are discussed in §5.3(14).

§4.7. *The records witness*

In today's trial environment, records are an increasingly common sight. Although always present in commercial cases, records are now often a significant part of personal injury and even criminal cases. Consequently, being able to present records witnesses and introduce records into evidence effectively is becoming an increasingly indispensable trial skill in every type of trial. This is so even though business records are frequently admitted by stipulation, or without opposition.

Business records, of course, are hearsay. Since the 1930s, however, when the first business records legislation appeared, all jurisdictions have enacted statutes that, when certain requirements are met, permit business records to be admitted in evidence. All these statutes, including the present federal rule in FRE 803(6), have the same underlying rationale: reliability. When a business has created documents on a recurring basis, has relied on their accuracy to conduct the affairs of the business, and has developed systems to store and retrieve those records, that rationale has been met.

The records witness has three principal functions at trial. First, he must be able to establish the foundation requirements to get the exhibit admitted in evidence. Second, he must do it in a way that maximizes the weight the jury will give to the exhibit. Finally, he must be prepared to read and explain the contents of the records to the jury.

There is a tendency to present such witnesses in summary fashion: quickly establish the witness as custodian of the pertinent documents, recite the foundation litany, and get the records into evidence. However, you should resist the temptation to treat such witnesses casually. Remember that the evidentiary impact of documents is affected primarily by how systematically the information on the documents is compiled, how accurately the records are prepared, and how carefully they are stored. Accordingly, what the witness has to say about the records, over and above merely laying the foundation for their admissibility, can be significant. Do not miss an opportunity to enhance the quality of this part of your proof.

How do you do this? Several separate considerations are involved:

1.   Thoroughly qualify your witness. Show that he has substantial knowledge of the records involved, works with them on a daily basis, and knows the storage and retrieval methods the business uses.

2.   Show how the records are made, who makes them, and the primary source of the information contained on them. The witness should be able to trace all the transactions contained in the records, from their initial creation by the first person who conducted the transactions to their inclusion in some permanent record.

3.   Show how the records are distributed, stored, and subsequently retrieved for use. Essential to the credibility of records is a showing that the records, once created, are stored in such a way as to minimize the risk of loss, destruction, or alteration.

4.   Show what use the records have for the business creating them. Where you can show that the business constantly uses the records, and that accurate and complete records are essential to the successful operation of that business, you will substantially enhance the impact those records will make at trial.

The following example illustrates the kind of development a records witness can provide in a direct examination. This should obviously not be done in every instance. When, however, the records are the primary evidence of a transaction, not merely corroborative evidence, and must stand on their own, you should always consider this kind of development for your qualifying witness.

Example:

The office manager has been called as a witness to qualify certain shipping documents of a trucking company.

Q. Ms. Doe, what is your occupation?

A. I am the branch manager of the Chicago office of the XYZ Trucking Company.

Q. How long have you been the branch manager of the Chicago office?

A. Approximately five years.

Q. Before becoming branch manager, what kind of work did you do?

A. I originally started as a supervisor in the loading dock area. I then moved to the Billing Department. I then became manager of the Billing Department before moving to my present job.

Q. How many years in all have you worked for XYZ Company?

A. Almost 12 years.

Q. Has that entire time been spent in the Chicago office?

A. Yes, it has.

Q. Ms. Doe, what kind of business does XYZ Trucking Company do?

A. We're what they call an over-the-road carrier; that is, we carry goods in tractor-trailers between major cities throughout the United States and Canada.

Q. How many offices does XYZ Trucking have?

A. We have 11 regional and 46 local offices.

Q. How many persons do you employ at the Chicago office?

A. Right now we have 14 full-time and 6 part-time employees. The number varies depending on the season.

Q. What kind of work does the regional office in Chicago do?

A. We receive orders for goods, pick them up, and deliver them to the designated locations. We also receive shipments from other cities and either store them for pickup by the consignee or deliver the goods directly to him. It all depends on the nature of the shipping contracts. As a large carrier we can work out almost any kind of shipping arrangement.

Q. What kind of records does your office regularly generate during the course of its business?

A. Our standard records that we make for each shipment are bills of lading, shipping orders, shipping invoices, and billings.

Q. Ms. Doe, did you recently receive a subpoena directing your company to produce certain records for this trial?

A. Yes, we did.

Q. Did you bring those records with you today?

A. Yes, I did.

Q. Mr. Reporter, please mark this document Plaintiff's Exhibit #1. (Reporter does so.) May the record reflect that I am showing Plaintiff's Exhibit #1 to defense counsel. (Shows exhibit to defense counsel.)

Q. Ms. Doe, I am now showing you what has just been marked Plaintiff's Exhibit #1. Do you recognize it?

A. Yes, I do.

Q. What do you recognize Plaintiff's Exhibit #1 to be?

A.   That is the record I brought here pursuant to the subpoena.

Q.   What kind of record is it?

A.   This record is what we call a shipping invoice.

Q.   What use does your company make of that kind of record?

A.   That is the basic record which contains all the information about one shipped order. We use that form so that we have a complete record of that shipment on one document. We also use it for billing purposes.

Q.   What kind of information is on a shipping invoice?

A.   It contains the date the shipment was picked up, where it was picked up, what the shipment consisted of, the weight of that shipment, delivery instructions, and billing instructions.

Q.   Who receives and enters the information that appears on the statement?

A.   Two people normally fill out the form. First, an office clerk who receives a shipping order, whether in person or on the telephone, fills out the entire form except the weight. The shipping invoice is then given to the driver. When the driver picks up the shipment, he weighs it on our scales and then writes in the weight on the form. Both the office clerk and driver must initial the form.

Q.   What then happens to the form?

A.   The form itself has four copies. The driver gives the first two copies to our office after weighing the shipment. He takes the other two forms with him. When the shipment is delivered, he gives a copy to the party receiving the shipment. On the other copy he gets the signature of the receiving party, and returns that copy to our billing department.

Q.   What does your office do with the copies?

A.   We send one copy to the party placing the order. We send the other one, the original, to the billing department. When the signed copy is received from the driver, we send out our bill.

Q.   What ultimately happens to the two bills, the original and signed copy?

A.   The original goes into our permanent records files which we maintain in a separate room. The Billing Department sends the signed copy along with a bill to the party to be billed.

The background development is now complete. The only remaining step is to complete the foundation litany required by FRE 803(6). This is most easily accomplished by tracking its language. This is the testimony that the judge wants to hear.

Q.   Ms. Doe, I am again directing your attention to the XYZ Corporation record marked Plaintiff's Exhibit #1 for identification: Was that record made by a person with knowledge of (or made from information transmitted by a person with knowledge of) the acts and events appearing on it?

A.   Yes.

Q. Was it made at or near the time of the acts and events appearing on it?

A. Yes.

Q. Is it the regular practice of the XYZ Corporation to make such a record?

A. Yes.

Q. Was that record kept in the ordinary course of a regularly conducted business activity?

A. Yes.

§4.8. *Preparation of expert witnesses*

Modern litigation is using experts with unparalleled frequency. No longer are experts used merely in personal injury cases, nor are they only physicians and surgeons. Injury cases now regularly use economists. Products liability cases often use reconstruction experts. Building construction cases regularly use engineers and architects. More and more frequently, trial lawyers are using experts to explain how and why things happened the way they did, or didn't happen the way they were supposed to. Because of this, being able to prepare and effectively present experts at trial is an essential skill every trial lawyer should have.

The basic reason that permits experts to give their opinions in court, despite the general evidentiary bar against opinions, is that the subject matter on which the expert is testifying is one on which the expert has knowledge beyond that of the average lay person. Hence, expert testimony is permitted because it aids the jury in reaching a proper decision.

The federal rules (FRE 702-705) leave unchanged the basic conceptual rationale for the expert opinion rules as they exist in most other jurisdictions. However, the Rules have been liberalized and expanded in several aspects. First, the Rules liberalize the definition of an expert. Under FRE 702, an expert is any person who possesses specialized knowledge through "knowledge, skill, experience, training, or education." This substantially expands the number of persons who qualify as experts as well as the areas in which they can testify. Second, the Rules eliminate the need for the traditional form of the opinion question (e.g., "Do you have an opinion, to a reasonable degree of medical certainty, whether the injuries you observed are permanent in nature?"). Under FRE 702, the expert can now give his testimony as an "opinion or otherwise." This permits you to elicit conclusions directly (e.g., "Are these injuries permanent?"). Third, the Rules eliminate the need to put in evidence, before the expert testifies, all the facts on which the expert will base his testimony. FRE 703 permits the expert to obtain the relevant facts outside of court and, if the facts or data are reasonably relied on by experts in that field, the facts or data need not be admissible in evidence. Fourth, FRE 705 now permits the expert to give his opinions without first disclosing the facts he relied on to reach the opinions. Finally, FRE 704 now permits an expert to testify on ultimate issues of fact.

The federal rules, expanding as they do the permissible scope of expert testimony, make knowing how to prepare and present such witnesses effectively in court an even more indispensable trial skill.

Expert witnesses present the same general preparation problems as lay witnesses. It is a mistake to assume that, simply because the witness may be a professional person and has probably appeared in court before, pretrial preparation can be abbreviated or dispensed with. Experts should be prepared in the same fashion as any other witness. Keep in mind that the whole purpose of experts is to apply knowledge that is beyond that of lay persons to the case to assist the jury in reaching a proper verdict. If anything, experts, because of the specialized nature of their testimony, require even more preparation than lay witnesses. This includes the following:

1. It is usually a good idea to let the jury know why the particular witness has been called.

Example:

Q. Dr. Johnson, you're a doctor practicing in New York City?
A. Yes.
Q. You specialize in heart conditions?
A. Yes.
Q. And you actually treated the plaintiff, Mrs. Jones?
A. Yes.
Q. Dr. Johnson, before we discuss how you treated Mrs. Jones' heart condition, we need to talk about your background as a doctor. First, where did you go to medical school?

2. Thoroughly but efficiently qualify your expert. Obtain a copy of his current résumé, then review with him the questions you will ask to qualify him as an expert. Determine what you will *not* ask (e.g., "Have you published papers in your field?" "No"). Your qualifying voir dire questions must run smoothly and avoid embarrassment, since the relative credibility of opposing experts may depend significantly on which has the more apparently impressive background. Consider introducing his resume as an exhibit to supplement the qualifications testimony.
3. Make sure your expert can spell and accurately define the technical terms he will use during his testimony. Make sure his definition is consistent with technical dictionaries and encyclopedias, and that he has read those definitions. Cross-examiners sometimes attempt to embarrass experts on these points.
4. Make sure your expert defines technical terms at the time he *first* uses them. However, have your expert use common terms whenever possible, as long as he can still testify accurately by using them.

5. Make sure your expert familiarizes himself with the most recent editions of standard treatises on his subject, as well as his own related publications. Tell him he can expect to be cross-examined from both sources. Show him how impeachment using treatises and his own publications is done.

6. Consider using any treatise that the expert has relied upon as an exhibit. Under FRE 803(18) any treatise or periodical that is established as a reliable authority during cross or relied upon by the expert during direct is a hearsay exception. You should be able to read the pertinent parts of the treatise into evidence during the expert's direct examination.

7. Consider what the expert can contribute to the case in addition to his opinion and basis for that opinion. He may have valuable additional information. Conversely, he may have damaging information you will want to steer clear of, or prepare for if you anticipate cross-examination on those points.

8. Remind your expert not to volunteer answers outside his area of expertise. Experts love to talk. Prepare your expert to deny his expertise on topics outside his specialized field (e.g., "I'm sorry, counsel, but I really can't give you an expert opinion in that particular area"). Remind him that cross-examiners love to get experts to stick their necks out.

9. Review *how* to testify. Experts often testify in a professionally arrogant or obviously condescending fashion that fails to respect the jury's intelligence. There is obviously a happy medium preferred here. The experts should, whenever possible, use layman's terms and language, without sounding demeaning or arrogant.

10. Use models and diagrams to illustrate testimony whenever possible. Expert testimony, even when well prepared, can be complex and difficult. Make the maximum use of visual aids.

11. If you must use, or if you decide to use, a hypothetical question, prepare it in advance and review it with your expert. Remember that hypotheticals should include all relevant facts in evidence. (See §4.12, p. 140.)

12. Explain what your opinion questions will be and how you will be required to phrase them. Explain how legal causation, which essentially covers precipitating causes, differs from medical or other scientific concepts of causation. Explain that a "reasonable degree of medical or scientific certainty" is neither total certainty nor speculation, but that level of certainty customarily relied on in making professional decisions.

13. Your opponent may offer to stipulate to your expert's qualifications. Unless your witness has marginal qualifications and is an otherwise effective witness, resist the offer. If your opponent's expert has superior qualifications, agree to stipulate only if your opponent will agree to the identical stipulation for his expert. If you reject the stipulation offer in open court, do so in a way that lets the Court and jury know why.

Example:

Your Honor, in light of Dr. Smith's extensive professional background and because his background is so directly related to the weight the jury will attach to his testimony, we feel that the jury is entitled to hear his qualifications.

14. Decide how to handle the issue of fees. Normally, where both sides have experts who are being paid for their work and court appearances, there is little to be gained by either side bringing out these details. If, as plaintiff, you have an expert witness and your opponent does not, consider volunteering the fee information during the direct examination before your opponent brings it out his way on cross.

Example:

Q. Dr. Smith, did you charge a fee for your consultation work in this case?
A. Yes, I did.
Q. How did you determine the amount of that fee?
A. In this case, as in all my consultation work, I bill at the rate of $100 per hour. That bill is submitted to the party that retained me regardless of which side, if anyone's, my opinion may favor.
Q. How much was your bill in this case?
A. It was $600.
A. Has that bill been paid?
A. Yes, it was paid in full some time ago.
Q. Are you being paid to appear and testify in court today?
A. I am being compensated for my time at my usual hourly rate.

§4.9. *Qualifying and examining expert witnesses*

The following checklists should be utilized in reviewing an expert's qualifications and preparing the direct examination questions that will qualify him as an expert in your case. It is particularly important to develop his background slowly and thoroughly, since the credibility of the expert will depend significantly on his professional credentials.

Keep in mind that an expert's professional background has two components. First, the expert's general background will include his education, degrees, licenses, and employment history. Second, the expert's specific background will include the special training, publications, and particular work experiences that directly bear on the situation about which he is testifying. While the first part is necessary, the second one is critical, because jurors will usually give greater weight to the expert who has more experience with the particular situation involved. The emphasis of your qualifications questions, therefore, should be directed to the specific experience area.

1. General qualifications checklist

a. *Name:*
   1. address
   2. personal background.
b. *Business or occupation:* what — how long — description of field — company or organization — capacity — how long — where located — prior positions — description of positions.
c. *Education:*
   1. undergraduate school — degree — when graduated.
   2. post-graduate school — degree — when graduated — area of study.
d. *Training:* formal courses — what — when — trained under recognized expert — who — when — how long.
e. *Licenses:* what — when reviewed — specialty certification — when — requirements.
f. *Professional association:* what — positions held.
g. *Other background:* teaching positions — publications — lectures — consulting work.
h. *Expert witness at trials:* how many — which side.
i. *Experience in specialty:*
   1. types of examinations commonly done — how many.
   2. ever perform a ____ test — how many.
   3. does that experience include ____.
   4. over these ____ years of practice, how many ____ have you (bought, sold, dealt with, installed, taken, examined, analyzed, etc.).
   5. over these ____ years, what is the total dollar value of all the ____ you have (designed, constructed, evaluated, appraised, bought, sold, etc.). (Try to develop big numbers showing substantial experience, particularly in the specific area involved.)

Developing an expert's professional qualifications can be tedious, and the expert can easily sound pompous and arrogant as you develop his credentials. There are two ways you can deal with this problem if it arises. First, use leading questions from time to time, because this breaks up the tone of the examination. The expert will sound less arrogant if *you* say what he's accomplished and the witness merely agrees. Because these are preliminary matters, the fact that these questions are leading does not matter.

Example:

Q. Doctor Johnson, you graduated from Northwestern University School of Medicine?
A. Yes.
Q. What year?

A. In 1970.
Q. You did your internship and residency at Massachusetts General Hospital?
A. Yes.
Q. Are you board-certified in orthopedics?
A. Yes.
Q. What does board-certified mean?
A. It means you have done all the study and work requirements and have passed the examination for that specialty.

In this example part of the background comes from a lawyer in leading form, and part from the witness. By mixing the questions, the witness appears more modest, and the questions go more quickly.

Second, try using the expert's resume as an exhibit to supplement and expand on his qualification testimony. The resume can probably be qualified as a business record under FRE 803(6), and should qualify as reliable hearsay under FRE 803(24), the residual hearsay exception. If the resume can be admitted as an exhibit, it will allow you to be more streamlined when you go through the qualification testimony. Of course, the exhibit will also be useful when you argue later that your expert is better qualified than your opponent's expert.

2. Treating-physician checklist

a. *Qualifications:*
1. licensed — where — when.
2. education and training: college/medical school — when — degree — internship — residency — military.
3. specialty: training — specialty boards — requirements.
4. hospital staff memberships.
5. teaching positions.
6. publications and lectures.
7. medical society memberships.
8. other honors.
9. previously testified as expert.
b. *Experience:*
1. description of his practice.
2. number of patients, particularly related to this case.
3. examinations of similar type.
4. experience with X rays, lab tests, etc.
c. *Examination of this patient:*
1. description of office records.
2. history of patient.
3. examination: (a) complaints ("symptoms"); (b) positive findings ("signs"); (c) negative findings (obviate congenital and pre-existing conditions)
4. X-ray findings
5. lab test findings

d. *Diagnosis:* tentative and definite
e. *Treatment (chronological)* hospitalization; operations; drugs; casts.
f. *Subsequent examinations.*
g. *Patient's present condition based on last examination.*
h. *Opinion on causation:*
   1. Opinion (See FRE 702 et seq.). "Do you have an opinion, based on a reasonable degree of medical certainty, on what caused the injury?" (State this question as forcefully and directly as is permitted in your particular jurisdiction, since establishing a direct causal connection between an accident and injuries is an element of plaintiff's proof in negligence cases.)
   2. Reasons for his opinion. "What is it?" "What are the reasons for your opinion/conclusions?"
i. *Prognosis:* Opinion on prospects for complete recovery, future pain, necessity of future treatment, permanency of disabilities, etc.
j. *Amount of present and future medical services:*
   1. bill to date/if paid — if bill usual and customary charge.
   2. necessary future medical expenses.

§4.10.   *Examples of expert direct examinations*

1.   Treating-physician — direct examination

In the following example the doctor is testifying about his examination, diagnosis, and treatment of an accident victim, as well as his professional bill and opinion on the victim's prognosis.

Example:

Q. Dr. White, please state your full name.
A. Paul White.
Q. Where do you live?
A. I live in Evanston, Illinois.
Q. What is your occupation?
A. I am a physician.
Q. Dr. White, you're the doctor who treated John Smith after he was struck by a car, correct?
A. Yes.
Q. Dr. White, I'm going to ask you some questions about your background as a doctor. Are you licensed to practice medicine in Illinois?
A. Yes, I am.
Q. How many years have you been licensed?

Note that the expert's qualifications are drawn out a little at a time. Avoid attempting to get everything out in one or two questions (e.g., "Doctor, tell us a little about your background and credentials"). Drawing out his background bit by bit also avoids the impression that the expert is impressed with himself.

A. Six years.

Q. Where did you receive your undergraduate education?

A. At Dartmouth College.

Q. What year did you graduate?

A. 1974.

Q. What medical school did you attend?

A. Northwestern University School of Medicine.

Q. Did you receive a degree from that school?

A. Yes, I received a Doctor of Medicine degree in 1978.

Q. Where did you do your internship?

A. At Cook County Hospital, in Chicago.

Q. What is an internship?

A. That is a one-year post-graduate training program at a hospital, where you spend several weeks in each of the major medical departments diagnosing illnesses and treating patients.

Q. Did you afterwards specialize in any particular field of medicine?

A. Yes, I did.

Q. What field was that?

A. After my internship, I began my specialty training in the field of orthopedic surgery.

Q. Where did you continue your residency training in orthopedics?

A. At Northwestern University Hospital.

Q. How long did your training and residency in orthopedics take?

A. The residency program in my particular specialty was three years, which I completed in 1982.

Q. What did the residency program consist of?

A. This is an intensive course of study, again at a hospital, in the diagnosis and treatment of illnesses in that particular medical specialty.

Q. Are you board-certified in the field of orthopedic surgery?

A. Yes, I am.

Q. What are the requirements for becoming board-certified?

A. You are required to complete a residency program at an accredited institution and successfully pass the board examination.

Q. Did you complete those requirements?

A. Yes, I did.

Q. By which board are you certified?

A. I am certified by the American Board of Orthopedic Surgeons as a diplomate.

Q. What is the American Board of Orthopedic Surgeons?

A. That is the official board in this country that examines and certifies specialists in the field of orthopedic surgery.

Q. Is a diplomate the highest certification one can obtain in the field of orthopedic surgery?

A. Yes, it is.

Q. How long have you been board-certified?

A. Since 1982.

Q. Dr. White, are you on the staff of any hospitals?

A. Yes, I am on the staffs of Northwestern Memorial and Rush Presbyterian Hospitals.

Q. Do you hold any teaching positions in your specialty?

A. Yes, I do.

Q. What are they?

A. I am a clinical lecturer in orthopedics at Northwestern University School of Medicine.

Q. For how long?

A. Since 1982.

Q. Are you a member of any medical associations?

A. Yes, I am.

Q. Which ones?

A. I am a member of the American Medical Association, the Illinois State Medical Society, the Chicago Medical Society and the American College of Orthopedic Surgeons.

Q. Dr. White, are you engaged in the private practice of medicine?

A. Yes, I am.

Q. What kind of practice do you have?

A. My practice is limited to orthopedics.

Q. What do you mean by the term orthopedics?

A. Orthopedics is that area of medicine which deals with the body's skeletal and muscular systems and related joints, tendons, and ligaments. It also involves traumatic, that

Notice how the board certification is developed in some detail, since it is probably the single most impressive credential in the doctor's background.

Notice what was *not* asked: lectures and publications, since the doctor has not done this kind of work; and other honors, since he has not received any.

The general background is now complete. The questions now focus on the witness' experience in the particular injury the case is involved with.

The basic terms in the specialty should always be defined in nontechnical terms.

is, accident-related, and nontraumatic conditions and diseases in these systems.

Q. Does your practice center on any particular aspect of orthopedics?

A. My main interest is in the area of traumatic injury, so my patients are generally restricted to that type.

Q. Has that experience in your practice included cases in which the traumatic injury was to the knees and related bones?

A. Oh, yes. Knee-type injuries are very common.

Q. How many patients have you treated during the course of your professional experience in which the medical condition related to traumatic injuries to the knee?

A. Oh, I have probably examined and treated 200 or 300 injuries of that type.

Q. Have you ever treated patients who have fractured a femur, the thigh bone, or dislocated a knee?

A. Yes, I've probably handled that type of injury perhaps 50 to 75 times.

Q. Dr. White, let's turn now to the events of December 13, 1984. You saw John Smith, the plaintiff, on that day, didn't you?

A. Yes, I did.

Q. Where did you see Mr. Smith on that day?

A. I saw him in the emergency room of Northwestern Memorial Hospital.

Q. Did you talk to the patient at that time?

A. Oh, yes. He was conscious.

Q. Did he talk to you about his injuries?

A. Yes, he did.

Q. What did he tell you?

A. He told me he had been struck on his left knee by a car while he was crossing a street. He also told me that he thought his left leg was broken.

Q. Did you take the patient's history?

A. Yes.

Q. What was his history relative to his left knee and leg?

A. He stated that he had never had any previous injuries, soreness, pain or problems with that knee or leg.

Q. Did you examine him at that time?

Always show that the doctor's actual expertise includes the specific type of injury involved in the case.

Big numbers, when you can get them, are always impressive.

The doctor has now been qualified as an expert. Note that in some jurisdictions the opposing counsel may conduct a voir dire on the expert's qualifications before you get to substantive testimony. In some jurisdictions you may ask the court to rule that the witness has been established as an expert in his field.

The patient's statements made for the purpose of diagnosis are admissible. (See FRE 803(4).)

A. Yes, I did.

Q. What did that examination consist of?

A. First, I cut away the clothing around the left leg. I then examined the left leg as well as the other areas of his body.

Q. What did you notice at that time?

A. The patient was in a great deal of pain. He could not move his leg. He complained constantly about the pain, particularly shooting pains in his leg. I observed the area near and above his knee. It was swollen and had obvious signs of trauma.

Q. When you say trauma, Doctor, exactly what do you mean?

A. By trauma we mean any externally caused damage or destruction to body tissue. In this case I could see some abrasions, that is, scratches and cuts on the exterior portion of the upper leg, swelling, and bruise marks in that general area.

Note that the doctor is asked to define terms in layman's language, if he does not do so on his own.

Q. What is the next thing you did?

A. I then ordered a series of X rays of that portion of the patient's body.

Q. Other than the X rays, were any other lab tests performed at that time?

A. We performed the usual preoperative tests; that is, the patient's pulse, blood pressure and respiration were checked and his blood was cross-typed.

Q. On the basis of your history of the patient and your examinations, did you reach a tentative diagnosis?

A. Yes, I did.

Q. What was that?

A. It was my tentative conclusion, based on how the trauma occurred, the patient's symptoms, and my examination, that in all likelihood he had suffered some type of fracture to either the knee joint or the long bones in his left leg, that is, the femur in the upper leg or the tibia and fibula in the lower leg.

Where appropriate, both a tentative and a definite diagnosis should be shown.

Q. On the basis of the X-ray findings, did you reach a definite diagnosis?

A. Yes, the X-ray findings confirmed my preliminary diagnosis. The patient had suffered a fracture of his left femur just above the knee joint. In addition, there appeared to be a moderate displacement of the knee joint itself.

Q. Exactly which bone is the femur?

A. The femur is the thigh bone that runs from the hip to the knee.

Q. On the basis of your diagnosis, Dr. White, did you begin a course of treatment?

A. Yes, I did.

Q. What did that treatment consist of?

A. The first thing I did was to initiate a reduction of the fracture. The patient was given a general anesthesia after which I did a closed reduction. A closed reduction consists of manipulating the bones at the fracture site so that they are realigned in their proper place. In this situation the patient had a transverse fracture, that is, a fracture straight across the left femur approximately nine centimeters from the knee joint. The bones were approximately one centimeter displaced. My reduction consisted of moving by hand the knee joint and femur until the two bone segments were in proper relation to each other.

Q. What did you do after that?

A. I then had X rays taken to make sure that the fracture was properly realigned. I then applied a plaster cast to the leg. The cast in this case was the normal type. The cast extended from the toes all the way up to the crotch of the left leg, the purpose being to totally immobilize all the bones in the left leg. The patient was then taken to a postoperative recovery room.

Q. Was Mr. Smith given any kind of prescription drugs?

A. I prescribed medication during the time he was in the hospital to help him cope with the pain, and anti-inflammatory drugs to reduce the swelling in the leg.

Q. How long did he remain at the hospital?

A. He was discharged on December 18, so he was there five days.

Q. How often did you see him during his hospital stay?

A. I saw him each day until he was discharged.

Q. Did his condition change during that period of time?

At this point the X rays could be introduced as exhibits and shown to the jury, to explain fully the fracture.

Note that the treatment is described in detail. This is important on the issue of pain and suffering and necessary to show that any permanent injury was not caused by inadequate treatment.

A. No, sir. In a fracture situation the healing process is quite slow. The hospitalization is primarily necessary to insure that the patient's general physical condition is stable.

Q. Dr. White, let's talk about Mr. Smith's progress after he was discharged from the hospital. Did you continue to see him as a patient?

A transition question again introduces a new topic.

A. Yes, I did.

Q. When was the first time you saw him?

A. I saw him in my office approximately six weeks later.

Subsequent treatment should be shown on a visit-by-visit basis.

Q. What was done at that time?

A. I removed the cast, had his leg x-rayed, reviewed the X rays, examined the leg, and applied a new cast on his leg.

Q. What did you observe at that time?

A. At that time the bone appeared to be healing satisfactorily. There was good callous formation at the fracture site. By callous I mean that there was good new bone growth that was beginning to cement the two bone fragments together. The leg had atrophied substantially, meaning that muscle tissue had shrunk in size through nonuse. This is a normal consequence of the immobilization of any sizable body structure.

Q. When was the next time you saw him?

A. I saw him approximately three months after his discharge from the hospital.

Q. Did you examine him at that time?

A. Yes, I did.

Q. What did your examination consist of at that time?

A. I followed the same procedure I employed during his first visit. I removed the cast, x-rayed the leg, and examined the X rays. In addition, of course, I examined the patient's leg.

Q. What were your observations during that examination?

A. Again, the leg at the fracture site was healing substantially. Callous formation was complete. Atrophy had progressed to the expected extent.

Q. Following this examination, what did you do next?

A. I prescribed a course of treatment and therapy for Mr. Smith. That program consisted of daily heat treatments from hot-water bags and hot towels to the knee area as often as possible and exercises to regain full mobility of the knee joint. This is necessary because the muscles and tendons shrink very quickly when the joint is immobilized. Consequently, when a cast or other restraint is finally removed, that joint is usually frozen, so to speak, and the patient has essentially no motion to the joint. I also prescribed a series of exercises, once motion in the knee joint was reestablished. This consisted of first applying the patient's body weight on the leg itself, followed by walking exercises once actual use of the leg was established. Thereafter he was to do a series of weight exercises to rebuild muscle strength.

Q. Since that examination, Dr. White, have you ever reexamined Mr. Smith?

A. Yes, I saw him approximately three weeks ago.

Q. What is Mr. Smith's condition at the present time as disclosed by your examination?

A. From my examination, I concluded that he had regained total extension and rotation, but that flexion, that is, bending the knee as far as possible, was not complete. In addition, the left calf and thigh were significantly smaller in circumference as compared to his right. The patient appeared to walk and use his leg in a tentative or apprehensive manner. I concluded, therefore, that despite the prescribed treatment the patient's leg had not recovered fully to its former condition. In addition, the patient was experiencing discomfort and pain at the fracture site during my examination. X rays disclosed an arthritis had formed at the fracture site.

The patient's present condition is critical, since a large part of any judgment will be based on permanent disability.

Q. Dr. White, do you have an opinion, based on a reasonable degree of medical certainty, whether the conditions you observed during your last examination are temporary or permanent?

A. Yes, I do.

Note that this is the traditional form of the opinion question.

Note that the doctor's conclusions can be asked directly under

Q. What is your opinion?

A. I concluded that in all likelihood Mr. Smith's leg will never completely return to its former condition, so the present conditions are permanent.

Q. What are the reasons for your opinion?

A. In cases of this type, a full recovery, if it is to occur at all, invariably does so quickly, usually within the first few months following removal of the cast. In this case, approximately 15 months have passed since I removed his cast. The muscles in his left leg are still significantly atrophied. While not impossible, it is highly unlikely that his leg will improve significantly from its present condition. The last series of X rays showed an arthritis at the fracture site. This sometimes happens as a result of fractures and is generally called a traumatic arthritis.

Q. Is such a traumatic arthritis capable of producing pain?

A. Yes.

Q. Is the pain the patient was experiencing a temporary or permanent condition?

A. In my opinion, he will probably continue having a moderate degree of pain indefinitely.

Q. Do you have an opinion, to a reasonable degree of medical certainty, whether the plaintiff's injuries you have described and treated were caused by the collision on December 13, 1984?

A. Yes, I do.

Q. What is your opinion?

A. In my opinion these injuries were directly caused by the collision.

Q. Dr. White, did you submit a bill for the professional services you rendered in this case?

A. Yes, I did.

Q. What was the amount of that bill?

A. My bill for all my professional services was $1400.

Q. Was that bill paid?

A. Yes, it has been paid in full.

Q. Is that bill consistent with the usual and customary charges in this area for professional services of that kind?

---

the federal rules (e.g., "Doctor, are the conditions you observed temporary or permanent?").

Keep in mind, however, that the doctor may feel more comfortable with questions which ask for his opinions, although the rules allow you to ask for conclusions. It is usually best to ask the opinion question in a way the doctor will feel comfortable with. Often this will be the traditional form.

This question and answer will support the plaintiff's testimony regarding pain.

The causation question must be asked to clearly establish the proximate cause element of plaintiff's cause of action. (The question referring to the "collision" is proper, since the patient's subjective symptoms to the doctor included the fact that he had been struck by a car while crossing the street.)

Since past medical expenses are an element of damages, this should be brought out.

(In many jurisdictions the fact that the bill

A. Yes, I believe it is.

Q. Will John Smith incur further medical expenses in the future?

A. Yes, he will.

Q. What kinds of medical treatment will he require?

A. I believe he will probably require further treatment for the arthritic condition he has.

Q. Can you estimate what the extent of that medical treatment will be?

A. No, I cannot. There is no way to tell at the present time what that would involve. The only thing to do is wait and see what his medical requirements will be.

was paid creates a presumption that its amount was reasonable.)

If the expert can demonstrate necessary future medical expenses, he should do so, since this is also a proper element of damages.

2. Ballistics expert — direct examination

In the following example the expert is testifying about a comparison he made between a revolver and a pellet recovered from a gunshot victim. Both revolver and pellet have already been admitted in evidence.

Example:

Q. Please tell us your full name.

A. Sandra Nicholson.

Q. Whom do you work for?

A. The Chicago Police Department.

Q. How long have you worked for the department?

A. Twelve years.

Q. What kind of work do you do for them?

A. I'm a firearms examiner working in the Criminalistics Department, commonly called the Crime Lab.

Q. How long have you been employed as a firearms examiner?

A. About 10 years.

Q. Officer Nicholson, what area does the field of firearms cover?

A. It covers the study of all kinds of weapons, their parts, and any projectiles associated with those weapons.

Q. What is meant by the term "ballistics"?

A. Ballistics is the study of projectiles, such as bullets, and their relationship to weapons.

Q. Did you attend any colleges or universities?

The background and qualifications are again drawn out bit by bit. Since ballistics is a learn-by-doing field, make sure this is clear to the jury.

A. I attended Northern Illinois University.

Q. Did you receive a degree?

A. I received a B.S. degree in physics.

Q. Are there any formal courses in the field of firearms and ballistics?

A. No, the training is received by studying under a recognized expert for two or three years.

Q. Whom did you train under?

A. I studied under Lt. John Long, the head of the Criminalistics Dept., and my father, Sgt. Nicholson, both of whom were firearms experts.

Q. What did that training consist of?

A. It began by my watching them do the various tests and analyses used in the field. After a while I performed the work under their supervision. After about two years I began working on my own, although our procedures always require that someone else confirm our conclusions.

Q. Are there any recognized texts in the field?

A. Yes.

Q. Have you read them?

A. Yes, sir.

Q. Officer Nicholson, what types of tests are commonly done in your field?

A. The most common are tests to determine if a weapon is working properly, trigger-pull tests, and bullet comparisons.

Q. What is a comparison test?

A. That's a test to determine if a bullet was fired from a certain gun.

Q. Have you ever performed such a test?

A. Yes, sir, I do several hundred every year.

Q. Have you ever testified in court as an expert on bullet comparisons?

A. Yes, I have.

Q. How many times?

A. Over the past nine years I'd say about 60 or 70 times.

Q. Are you a member of any professional organizations?

A. Yes, sir.

Q. Which one?

A. I'm a member of the American Academy of Forensic Sciences, and the Illinois branch of the Academy.

Note that the types of tests commonly done are then narrowed down to the specific test involved in the case. The expert then shows he has performed the identical test numerous times, and has testified to his conclusions in court. The big numbers are always impressive to the jury.

Q. Do you hold any teaching positions in your field?

A. Yes, for the past three years I've been teaching the new people in the firearms section. I also lecture from time to time at the department's training academy and at professional seminars in my field.

Q. Have you published any papers in the area of firearms and particularly ballistics?

A. Yes, I've published five papers in professional journals. Two of these dealt specifically with bullet comparisons.

> Since this witness has published, that additional qualification should be demonstrated.

Q. Officer Nicholson, please describe the basic principles involved in making a ballistics comparison between a weapon and a bullet.

A. Yes. The purpose, of course, is to determine if the bullet, or projectile, came from the suspect weapon. Guns have two basic characteristics, called class and accidental.

Q. What are class characteristics?

A. These are: first, the caliber, such as a .22, .38, or .45 caliber, which refers to the diameter of the bullets. Second, lands and grooves, which refers to the impressions made on a bullet from the spiral ridges in a gun barrel which spins a bullet as it is forced out of the barrel and gives the bullet stability in flight. Different guns have different numbers of ridges, such as four or five. Third, width and depth, which refers to the size and shape of the barrel ridges, which vary depending on the weapon. Fourth, the ridges can be twisted to the right or left, in what is known as a right-hand or left-hand twist. Finally, the degree of the twist can vary, again depending on the particular gun involved. All of these are all known as class characteristics.

> The witness now goes into a detailed explanation of the principles that make ballistics comparisons an accepted scientific method. This should be detailed, because the jury will more readily accept the expert's conclusions if it understands why the method is valid and reliable.

Q. What is meant by accidental characteristics?

A. All weapons develop unique characteristics which make exact identification possible. Some of these are created during manufacture when minute imperfections are created in the inside of a gun barrel, that are never exactly repeated again. In addition, the use of a weapon will impart additional characteristics, since each time a weapon is fired, small traces of metal are scooped away as the bullet passes through the barrel. Finally, such things as rusting, abuse, improper cleaning, and misalignment of the barrel and cylinder will change the weapon's characteristics.

Q. How do these class and accidental characteristics assist in performing ballistics comparison tests?

A. These class and accidental characteristics are then forced into the sides of the bullet as it passes through the barrel of the weapon. All these factors combine to give a weapon unique characteristics that enable an expert to match the particular weapon to a particular bullet.

Q. What is involved in making such a comparison?

A. First, we check the weapon to see if it is operable. If so, we load the weapon with a bullet of the same caliber and characteristics as the suspect bullet. We then fire the gun into a bullet trap, which is a long box filled with cotton, which enables us to recover the bullet in undamaged form. We then take the test bullet and suspect bullet and compare them on a comparison microscope. This is a microscope that allows you to see both bullets at the same time, to see the markings on the sides of both, to see if they match. The microscope allows you to rotate the bullets and allows you to see both on a split screen. If the bullets match, you will see the same markings or striations at the same locations on both bullets. After making the comparisons, we inventory the gun and the suspect bullet, and write a report on our findings.

Q. Officer Nicholson, I show you what has been previously admitted in evidence as People's Exhibit #1, and ask you to examine it. Do you recognize it?

A. Yes, I do.

Q. Have you seen People's Exhibit #1 before?

A. Yes.

Q. When was the first time you saw it?

A. I saw it when it was submitted to the lab on December 18, 1984.

After the scientific basis has been established, the actual testing methodology should be demonstrated.

Witness next identifies the two exhibits he compared.

(#1 is the gun; #2 is the bullet.)

Q. I now show you what has previously been admitted in evidence as People's Exhibit #2, and ask you to examine it. Do you recognize it?

A. Yes, I received this at the lab on December 20, 1984.

Q. Did you perform any tests on these two exhibits?

A. Yes, I did.

Q. Which were those?

A. I test-fired Exhibit #1 and found it to be in operable condition. I then performed a comparison test between a bullet fired from Exhibit #1 and Exhibit #2.

Q. When did you perform that test?

A. On December 21, 1984.

Q. How was that test performed?

A. I used the same method that I described previously. The weapon, a .38 caliber revolver with four lands and grooves with a right hand twist, was test fired using a .38 caliber lead bullet. The pellet was recovered from the cotton trap. I then placed this test pellet on one side of the comparison microscope and the suspect pellet, Exhibit #2, on the other side. I then completed the comparison.

Note that in this example the test pellet was not marked or offered in evidence. The introduction of the pellet is not essential to the comparison. However, you may well decide that you will want to introduce the pellet to make the testimony more complete.

Q. As a result of the comparison test, Officer Nicholson, did you reach any conclusions?

A. Yes, I did.

Q. What were those?

A. I concluded that the suspect pellet, Exhibit #2, was fired from the same weapon as the test pellet, that is, from Exhibit #1.

Q. What are the reasons for your conclusion?

A. (Explains basis for conclusion.)

Q. After completing the comparison test, what did you do?

A. I prepared a written report, and returned the weapon, Exhibit #1, and pellet, Exhibit #2, to the police inventory section.

Q. What did you do with the test pellet?

A. I marked it, but retained it, as we always do, in the ballistics lab files.

Q. How did you return those items to the inventory section?

A. I tagged the weapon, Exhibit #2, initialed the tag, and placed it into a sealed, labeled

In practice, there will usually be photographs taken of the test and suspect pellets, which would be introduced as exhibits, so the expert can use them to explain the reasons for the match.

Before concluding the direct examination,

manila envelope. The pellet, Exhibit #2, I placed in a standard pellet box, sealed the box, labeled it, and initialed it. I then had a messenger take both exhibits to the inventory section of the lab.

the integrity of the exhibits should be demonstrated.

§4.11. *Opinions of the lay witness*

While in general only experts can give opinions in areas beyond the knowledge and experience of ordinary laymen, certain exceptions exist. Several kinds of facts, while perhaps technically opinions, are facts that repeatedly occur in the experiences of lay witnesses. For that reason, the lay witnesses are permitted to give opinions, if based on the perception of the witness and helpful to a clear determination of a fact in issue. (See FRE 701.) Common facts on which such opinions are allowed include age, speed, sobriety, and handwriting.

Example:

The witness is testifying that he saw the driver of a car involved in an accident and that the driver appeared to be under the influence of alcohol. First establish the witness' background and his presence at the accident; then:

Q. Mr. Doe, were you able to watch the driver after he got out of the car?
A. Yes.
Q. How long were you able to watch him?
A. About two minutes.
Q. What was he doing during that time?
A. He was kind of walking and talking to various people.
Q. Did you notice anything about his walk?
A. Yes, he was walking in a hesitant, stumbling sort of way. He almost tripped once or twice.
Q. What did he look like during this time?
A. Well, his face was red and sweaty, and his eyes looked kind of glazed.
Q. Were you able to hear him talk?
A. Yes.
Q. Did you notice anything about his speech?
A. His speech was very slurred and halting.
Q. Mr. Doe, have you ever seen persons when they were under the influence of alcohol?
A. Of course.

Q. How many times during your adult life have you seen persons under the influence of alcohol?
A. Probably a few hundred times.
Q. Mr. Doe, were you able to tell what condition the driver of that car was in?
A. Yes, sir, I could.
Q. What was it?
A. He was under the influence. I'd say he was drunk.

§4.12. *Hypothetical questions*

Before the Federal Rules of Evidence were enacted, the hypothetical question was the required method for getting opinions from nontreating or consulting experts. This was because such experts had no first-hand knowledge of the facts necessary to support their opinions. To get around this problem, experts were asked to "assume" certain facts were true, and then were asked their opinions about the assumed facts. Since the hypothetical question needed a proper foundation, there had to be evidence admitted to support each assumed material fact. If there was none, the hypothetical question was improper, and the expert, having no first-hand knowledge of the relevant facts, could not testify to his opinions. Needless to say, lawyers often fought over whether all material facts were properly included in the hypothetical questions and over other technical requirements of this rule.

These requirements were justifiably criticized as being both cumbersome and unnecessary. Consequently, the Federal Rules of Evidence have substantially reduced the circumstances under which the hypothetical question is necessary. FRE 703 now permits an expert to testify to an opinion or inference, if he attended the trial and heard the testimony establishing the facts, or was presented the underlying facts from reliable sources outside of court. FRE 705 permits the expert, unless the court requires otherwise, to give his opinions and inferences without previously disclosing the facts underlying the testimony. Hypothetical questions are apparently necessary only where the facts and data upon which the expert will base his testimony were *not* either perceived by him or made known to him at or before the trial, a situation that will rarely exist if the expert is properly prepared.

Despite these changes, hypothetical questions are still used at trial. Some state jurisdictions still require them. Many lawyers, having been raised on hypothetical questions, still use them even though they are no longer required in many situations. Finally, hypothetical questions still are useful as vehicles of persuasion. They allow you to effectively summarize all the evidence introduced at trial the way you want it summarized, and elicit an expert opinion on a critical issue at trial, such as causation or permanence of injuries. For that reason, the hypothetical question can be an effective way to finish your case in chief, particularly in a personal injury case.

Checklist for hypothetical when questioning a consulting physician

Dr. ____ , I am now going to ask you to assume certain facts as true. (Don't tell him you're giving him a hypothetical.) *I will then ask your opinions based on these facts. Assume:*

   1. a man/woman/child
   2. age, height, weight
   3. previous conditions of health (work, play, around house)
   4. date
   5. scene
   6. how accident happened
   7. symptoms immediately after occurrence
   8. diagnosis and treatment
   9. present condition ("*He can't. . . . He can't. . . . He can't. . . . This is his condition to the present day.*")
  10. Hypothetical
       a. *Dr. ____ , based on these facts, do you have an opinion, to a reasonable degree of medical certainty, whether (there is a causal connection between the collision and injuries sustained) (the injuries are temporary or permanent)?*
              or (as permitted by FRE 702):
           Dr. ____ , based on these facts (is there a causal connection between the collision and the injuries sustained) (are the injuries temporary or permanent)?
       b. *What is your opinion?*
       c. *Please tell the court and jury the basis for your opinion.*

Example:

Thoroughly qualify your consulting physician as an expert in the appropriate specialty. Establish that he did not examine or treat the patient himself. Then:

   Q. Dr. Black, I am now going to ask you to assume that certain facts are true. I will then ask you your opinions based on these facts. Assume the following:
       a. A man is 30 years old, 5 feet 10 inches tall, and weighs 175 lbs.
       b. Before December 13, 1984, he was in perfect health. He was able to work as a school teacher and coach a basketball team. He enjoyed hiking and camping with his wife and daughters, enjoyed playing basketball on a team, and did the usual work around his house.
       c. On December 13, 1984, while crossing the street, he was struck by a car on his left side near the knee and thrown down on the pavement.

    d.   Immediately after being struck he was unable to move his left leg, was under considerable stress, and experienced constant shooting pains in the leg.

    e.   He was taken by ambulance to a hospital, where he was examined and X-rayed. The diagnosis was a transverse fracture of the left femur approximately nine centimeters above the knee.

    f.   The fracture was reduced and the leg placed in a cast. About six weeks later the leg was reexamined and a new cast was applied. That cast was kept on six more weeks. When the cast was removed, the healing process appeared to be progressing normally.

    g.   Three weeks ago the leg was examined again. At that time the leg was still substantially smaller, the man experienced considerable pain in the leg whenever he was physically active, and the examination disclosed that arthritis had developed at the fracture site.

    h.   He can't engage in sports activities, can't work around the house, can't go hiking, and can't do other physical activities involving use of his legs because of pain. That is his condition to the present day.

Q. Dr. Black, based on these facts, do you have an opinion, to a reasonable degree of medical certainty, whether there is a causal connection between the injuries sustained and the development of arthritis?

A. Yes, I have.

Q. What is that opinion?

A. (Dr. gives opinion.)

Q. What is the reason for your opinion?

A. (Dr. explains why.)

Ask the same questions for every other issue that you can and wish to elicit an opinion on, such as:

1. whether there is a causal connection between the arthritis and the pain.

2. whether the leg atrophy is a permanent condition.

3. whether the arthritis is a permanent condition.

4. whether the pain is a permanent condition.

Where the hypothetical has been outlined in advance and reviewed with the expert, it can be an effective persuasive tool at trial. Keep in mind that the hypothetical question should be as brief as possible and delivered in a style that parallels the picture portion of the opening statement. If the hypothetical is too long, too technical, or too dull, the jury will simply get bored and stop listening. In addition, remember that hypotheticals can be dangerous. If the witness becomes confused, or bases his opinion on facts not included in the hypothetical, the entire examination can fall apart. When you decide to use a hypothetical question, you should be reasonably sure this can be done safely and efficiently.

§4.13. *Character witnesses*

1. Law

Character witnesses occupy a unique niche in trials. Infrequently used and, when called, usually appearing in criminal cases, such witnesses are nevertheless potential witnesses in any trial. The law of character evidence must be clearly understood before an intelligent decision to present such evidence at trial can be made. Substantial differences exist between federal and state courts regarding the admissibility, presentation, and examination of such evidence. Since the Federal Rules of Evidence were enacted, these differences have been substantially broadened. You should always review FRE 404 and 405 beforehand, because the procedural rules are technical.

Character evidence is of two distinct types: evidence of specific character traits, admissible as direct or circumstantial evidence; and evidence of truthfulness, admissible only to affect the credibility of witnesses who have testified. Each is properly admissible in limited situations after certain foundation requirements have been met.

a.   Evidence of specific character traits can be either direct or circumstantial. Where a character trait is an "essential element" of a claim or defense, it is direct evidence and can introduced in both civil and criminal cases. This use of specific character traits evidence is rarely used. For example, in a libel action where the defendant called the plaintiff a drug addict, and the defense is truth, it raises as an essential element of the defense whether the plaintiff is in fact an addict. In an employment discrimination action, where the defendant claims the plaintiff was fired for being a thief and a drunk, the defense raises as an essential element whether the plaintiff is in fact a thief or drunk. When the specific character is an essential element of a claim or defense, it can be shown by reputation, opinion, or specific instances of conduct.

Evidence of specific character traits of the defendant and victim is also admissible as circumstantial evidence, but in criminal cases only. This is allowed because a person's reputation for a specific character trait shows that on the pertinent date that person probably acted consistently with that character trait. For example, showing that a defendant has a good reputation for honesty makes it less likely that he committed a theft. In an assault case where the defense is self-defense, showing that the defendant has a good reputation for peacefulness, or that the victim has a bad reputation for peacefulness, is circumstantial proof supporting the defense.

The procedure for use of specific character trait evidence as circumstantial evidence is important. Only the defendant in a criminal case may initiate character trait evidence. He does this by calling a witness who testifies, in either a reputation or opinion form, to the pertinent character trait of the defendant or victim. Once the defendant has initiated this proof, the prosecution can rebut with the same type of proof. (The only exception is homicide cases involving the defense of self-defense.)

b.   Evidence of truthfulness is governed by different rules. Evidence of *bad* reputation for truthfulness, or personal opinion of untruthfulness, may be introduced by the opposing party, after a witness has testified, to attack the credibility of that witness. The evidence is admitted solely to diminish the credibility and weight of the witness' testimony. This rule applies to any witness, including any party, who has testified at trial. A party always has the right to attack any witness called by the opposing party with such evidence. Once a witness' reputation has been attacked the proponent of the witness thereafter can offer contrary reputation or opinion evidence.

The procedural differences between evidence of truthfulness and specific character traits must be kept clear. Where the trait evidence is involved, the defendant has the exclusive right to decide whether to raise the relevant trait as an issue. The defendant does this by presenting evidence of that trait. Only after he has done so can the prosecution present opposing evidence.

Where evidence of truthfulness is involved, different rules apply. Here both sides have the right to attack any witness who has testified for the opposing party by presenting evidence of that witness' bad reputation, or personal opinion, for truthfulness. Moreover, only after the witness has been attacked by such evidence can the party initially calling that witness present contrary evidence.

2.   Foundation

Several foundation requirements must be met before character trait evidence is properly admissible at trial. Although certain differences exist, the foundations for specific trait evidence and truthfulness evidence are essentially similar.

First, the evidence must come from a qualified witness. Where reputation evidence is involved, the witness must be able to testify that he has heard the reputation discussed by other persons in the community. Where personal opinion is involved, the witness must be able to testify that he has had periodic contacts with the person about whom he is testifying. In both situations there must be an adequate basis shown for either the reputation or personal opinion.

Second, the evidence must be based on a relevant community or neighborhood. Any identifiable community of substantial population in which the person spends a considerable period of time — residence, work, school, organizations — can be an appropriate community for supporting such evidence.

Third, the evidence must be based on a proper time period. Where the issue is a specific character trait, the relevant time period is the date the act charged was committed or a reasonable prior period. When the issue is truthfullness, the relevant time is the date the person to whom the reputation, or opinion, applies testified at trial or a reasonable prior period.

3. Tactics

Several factual considerations should be weighed before deciding to present character evidence at trial. A list, by no means exhaustive, includes the following:

a. How effective will the character evidence be in the type of case on trial? (It is probably more effective in primarily circumstantial cases.)
b. Is the character evidence consistent with other evidence at trial?
c. Will the reputation witnesses be able to testify about the reputation in all relevant communities? (Incomplete reputation evidence is always suspect.)
d. Will the defendant testify? (Jurors may resent a defendant who does not testify, yet calls character witnesses that attack the other side's witnesses.)
e. Are the character witnesses vulnerable on cross?
f. Is the person to whom the reputation applies vulnerable on cross?

Once the decision to present character evidence has been made, appropriate witnesses must be selected. For this purpose the following should be considered:

a. Objective, nonfamily witnesses with diverse backgrounds and no financial relationship to the person in question are preferable.
b. Witnesses should be selected who can collectively testify to the person's reputation in every relevant community—residence, work, or other qualified areas.
c. Witnesses should never be called unless they are intimately familiar with the person's reputation.
d. Witnesses should be selected that a jury feels comfortable with, who have backgrounds similar to the jurors.

If, after the above considerations have been weighed, the decision to present such evidence is made, then a direct examination can be conducted along the following lines:

Example (reputation for peacefulness):

Q. Please state your name.
A. Robert Smith.
Q. Where do you live?
A. I live at 123 Rose Lane, Oak Park, Illinois.

Q. Who lives there with you?

A. My wife, Mary, and three children, Tom, Ted, and Betsy.

Q. How long have you lived there?

A. Fourteen years.

Q. What kind of work do you do?

A. I'm a typographer.

Q. How long have you been a typographer?

A. Fifteen years.

Q. What are your duties as a typographer?

A. I set the type for printing and design the ad layouts.

Q. What company do you work for?

A. The Donnelly Press.

Q. What kind of business is the Donnelly Press engaged in?

A. It publishes all kinds of advertising catalogs and pamphlets.

Q. How long have you worked for the Donnelly Press?

A. Six years.

Q. What is your present title?

A. I'm the assistant manager of the typography section.

Q. Do you know John Doe?

A. Yes, I do.

Q. How long have you known him?

A. Fourteen years.

Q. Are you related to him in any way?

A. No.

Q. Do you have any business dealings with him?

A. No.

Q. During the fourteen years you have known him, how often would you come into contact with him?

A. Two or three times a week, on the average.

Q. Do you know where he lives?

A. Yes.

Q. What is his address?

A. 136 Tulip Lane, Oak Park.

Q. How long has he lived at that address?

A. About ten years.

Q. Where is that address in relation to your home?

A. It's on the next block west of my block.

Q. How long have you lived that distance from him?

A. About ten years.

Q. During the years you have known John Doe, have you known other people in the community in which he lives who also know him?

A. Yes.

Q. Who are these people?

A. Other people who live in the neighborhood.

Q. Have you ever been present when those people discussed John Doe?

A. Yes, I have.

Q. How many persons have you heard discuss John Doe?

A. Probably a couple dozen.

Q. How many times have you heard them discuss John Doe?

A. Probably at least a hundred times over the past 14 years.

Q. Have you heard the reputation of John Doe for peacefulness in the community in which he lives, as it was around April 1, 1985?

A. Yes, I have.

Q. What is that reputation?

A. It's excellent. He's known as a peaceful guy.

If the witness can also give a personal opinion, that can be quickly obtained.

Example (personal opinion):

Q. Mr. Smith, other than having heard about John Doe's reputation, do you have a personal opinion whether Mr. Doe is a peaceful person?

A. Yes.

Q. What is your opinion?

A. I think he's an extremely peaceful, quiet, gentle kind of guy.

§4.14. *Adverse witnesses*

This chapter has evaluated the direct examinations of witnesses that are presumably favorable to the direct examiner. In those situations the witness will cooperate in the development and presentation of his testimony, since his interest is in maximizing the impact of that testimony.

A diametrically different situation exists with adverse witnesses. An adverse witness is any witness who, because of his position as a party or because he has special relationships to a party, will be presumed to give testimony detrimental to the other parties. As the name implies, such a witness favors your opponent. He will use every available opportunity to hurt you. Accordingly, it is usually preferable not to call a witness who is adverse unless necessary to establish an element of a claim or defense.

When you do call a witness that is adverse, you have a witness outside of your control. Because of this, you are permitted to examine the witness as if on cross-examination, so you can control the witness by leading him.

Determine in advance whether the court will permit you to call someone as an adverse witness. Party opponents are adverse witnesses, as well as officers, directors, and managing agents of parties. These can usually be presumed to be identified with an adverse party. However, many times a witness' status is unclear. FRE 611(c) speaks of "a witness identified with an adverse party," which enlarges the traditional scope of the definition of an adverse witness. In multiparty litigation, a witness may be adverse to some, but not all, parties. Make sure you determine in advance that you will be allowed to treat the witness as if on cross-examination.

When you do call an adverse witness to the stand, make sure you let the court know what you are doing.

Example:

Your Honor, at this time we will call the defendant, Frank Smith, as an adverse witness.

As noted earlier, don't call an adverse witness unless necessary to prove a claim or defense. If the witness is critical, and must be called, it is safer to call him in the middle of your case where he will be sandwiched between favorable witnesses. Make his testimony as brief as possible by leading directly to the necessary facts, draw them out, and stop. The longer such a witness is on the stand, the greater the opportunity he has to hurt your case. When dealing with adverse witnesses, brevity is the safest approach.

§4.15. *Hostile witnesses*

A hostile witness is one who surprises you and unexpectedly turns against you during his testimony at trial. When a witness becomes hostile, the same rules as those on adverse witnesses apply: You may examine that witness as if on cross-examination. (See FRE 611(c).)

The hostile-witness rule stems from the traditional rule that a party calling a witness vouched for his credibility. Since he was presumably favorable to your side, you were in essence stuck with his testimony, for better or worse. Only if the witness unexpectedly failed to give the testimony you anticipated could you have the witness declared hostile. The Federal Rules of Evidence have swept away this questionable presumption, so that a party does not vouch for the credibility of the witnesses it calls. (See FRE 607.) The Rules, therefore, accept the reality that parties are generally stuck with the witnesses that are available, and that these are called at trial from necessity, hardly by choice or design. When such a witness is hostile, he can be asked leading questions. (FRE 611(c).)

In those jurisdictions adhering to the traditional rule, having a witness declared hostile, so that you can lead him, requires a showing of surprise. The usual procedure is as follows: When the witness surprises you at trial by giving totally unexpected answers adverse to your side, ask enough additional questions so that your surprise is made apparent to the court. Ask for a side-bar conference or a short recess. Once you are out of the presence of the jury and witness, explain to the judge that you have been surprised and that you had anticipated substantially different testimony. In many jurisdictions you must show surprise *at trial.* In those jurisdictions, where you learn in advance of the trial (usually at the final trial preparation stage) that the witness intends to change his testimony, you cannot make an adequate showing of surprise. You must also demonstrate that you anticipated the witness' testimony to be materially different. Tell the court what your pretrial interviews showed. Where you have interview notes, or the witness made previous written statements, make these available to the judge. You might also conduct a voir dire examination of the witness, still out of the jury's presence, about any prior inconsistent statement. If the witness admits making it, you have demonstrated hostility.

In the presence of the jury, have the witness again admit making the prior inconsistent statement, then proceed with a cross-examination of the witness. Lead, elicit the wanted information, and stop. As with adverse witnesses, the safer approach is to conduct as short an examination as can be done under the circumstances.

§4.16. Using deposition transcripts

Most trials involve "live" witnesses. Sometimes, however, witnesses are unavailable by the time the trial begins. Where this is the case, you can introduce a transcript of the witness' trial testimony if the requirements of FRE 804(b)(1) are met. Basically, the witness must be "unavailable" under FRE 804(a), and the party against whom the former testimony is introduced must have had an opportunity to question the witness, and the same motive for questioning the witness, at the earlier proceeding. The most commonly introduced former testimony is deposition transcripts.

When you plan to use a witness' deposition transcript at trial, you must determine two things: what parts of the transcript will be submitted to the jury, and how you will be permitted to present the transcript in court.

First, advise the court which parts of the transcript you intend to read. Opposing counsel should then designate which additional parts he wants read. All evidentiary objections should be made and ruled on in advance. By raising and obtaining rulings on these matters in advance, you will be able to read the transcript to the jury uninterrupted by objections.

Second, advise the court in advance how you intend to read the transcript. The most effective method is to have someone play the role of the witness and actually take the witness stand. You play the role of the questioner. Since both you and the witness will have a copy of the transcript (marked to show what parts will be read), you can now reenact the testimony for the jury. Using this approach is the best way to make a cold record come alive, with a reading that can closely approximate what the actual testimony was like. This works particularly well if the person playing the role of the witness is of the same age and sex as the witness.

When the deposition is of a party in the case, the deposition can be used in two different ways. First, the deposition can be used to impeach the party witness if he testifies at trial inconsistently with the transcript. Second, the deposition, being a party admission, can be introduced as substantive evidence in your case in chief.

If you decide to use the party's deposition in your case in chief, proceed the same way as with unavailable witnesses. Determine what parts you want read to the jury, have any evidentiary objections ruled on in advance, and have someone else play the role of the party when the transcript is read to the jury. The only difference is that, while all or most of the transcript of an unavailable witness is usually read to the jury, only those parts of the transcript of a party that contain the admissions are normally read. Consequently, reading admissions of a party to the jury is usually accomplished quickly.

§4.17. *Judicial notice and stipulations*

1. Judicial notice

Judicial notice is the procedure, governed by FRE 201, by which the trial judge is asked to rule that certain facts are true. Its purpose is to increase trial efficiency and admit indisputable evidence where formal proof of these facts would be both difficult and time consuming.

Judicial notice can be taken in three areas. First, the court can take judicial notice of facts that are generally known in that particular geographic area. In San Francisco, for example, it is generally known that the Golden Gate Bridge is between San Francisco and Marin County. Second, the court can judicially notice facts that can be accurately and easily verified from a reliable source. Common examples are Department of Labor actuarial tables showing life expectancy, and almanac facts, such as when a full moon or high tide occurred, or what day of the week a certain date was. Third, the court can take judicial notice of the scientific basis for accepted scientific tests, such as that radar machines can measure speeds of objects, or that certain blood tests can show the possibility or impossibility of paternity.

The party wishing to have the court judicially notice a fact must ask the judge to take judicial notice, and the opposing party must have an opportunity to state objections. If the court takes judicial notice of the fact, the jury is informed of the fact through an instruction. In civil cases the jury must take a fact judicially noticed as being true, but this is not so in criminal cases. Because of due process problems, juries in criminal cases are instructed that they may, but are not required to, accept a judicially noticed fact as being true.

Example:

In a civil case, the court would tell the jury: *In this case, you must accept as a fact that. . . .*

In a criminal case, the court would instruct: *In this case, you may, but are not required to, accept as a fact that. . . .*

In practice, judicial notice is not commonly used. If a fact is so obvious that it can be judicially noticed, the standard way of getting the fact before the jury is through a stipulation.

2. Stipulations

A stipulation is simply an agreement between the parties that certain facts are true. If the stipulation involves an absent witness, the agreement usually states that if the witness were called at trial, he would testify to certain things. Regardless of what the stipulation is about, it must be brought to the attention of the jurors. The usual, and best, procedure is to prepare the stipulation in writing, have the lawyers sign it, and present it to the court in advance. The stipulation is then usually marked as an exhibit and read to the jury at an appropriate time. (See §5.3(18)).

§4.18. *Redirect examination*

When the cross-examination of a witness has been completed, the direct examiner may conduct a redirect examination of that witness. The purpose of the redirect examination is to explain or further develop matters that were raised during the cross-examination. This means that the scope of the redirect will be limited to what the cross-examiner chooses to raise during his examination. Courts vary widely on the latitude they permit during the redirect examination. Some will strictly forbid going beyond the scope of the cross-examination. Others will give the redirect examiner a free rein.

Regardless of the judge's tendencies in your case, it is always dangerous to withhold part of the direct examination to save it for the redirect. "Sandbagging" is great when it works, but is a disaster when it fails. Holding back a choice piece of information from the direct examination in the hope that the cross-examiner will ask about it and choke on it is a dangerous tactic. The cross-examiner, either through design or luck, may decide not to cross-examine at all, or probe areas totally divorced from the withheld topic, thereby preventing you from eliciting the testimony at all. (If this happens, you can always try asking the court for permission to reopen the direct examination or recall the witness later. This is discretionary with the court. Even if permitted, however, the testimony will not appear as convincing, since the jury will view it as an afterthought.) The safer approach is always to bring out the entire testimony during the direct examination.

Another common tendency is for the direct and cross-examiners to constantly ask "just one more question," under the theory that it is always advantageous to have the last word. Keep in mind that constantly seesawing back and forth, so that the re-redirect is followed by the re-recross, inevitably develops no further information and is viewed by the jury as boring and nit-picking. If you have nothing substantial to develop, don't redirect solely to rehash already existing testimony. Tell the court you have no further questions of the witness. The jury will appreciate both your professionalism and brevity.

The most common redirect examinations involve situations where the cross-examination has called into question the witness' conduct, or where the cross-examination has brought out only the favorable parts of a conversation or occurrence, or the witness has been impeached with a prior inconsistent statement. In each situation the redirect examination can develop additional facts that tell the complete story or explain why the inconsistency occurred.

Example:

The cross-examination of a rape victim has stressed the fact that the victim waited two hours after the rape before she called the police. The implication is that a rape really never occurred. On redirect the following question is proper:

Q. Why didn't you call the police for two hours?
A. I was upset and afraid. He said he'd come back and kill me if I called the police.

Example:

The cross-examination has elicited part of a conversation, that part that helps the cross-examiner. On redirect the following question is proper:

Q. Other than "I'm sorry this whole thing happened," did you say anything else to Mr. Smith at that time?
A. Yes, I also said: "However, if you don't pay me the money you owe, I'll have to hire a lawyer to collect it."

When a witness has been impeached by a prior inconsistent statement, it is proper on redirect to "rehabilitate" the witness. This is done by having the witness explain how or why the inconsistency occurred. If there is a sensible, logical explanation for the inconsistency, the impact of the inconsistency will be significantly lessened.

Example:

On direct examination a police officer has testified that the defendant he arrested stated "I shot John Doe and he deserved it." The cross-examiner impeached the police officer by showing that the defendant's statement does not appear on the officer's initial case report (impeachment by omission). On redirect the following questions are proper:

Q. Did you make out any other case reports?

A. Yes, I made two supplementary reports.

Q. Did you put the defendant's statement in those reports?

A. Yes, in both of them.

Q. Is there a reason the statement wasn't put in your initial report?

A. Yes. The initial report covered only the events up to the defendant's arrest at his house. He made the statement at the station, and what happened there is covered by the supplementary reports.

Under certain circumstances a witness impeached by a prior inconsistent statement can be rehabilitated with a prior consistent statement. This is proper when the cross-examination both suggests a recent fabrication of testimony or improper influence or motive, and the prior consistent statement was made when no motive to lie existed. Under FRE 801(d)(1)(B) the prior consistent statement is then admissible. The following example illustrates the technical circumstances that are necessary to permit the introduction of a prior consistent statement.

Example:

1. On September 1, 1984, defendant is arrested for a crime. A witness gives a statement to police: "I didn't do it, the defendant did."

2. On December 1, 1984, the witness is arrested for being the defendant's accomplice.

3. On January 1, 1985, the witness is interviewed by the defendant's investigator and gives him a statement: "I didn't do it, and neither did the defendant."

4. On August 1, 1985, the witness is immunized and agrees to be a witness at the defendant's upcoming trial. The witness' charges are dropped.

5. On September 1, 1985, the witness testifies at trial: "I didn't do it, the defendant did."

The defense lawyer then cross-examines the witness, impeaching his testimony with the prior inconsistent statement made to the defendant's investigator, on January 1, 1985, as well as with the recent deal he made with the prosecutors. The necessary inference of the cross-examination is that the witness' testimony at trial is false and came about as a result of the deal with the prosecutors. Under these circumstances the prosecution on redirect can bring out the witness' original statement to the police, on September 1, 1984, which was made prior to the immunization, and hence prior to a time when a motive to fabricate existed.

V

EXHIBITS

§5.1. Introduction

Ours is the age of visual media. Television has become the dominant information-transmitting source in our society. Printed and aural communications have taken a back seat to the visual media. A whole generation of Americans has been raised and educated primarily by seeing. Children learn by watching TV, not by reading. Critics complain that the art of clear speaking and clear writing is becoming lost.

Whether this change is desirable can be debated, but not its existence. Visual communications have grown by leaps and bounds. Advertising on TV, magazines, and billboards is often predominantly nonverbal, influencing its viewers by subconscious appeals. Studies have shown that the preponderant quantity of learning and memory is related to sight, the remainder to hearing and the other senses.

These changes have hardly gone unnoticed in the courtroom. Led by imaginative personal injury lawyers, other lawyers began to realize that, in the courtroom as well, a picture was indeed worth a thousand words. If a picture was so useful, so too could be a map, chart, diagram, model, movie, experiment, or in-court demonstration. Trial lawyers began using aerial photographs. Automobiles and machinery were reassembled in court. "A day in the life of" movies portrayed personal injury plaintiffs. Elaborate models of buildings and accident sites appeared. In-court demonstrations became common. In short, exhibits assumed a new importance.

What can be an exhibit? In its broadest sense an exhibit can be anything, other than testimony, that can be perceived by the senses and be presented in the courtroom. Any trial lawyer who has ever been involved in a case that used exhibits creatively knows the impact they have on the jury.

The exhibits become the center of attention. They make an immediate and lasting impression on the jury. It sees the exhibits as not only more interesting, but also more reliable. Accordingly, an aspiring lawyer must learn more than how to establish the foundation for common as well as more dramatic exhibits. He must also learn when to use them, and how to present them effectively at trial.

This chapter will discuss the proper procedures for having exhibits admitted in evidence, how and when to use them effectively, and the foundation requirements of exhibits commonly encountered during trials.

§5.2. *How to get exhibits in evidence*

Exhibits can be admitted in evidence only when a sequence of procedural steps has been followed. These steps are part of a litany that should be smoothly and efficiently demonstrated for each exhibit, using a qualified witness.

Your preliminary consideration is witness selection. Many times you will have more than one witness who is competent to qualify an exhibit for admission in evidence. When this is so, you will ordinarily select the witness who has the most knowledge of the exhibit and makes the best impression on the jury. Call the witness early in your case in chief, since it is usually advantageous to get your exhibits before the jury as soon as possible. (If you have witnesses who may become confused by the exhibits, consider calling them *before* the exhibits are introduced.) Keep in mind that some exhibits may need more than one witness to establish a proper foundation. In such cases, do not offer the exhibit in evidence until the last necessary witness has testified.

The following steps for getting exhibits into evidence constitute the most complete procedure. Various courts have relaxed some of the requirements. For instance, many courts permit marking exhibits before trial. Many do not require asking permission to approach the witness. Nevertheless, you must be familiar with the most formal procedural requirements, then determine in advance of trial which ones have been relaxed or eliminated by your particular court.

Step 1.   Have the exhibit marked

Every exhibit must be marked so it can be differentiated from all others. Exhibits are most commonly given sequential numbers or letters (e.g., 1, 2, 3). Where certain exhibits are part of a series, they can be marked 1A, 1B, 1C, or 1-1, 1-2, 1-3. Sets of exhibits that should remain together should be marked as group exhibits. Use any numbering system that logically marks the exhibits in your type of case. Exhibits should be designated to show which party offered them (e.g., Plaintiff, Defendant, Government, Defendant Smith). Many jurisdictions do not put "for identification" on the label.

Example:

> *Counsel:* Ms. Reporter, please mark this Plaintiff's Exhibit #1 for identification. (Hand the exhibit to the reporter, who will

attach a label to the exhibit, mark it "Plaintiff's Exhibit #1 for identification," and return it to you.)

If your jurisdiction permits premarking exhibits, make sure your labels clearly designate which party's exhibits they are. If the exhibit has previously been used during the trial, it will already be marked, so this step is unnecessary.

Step 2.   Show the exhibit to opposing counsel

Example:

> *Counsel:*   Your Honor, may the record reflect that I am now showing Mr. Smith Plaintiff's Exhibit #1 for identification. (Hand the exhibit to counsel, who should have a reasonable opportunity to inspect or read the exhibit, and get the exhibit back.)

In a few jurisdictions the practice is to show the exhibit to the opposing counsel only when the exhibit is offered in evidence. This is not the preferred approach, however, since it does not give the opposing counsel a timely opportunity to examine the exhibit to determine what the proper foundation for that exhibit is, or to make an early objection.

Step 3.   Ask the court's permission to approach the witness

Example:

> *Counsel:*   Your Honor, may I approach the witness?
> *Court:*   You may.

This formal requirement has been eliminated in most jurisdictions. In addition, the court bailiff in some jurisdictions hands exhibits to the witnesses.

Step 4.   Show the exhibit to the witness

Example:

> *Counsel:*   Mr. Witness, I am handing you Plaintiff's Exhibit #1 for identification. (Walk to the witness and hand the exhibit to him or place it in front of him.)

You should hand the exhibit to the witness so that the jury cannot see what the exhibit contains, since the jury is not entitled to see the exhibit unless it has been admitted in evidence. If the opposing lawyer has indicated that he has no objection to the exhibit, there is no problem. However, if you expect the opposing lawyer to object, this is important. Photographs, documents, and records can easily be handed to the witness without the jury seeing their contents. Physical objects and large diagrams, however, cannot be handled in the courtroom without the jury seeing them. As the opponent, if you have a serious objection to the exhibit, ask the judge to require that the foundation for such an exhibit be first made out of the jury's presence and that you be permitted to cross-examine the witness. If the judge sustains your objection, the jury never sees the exhibit and cannot be improperly influenced by it. This is a useful procedure when potentially inflammatory or misleading exhibits are involved.

Step 5.   Lay the foundation for the exhibit

(Section 5.3 of this chapter will cover the foundations necessary for different types of exhibits commonly introduced in trials.)

Step 6.   Move for admission of the exhibit in evidence

Example:

> *Counsel:*   Your Honor, at this time we move that Plaintiff's Exhibit #1 for identification be admitted in evidence as Plaintiff's Exhibit #1.
>
> *Court:*   Any objections, counsel?
>
> *Opposing Counsel:*   (States legal objections, if any. The opponent should ask for a side-bar conference if he wishes to make a lengthy argument.)
>
> *Court:*   It will be admitted.

Show the exhibit to the judge when you offer it in evidence, since the judge may need to see the exhibit to rule on any objections. After the court has admitted into evidence the offered exhibit, be sure you note this on your exhibit chart.

If you have a serious objection, or you think you can destroy the foundation for the exhibit, as the opposing counsel you can ask the judge for permission to cross-examine the witness on the exhibit's foundation. This is sometimes done out of the jury's presence.

Example:

> *Opposing counsel:*   Your Honor, may I voir dire the witness on the exhibit?
>
> *Court:*   You may. The jury will be excused for a few minutes while we take up a legal matter.

Whether a proper foundation can be established can only be determined at trial, since a witness must establish a proper foundation. However, other objections such as privilege or hearsay can often be ruled on in advance. Where this is the case, you should make a motion in limine before trial to raise the objection and get a ruling.

Step 7. Have the exhibit marked in evidence

In most jurisdictions the clerk now marks the exhibit label "admitted" and notes the date and time the exhibit was admitted in evidence. In some jurisdictions the older method is still used. There the court reporter crosses out the "for identification" portion of the label.

Example:

> *Counsel:* Your Honor, may we have the "for identification" symbol struck from the exhibit?
> *Court:* You may.
> (Hand the exhibit to the court reporter, who will cross out the "for id." part of the label, showing that the exhibit is now in evidence.)

There are many variations of this procedure. For example, in some jurisdictions the exhibit is stamped "admitted" or "received." Whatever the procedure, make sure you follow it so that the record clearly shows that the exhibit is now in evidence.

Step 8. Have the witness use or mark the exhibit

Once the exhibit has been admitted in evidence, you should always consider how the exhibit can be used or marked to increase its usefulness. Tangible objects can be held to show how they were used. Diagrams and photographs can be marked to show locations and distances. Documents and records can have their significant sections underlined. The various techniques for marking and using exhibits effectively are discussed in §5.4.

Keep in mind that some judges do not allow documents and records to be marked, on the theory that underlining or circling important terms or sections alters exhibits.

Step 9. Obtain permission to show or read the exhibit to the jury

Example:

> *Counsel:* Your Honor, may we show Plaintiff's Exhibit #1 in evidence to the jury at this time?
> *Court:* You may.

Step 10. "Publish" the exhibit

How and when an exhibit should be "published" with maximum effectiveness will be discussed in detail in the next section. In general, however, how you publish the exhibit depends for the most part on what kind of exhibit it is. Many exhibits, such as photographs and tangible objects, are usually shown to the jury.

Example:

> *Counsel:* Your Honor, may we show Plaintiff's Exhibit #1 now in evidence to the jury?
> *Court:* You may.
> (Then hand the exhibit to the first juror, who will look at it and pass it on to the next juror until all jurors have seen it. Then get the exhibit back.)

Other exhibits, principally documents and records, can be published either by showing or reading them to the jury. Where the documents are simple, such as with checks or promissory notes, the exhibit can easily be shown or read to the jury. If read, either the counsel or the witness can read it.

Example (counsel):

> *(Counsel stands before the jury.)*
> *Counsel:* Ladies and gentlemen, Plaintiff's Exhibit #1 in evidence reads as follows:
> (Then read the exhibit to the jury.)

Example (witness):

> *Q.* Mr. Smith, please read Plaintiff's Exhibit #1 in evidence to the jury.
> *A.* (Witness then reads the exhibit.)

Many records, however, are lengthy or complicated, and showing or reading them to the jury may be ineffective. The better technique is to ask the witness to read the important parts of the record to the jury. The jury can then look at the entire exhibit during a recess.

Example:

> *Q.* Mr. Smith, does that invoice, Plaintiff's Exhibit #1, show on what date the shipment was made?
> *A.* Yes, it was made on December 12, 1984.
> *Q.* Does it reflect the gross weight of the shipment?

A. Yes, it was 1,936 lbs.
Q. Does the invoice have a place where the addressee acknowledges receipt of the shipment?
A. Yes.
Q. What is contained in that place on the invoice?
A. The place is captioned "Received the above shipment." It bears the signature R. Schwartz and the date of December 14, 1984.

At the conclusion of your case in chief, it is always a sound procedure, before resting, to reoffer your exhibits in evidence or check with the judge that you have correctly recorded the admission of the exhibits. The judge will then usually run down his list of exhibits and report what his ruling was on each one. This creates a clear record and avoids possible confusion later in the trial or on appeal.

These steps are the most formal requirements for admitting exhibits in evidence. Many jurisdictions, including federal courts, have eliminated some of the formalities. For instance, having the court reporter or clerk mark exhibits, marking them "for identification," or asking for permission to approach the witness are frequently no longer required. You should use the most efficient procedure allowed in your court.

The following example illustrates the exhibits procedure usually followed in federal courts.

Example:

Q. Your Honor, may the record reflect that I am showing Plaintiff's Exhibit #1 to counsel?
Court: It will.
Q. Mrs. White, I'm showing you Plaintiff's Exhibit #1. Do you recognize it?
A. Yes.
Q. What scene does that photograph show?
A. It shows the corner of Elm and Maple Streets where the accident happened.
Q. Does the photo fairly and accurately show how that intersection looked at the time of the accident?
A. Yes, it does.
Q. Your Honor, we offer Plaintiff's Exhibit #1 in evidence.
Court: Any objections, counsel?
Counsel: No, your Honor.
Court: It's admitted.
Q. Mrs. White, does the photograph show where the two cars collided?
A. Yes.
Q. Using this red felt pen, please put an "X" where the cars collided.
(Witness marks photograph.)

> *Q.* Does the photograph show where you were standing when the cars collided?
> *A.* Yes.
> *Q.* Using this blue felt pen, please put a "W" in a circle where you were standing.
> (Witness marks photograph.)
> *Q.* Your Honor, may we show Plaintiff's Exhibit #1 to the jury?
> *Court:* You may.
> (Hand photograph to first juror.)

§5.3. *Foundations for exhibits*

Every exhibit must meet three basic requirements before it can be admitted in evidence. These are:

1. The qualifying witness must be competent.
2. The exhibit must be relevant.
3. The exhibit must be authenticated.

The first two requirements rarely cause problems. The witness will ordinarily have first-hand knowledge because he previously saw the exhibit, or knows the facts underlying the exhibits. Relevance can usually be established by having the judge examine the exhibit and comparing it to the issues raised by the claims and defenses.

Authentication is the principal issue raised at trial. Authentication, governed primarily by FRE 901 and 902, involves establishing that the exhibit is in fact what it purports to be. In trial lawyer's language, you must "lay a foundation" for the exhibit. This section sets out the necessary foundations for the kinds of exhibits frequently introduced at trial.

Keep in mind that you are establishing a foundation for both the judge and jury. The judge, concerned only with admissibility, is interested in seeing if you have made a prima facie showing under FRE 901(a) that the exhibit is what it purports to be. The jury, concerned only with credibility and weight, is interested in how persuasive your witness and foundation testimony is. Hence, your foundation must be technically adequate, to satisfy the judge, and factually persuasive, to convince the jury.

Although there are numerous kinds of exhibits, almost all of them fit into one of four categories, and the basic foundation requirements are the same for all exhibits within a category. These categories are as follows:

1. *Real evidence.* Since "real evidence" is the actual tangible object involved, the exhibit is admissible if it is actually what it purports to be. Common examples are weapons, clothing, blood, and other objects. Hence, the witness must testify that the exhibit is the actual one, and not a substitute, and that it is in basically the same condition now as it was on the relevant date.

2. *Demonstrative evidence.* "Demonstrative evidence" is not the actual object itself, but is evidence that represents or illustrates the real thing.

Common examples are photographs, diagrams, maps, and models. Hence, demonstrative evidence is admissible if it fairly and accurately represents the real thing, and helps explain the facts of the case.

3. *Writings.* Writings are documents that have legal significance. As such, the documents are nonhearsay. Common examples are written contracts, letters that form contracts, promissory notes, checks, and wills. These writings are admissible if they were in fact executed by the person they appear to have been signed by. Hence, the signatures must be identified as being genuine before these writings are admissible.

4. *Records.* Business records are hearsay, and are admissible as hearsay exceptions only if the foundation requirements of FRE 803(6) are met. Business records include not only common records like invoices, shipping documents, and bills, but can also include things like telephone memos and diaries. A custodian or other qualified witness must testify that the record involved was made under the requirements of that rule, since this shows that the record was accurately made and maintained by the business.

The following exhibit types described in this section expand on these four basic categories and demonstrate the foundation requirements necessary for admission. Keep in mind that each required step of the admissions procedure, from marking the exhibit to reading or showing the exhibit to the jury, must be followed each time an exhibit is introduced into evidence.

The admissions procedure and foundation should be done smoothly and efficiently. Leading questions are proper when doing this since there is no nonleading way the foundation information can reasonably be obtained from the qualifying witness. Hence, leading questions that use the words of the foundation requirements are proper, and this is the standard way of establishing the necessary foundation.

1. Tangible objects

Elements:

a. Exhibit is relevant.
b. Exhibit can be identified visually, or through other senses.
c. Witness recognizes the exhibit.
d. Witness knows what the exhibit looked like on the relevant date.
e. Exhibit is in the same condition or substantially the same condition now as when the witness saw it on the relevant date.

The above elements pertain to any tangible object that can be positively identified, usually because the witness previously saw it. Common examples are weapons, clothing, and other objects that can be identified visually, either because the article is inherently unique in appearance, or because a serial number, markings or identifying symbols make it unique. In these situations a chain of custody is not required.

Example:

A police officer has testified that he found a handgun at the defendant's house.

> Q. Please describe the weapon you saw on the dresser in the bedroom.
> A. It was a .38 caliber blue steel Colt revolver, 5-shot, with a brown wood handle and a 2 inch barrel.

Step 1.   Have exhibit marked.
Step 2.   Show exhibit to opposing counsel.
Step 3.   Ask permission to approach witness.
Step 4.   Show exhibit to witness.
Step 5.   Establish foundation:

> Q. Officer Doe, I show you Plaintiff's Exhibit #1 for identification and ask you to examine it. (Witness does so.) Have you seen it before?
> A. Yes, I have.
> Q. When was the first time you saw this exhibit?
> A. When I saw it on the dresser in the bedroom on December 13, 1984.
> Q. How are you able to recognize this as being the same revolver?
> A. Well, I remember what kind of gun it was and what it looked like. I can remember the notches that were cut in the wooden handle (pointing). I also recorded the serial number appearing on the barrel in my report. In addition, I scratched the date and my initials on the trigger guard, and they're still there: "12/13/84, T.A.D."
> Q. Is Plaintiff's Exhibit #1 for identification in the same or substantially the same condition today as when you first saw it on December 13, 1984?
> A. Yes, sir, it is.
> Q. Is there anything different about this exhibit today compared to when you first saw it?
> A. Other than where I scratched the date and my initials, no, sir.

Step   6.   Move to admit exhibit in evidence.
Step   7.   Have exhibit marked in evidence.
Step   8.   Have witness use exhibit.
Step   9.   Ask permission to show exhibit to jury.
Step 10.   Show exhibit to jury.

If the physical object is so large that it cannot be brought into the courtroom, or if aids such as photographs and diagrams do not adequately show a scene, the jury can be taken to the object or scene. This is called a "view." The procedure is sometimes regulated by statute, but otherwise deciding whether to permit a view and how it should be conducted is usually within the discretion of the trial judge.

2. Tangible objects — chain of custody

Where an object cannot be uniquely identified through the senses, a chain of custody must be established to demonstrate that it is the same object that was previously found. Although most common in cases involving narcotics such as pills or powdered drugs, a "chain" may be necessary in many other circumstances. A bullet, wire, rubber tubing, paint chips, and dirt samples may have no identifying markings and are too small to be marked. Liquids such as blood or brake fluid cannot be marked. In all these cases a chain of custody must be established to prove that the object is the same one, and has not been switched, altered, or tampered with, before it can properly be received in evidence.

Elements:

There are two basic methods to show a chain of custody:

a. Show that the exhibit has been in one or more persons' continuous, exclusive, and secure possession at all times.
b. Show that the exhibit was in a uniquely marked, sealed, tamperproof container at all times.

Example (method a):

A police officer has testified that he removed a broken hydraulic brake-fluid tube from a car immediately after an accident.

Q. Officer Doe, what did that tubing look like?
A. It was a black rubber tube, 8 inches long, 1 inch in diameter. It was covered with a black fluid and had a large crack running lengthwise.
Q. What did you do with the tubing after you removed it from the car?
A. I put it in a small cardboard box, labeled the box, and placed it in my evidence locker.
Q. Was the tubing in your possession from the time you removed it from the car to the time you put it in your evidence locker?
A. Yes, sir.
Q. Did anyone else handle it?
A. No, sir.
Q. Did you do anything to or with the tubing during this time?
A. No, sir.
Q. What does your evidence locker consist of?
A. There's a room in the station we reserve to store evidence. Every officer has his own steel locker with a lock on it. It's about the size of a file drawer.
Q. Who has access to your evidence locker?
A. Only me. I've got the only key to the lock.

Q. After placing the tubing in your locker, what's the next thing you did?

A. I locked the door to it.

Q. Between December 13, 1984, and today, did you ever remove the box or tubing from your locker?

A. No.

Q. Did you ever allow anyone else to open and enter your locker?

A. No.

Q. Did you ever give your locker key to anyone else?

A. No.

Q. Did you do anything with the tubing today?

A. This morning I went to my locker, unlocked it, took out the box with the tubing, and took it with me to court.

Q. Has the tubing been in your possession since you removed it from your locker this morning?

A. Yes, it has.

Q. Did you do anything to or with the tubing today?

A. No, sir.

Q. May I have the tubing, please? (Obtain tubing from witness.)

Step 1.   Have exhibit marked.

Step 2.   Show exhibit to opposing counsel.

Step 3.   Ask permission to approach witness.

Step 4.   Show exhibit to witness.

Step 5.   Establish foundation:

Q. Officer Doe, I show you what has just been marked Plaintiff's Exhibit #1 for identification. Is this the tubing you removed from your evidence locker and brought to court today?

A. Yes, it is.

Q. Is it in substantially the same condition now as when you first saw it on December 13, 1984?

A. Yes.

Step 6.   Move to admit exhibit in evidence.

Step 7.   Have exhibit marked in evidence.

Step 8.   Have witness use exhibit.

Step 9.   Ask permission to show exhibit to jury.

Step 10.   Show exhibit to jury.

Notice that the witness was *not* asked if this tubing was the same tubing that he obtained on December 13, 1984. The answer to that question necessarily follows from the testimony.

Example (method b):

A quantity of powdered heroin in a plastic bag was seized by a police officer, given to a laboratory custodian, and then to a chemist.

Police officer testifies

Q. Officer Doe, after seizing the bag containing the brown powdery substance on December 13, 1984, what did you do with it?

A. I kept it in my possession and took it with me to headquarters. I then placed the bag containing the powder in one of our plastic evidence bags, labeled it, and sealed it.

Q. How did you label the evidence bag?

A. The bag has a special texture on the inside of the opening where you can write. I put the date, subject's name, address, and time of seizure, my name, badge number, and the case number.

Q. How did you seal the evidence bag?

A. We have a special machine which seals the opening by heating it so the two sides melt into each other. It's sort of like laminating plastic. The sealed strip is about 1½ inches wide, and it also seals in the identifying marks I made.

Q. What did you do with the bag after labeling and sealing it?

A. I carried it to the chemistry section of our crime laboratory.

Q. What did you do with it there?

A. I gave the bag to the record custodian, who gave me a receipt.

Q. At the time you gave the evidence bag to the custodian, what was its condition?

A. It was still in a sealed condition.

Step 1. Have exhibit marked.

Step 2. Show exhibit to opposing counsel.

Step 3. Ask permission to approach witness.

Step 4. Show exhibit to witness.

Step 5. Establish foundation:

Q. Officer Doe, I show you what has been marked Plaintiff's Exhibit #1 for identification. (Witness examines it.) Do you recognize it?

A. Yes, I do.

Q. What do you recognize it to be?

A. That's the evidence bag in which I placed the plastic bag containing the powder I seized on December 13, 1984.

Q. How can you recognize it to be the same particular bag?

A. I can see the label I placed on it by the heat seal.

Q. Is that heat seal in the same condition today as when you placed it on the bag on December 13, 1984?

A. Yes, sir.

Q. Is there anything different in the condition of the evidence bag today from the time when you delivered it to the crime lab on December 13, 1984?

A. Yes, sir. There's another heat seal on the opposite side of the bag from the one I made.

Q. Did you make that second seal?

A. No, sir.

Q. From December 13, 1984, until today, did you ever see that evidence bag?

A. No.

Chemist testifies

Q. Ms. Rae, I show you what has been previously marked Plaintiff's Exhibit #1 for identification. (Witness examines it.) Have you ever seen it before?

A. Yes, I have.

Q. When was the first time you saw it?

A. On December 16, 1984.

Q. Where did you first see it?

A. I saw it in the evidence room of the chemistry section when our custodian removed it and gave it to me.

Q. When you first received Plaintiff's Exhibit #1 for identification, what condition was it in?

A. It was in a sealed condition.

Q. Where was it sealed?

A. It had only one seal — on the right side.

Q. What was the condition of the bag itself?

A. It was in the normal condition. It had no signs of tampering or alteration.

Q. What did you do with the exhibit?

A. I cut open the side opposite from the seal, removed the contents, and weighed it. I removed a small portion of the contents on which I performed certain chemical tests. The remainder I put back in the same bag.

Q. What did you do after putting the contents back in the bag?

A. I labeled the bag and heat-sealed the edge I had opened.

Q. What did you do with the bag?

A. I returned it to our evidence locker.

Q. When did you next see Plaintiff's Exhibit #1 for identification?

A. This morning the custodian removed it from the evidence locker, and I brought it to the courtroom.

Q. When you received the bag this morning, what was its condition?

A. It was sealed.

Q. Was there anything different about the bag this morning from the way it was when you returned it to the evidence locker on December 16, 1984?

A. No, the bag was still sealed, looked the same, and had no signs of tampering.

Step 6. Move to admit exhibit in evidence.
Step 7. Have exhibit marked in evidence.
Step 8. Have witness use exhibit.
Step 9. Ask permission to show exhibit to jury.
Step 10. Show exhibit to jury.

Note that you have traced the bag from the moment the officer obtained it to the time the chemist received it, tested it, and brought it to court.

The evidence custodian is *not* a necessary witness because the evidence bag was still sealed when the chemist received it, nor is it necessary to show that no one else handled the bag. The important point is that no one, other than the chemist, had access to the bag's contents. This is conclusively demonstrated by showing that the bag remained sealed and had no signs of tampering from the time the police officer delivered it to the crime laboratory to the time the chemist received it. Hence, you have proved that the evidence is what it purports to be. Of course, if your opponent seriously challenges your chain of custody, the evidence custodian should be available as a witness.

3. Photographs and motion pictures

Elements:

    a. Photograph is relevant.
    b. Witness is familiar with the scene portrayed in the photograph.
    c. Witness is familiar with the scene at the relevant date (and time, if important).
    d. Photograph "fairly and accurately" shows the scene as it appeared on the relevant date.
    e. Probative value of the photograph exceeds any prejudicial effect. (This is, strictly speaking, not an element, but an objection the opponent can raise where appropriate. This objection is common only where the photographs are of homicide or accident victims.)

Example:

    Q. Mr. Doe, have you ever been at the intersection of North and Clark Streets?
    A. Yes.
    Q. How many times have you been there?
    A. About 50 times.
    Q. Are you familiar with the intersection as it looked on December 13, 1984?
    A. Yes, I am.
Step 1. Have exhibit marked.
Step 2. Show exhibit to opposing counsel.
Step 3. Ask permission to approach witness.
Step 4. Show exhibit to witness.
Step 5. Establish foundation:
    Q. I show you what has been marked Plaintiff's Exhibit #1 for identification and ask you to examine it. Do you recognize the scene in that photograph?
    A. Yes.
    Q. What scene is shown in the photograph?
    A. It shows the intersection of North and Clark Streets.

Q. Mr. Doe, does Plaintiff's Exhibit #1 for identification fairly and accurately show that intersection as it appeared on December 13, 1984?

A. Yes, sir, it does.

Step 6. Move to admit exhibit in evidence.

Step 7. Have exhibit marked in evidence.

Step 8. Have witness mark exhibit.

Step 9. Ask permission to show exhibit to jury.

Step 10. Show exhibit to jury.

In recent years motion pictures have been used with increasing frequency at trial, particularly in personal injury cases. Plaintiff's lawyers use movies to illustrate graphically how the plaintiff's injuries have affected his life-style. These a-day-in-the-life-of movies show the plaintiff's activities during a typical day much more effectively and dramatically than is possible through oral testimony. Defense lawyers, on the other hand, have used movies of the plaintiff to demonstrate that the plaintiff's injuries and subsequent limitations have been exaggerated or even fabricated.

Where motion pictures are introduced, the foundation elements are essentially identical to that for still photographs. However, the mechanical procedures in establishing those foundation elements parallel that for sound and video recordings. (See subsection 8 below.)

4. Diagrams, models, and maps

Elements:

a. Diagram, model, or map is relevant.

b. Witness is familiar with the scene represented by the diagram, model, or map.

c. Witness is familiar with the scene at the relevant date (and time, if important).

d. Diagram, model, or map is useful in helping the witness explain his testimony to the jury.

e. Diagram, model, or map is reasonably accurate or to scale.

Keep in mind that jurisdictions can differ in their treatment of these exhibits, depending on the accuracy of the exhibit itself. When an exhibit is "to scale," all jurisdictions will admit the exhibit in evidence.

When the exhibit is "reasonably accurate," courts differ in their approach. Most still admit the exhibit in evidence since its probative value is still substantial. A few still take the view that the exhibit is merely an "illustrative" aid to help the witness explain his testimony to the jury, so the exhibit is not admitted in evidence. Hence, it does not go to the jury at the close of the case. Make sure you learn in advance what your judge's approach to a diagram not drawn to scale is.

Example (exhibit not to scale):

Q. Mr. Doe, are you familiar with the intersection of North and Clark Streets?

A. Yes.

Q. Are you familiar with that intersection as it looked on December 13, 1984?

A. Yes.

Step 1. Have exhibit marked.

Step 2. Show exhibit to opposing counsel.

Step 3. Ask permission to approach witness.

Step 4. Show exhibit to witness.

Step 5. Establish foundation:

Q. I show you Plaintiff's Exhibit #1 for identification. Is that diagram a reasonably accurate representation of the intersection of North and Clark Streets as it existed on December 13, 1984?

A. Yes, sir. I'd say it is.

Q. Would that diagram help you explain what happened?

A. I think so.

Step 6. Move to admit exhibit in evidence.

Step 7. Have exhibit marked in evidence.

Step 8. Have witness mark exhibit.

Step 9. Ask permission to show exhibit to jury.

Step 10. Show exhibit to jury.

If the exhibit has been prepared to scale, the person preparing it could testify as follows:

Example (exhibit to scale):

Q. Mr. Doe, were you at the intersection of North and Clark Streets on approximately December 30, 1984?

A. I was.

Q. At whose direction did you go there?

A. You asked me to.

Q. When you got to the intersection, what did you do?

A. I measured every important distance such as street widths, sidewalk widths, crosswalks, traffic controls, and so forth.

Q. After completing these measurements, what did you do next?

A. I went to my office and prepared a diagram of the intersection.

Step 1. Have exhibit marked.

Step 2. Show exhibit to opposing counsel.

Step 3. Ask permission to approach witness.

Step 4. Show exhibit to witness.

Step 5. Establish foundation:

Q. Mr. Doe, I show you what has been marked Plaintiff's Exhibit #1 for identification. Do you recognize it?

A. Yes, that's the diagram I prepared.

Q. Does that diagram accurately portray the intersection of North and Clark Streets as it existed on December 30, 1984?

A. Yes, it does.

Q. Is the diagram to scale?

A. Yes, it is.

Q. What scale is it?

A. I prepared the diagram using a scale of one inch equaling five feet.

Step 6. Move to admit exhibit in evidence.

Step 7. Have exhibit marked in evidence.

Step 8. Have witness mark exhibit.

Step 9. Ask permission to show exhibit to jury.

Step 10. Show exhibit to jury.

Note that since the witness obviously prepared the "to scale" diagram some time after the occurrence, it may be necessary to have another witness testify that the intersection looked the same on the date of the occurrence as it looked on the date the diagram was prepared.

The requirement that the diagram helps explain the witness testimony is derived from older notions of relevance. Since the diagram was not the "real thing," but only "illustrative," it was viewed as only a supplement to the witness' oral testimony and was properly in court only if the witness used it to explain his testimony. In most jurisdictions this concept has been discarded, and illustrative exhibits are treated for relevancy purposes like any other evidence. Hence, you can usually dispense with the "does the diagram help you explain what happened" type of question, since this is not a logical requirement for the exhibit's admission.

5. Drawings by witnesses

Drawings by witnesses in court are usually things to be avoided. It is difficult to create an adequate record, particularly where the witness uses a blackboard. Moreover, witness drawings are usually inaccurate and often misleading. The better practice is to prepare a diagram and have the witness prepared to qualify it. If you must have an in-court drawing, use artist's paper so that the drawing can be preserved as part of the record.

Elements:

a. Drawing is relevant.

b. Witness is familiar with the scene at the relevant date.

c. Drawing is useful in helping the witness explain what he saw.

d. Drawing is reasonably accurate and is not misleading.

Example:

> Q. Mr. Doe, are you familiar with the intersection of North and Clark Streets as it looked on December 13, 1984?
> A. Yes, I am.
> Q. Mr. Doe, would making a drawing of the intersection of North and Clark Streets help you explain what happened?
> A. Yes, I think so.
> Q. Your Honor, may the witness step down from the witness stand and approach the exhibit stand?
> *Court:*   He may.
> Q. Using the black felt pen, please make a drawing of that intersection on the artist's paper, which is marked Plaintiff's Exhibit #1 for identification. (Witness does so.) What does this line represent? (pointing)
> A. That's the curb line between the sidewalk and street. (Have the witness identify the major parts of the drawing, and label as is necessary. Then:)

Step   6.   Move to admit exhibit in evidence. (If the Court will admit in evidence a drawing that is not to scale.)

Step   7.   Have exhibit marked in evidence.

Step   8.   Have witness mark exhibit.

Step   9.   Ask permission to show exhibit to jury.

Step 10.   Show exhibit to jury.

6.   Demonstrations by witnesses

Witnesses are generally allowed to display body parts to the jury, demonstrate physical acts, or reenact an event. This is usually done by having the witness step down, stand before the jury box, and display the body part (such as a foot), or demonstrate a physical act (such as bending a knee), or act out an event.

Keep in mind, however, that some personal injury lawyers disapprove of having their clients display injuries to the jury. They feel that this runs a grave risk of offending the jury, and that the injuries can better be demonstrated by using photographs. In addition, the opponent can object that the demonstration's inflammatory effect outweighs its probative value.

Making an accurate record of the demonstration is also difficult. If you must use a witness demonstration, be sure that you narrate for the record exactly what the witness does, and ask the judge to confirm the basic accuracy of your narration.

Elements:

a. Demonstration is relevant.
b. Probative value of the demonstration exceeds any prejudicial effect.

Example:

Q. Your Honor, may the witness step down from the stand and approach the jury box?

Court: He may.

Q. Mr. Doe, would you please step down and stand before the jury? (Witness does so.)

The scars on your face that you have previously described, would you please point them out to the jury?

A. The scar over my left eye is right here (witness points, while facing jury). The scar on my left cheek is right here (pointing).

Q. Your Honor, may the record show that Mr. Doe has pointed to a white scar approximately two inches long, running horizontally about one inch over his left eye, and a reddish scar approximately four inches long, a half inch wide, which runs vertically starting about one inch below his left eye?

Court: That looks pretty accurate to me. Any objection to that description, counsel?

Counsel: No, your Honor.

Q. Thank you, Mr. Doe. Please return to the witness stand. (Witness does so.)

Example:

Q. Your Honor, may the witness step down and approach the jury box?

Court: Of course.

Q. Mr. Doe, would you please step down and stand before the jury? (Witness does so.) Before the collision, how far could you bend forward?

A. I could bend all the way over and touch my toes.

Q. Since the collision, how far have you been able to bend your back?

A. Just a little bit, not nearly as far as before.

Q. Mr. Doe, please demonstrate to the jury the extent to which you can now bend your back. (Witness does so.) Your Honor, may the record show that the witness has bent over and touched his legs so that his fingertips reach his thighs about six inches above the knees?

Court: The record will so show. Any objection, counsel?

Counsel: No, your Honor.

Q. Is that the furthest you are able to bend over at the present time?

A. Yes, sir.

Q. How long has that condition existed?

A. It's been that way for over a year now.

Q. Thank you. Please return to the witness stand.

7. X-ray films

X-ray films can usually be admitted in evidence using either of the two following approaches. First, the X ray and accompanying label can be qualified as a business record, since doctors and hospitals routinely take, label, and maintain X rays under established procedures and rely on them for diagnosing and treating patients. Second, the X ray is like a photograph and a qualified witness, usually the treating physician, can identify the X ray as being of the particular patient.

Old case law sometimes required that a witness testify that the X-ray machine was in good working order and that the machine was properly used. Since the scientific basis for X-ray technology is now clearly established and accepted, this type of foundation is unnecessary.

Elements (business records):

    a. X ray is relevant.
    b. X ray is a "record" of the hospital.
    c. Witness is the "custodian or other qualified witness."
    d. X ray and the label was "made by a person with knowledge" of the facts, or was "made from information transmitted by a person with knowledge" of the facts.
    e. X ray was "made at or near the time" of the "conditions" appearing on it.
    f. X ray was made as part of "the regular practice" of the hospital.
    g. X ray was "kept in the course of a regularly conducted business activity."

Example:

(See the examples in subsection 12 dealing with business records.)

Elements (photographs):

    a. X ray is relevant.
    b. Witness is familiar with the patient's physical condition at the relevant date.
    c. X ray "fairly and accurately" shows the condition of the patient's body as it was at the relevant date.

Example:

The treating physician is testifying. He has already described his initial examination of the patient.

Q. Dr. Doe, did you order any X rays of John Smith during the course of your examination and treatment on December 13, 1984?

A. I did.

Q. What parts of the body did you order X rays of?

A. I ordered two X rays of the left knee, a lateral view and an anterior-posterior view.

Step 1.   Have exhibit marked.

Step 2.   Show exhibit to opposing counsel.

Step 3.   Ask permission to approach witness.

Step 4.   Show exhibit to witness.

Step 5.   Establish foundation:

Q. Dr. Doe, I show you Plaintiff's Exhibit #1 for identification. Do you recognize it?

A. Yes.

Q. What do you recognize it to be?

A. This is an X-ray film of John Smith's left knee I had taken on December 13, 1984.

Q. How are you able to recognize this particular X-ray film as being of John Smith?

A. Well, the corner label is exposed on the film when the X rays are taken. The label always has the patient's name, date, and hospital on it. This X ray's label in the corner shows it to be of John Smith and taken on December 13, 1984. In addition, I remember seeing this particular plate, the anterior-posterior view, with these fracture lines on December 13, 1984, and can identify the plate on that basis. Finally, my examination of the patient disclosed a probable fracture of Mr. Smith's left femur just above the knee, which corresponded to the fracture disclosed on the films.

Q. Does Plaintiff's Exhibit #1 for identification fairly and accurately portray the bones and other internal structures of John Smith's left knee as they were on December 13, 1984?

A. Yes, it does.

Step 6.   Move to admit exhibit in evidence.

Step 7.   Have exhibit marked in evidence.

Step 8.   Have witness use exhibit.

Step 9.   Ask permission to show exhibit to jury.

Step 10.   Show exhibit to jury.

8. Sound and video recordings

Sound and video recordings present complex authentication problems. A witness must be able to testify that the recording is an accurate reproduction of the events involved. Therefore, the equipment used to record the original event, as well as the equipment used to show it, must be in good working condition. In addition, a qualified witness must be able to identify the scenes, persons, or voices on the tape. Finally, the tape recording itself must be securely stored, to prevent the possibility of erasing, editing, or other tampering.

Elements:

a. Recording is relevant.
b. Recording machine was tested before being used and was in normal operating condition.
c. Recording machine that was used can accurately record and reproduce sounds/images.
d. Operator was experienced and qualified to operate the recording machine that was used.
e. Witness heard/saw what was being recorded.
f. After the recording was made, the operator replayed the tape and the tape had accurately recorded the sounds/images.
g. Tape was then labeled and sealed, placed in a secure storage vault to guard against tampering, and later removed for trial, still in a sealed condition.
h. Recording machine in court is in normal operating condition and can accurately reproduce the sounds/images on the tape.
i. Witness recognizes and can identify the voices on the tape/locations and persons seen on the tape.

Note that more than one witness may be necessary to completely qualify a recording. For instance, in a sound recording of a telephone conversation, you may need three witnesses, each of whom can testify to one of the following required elements: (1) qualify the machines and recording; (2) demonstrate the custody of the tape; and (3) identify the voices on the tape.

Example:

The following example involves a police officer who made a sound recording of a telephone conversation.

Q. Officer Doe, what kind of sound-recording machine did you use to record this telephone conversation?
A. A Uhr tape recorder, using a half-inch magnetic tape.
Q. Are you familiar with the operation of that machine?
A. Yes, sir.
Q. How many times have you used it?
A. I've used this particular type of machine probably 200 to 300 times.
Q. Did you do anything with the machine before recording the call?
A. Yes, I tested it.
Q. How did you test it?
A. I attached the microphone of the tape recorder to the telephone, dialed the number of our department, and talked shortly

to our receptionist. I recorded the call and then played it back on the machine.

Q. What was the result of your test?

A. The machine was working properly. It was accurately recording and playing back.

Q. What happened next?

A. I turned the machine on again. Mr. Smith picked up the receiver, dialed a number, and engaged in a conversation for about two minutes. He then put down the receiver and I turned off the machine.

Q. Did you do anything during the conversation?

A. Yes, I was listening to the conversation on an extension phone.

Q. Did you recognize the voice on the other end?

A. Yes.

Q. Had you ever heard it before?

A. Oh yes, lots of times.

Q. Whose voice did you recognize it to be?

A. Mr. Jones'.

Q. After the conversation, what is the next thing you did?

A. Immediately after the conversation, I rewound the tape and played it.

Q. Did the tape truly and accurately record the conversation you had just heard?

A. Yes, it did.

Q. What did you do with that tape?

A. I labeled it, put it in an evidence bag, sealed the bag, and placed the bag in my evidence vault.

Q. Did you ever see the tape again?

A. Yes, this morning.

Q. Where did you see it at that time?

A. I took it out of my evidence vault.

Step 1.   Have exhibit marked.

Step 2.   Show exhibit to opposing counsel.

Step 3.   Ask permission to approach witness.

Step 4.   Show exhibit to witness.

Step 5.   Establish foundation:

Q. Officer Doe, I show you what has been marked Plaintiff's Exhibit #1 for identification. Do you recognize it?

A. Yes.

Q. What do you recognize it to be?

A. That's the tape I previously made on December 13, 1984.

Q. What is the condition of the bag at this time?

A. It's still in a sealed condition.

Q. Is this bag with the tape in it in the same condition now as when you sealed it on December 13, 1984?

A. Yes, sir, it is.

Q. Your Honor, at this time we move that Plaintiff's Exhibit #1 for identification be admitted in evidence.

Court: It will be admitted.

Q. Officer Doe, do you recognize the machine on the table in front of you?

A. Yes, sir,

Q. What is it?

A. That's a Uhr cassette tape recorder. In fact, that's the same kind of machine I used to record the telephone conversation.

Q. Is this machine in proper working order?

A. Yes. I tested it just before bringing it to the courtroom.

Q. Your Honor, may the witness unseal Plaintiff's Exhibit #1 in evidence, and play it on the machine for the jury?

Court: He may.

(Witness sets up machine, unseals the tape, puts it on the machine.)

Q. Officer Doe, before playing the tape, would you describe which voice is Mr. Smith's and which is Mr. Jones'?

A. Smith has a very low, deep voice. Jones has a high-pitched voice with a slight accent.

Q. Please play the tape for the court and the jury. (Witness plays tape.)

Where the voices cannot be easily described, it may be preferable to play the first few seconds of the tape, stop the machine, then ask the witness to identify the voices which were just heard.

Example:

Q. Officer Doe, please stop the tape. (Witness does so.) Whose voice said "Hello"?

A. That was Mr. Jones.

Q. Whose voice said "Frank, it's me"?

A. That's Mr. Smith.

Q. Please continue playing the tape.

Where sound recordings are involved, it is usually advantageous to offer in evidence a transcript of the recording. A copy of the transcript can then be given to each juror to read as the recording is played. Following along on the transcript while the tape is being played makes the tape much easier to understand. Whether the transcript can be used in addition to the recording, or whether it goes to the jury during deliberations, rests in the sound discretion of the trial judge. Where allowed, the witness who prepared the transcript must testify that it is a true and accurate verbatim transcript of the recording involved.

Finally, remember that establishing the foundation for a recording and presenting it in court is a complicated procedure. For this reason, many courts will require you to demonstrate the complete foundation out of the jury's presence before permitting you to present it before the jury.

9. Signed instruments

Signed instruments such as wills, contracts, and promissory notes are writings that have independent legal significance, and are nonhearsay. Whenever a signed instrument is introduced at trial, such as in a contract action, the authentication requirement must be met by proving that the party actually signed the instrument involved. If this is shown, the instrument is admissible against the party that signed it. This requirement protects against fraudulent claims based on forged instruments.

There are a variety of ways to prove that the signature on the instrument was made by the person whose signature it purports to be. These include:

1. Call a witness who saw the party place his signature on the document.
2. Call a witness who is familiar with the party's signature and can identify it.
3. Call the signing party as an adverse witness to admit the signature as being his.
4. Call a handwriting expert who can testify that, based on handwriting comparisons, the signature was made by the party.

Keep in mind that any kind of writing that has independent legal significance is nonhearsay. Therefore, trying to establish the writing as a business record under FRE 803(6) does nothing. Whenever the instrument is being introduced against a signator, you must prove that the signature on the instrument was in fact made by the signator.

Elements:

a. Document is relevant.
b. Document bears a signature (or is handwritten.)
c. Signature (or handwriting) is that of the party or his agent.
d. Document is in the same condition now as when it was executed.

Example:

The witness saw the promissory note signed by a party.

Step 1. Have exhibit marked.
Step 2. Show exhibit to opposing counsel.
Step 3. Ask permission to approach witness.
Step 4. Show exhibit to witness.
Step 5. Extablish foundation:
Q. Mr. Doe, I show you what has been marked Plaintiff's Exhibit #1 for identification. Have you seen it before?
A. Yes.
Q. When was the first time you saw it?

A. I saw it on December 13, 1984.

Q. Where were you at that time?

A. In my office.

Q. Did you see who prepared Plaintiff's Exhibit #1 for identification?

A. Yes, I prepared that note myself.

Q. After preparing it, what did you do with it?

A. I gave it to Mr. Jones, who was sitting in my office.

Q. What did Mr. Jones do with it?

A. He signed it at the bottom.

Q. Did you actually see him sign it?

A. Yes.

Q. After Mr. Jones signed Plaintiff's Exhibit #1 for identification, what did you do with it?

A. I took the signed note and put it in my files.

Q. Is Plaintiff's Exhibit #1 for identification in the same condition now as when Mr. Jones signed it?

A. Yes, sir, nothing's been done to it since he signed it.

Step   6.   Move to admit exhibit in evidence.

Step   7.   Have exhibit marked in evidence.

Step   8.   Have witness mark exhibit.

Step   9.   Ask permission to show/read exhibit to jury.

Step 10.   Show/read exhibit to jury.

Example:

The witness sent a contract to a party, who returned the contract signed. The witness can identify the party's signature.

Step 1.   Have the exhibit marked.

Step 2.   Show the exhibit to opposing counsel.

Step 3.   Ask the Court's permission to approach the witness.

Step 4.   Show the exhibit to the witness.

Step 5.   Establish foundation:

Q. Mr. Doe, I show you Plaintiff's Exhibit #1 for identification. Have you seen it before?

A. Yes.

Q. When was the first time you saw it?

A. On December 13, 1984, when I prepared it.

Q. What did you do with it?

A. I mailed it to Mr. Jones.

Q. Did you see it again?

A. Yes.

Q. When was that?

A. About one week later I received it in the mail.

Q. Was anything different about Plaintiff's Exhibit #1 for identification at that time?

A. Yes, it had been signed at the bottom.

Q. Did you recognize the signature?
A. Yes.
Q. Had you ever seen that signature before?
A. Oh yes, many times.
Q. Under what circumstances had you seen it?
A. I've seen it on correspondence and contracts. Several times I've actually seen Mr. Jones sign his name.
Q. Mr. Doe, showing you Plaintiff's Exhibit #1 for identification, do you recognize the signature that appears at the bottom of page 2?
A. Yes, that's Mr. Jones' signature.
Q. Is this document in the same condition now as when you received it on approximately December 22, 1984?
A. Yes, sir.

Step 6. Move to admit exhibit in evidence.
Step 7. Have exhibit marked in evidence.
Step 8. Have witness mark exhibit.
Step 9. Ask permission to show/read exhibit to jury.
Step 10. Show/read exhibit to jury.

Note that a qualified witness can identify the signature on the document, even if that witness had nothing to do with the preparation or execution of the document itself.

10. Checks

Checks are negotiable instruments and therefore have independent legal significance. Since checks are nonhearsay, they must be authenticated the same way as all instruments. A witness must be able to identify the signature of the drawer before the check is admissible as proof that the drawer made the payment. A witness must be able to identify the endorsement signature of the payee to prove receipt by the payee.

Checks are commonly used at trial as proof of payment from drawer to payee. There are several ways the signatures of the drawer and payee can be authenticated, so that the check can be admitted to prove payment.

a. Call the drawer of the check to testify that he personally gave the check to the payee or his agent.
b. Call the payee or his agent as an adverse witness to prove his receipt, endorsement, and cashing of the check.
c. Call a handwriting expert to testify that the endorsement on the back of the check is in the payee's handwriting.
d. Call a representative of the payee's bank to qualify a microfilm of the canceled check as a business record and show that the check was deposited to the payee's account.

Of these methods, the most common approach involves calling the drawer of the check as the only or primary witness.

Elements (drawer of check):

    a. Check is relevant.
    b. Witness made payment by check.
    c. Witness prepared the check and signed it.
    d. Witness gave the check to the payee.
    e. Witness received canceled check from his bank some time later.
    f. Canceled check had payee's endorsement on the back.
    g. Witness recognizes handwriting of endorsement as payee's.
    h. Canceled check is in the same condition now except for the endorsement and markings on the back of the check.

Example (drawer of the check is testifying):

Q. Mr. Doe, did you pay the bill sent to you by the XYZ Hardware Co.?
A. Yes.
Q. How did you pay the bill?
A. By check.
Q. What bank was that check drawn on?
A. That was on my account at the First National Bank.

Step 1. Have exhibit marked.
Step 2. Show exhibit to opposing counsel.
Step 3. Ask permission to approach witness.
Step 4. Show exhibit to witness.
Step 5. Establish foundation:

Q. Mr. Doe, I show you Plaintiff's Exhibit #1 for identification. Do you recognize it?
A. Yes, I do.
Q. What kind of document is it?
A. It's a check.
Q. Do you recognize the drawer's signature on the front?
A. Yes, it is my signature.
Q. Do you recognize the handwriting on the face of the check?
A. Yes, it's all in my handwriting. I prepared that check.
Q. What did you do with Plaintiff's Exhibit #1 for identification after you prepared it?
A. I gave it to Mr. Roe at the hardware store.
Q. Are you familiar with Mr. Roe's signature?
A. Oh yes, I've seen him write his name many times.
Q. Mr. Doe, please look at the back of the check. Do you recognize the signature appearing there?
A. Yes, I do.
Q. Whose signature do you recognize it to be?
A. That's Mr. Roe's signature.
Q. After giving that check to Mr. Roe, did you ever see it again?
A. Yes.
Q. When did you see it next?

> A. The following month I got the check from my bank, as part of that month's batch of canceled checks.
>
> Q. Was there anything different about the check when you got it from your bank?
>
> A. Yes.
>
> Q. What was that?
>
> A. The back of the check had Mr. Roe's signature on it and various bank stamps.
>
> Q. Other than those added items, did the check appear in the same condition as when you gave it to Mr. Roe?
>
> A. Yes.

Step 6. Move to admit exhibit in evidence.

Step 7. Have exhibit marked in evidence.

Step 8. Have witness mark exhibit.

Step 9. Ask permission to show exhibit to jury.

Step 10. Show exhibit to jury.

(Make sure you offer *both* sides of the check in evidence.)

Note that in the above example one witness was able to testify to both preparing and presenting the check as well as to the identity of the endorser. Many times, of course, two or more witnesses would be necessary to complete the required proof.

In criminal cases, checks are sometimes introduced at trial, most commonly in forgery cases. In such cases, the identity of the handwriting on the face of the check as well as the endorsement may be in issue. Since the defendant cannot be called as a witness by the prosecution, proof of these facts can be through:

a. a witness who recognizes the handwriting on the check as the defendant's

b. a witness who saw the defendant write out the check or endorse it

c. a handwriting expert who can testify that the handwriting is the defendant's

Note that while the operative portions of the check have independent legal significance and are nonhearsay, this is not the case with other parts of the check. The "memo" portion of a check, which is frequently filled out to show the purpose for writing the check, is probably hearsay. The bank stamps on the back of a check, which show the clearing process, are probably hearsay as well.

11. Letters

Letters can present complicated evidentiary issues. First, letters can be hearsay or nonhearsay, depending on their contents and use. Where an exchange of two letters forms a contract, the letters, being words of offer and acceptance, have independent legal significance and are nonhearsay. If not, facts asserted in a letter will be hearsay, and some exception, most commonly party admissions, must be applicable to make the letter admissible. Second, letters must be authenticated. A witness must be able to identify the signature on the letter as being in fact that of the person it purports to be. This authentication requirement is designed to prevent the possibility of forgery. Third, letters may not be relevant unless it can be shown that the intended addressee actually received the original. This is required where the letters form a contract, or a letter constitutes notice to the addressee. Fourth, where the original has been sent out and is unavailable, and there is a dispute over authenticity, the best evidence rule, FRE 1001-1004, may require production of the original or that its absence be explained before a copy is admissible. All these issues — hearsay, authentication, proof of receipt, best evidence, and copies — can arise whenever a letter is offered in evidence at trial.

The following examples illustrate what are probably the two most common authentication, receipt, and copy problem areas; both involve letters sent between parties.

a.   Letter sent to your party by another party

Elements:

a.   Letter is relevant.
b.   Witness received the letter.
c.   Witness recognizes the signature as the other party's.
d.   Letter is in the same condition today as when first received.

Note that the receipt of the letter and the identity of the signature can be established by separate witnesses. If the witness who can testify to receiving the letter cannot identify the signature, the signature must be proved by a witness who can identify the handwriting, or by expert handwriting comparisons.

Example:

The witness can testify that he received a letter and can identify the signature on it.

Step 1.   Have exhibit marked.
Step 2.   Show exhibit to opposing counsel.
Step 3.   Ask permission to approach witness.
Step 4.   Show exhibit to witness.
Step 5.   Establish foundation:
    Q.   Mr. Doe, I show you Plaintiff's Exhibit #1 for identification. Do you recognize it?
    A.   Yes.
    Q.   Have you seen it before?
    A.   Yes, I received this on approximately December 13, 1984.
    Q.   Do you recognize the signature at the bottom?
    A.   Yes, I do.

Q. Have you seen that signature before?

A. Yes, sir, lots of times.

Q. Under what circumstances?

   (Witness explains how he has acquired personal knowledge.)

Q. Whose signature is it?

A. It is Frank Jones' signature.

Q. Is this letter in the same condition today as when you received it on approximately December 13, 1984?

A. Yes, sir. It looks the same.

Step 6. Move to admit exhibit in evidence.

Step 7. Have exhibit marked in evidence.

Step 8. Have witness mark exhibit.

Step 9. Ask permission to show/read exhibit to jury.

Step 10. Show/read exhibit to jury.

b. *Letter sent by your party to another party*

The more difficult situation involves the mailing of a letter to another party. This presents two problems. First, there is usually no direct way to prove receipt by the addressee, absent an admission. Second, unless the original of the letter has been produced by the addressee, it will be necessary to introduce a copy of that letter at trial. The essential element is proof of proper mailing, to raise the inference of receipt. A copy of the original can then be introduced.

Elements:

   a. Letter is relevant.

   b. Witness dictated the letter, addressed to a party.

   c. Witness saw the typed original and copy (carbon or photocopy) of the letter.

   d. Witness signed the original letter.

   e. Original letter was placed in a properly addressed and postmarked envelope, bearing a proper return address.

   f. Envelope was deposited in a U.S. mail depository.

   g. Carbon or photocopy of original is a true and accurate copy of original.

   h. Original letter and envelope were never returned to sender.

Example:

Witness is the secretary who typed and mailed the original letter.

Step 1. Have exhibit marked.

Step 2. Show exhibit to opposing counsel.

Step 3. Ask permission to approach witness.

Step 4. Show exhibit to witness.

Step 5. Establish foundation:

Q. Ms. White, I show you what has been marked as Plaintiff's Exhibit #1 for identification. Have you ever seen it?

A. Yes, I have.

Q. What kind of document is it?

A. It is a carbon copy of a letter.

Q. Did you have anything to do with the preparation of this copy?

A. Yes, I did.

Q. What was that?

A. I took the dictation for this letter from Mr. Smith and typed an original and a carbon copy of the letter.

Q. When did you prepare the original and copy?

A. The same date that is on the letter, December 13, 1984.

Q. What did you do after you prepared the original and copy?

A. I gave the original to Mr. Smith. He signed it and gave it back to me.

Q. What did you do next?

A. I prepared an envelope that had the same address as appeared on the letter. I then put the signed original in the envelope, sealed the envelope, and put a first-class stamp on it.

Q. What happened next?

A. At the end of the day I mailed the letter by putting it in the mailbox in front of our building.

Q. Did that envelope contain a return address?

A. Yes, it did.

Q. What was that address?

A. Our office stationery, including the envelopes, has our complete office address on it.

Q. Who is in charge of incoming mail in your office?

A. I am.

Q. Did you ever receive back the letter and envelope you sent Mr. Smith?

A. No, that letter never came back to us.

Q. After mailing the original, what did you do with the copy?

A. I put it in our files.

Q. The copy of that letter, Ms. White, is that the same document that has been marked Plaintiff's Exhibit #1 for identification?

A. Yes, sir. That is the copy.

Q. Is Plaintiff's Exhibit #1 for identification a true and accurate copy of the letter you sent to Mr. Jones on December 13, 1984?

A. Yes, sir, it's identical.

Q. How are you able to recognize this copy as a copy of the letter you prepared and sent that day?

A. Because both Mr. Smith's initials and mine appear in the lower lefthand corner of the copy. This shows that I typed this particular letter for Mr. Smith on that date.

Q. Is this copy in the same condition now as when you mailed the original to Mr. Jones on December 13, 1984?

A. Yes, it is.

Step   6.   Move to admit exhibit in evidence.
Step   7.   Have exhibit marked in evidence.
Step   8.   Have witness mark exhibit.
Step   9.   Ask permission to show/read exhibit to jury.
Step 10.   Show/read exhibit to jury.

Preparation is rarely a problem because the secretary will routinely place initials on every letter typed. In many cases, however, the secretary cannot independently remember having mailed the particular letter to the addressee. In those instances, it is necessary to show the usual established business practice of the office in mailing letters, to prove by inference that the letter in question was, in fact, mailed to the addressee.

Example:

> *Q.* Ms. White, do you remember what you did with the original of this letter after you prepared it?
> *A.* I cannot tell you what I did with this particular letter. It's just been too long ago.
> *Q.* Do you have a standard established office procedure in preparing and handling letters?
> *A.* Yes, we do.
> *Q.* Was that procedure employed in December of 1984?
> *A.* Oh yes, we've been doing it the same way for years now.
> *Q.* Please describe that procedure to the jury.
> *A.* Well, after I type the original and make one copy I give it to the proper person for signing. I never mail a letter unless it has been signed by the person indicated. I then put the original in an envelope that has the same address as appears on the letter. The envelope bears the return address of our office. I then seal the envelope and put it in our office mailbox.
> *Q.* What happens next?
> *A.* Around 5:00 P.M. I take all the letters that have been prepared that day, stamp them with the proper postage on our stamp machine, and tie all the letters together. When I leave the office, I take that mail package and put it in the mailbox located in front of the building.
> *Q.* Did you go through that procedure on December 13, 1984?
> *A.* Yes, sir. I do that every day I work, and I worked that day.

12.   Business records

Business records are the most common type of documentary evidence introduced in trials. Introducing such records in evidence can be accomplished simply by following the litany set out in FRE 803(6).

The federal business records rule has substantially relaxed certain requirements previously required under older statutes. The witness no longer need be the records custodian, but also can be any "other qualified witness." A business now includes any "business, institution, association, profession, occupation, and calling of any kind, whether or not conducted for profit." A record can be any "memorandum, report, record or data compilation, in any form, of acts, events, conditions, opinions or diagnoses." The record must be "made by . . . a person with knowledge" or "made . . . from information transmitted by a person with knowledge." The witness in court should be able to identify the type of person working for the business who had firsthand knowledge of the facts and initially received, recorded, or transmitted the information that ultimately appeared on the record.

Elements:

    a. Record is relevant.
    b. Record is a "memorandum, report, record or data compilation in any form."
    c. Witness is the "custodian or other qualified witness."
    d. Record was "made by a person with knowledge" of the facts or was "made from information transmitted by a person with knowledge" of the facts.
    e. Record was "made at or near the time" of the "acts, events, conditions, opinions, or diagnoses" appearing on it.
    f. Record was made as part of "the regular practice of that business activity."
    g. Record was "kept in the course of a regularly conducted business activity."

The following example shows how easily the required technical elements of FRE 803(6) can be met.

Example:

    Q. Mr. Doe, please state your occupation.
    A. I'm the records keeper of the XYZ Corporation.
    Q. What does your job involve?
    A. I collect, keep, and maintain all the company records according to our indexing system.
Step 1. Have exhibit marked.
Step 2. Show exhibit to opposing counsel.
Step 3. Ask permission to approach witness.
Step 4. Show exhibit to witness.
Step 5. Establish foundation:
    Q. Mr. Doe, I am showing you what has been marked Plaintiff's Exhibit #1 for identification. Do you recognize it?
    A. Yes, it's one of our records.

Q. Was that record made by a person with knowledge of, or made from information transmitted by a person with knowledge of, the acts and events appearing on it?

A. Yes.

Q. Was the record made at or near the time of the acts and events appearing on it?

A. Yes.

Q. Is it the regular practice of the XYZ Corporation to make such a record?

A. Yes.

Q. Was that record kept in the course of a regularly conducted business activity?

A. Yes.

Step 6. Move to admit exhibit in evidence.
Step 7. Have exhibit marked in evidence.
Step 8. Have witness mark/explain exhibit.
Step 9. Ask permission to show/read exhibit to jury.
Step 10. Show/read exhibit to jury.

The above example illustrates how quickly the minimum foundation requirements can be established. As a vehicle of persuasion, of course, it may not be adequate. Where the record is an important part of your case, the credibility of the witness and the record should be enhanced by developing both fully. Developing the witness' background has been previously shown. (See §4.7 and the accompanying example.) The following example demonstrates how the exhibit itself can be enhanced, and how the requirements of FRE 803(6) can be met without using the technical language of the rule.

Example:

Step 1. Have exhibit marked.
Step 2. Show exhibit to opposing counsel.
Step 3. Ask permission to approach witness.
Step 4. Show exhibit to witness.
Step 5. Establish foundation:

Q. Mr. Doe, I am showing you Plaintiff's Exhibit #1 for identification. Do you recognize it?

A. Yes, I do.

Q. What kind of record is it?

A. This is a monthly statement for a checking account.

Q. What use does the bank make of the monthly statement?

A. It's the basic record on which we record all transactions involving that account. We also send it to our customers to advise them of the current status of their accounts.

Q. What kind of information is recorded on a monthly statement?

A. It contains all the checks, deposits, charges, and other debits and credits for that account, as well as a daily balance for the particular month involved.

Q. Who receives and enters the transactions that appear on the statement?

A. That's done by a clerk in our accounting department. The clerk receives all checks and deposits and enters them on the appropriate account ledger.

Q. When are the transactions entered on the ledger?

A. All transactions, like checks, deposits, and other charges, are posted on the account ledger within 24 hours of their receipt by the bank.

Q. When are these transactions entered on the monthly statements?

A. At the end of every month all transactions entered on the account ledger are printed on the monthly statement form.

Q. What's the difference between the account ledger and the monthly statement?

A. They both contain the same information, but the ledger is a continuous record. The statement simply takes this month's ledger transactions and prints them on an almost identical form. The statement is really just a reprint of the last part of the ledger.

Q. What happens to the statement after it is printed?

A. One copy is mailed to the customer. The other copies are kept in the bank's auditing department.

Q. Mr. Doe, again directing your attention to Plaintiff's Exhibit #1 for identification: Was that record made by a person with knowledge of, or from information transmitted by a person with knowledge of, the acts and events appearing on it?

A. Yes.

Q. Was it prepared at or near the time of the acts and events appearing on it?

A. Yes.

Q. Is it the regular practice of the bank to make such a record?

A. Yes.

Q. Was that record kept in the course of a regularly conducted business activity?

A. Yes.

Step 6. Move to admit exhibit in evidence.
Step 7. Have exhibit marked in evidence.
Step 8. Have witness mark/explain exhibit.
Step 9. Ask permission to show/read exhibit to jury.
Step 10. Show/read exhibit to jury.

Note how the first part of the example established the required elements of FRE 803(6) without using the rule's technical language. The record was explained in language any layman can understand. However, the second part of the example established the requirements using the language of the rule. This is done essentially for the court's benefit. Judges are used to hearing business records foundations established using the technical language of the rule. By meeting the rule's requirements in both layman's and technical language, you will satisfy both the jury and judge, and create a clear, complete record.

Finally, as the party opposing the admission of the record, always keep in mind that many objections to its admission can be made. In addition to a lack of foundation, you can object on grounds of relevance or "lack of trustworthiness" of the record. You can object to parts of the record if it contains double hearsay or violates some other evidentiary rule, such as mentioning insurance, settlement offers, or privileged communications. For these reasons, you must carefully review the contents of the records for additional bases for objections to their admission in evidence.

The absence of a business record can be admissible evidence. Under FRE 803(7), if an event or transaction had occurred, and the business would create a record of the event or transaction had it actually occurred, proving that the event or transaction never occurred can be done by showing that there is no business record for the claimed event or transaction.

Proving the absence of a record is done by calling a custodian or other qualified witness to testify about how the business creates records to record events and transactions. The witness can then testify that he searched the business records, but could find no record for that event or transaction.

13.   Computer records

The use of computers by business organizations is rapidly eliminating traditional methods of record-keeping. Even where traditional account books and ledger systems are still employed, such data is often periodically transferred to computer banks and the original systems are destroyed. Where computers are used to store business records, the retrieval of such information is done through a computer printout. Hence, such computer printouts are becoming increasingly common evidence in trials.

Since FRE 803(6) includes "data compilations," computer printouts can be qualified for admission like any other business record. It is not necessary to prove that the computer printout was made at or near the time of the transaction involved, since frequently this will not have been the case. However, so long as the data was initially recorded on some record, at or near the time the event or transaction occurred, either as input into the computer's data bank or on a traditional paper record, the reliability requirement of the business records rule has been substantially met. When the computer printout was actually printed, or when the data was transferred from a paper record to the computer's data bank, should not matter, at least as far as admissibility of the printout is concerned. Keep in mind that some courts require pretrial disclosure of intent to use computer records, much like that required by FRE 1006.

In most jurisdictions the electronic capabilities of a computer's input, storage, and output systems have been scientifically accepted as valid and reliable, so it is no longer necessary to have a knowledgeable witness testify to the computer's methodology and reliability. In those few jurisdictions where this type of foundation may still be necessary, see United States v. Scholle, 553 F.2d 1109 (1977), and United States v. Russo, 480 F.2d 1228 (1973).

A more current issue is whether the computer printout offered in evidence is the complete record. Since computers are capable of printing out data in any form, and selectively, there is always a question whether the printout offered in evidence is the complete record of a transaction, or whether it selectively shows only certain facts. The rule of completeness, FRE 106, requires that when a writing is offered in evidence, all parts of that writing that in fairness should be considered at the same time must also be offered in evidence. This rule prevents offering parts of writings taken out of context. In the computer printout area, this is of major concern, since the printout itself does not show whether it is only part of the record of a particular transaction. These problems are often worked out at the discovery stage when business records are first produced and the completeness problem first arises.

Another approach is to treat computer printouts that show only selected information as a summary, which is admissible if the requirements of FRE 1006 are met. If this is the approach, the rule requires that the records on which the summaries are based be available for examination and copying. This ensures that opposing parties can check the accuracy of the summary chart.

14. Recorded recollection

Past recollection recorded exhibits are the other side of the present recollection refreshed coin. (See §4.6 p. 113.) Under FRE 803(5), a memorandum or record is admissible as a recorded recollection if the record was made when the facts were fresh in the witness' mind, the record was accurate when made, and the witness now has insufficient recollection "to testify fully and accurately." This exception to the hearsay rule should be considered whenever the witness has a partial memory failure and the memorandum does not qualify as a business record.

If properly qualified, the record may be admitted and read into evidence. However, the exhibit itself does not go to the jury unless offered by an adverse party.

Elements:

    a. Exhibit is relevant.
    b. Witness has no full or accurate present recollection of the facts.
    c. Witness had firsthand knowledge of facts when they occurred.
    d. Witness made a record of the facts at or near the time the facts occurred.
    e. Record was accurate and complete when made.
    f. Record is in the same condition now as when made.

Example:

Witness has testified that he recorded the serial numbers of every automobile on a dealership lot on a certain date.

Q. Mr. Doe, how many cars did you see on the lot that day?
A. About 300.
Q. Did each car have a serial number?
A. Yes.
Q. Can you tell the jury what the serial numbers on the cars were?
A. No, sir, I can't possibly remember them.
Q. Did you make any record of those serial numbers?
A. Yes, sir, I made a list.
Q. When did you make that list?
A. I made it at the time I was on the dealership lot.
Q. Was the list you made accurate and complete?
A. Yes, sir.
Q. Mr. Doe, would that list refresh your recollection as to what those serial numbers were?
A. No, I couldn't possibly remember them, even if I reviewed the list.

Step 1. Have exhibit marked.
Step 2. Show exhibit to opposing counsel.
Step 3. Ask permission to approach witness.
Step 4. Show exhibit to witness.
Step 5. Establish foundation:
   Q. I show you what has been marked Plaintiff's Exhibit #1 for identification. Do you recognize it?
   A. Yes.
   Q. What is it?
   A. That's the list I made of the serial numbers on the cars I saw at the car dealership.
   Q. Is the record in the same condition now as when you made it?
   A. Yes, nothing on it has been changed.
Step 6. Move to admit exhibit in evidence.
Step 7. Have exhibit marked in evidence.
Step 8. Have witness mark exhibit.
Step 9. Ask permission to show/read exhibit to jury.
Step 10. Show/read exhibit to jury.

15. Copies

Under the Federal Rules of Evidence copies of records are usually just as admissible as the originals. FRE 1001-1004, the best evidence rule, provides that copies, now called "duplicates," are just as admissible as an original, unless there is a genuine dispute over authenticity, as would be the case where an important document is alleged to be a forgery. Only in this situation must an original be produced. If an original cannot be produced, its absence must be satisfactorily explained before a copy is then admissible. Duplicates include carbon copies, photocopies, or any accurate reproduction of an original.

The federal rule generally permits copies to be introduced in any trial. Keep in mind, however, that some states that have not adopted the federal rules may still require originals, unless their unavailability is explained, in which case copies and other degrees of evidence such as oral testimony may be admissible.

Where the absence of the original must be explained before the copy is admissible, the following foundation should be established.

Elements:

    a. Copy is relevant.
    b. Executed original once existed.
    c. Copy of the original was made.
    d. Copy was a true and accurate copy.
    e. Original was unintentionally lost, is unavailable, etc.
    f. A thorough search for the original in every possible location failed to produce it.

Example:

Step 1. Have exhibit marked.
Step 2. Show exhibit to opposing counsel.
Step 3. Ask permission to approach witness.
Step 4. Show exhibit to witness.
Step 5. Establish foundation:

Q. Ms. White, I show you what has been marked as Plaintiff's Exhibit #1 for identification. Do you recognize it?
A. Yes, I do.
Q. What kind of document is it?
A. It is a photocopy of an agreement.
Q. Was there an original to the copy?
A. Yes, there was.
Q. What did you have to do with the creation of the original and the copy of the agreement?
A. I typed the original and made two photocopies of it.
Q. What did you do with the original?
A. After it was signed I put the original in the appropriate file in the file cabinets.
Q. What did you do with the copies?
A. One I put in our files with the original. The other I mailed to Mr. Jones.
Q. Ms. White, did you receive a subpoena calling for the production of that agreement?
A. Yes, I did.
Q. Pursuant to the subpoena did you locate the original?

A. No, I couldn't.
Q. Where should the original have been?
A. It should have been in our files with the copy, but when I went to get it, only the copy was there.
Q. Did you conduct a search of your office to find the original?
A. Yes, I did.
Q. What did that search consist of?
A. I notified everybody in the office to look for it. I personally went through every file in every cabinet in the office and every desk in our clerical area to look for it.
Q. How long did you search for the original?
A. I spent about 12 hours looking for it.
Q. Did you or anyone else find the original?
A. No, we finally had to give up. I just don't know where it could have gone.

Step 6. Move to admit exhibit in evidence.
Step 7. Have exhibit marked in evidence.
Step 8. Have witness mark exhibit.
Step 9. Ask permission to show/read exhibit to jury.
Step 10. Show/read exhibit to jury.

16. Certified records

Under FRE 902, certified copies of public records are self-authenticating. A record is certified when there is a statement attached to it stating that the record is in fact a record from that public agency. It usually bears the seal of the agency and has a blue or red ribbon attached. Hence, no witness is necessary to qualify the exhibit for admission. It need only be offered, then published to the jury. The only evidentiary objection possible is relevance.

Example:

> *Counsel:* Your Honor, we offer for admission in evidence Plaintiff's Exhibit #1 for identification. It is a certified copy of a State of Illinois Department of Motor Vehicles vehicle registration. (Hand the exhibit to the judge.)
>
> *Court:* Any objection, counsel?
>
> *Opposing counsel:* No objection, your Honor.

Ask for permission to read or show it to the jury.

17. Summaries

In an age when trials are becoming increasingly complex, it is hardly surprising that summary charts of technical evidence and other data are be-

coming increasingly common. Such charts can effectively compile
financial records and other statistical data, clearly depict a chronological
sequence of events, or graphically illustrate any number and type of
transactions and relationships. When properly qualified as exhibits and
admitted in evidence, such charts can be persuasive weapons.

There are two types of summary charts that are admissible at trial:
summary charts of evidence produced at trial and summaries of voluminous records. The usual procedure in establishing the necessary foundation for a summary chart of evidence is to have it prepared by a witness
who will actually sit in court while the evidence is being presented. Each
fact appearing on the chart must then be related to the exhibit or witness
that established the particular fact. This is usually done on the chart itself. At the appropriate time this witness can be called to demonstrate the
evidentiary sources of the facts as well as any resulting mathematical com-
putations he performed. When so qualified, the chart is admissible if it
will aid the jury in understanding the evidence.

Example:

The following summary chart shows the cash loss to a bank following
a robbery. A summary witness will be necessary to explain the audit procedures employed on the chart. (GE# refers to the government exhibits
in evidence that prove each entry.)

	Second Federal Savings & Loan Association **Cash Loss Audit on 5/2/84**		
	Teller #1	*Teller #2*	*Teller #3*
Cash on hand	$12,101.86	$6,388.96	$25,162.00
4/30/84	(GE# 20E)	(GE# 20C)	(GE# 20A)
Cash deposits	100.00	340.00	0
5/2/84	(GE# 21D)	(GE# 21D)	
Cash withdrawals	427.50	0	0
5/2/84	(GE# 22A, 23)		
Net change	$11,774.36	$6,728.96	$25,162.00
	(GE# 20F)	(GE# 20D)	(GE# 20B)
Cash on hand	11,774.36	6,728.96	9,162.00
	(GE# 20F)	(GE# 20D)	(GE# 20B)
Difference	0	0	$16,000.00 loss

Summaries of voluminous records are governed by FRE 1006.
Under FRE 1006, summaries of writings, recordings, or photographs that
cannot be conveniently produced in court can be admitted without first
producing in court and getting into evidence the writings, recordings, or
photographs. The underlying sources for the summaries can be exam-

ined and copied by the parties prior to trial, and the court can still require their production at trial if appropriate.

Summary charts of evidence and summaries of voluminous records should be distinguished from charts, diagrams, or drawings that lawyers may make on blackboards or sketch pads during closing arguments. When made by the lawyers during closing arguments, the charts and drawings are not evidence, are not marked as exhibits, and do not go to the jury during deliberations. They are merely illustrative aids that the lawyers may use to supplement their closing arguments.

18. Stipulations

Stipulations can be both oral and written, although they are usually in a written form. Where written, they should be marked as an exhibit for purposes of the record and offered in evidence. The stipulation is usually read to the jury by the attorney who requested the stipulation.

Example:

> *Counsel:* Your Honor, may we read a stipulation, which has been marked Plaintiff's Exhibit #1, to the jury at this time?
>
> *Court:* Have you agreed to this stipulation?
>
> *Opposing counsel:* We have, your Honor.
>
> *Court:* Very well. Read the stipulation.
>
> *Counsel:* Ladies and gentlemen of the jury, this stipulation, or agreement, between the parties, states as follows: (Read the entire stipulation.) At the bottom is my signature as attorney for Mr. Smith, the plaintiff, and the signature of Mr. Doe as attorney for Mr. Jones, the defendant. (Give the executed original to the court for inclusion in the record.)

Stipulations are customarily drafted in either fact or witness form. A stipulation in fact form usually states that "the parties agree that the following facts are true:" and recites the agreed facts. A stipulation in witness form usually states that "the parties agree that if Jane Smith were called as a witness she would testify to the following:" and recites what the witness would say. When you use the witness form, make sure you include appropriate backgrounds for both lay and expert witnesses because the jury needs a basis for determining the witness' credibility.

19. Pleadings and discovery

Pleadings and discovery answers, when they contain admissions, may be shown or read to the jury. The most common examples are the answers to the complaint and interrogatory answers. Since the papers were previously filed with the court, they have already been authenticated as coming from a particular party. Consequently, they need only be "published" to the jury. Since introducing such court papers is not a common procedure, perhaps it is best to ask for a side-bar conference to determine how to publish the exhibit. Before it is published, the judge will usually explain what the exhibit is and how it was made. The lawyer then reads the appropriate parts to the jury.

Example:

> *Counsel:* Your Honor, at this time we offer in evidence the contract attached to our complaint as Exhibit A. The existence and execution of this contract have been admitted in the defendant's answer.
>
> *Court:* It may be admitted.

The contract can then be shown to the jury like any other exhibit.

Example:

The defendant will introduce one of the plaintiff's interrogatory answers.

> *Counsel:* Your Honor, before reading the pertinent part of the exhibit to the jury, we ask that the jury be instructed as to the significance of interrogatories and interrogatory answers.
>
> *Court:* Very well. Members of the jury, before trial the parties customarily send each other what one calls interrogatories, which are simply written questions about the case. Their purpose is to permit the parties to learn more about the case and find out what facts are not disputed. The party answering the interrogatories must answer in writing, under oath, and sign the answer. Please proceed, counsel.
>
> *Counsel:* Ladies and gentlemen, Defendant's Interrogatory #3 reads as follows: "State whether the plaintiff's vehicle involved in the accident had been inspected at an official motor vehicle inspection station within 12 months of the accident, and if so, where and when was it inspected?" The plaintiff's answer to Interrogatory #3 reads as follows: "The vehicle was not inspected within 12 months of the accident."

Before attempting to introduce a pleading or discovery answer, research the applicable law. In general, verified pleadings ("judicial admissions") and unverified pleadings ("evidentiary admissions") are both admissible. However, parties often amend pleadings and other discovery responses prior to trial. Under certain circumstances, the original pleading or response, particularly if unverified, may not be introduced as an admission.

§5.4. *Preparing and using exhibits*

Before deciding how and when to use exhibits, a threshold decision must be made: What exhibits will you seek to introduce at trial?

The general answer to this question is clear. Since exhibits are usually dramatic and persuasive, always consider using them when it can be done effectively. Most trial lawyers accept the adage that if a fact appears on a record, no amount of contrary testimony will persuade the jury that the record is erroneous. While exhibits can be both overused and misused, you should always explore ways in which you can use any available exhibits in any case.

This general approach, however, calls for certain caveats. First, exhibits should not be so voluminous that they become repetitive and boring to the jury. This is usually a consideration only in documentary exhibits, where voluminous and repeatedly cumulative exhibits become counterproductive. In those cases the records should be reviewed to cull the most pertinent documents, and only these should be introduced at trial. Second, make sure that the exhibit is actually probative on some issue. Exhibits that are merely interesting should be avoided, because introducing them opens you to an attack that you are short on proof and are introducing these peripheral exhibits to pad and bolster a weak case. Third, examine the exhibits carefully to see if any conflicts appear between the exhibits themselves, or the exhibits and your witnesses. Exhibits, particularly documents, can have a wealth of information, some of which can be contradictory, inconsistent, and impeaching. Finally, review the exhibits to determine if there is anything, directly or inferentially, that your opponent can use to support his positions. Exhibits can cut both ways. Few things are as embarrassing as an opponent who effectively uses one of your exhibits, then points out in closing arguments that you are the person who introduced it. A careful review of the exhibits, and playing devil's advocate with them, will avoid these kinds of problems.

Having reviewed the available exhibits and decided on those you will introduce as evidence, you are now ready to consider how and when to use them effectively at trial.

1.   How to prepare exhibits

Exhibits that you intend to introduce at trial should be prepared in such a way that they are visually attractive and clear. Exhibits frequently suffer from three defects: the exhibit is too small, its lettering is too small, and it is too cluttered.

To avoid these defects, keep in mind several generalizations that apply to trial exhibits. First, larger is better. Second, using color is better than black and white. Third, there is a limited amount of information the jury can absorb from a single exhibit. Fourth, jurors' visual capabilities necessarily define how exhibits must be prepared.

a. Photographs and records

Photographs are more attractive when they are enlarged and are in color. Hence, the originals should be taken so that they can be enlarged to 8″ × 10″ size without loss of contrast. The enlargements should be mounted on stiff backing. Color photographs are preferable, particularly where the scene has low contrast. If a particular photograph is critically important, consider having it enlarged, or the essential part of it enlarged, to 30″ × 40″ size and having it mounted on poster board. Commercial photography companies can do this easily.

Records and documents are usually dull reading, so thought must be given to how such exhibits can be made more attractive to the jury. Two techniques are frequently used. First, an overhead projector can enlarge the record, allowing every juror to see the same page at the same time. It allows the witness to point out important sections of the record, and underline or circle them. Photocopy stores can easily make transparencies for the overhead projector from the records. Second, a photographic enlargement of a particularly important document, or page of a record, can be an effective way of keeping the jury's attention focused on it.

b. Diagrams and charts

The trial lawyer has the most latitude in preparing diagrams and charts. Hence, the only consideration is what will be effective before the jury. First, use a poster board that is large enough. The standard is 30″ × 40″ poster board that has a rigid Styrofoam sandwich center. These are available at art supply stores. Second, a totally white board provides too strong a contrast for black lines and letters. A board with a very light gray, blue, or tan tone is preferable. The poster board should have a dull matte finish to minimize glare and reflection.

Second, in addition to black, use color for lines, lettering, and other markings. However, keep in mind that a significant number of persons have color deficiencies. The most confusing colors are bland reds and greens; bright colors are the most easily seen. An effective method is to use black for the basic diagram, then use colors when the witness marks on the exhibit.

Third, how lines and lettering are made are critical to the diagram or chart's effectiveness. Obviously they must be large enough to be seen easily by everyone. Since a juror may be as much as 20 feet from the exhibit, lines and letters must be at least ⅛ inches thick and at least 1 inch high. The standard lettering that meets these requirements is called 120-point Helvetica type, and is available at art supply stores in both stick-on and rub-on lettering.

Fourth, be careful not to clutter the diagram with too much information. Diagrams are more effective if kept simple. Put only those lines on it that are necessary, and label only the important parts. When the witness stands by the diagram, he can add additional information, such as locations of vehicles, people, and distances, using appropriately colored felt pens.

Finally, informational charts such as summaries, chronological sequences, and damages charts must be carefully composed so that they can be easily read and comprehended. Graphic arts designers have several rules of thumb that are useful when creating a chart on a standard-sized 30″ × 40″ poster board. First, use a border of at least 2 inches of blank space. Second, use standard 120-point Helvetica type. The lower-case letters are 1 inch high, capital letters are 1⅓ inches high. Do not use all capital letters, since these are more difficult to read. Use a capital to begin a line or a single word, otherwise use lower-case letters. For a diagram heading, use the same type style as in the diagram body, except with thicker lettering. The heading should be in medium weight letters (¼ inch thick), while the rest of the wording should be in light weight (⅛ inch thick). Third, spacing between letters and lines is important. As a general rule the distance between letters should be about equal to the thickness of the lettering. The spacing between lines should be at least the distance of the height of capital letters (1⅓ inches), except that the spacing between the heading and the next line should be twice the usual spacing. Fourth, the left margin should be justified, the right margin ragged. If each line has a separate item of information, numbering on the left margin is useful.

Using these guidelines, a diagram on a 30″ × 40″ poster board can contain a heading and up to eight lines of print. Each line can contain about 39 characters (letters, punctuation, and spaces). If you have more information than can be contained in this format, use a second diagram, not a larger single diagram, otherwise there will be too much information on one. Knowing these format guidelines will help you sketch out a rough diagram, and will be useful whether you or a graphic artist prepares the actual courtroom diagram. Such a diagram will be clean, organized, and persuasive, and it will demonstrate to the jury how thoroughly you have prepared this case for trial.

2. When to use exhibits

Understanding the psychological impact of exhibits on the jury is important. Exhibits are interesting, even exciting. That is precisely why you want to use them as much as possible. On the other hand, their very attractiveness can be a problem. Exhibits draw attention away from oral testimony. They win the battle for the jury's attention. That is why the exhibits should complement the testimony, rather than compete with it. How you should use exhibits in a case depends on the nature of the witness' testimony, the kind of exhibit, and how the trial judge wants the exhibits presented to the jury.

Earlier chapters discussed why, during direct examinations, descriptive testimony ("the scene") should precede and not interrupt occurrence testimony ("what happened"), since occurrence testimony is most effectively presented in a well-paced, uninterrupted way. The same approach should be taken whenever possible where exhibits are involved. Do not let the exhibits interrupt the pace and flow of the occurrence testimony.

Exhibits, for the purpose of determining when to use them, can be classified in the following categories: exhibits that are self-explanatory (physical objects such as weapons, clothing, and machine parts); exhibits that are best shown to the jury (photographs, maps, charts, and diagrams); and exhibits that should be read to or by the jury (letters, documents, and other records). These classifications are significant because, once these objects are produced in the courtroom, jurors usually want to handle and examine the exhibits themselves. They will be frustrated by anyone who introduces an exhibit in evidence and then fails to give the exhibit to them. This will not be a serious consideration in the case of physical objects and large models and diagrams, which the jurors can readily see and understand the moment you bring them into the courtroom. However, photographs, small objects, and documents present different problems. These the jurors cannot understand unless they actually see or read them. Don't fail to give them that opportunity as soon as permissible.

Trial judges can vary significantly in their approach to exhibits. Some will give counsel a free rein in deciding how and when the exhibits will be published. Others seem to view exhibits, particularly documents, as disruptive influences, something the jury can view in the jury room during recesses or other convenient times. Learn what your judge's attitude is on your types of exhibits. If he will not let you publish the exhibits immediately after their admission in evidence, or in the way you would like to publish them, you must plan accordingly. Let the jury know the reason why they cannot see the exhibits now.

Example:

> *Counsel:* Your Honor, may we show Plaintiff's Exhibit #1 in evidence to the jury at this time?
>
> *Court:* We'll do that during the next recess. Please continue with your examination.

Despite these differences in judicial attitudes, there are three basic ways to use exhibits during direct examinations.

a. *During the direct examination*

Where witnesses are occurrence witnesses and the exhibits are tangible objects, the exhibits can be introduced when they are first mentioned during the direct examination. This method can work well for exhibits such as weapons, clothing, and other larger objects. The foundations for these exhibits can be quickly established without significantly interrupting the flow of the direct examination. From their very nature, they need not be immediately shown to the jury, since the jury saw each exhibit while its foundation was being developed. As the opponent, if you intend to resist the admissibility of such exhibits and question whether a proper foundation can be established, make a timely request that the foundation be initially established outside the jury's presence.

In some situations an exhibit must be introduced in the middle of the direct examination. Where the exhibit must be explained, or later testimony depends for its relevance on the admission of the exhibit, that exhibit must be introduced first. This often occurs where documents are involved, since the qualifying witness may have to explain technical aspects of the records and testify further about transactions appearing in the records.

b. At the end of the direct examination

The second, and generally preferred method, is to wait until the direct examination is essentially completed before introducing and qualifying any exhibits. This has several tactical advantages. First, it avoids interrupting the pace and flow of occurrence testimony. Second, it allows you to publish the exhibits to the jury immediately after they are qualified, and allows the witness to explain the exhibits if necessary. Third, it keeps the exhibits out of the way, where they will not compete with, and draw attention away from, the testifying witness. Finally, using exhibits at the end of the direct examination allows you to repeat the highlights of the direct, since the exhibits will often operate as summaries of events just described. While this is repetitive, the jury is seldom bored, because the exhibits themselves are usually interesting, and the repetition will only touch on the examination's central points.

Using exhibits at the end of the direct examination works particularly well with occurrence witnesses. With these witnesses the central part of testimony must have pace and must flow. Once the occurrence has been described, the witness can then be used to qualify the physical evidence, photographs, and diagrams these cases will require. The witness can then mark the photographs and diagrams to demonstrate the locations of parties and events he previously described. When the witness is through with the exhibits, they can immediately be given to the jury.

c. Handling multiple exhibits

Where only a few exhibits need to be shown to the witness and qualified for admission in evidence, each exhibit is usually handed to the witness individually, and the foundation for its admission is established before moving on to the next exhibit.

In certain cases, however, this procedure is unsatisfactory. Establishing the foundation for numerous exhibits separately is both needlessly time-consuming and boring to the jury. Particularly where large numbers of documents and records are involved, the witness can identify the documents individually, then qualify them for admission as a group. This should be considered whenever a substantial number of exhibits are of the same generic type and have identical foundation requirements.

Example:

Where a custodian of the records has been called to qualify 20 bills of lading, show all 20 to the witness successively. After he has looked at each bill of lading and has stated that they are documents of the XYZ Company, ask the FRE 803(6) foundation requirements once for the whole group.

3. How to use exhibits

Having decided when to introduce your exhibits, you must next decide how they can be most effectively presented at trial. This involves the mechanics of bringing the exhibit to the witness, and presenting the exhibit most effectively to the jury. Keep in mind that the evidentiary rules vary concerning the showing of exhibits to witnesses and publishing them to the jury, depending on the kind of exhibit involved and the attitude of your particular judge. Whenever the possibility of uncertainty or confusion exists, make sure you determine how the judge wants you to proceed, so that your procedure will smoothly qualify and publish the exhibits during the case in chief. There are three basic methods of giving the witness an exhibit.

a. *Having the witness hold the exhibit*

The easiest method is to walk to the witness, hand him the exhibit, and return to your normal position at the far end of the jury box to ask the foundation questions for the exhibit. Once the foundation has been established, you can retrieve the exhibit from the witness. In some jurisdictions the court bailiff hands exhibits to the jury.

b. *Having the witness mark or read from the exhibit*

The second method is employed where the witness will have to mark or read parts of the exhibit. In these situations the lawyer will need to remain by the witness stand. Two rules should be followed. First, never block the jury's view of the witness. You can avoid this by standing at either of the places indicated on the diagram.

Either of these positions gives the jury an unobstructed view of the witness. You will still be able to speak and look toward the jury when asking questions, yet be immediately next to the witness and the exhibit. This is important, since you should never turn your back to the jury during a direct examination.

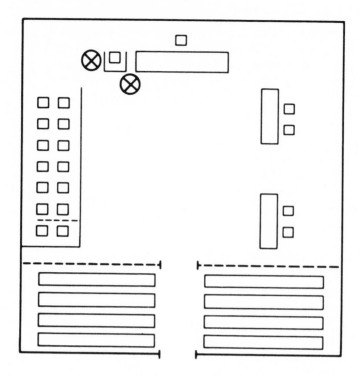

Second, make sure the record reflects what the witness is doing to an exhibit. When the witness points to or, preferably, marks the exhibit, make sure the record accurately reflects what has occurred.

Example:

The witness has established the foundation for a photograph of a lineup he attended, and the photo has just been admitted in evidence.

Q. Mr. Doe, does Plaintiff's Exhibit #2 in evidence show the person you identified at the lineup?
A. It does.
Q. Using this red pen, please draw a circle around the head of the person you identified, and place your initials next to the circle. (Witness does so.) Your Honor, may the record reflect that Mr. Doe has placed a red circle around the head of the third person from the left, and has placed the initials "TD" next to the circle.
Court: The record will so reflect.

Example:

The witness has testified to seeing a pedestrian struck at an intersection. A photo or diagram of the intersection has been admitted in evidence.

Q. Mr. Doe, does Plaintiff's Exhibit #2 in evidence show where Mr. Smith was standing when he was struck by the car?

A. Yes, sir, it does.

Q. Using this blue pen, please place an "X" in a circle at that location. (Witness does so.) Your Honor, may the record show that the witness has placed an "X" in a circle in what appears to be a crosswalk, near the bottom right corner of the exhibit?

Court: The record will so show.

c. *Using enlargements of photographs, documents, and illustrations*

The third technique is to use enlargements of photographs, overhead projections of documents, and large maps, plats, diagrams, or charts in the courtroom. Such evidence is dramatic, holds the jury's attention, and allows the witness to step down from the witness stand and illustrate his testimony using the exhibit.

Ordinarily an exhibit should first be admitted in evidence before it can be shown to the jury, although not all judges require this. Where it is apparent that you can establish a foundation, the court may allow you to place the exhibit before the jury on a stand while the foundation for its admission is being established. (As the opponent, if you intend to oppose the admission of the exhibit, ask that the other side be required preliminarily to establish the foundation for the exhibit out of the jury's presence.) Place the stand and diagram in the most advantageous position. When possible, this is directly centered before the jury, about 10 feet away. This treats all jurors equally, and places the diagram at a distance where jurors wearing bifocal glasses can see it easily. Of course, the judge and lawyers may not be able to see the exhibit from the bench or counsel table. If this happens, the usual solution is for the judge and the other lawyers to position themselves so they can see. If the judge will not allow this, you must, of course, place the exhibit where he directs.

Establish the foundation for the exhibit while the witness is still on the stand. Move the exhibit in evidence. After it has been admitted, ask the court for permission to have the witness leave the stand and go to the exhibit.

Example:

Counsel: Your Honor, may the witness leave the stand and continue his testimony by the exhibit?

Court: He may.

The witness should then step down and stand at one side of the exhibit. As always, the key is not to block the jury's view. Remind him to speak loudly, in the jury's direction. To force the witness to speak up and look at the jury when talking, you should ask questions from your usual position at the end of the jury box. Don't stand by the diagram. Have him use the exhibit to illustrate his testimony and mark the exhibit whenever possible.

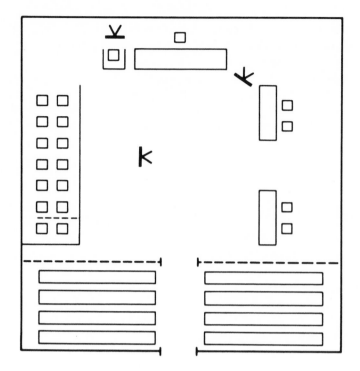

Example:

The witness is standing next to a large diagram of an intersection. The diagram has been admitted in evidence.

Q. Mr. Doe, is the grocery store that you left just before you saw the collision shown on this diagram, Plaintiff's Exhibit #2 in evidence?

A. Yes, it is.

Q. Please point to it. (Witness does so.) Your Honor, may the record show that the witness has pointed to the building at the northwest corner of the intersection?

Court: The record will so reflect.

Q. Does this diagram show where you stood at the time of the collision?

A. It does.

Q. Please place an X at that spot with this red felt pen. (Witness does so.) For the record, your Honor, the witness has placed an "X" at the northwest corner of the intersection at the curb line.

How the witness marks exhibits has a substantial impact on the exhibit's effectiveness. Use your imagination. Documents or records can be underlined with felt pens, or certain information can be circled, to highlight the critical facts. Appropriately selected colors and symbols logically connect information on a diagram to the evidence. For example, if the cars involved in a collision were blue and green, use the same colors to show their locations on the diagram. Appropriately selected symbols can enhance the exhibit's usefulness. Use pointed boxes to represent cars. Stick figures can represent persons, particularly where their body positions are important. Other important features, such as lights, can and should be marked. There are many ways to designate objects and locations other than the standard "X" markings.

Exhibits such as diagrams, maps, and photographs can also be marked to show distances and times. For example, if the distance from a witness to the scene of an event is important, and good for your side, have the witness draw a line between the two points and mark the distance on it. The same approach can be used to show time. For example, if a car went a given distance in a certain amount of time, and the time is important, have the witness draw a line between the two points and label the time involved.

Finally diagrams can be used to show sequences much like a stop-action movie. In automobile collision cases, for instance, it is often effective to use colored boxes to represent the cars involved. The boxes can then be drawn on the diagram to represent three time sequences: where the cars were when the witness first saw them, at the point of impact, and where they finally came to rest. Numbers should be put in each box to show the first, second, and third positions. Dotted lines can show the path of the cars, and distances can be marked on them. While doing this effectively requires rehearsing the sequences with the witness, it can prove to be a persuasive trial technique. The possibilities are limited only by the limits of your imagination.

Your opponent has a right to cross-examine the witness and to have the witness mark other things on the diagram. To preserve the integrity of your diagrams, it is often useful to have a plastic overlay available and to ask the judge to require that the cross-examiner's markings be made on the plastic overlay.

VI

CROSS-EXAMINATION

§6.1. Introduction

Cross-examination. The term itself commands respect and even generates fear among seasoned trial lawyers. Certainly, as far as the novice is concerned, no other area of trial work generates as much uncertainty and mystery. How many times, at the conclusion of a direct examination, has the thought flashed through every cross-examiner's mind: "My God! What do I do now?"

That countless writers have called cross-examination an art or intuitive skill hardly helps. Copying a model cross-examination from a "how to" text rarely helps, because every witness, in the context of a particular trial, is unique and must be treated as such. That 20 to 25 jury trials are usually necessary to acquire the experience essential for a moderate degree of polish in cross-examinations (as well as other aspects of trials) is hardly comforting. The novice trial lawyer needs help and he needs it now.

Because of this, the purposes of this chapter are twofold. First, it presents an analytical approach to threshold decisions and organization. Second, it presents a conceptual approach to the realistically attainable purposes of cross-examination.

§6.2. Should you cross-examine?

The decision to cross-examine cannot be intelligently made unless you have prepared the cross-examination in advance and have a realistic understanding of what you can expect to achieve during the cross-examination of any given witness. The key, as always, is thorough preparation before trial. You know what your opponent's theory of the case will probably be. Through discovery you know what the witness will testify to at trial. Therefore, you can decide on your purposes in a cross-examination, then plan it and organize it in advance.

Since modern discovery in civil and, to an increasing extent, criminal trials is essentially complete discovery, the element of surprise has been greatly reduced. Correspondingly, the need for thorough preparation to achieve an effective cross-examination has been greatly increased. The days of "let's see what he says on direct" are over, and a "wait-and-see" attitude will usually guarantee failure.

Although you have prepared your cross-examination in advance, this does not invariably mean that you will undertake it at trial. No one is required to cross-examine every witness who testifies at trial. Ask yourself the following questions whenever a witness has finished his direct testimony, before automatically rising to begin your cross-examination.

1. Has the witness hurt your case?

Not every witness will have a devastating impact at trial. Some witnesses may only establish a required technical element of a claim or defense, or provide the foundation for exhibits not in dispute. Others will simply be corroborative witnesses, and you have already established your points with earlier ones. Where the witness has not damaged your position, cross-examining him is not essential.

2. Is the witness important?

Keep in mind that jurors have certain preconceived notions about trials, which include the notion that every witness can and will be cross-examined by the opposing counsel. You must acknowledge and accommodate the jury's expectations. Where the witness has a significant role in the trial, this ordinarily means that you should undertake some type of cross-examination. Failure to do so will necessarily generate negative impressions for the jury and invite negative comments from opposing counsel during closing arguments.

3. Was the witness' testimony credible?

Sometimes a witness will not "come off right" and both the witness and his testimony are unbelievable. Other times a witness will be substantially contradicted by other witnesses. In those situations the damage has been done before you can do anything, so leaving well enough alone may be the soundest approach.

4. Did the witness give less than expected on direct?

Has the witness (or his lawyer) forgotten an important part of his testimony? If so, conducting a cross-examination may give the witness (or his lawyer) time to realize the mistake and attempt to repair it on redirect. Don't give the opposition a second chance.

Do you think the witness has intentionally withheld a damaging part of his testimony on direct, hoping you will pursue it on cross? In other words, is the witness (or his lawyer) "sandbagging"? Remember that damaging testimony is twice as damaging if elicited during the cross-examination. Where you think the opposition is sandbagging on an important point, consider foregoing cross-examination, in whole or in part.

5. What are your realistic expectations on cross?

Do you have any real ammunition to use during cross-examination? If the witness is credible and your ammunition is weak, consider avoiding cross-examination altogether or conducting a cursory cross on a peripheral point. Remember that during cross-examinations, where a witness has made a reasonable impression on direct, the jury will side with the witness. The jury sees the lawyer as sharp, crafty, and battle-tested, the witness as inexperienced, frightened, and in need of protection. While these attitudes may not always accurately reflect the true situation, they result in the same conclusion by the jury: In the cross-examination game, ties go to the witness. Accordingly, unless you can realistically expect to score points during your cross-examination, avoid it or conduct a cursory inquiry.

6. What risks do you need to take?

Trial lawyers always dream of taking to trial an invincible case, one where witness upon witness simply overwhelms the opposition. This rarely happens, because perfect cases, if they exist at all, are usually settled. Consequently, trials invariably involve calculated risks. The number and extent of the risks depend on how good your case is. If your case is solid and you can reasonably expect to win, keep your risks to a minimum. If, on the other hand, your case is a probable loser that cannot be settled, you can cast caution to the winds and conduct a risky cross that searches for the break that might turn the case around. If, as is likely, that never occurs, your case will hardly be worse off than before. Accordingly, "safe" cross-examinations should always be utilized in those cases where the facts are close or favor your side. However, where your facts are bad and, barring luck, you can confidently expect to lose, conducting "risky" cross-examinations is something you can consider.

§6.3. *Purposes and order of cross-examinations*

There are two basic approaches to cross-examinations:

a. *Elicit favorable testimony (the first purpose)*. This involves getting the witness to agree with those facts that support your case in chief and are consistent with your theory of the case.

b. *Conduct a destructive cross (the second purpose)*. This involves asking the kinds of questions that will discredit the witness or his testimony so that the jury will minimize or even disregard them.

Understanding these two basic, broad categories, and their order of use, is essential to conducting effective cross-examinations. While you may utilize only one of the approaches with some witnesses, you should always consider eliciting favorable testimony from the witness before you attempt a destructive cross-examination.

Why this order? At the end of the direct examination, most witnesses will have testified in a plausible fashion and their credibility will be high. This is the time to extract favorable admissions and information from the witness, since the witness' credibility will enhance the impact of the admissions. Such admissions will have less impact, and be less likely to occur, if you have previously attacked the witness.

Should you always undertake a destructive cross-examination? Not necessarily. Remember that a destructive cross is one that attempts to discredit a witness or his testimony, so that the jury will minimize or even disregard what the witness has stated. If you have been successful in obtaining significant admissions, you may well decide to omit any discrediting cross at all. Remember that trials make it difficult to have your cake and eat it too. Juries will be understandably skeptical if you argue that a witness' favorable testimony should be believed, while that part of the testimony you attempted to discredit should be disbelieved. Accordingly, where the witness' admissions have been helpful, thereafter conducting a destructive cross-examination will only undermine the admissions. Discretion is often the better part of valor in such situations.

§6.4. *Elements of cross-examinations*

1. Structure

Successful cross-examinations are invariably those that follow a preconceived structure that gives the examination a logical and persuasive order. That structure is based principally on the following considerations.

a. Have your cross-examination establish as few basic points as possible

Your cross should preferably have no more than three or four points that support your theory of the case. Why no more? Always remember the jury's finite capacity to retain information. The jury receives facts aurally, and it receives them only once. Attempting too much on cross-examination will invariably create two problems: the impact of your strongest points will be diluted, and the less significant points will be forgotten entirely by the time the jury deliberates on its verdict. Therefore, stick with the strongest ammunition and avoid the peripheral material.

b. Make your strongest points at the beginning and end of your cross-examination

Open with a flourish and end with a bang. Why? Again, the nature of the jury dictates this approach. Jurors remember best what they hear first and last. These are the principles of "primacy" and "recency." Their first and last impressions made during the cross-examination will be the lasting ones.

c. Vary the order of your subject matter

Successful cross-examinations are usually based on *indirection* — the ability to establish points without the witness perceiving your purpose or becoming aware of the point until it has been established. Varying the order of your topics will make it less likely that the witness will realize the purpose of a given line of questions. On the other hand, constantly jumping from point to point is ineffective, since usually the jury and you become more confused than the witness.

d. Don't repeat the direct examination!

This may be the most commonly violated maxim of good cross-examinations. Many are the lawyers whose standard approach is to have the witness "tell it again," in the invariably groundless hope that the witness' testimony will somehow fall apart during the second telling. This approach almost invariably fails. It has merit only in situations where the witness' testimony appears memorized, or where certain parts of the direct examination support your theory of the case.

2. Rules for cross-examinations

Your chances of conducting successful cross-examinations are maximized when you follow certain rules that have withstood the test of time. While these, like any other rules, can be ignored or violated in appropriate situations, following them is usually the safest approach. These rules include the following.

a. Know the probable answer to your questions before you ask the questions

Play it safe. The witness will seize every opportunity to hurt you. Cross-examination is not a discovery deposition. This is not a time to fish for interesting information or to satisfy your curiosity. Its sole purpose is to elicit favorable facts or minimize the impact of the direct testimony.

Accordingly, your questions should tread on safe ground, by asking questions that you know the witness should answer a certain way.

b. *Listen to the witness' answers*

This may appear to state the obvious, but the fact remains that lawyers often forget to do just that. Witnesses constantly surprise you. Unless you are watching and listening, you will miss nuances and gradations in the witness' testimony. Reluctance and hesitation in answering will be overlooked. Don't bury your face in your notes, worrying about the next questions while the witness is answering the last one. Organize your notes into cross-examination topics, then formulate your actual questions spontaneously. This way you can watch the witness as he listens and answers, gauge the witness' reaction to your question and the tone of his answer, and intelligently formulate follow-up questions.

c. *Don't argue with the witness*

Cross-examination can be frustrating. The answers will often not be to your liking. The temptation, therefore, to argue with the witness is always present. Resist the temptation. Arguing is legally improper. It is also unprofessional. In terms of maintaining your credibility with the jury, it is a disaster. Lawyers who succumb to this weakness are usually those who conduct cross-examinations like fishing expeditions. Repeatedly getting bad answers, they begin to argue with the witness. The possibility of this happening can be substantially reduced simply by carefully organizing and structuring your cross-examinations in advance.

d. *Don't let the witness explain*

Open-ended questions are disastrous on cross-examinations. Hostile witnesses are always looking for an opening to slip in a damaging answer. Questions that ask "how" or "why" or elicit explanations of any kind invite disaster. These kinds of questions are best avoided altogether.

e. *Keep control over the witness*

Control comes in large part by asking precisely phrased leading questions that never give the witness an opening to hurt you. But it has another facet. Control means forcing the witness to obey evidentiary rules, particularly those involving nonresponsive answers. When the witness continuously gives such answers, move to strike the answer and, if warranted, ask the court to admonish the witness.

Example:

Q. You recognized the driver of the car, didn't you?
A. Yes.

Q. It was Frank Jones, wasn't it?
A. Yes. He was weaving and looked drunk.
Q. Your Honor, we ask that the answer after "yes" be struck as nonresponsive, and the jury be instructed to disregard it.
Court: The answer will be stricken. The jury will disregard it.

Of course the jury cannot disregard it, since you cannot "unring a bell." However, it does serve a valuable purpose by letting the jury know that the witness' conduct is improper. If the witness repeatedly gives nonresponsive answers, ask the court to admonish him.

Example:

Q. Your Honor, could the witness be admonished to answer the question and only the question?
Court: Yes. Mr. Smith, you will only answer the questions asked. This is not the place for speeches.

If after such an admonition the witness continues to volunteer answers, the jury will realize how biased and partial the witness is and judge his testimony accordingly.

Another approach to controlling the witness is to repeat the question the witness answered unresponsively. It lets the witness know you cannot be put off with a nonresponsive answer. The jury will also understand that the witness is evading a hard question.

Example:

Q. Mr. Jones, between 8:00 and 9:00 P.M., you drank five bottles of beer in the tavern, didn't you?
A. Well, we were all drinking.
Q. Mr. Jones, my question is, you drank five bottles of beer during that hour, didn't you?
A. I guess so.

Another method of control is to let the witness know that you have total command of the facts and will immediately know if the witness is telling you anything less than the total truth.

Example:

Q. Mr. Jones, there were three other persons sitting at your table in the tavern, weren't there?
A. Yes.
Q. They were Jimmy Smith, James Oliver, and Wilbur Franklin, correct?
A. Yes.

> Q. Wilbur was sitting across from you, wasn't he?
> A. Yes.
> Q. And he's tall, thin, and has a deep voice, isn't that right?
> A. Yes.
> Q. And it was during that time in the tavern that you told Wilbur and the others, "I ditched the stolen car in the parking lot"; isn't that right?
> A. I guess so.

By demonstrating to the witness, before asking the important question, that you know the facts — because you probably talked to the other persons present in the tavern — you have a much lesser risk that the witness will give you an inaccurate or altogether false answer under the mistaken impression that you don't really know the true facts.

f. Don't ask the one-question-too-many

The traditional theory of cross-examinations was to make all your points during the cross-examination itself. The modern theory has an entirely different emphasis and level of subtlety. You ask only enough questions on cross-examination to establish the points you intend to make during your closing argument. This means that you will avoid asking the last question that explicitly drives home your point. Instead, your cross will merely suggest the point. During the closing argument you will rhetorically pose that last question and answer it the way you want it answered, when the witness is not around to give you a bad answer.

Example:

You want to establish that the witness did not see the collision until *after* the initial impact and therefore really doesn't know how the accident happened.

> Q. You weren't expecting a collision at the intersection, were you?
> A. No.
> Q. You'd gone through that corner many times without any collisions occurring, hadn't you?
> A. Yes.
> Q. The weather was good.
> A. Yes.
> Q. The traffic was normal.
> A. Yes.
> Q. As you approached the corner you were talking with your passenger, isn't that right?
> A. Yes.
> Q. The first unusual thing you heard was the sound of the crash, wasn't it?
> A. Yes.

> *Q.* And that's when you noticed that a crash had just occurred, isn't
>   that true?
> *A.* Yes.

At this point, stop! You've made your point. Don't ask the last obvious
question: "So you didn't really see the cars *before* the crash occurred, did
you?" The witness will always give you a bad answer. Instead, save it for
your closing argument:

Example:

> *Remember what Mr. Doe said on cross-examination? He testified that the first*
> *unusual sound he heard was the crash, and then he noticed that a crash between*
> *the two cars had just happened. Did he see the crash itself? Of course not. Did he*
> *see where the cars were before the crash? Of course not.*

The problem is always recognizing what that last question you shouldn't
ask is, before you inadvertently ask it. Perhaps the best safeguard against
doing this is to ask yourself: what's the final point about this witness that
I'll want to make during closing arguments? When you decide on the
point, make sure you don't ask it as a question during the cross-
examination.

g. *Stop when finished*

Cross-examination continuously tempts you to keep going on. There
is always one more question you could ask. There is always one more point
that you might be able to establish. Resist this natural temptation to fish
for additional points. It's dangerous. Moreover, the jury has a limited attention span. Stick with your game plan and get to your last big point
before the jury gets restless or bored. Make your point, stop, and sit down.

3. Verbal approach

Cross-examination requires a different attitude and verbal approach by
the lawyer from those on direct examination. Effective direct examinations normally require you to assume a secondary role, remain in the
background, and ask open-ended questions that let the witness dominate
the jury's attention. Cross-examination, in terms of the lawyer's position
and manner of questioning, is the mirror opposite of direct examinations. Accordingly, you should follow certain rules when conducting
cross-examinations.

a. *Make your questions leading*

This is an oft-violated rule. Questions like "What's the next thing you
did?" and "Describe what the intersection looked like" have little place on

cross, particularly where important testimony is involved. A leading question is one that suggests the answer and is the basic form you should use for cross-examinations. Inexperienced trial lawyers usually make two interrelated mistakes: they lead too much on direct and too little on cross. The best way to cure such mistakes is to consciously avoid them before they become an irreversible habit.

Example (proper leading forms):

> Q. Mr. Doe, on December 13, 1984, you owned a car, didn't you?
> Q. You left that intersection before the police arrived, isn't that correct?
> Q. You had two drinks in the hour before the collision, right?

The only time you can safely ignore the rule is when the answer is not important — you know that the witness must give a certain answer because he has been previously committed to that answer by prior statements — or because any other answer will defy common sense or other evidence. You can then safely ask a nonleading question, because you can effectively impeach any unexpected answer.

Asking nonleading questions can break up the monotony of constantly leading questions. However, whenever you get near important, contested matters, the leading form is the only safe questioning method.

b. *Make a statement of fact and have the witness agree to it*

During cross-examination you are the person who should make the principal assertions and statements of facts. The witness should simply be asked to agree with each of your statements. By phrasing your questions narrowly, asking only one specific fact in each question, you should be able to get "yes," "no," or short answers to each question. Keep in mind that whenever the witness is given the chance to give a long, self-serving answer, he will.

c. *Use short, clear questions, bit by bit*

Cross-examination is in part the art of slowly making mountains out of molehills. Don't make your big points in one question. Lead up to each point with a series of short, precise questions.

Example:

Don't ask: "You didn't really see the pedestrian get hit by the car, did you?" This is the classic "one-question-too-many." It's the point you will argue later in closings. The witness will always give you an unfavorable answer, and it's much better to lead up to that point by several short questions.

Q. You're familiar with the intersection of North and Clark, aren't you?

A. Yes.

Q. In fact, you've driven through that intersection over the past five years, haven't you?

A. Yes.

Q. You usually go through the intersection on your way to and from work, don't you?

A. Yes.

Q. So over the past five years, you've driven through the intersection over a thousand times, haven't you?

A. Probably.

Q. You never saw a pedestrian hit by a car there before, did you?

A. No.

Q. On December 13, 1984, the weather was clear and dry, wasn't it?

A. Yes.

Q. The traffic was pretty much the way it always is at that time of day, wasn't it?

A. Yes, I'd say so.

Q. Nothing was going on that made you pay more than your usual attention to the road, was there?

A. No.

Q. In fact, just before the accident you were thinking about what you were going to do at work that morning, weren't you?

A. I might have been.

Q. So the first unusual thing that you noticed that morning was the sound of the crash, wasn't it?

A. Yes.

Q. And that's when you saw that someone had been hit by a car, wasn't it?

A. Yes.

Notice that by a series of interrelated, progressive questions you have demonstrated that the witness was not expecting a crash and really did not notice anything until after hearing the sound of the crash. You have made your point by indirection. Notice that what would be a last question, "So you didn't really see the pedestrian before the crash, did you?" was not asked. The witness will invariably say "yes," or something even more damaging. As noted above, that is the question you want to save and answer in your closing argument.

d. Project a confident, take-charge attitude

On cross-examination, you should be the center of attention. Consistent with proper procedure and good taste, act the role. Ask questions in a voice and manner that projects confidence, both to the jury and the witness. Let the jury know your attitude about the facts. On direct examination, how a witness answers is as important as the answer itself. On cross-examination, how you ask a question is as important as the question itself. Projecting humor, incredulity, and sarcasm are all a proper part of cross-examination. Use them in appropriate situations. Above all, make sure the witness understands and feels your attitude about the facts of the case and your expectations in your questioning. Projecting that attitude usually has a significant impact in obtaining the answers you want.

e. Be a good actor

Every cross-examiner, no matter how experienced, careful, and talented, will get bad answers to questions. When this happens, a good poker face is invaluable. Juries, when they hear what appears to be a devastating answer, will look around the courtroom and gauge the reaction of the judge, lawyers, and spectators. When the witness does drop a bomb, don't react to it. Simply go on as if nothing really happened. If you refuse to make anything of the answer, you have minimized its impact, and the jury may well conclude that the answer was not as damaging as it first appeared to be.

f. Use a natural style

While trying cases requires you to conform your conduct as a lawyer to certain rules, there is a great deal of latitude that permits the personalities of the lawyers to come out. As in other phases of trial work, there are many styles with which you can conduct cross-examinations. However, there is only one solid rule you should follow: Use the style that is natural to you, that you feel comfortable with. Juries will immediately spot any lawyer who is attempting to copy someone else's style. The style that is natural for you will invariably be the one that is the most effective as well.

4. Lawyer's position

Yours should be the dominant physical presence during the cross-examination, since you want to capture the jury's attention. Staying in the jury's line of sight will force them to watch you and concentrate on your questions. Where local rules do not restrict you to a council table or a lectern, standing directly before the jury, as you would during opening statements and closing arguments, is the most dominant position.

Use your voice and appropriate gestures to maintain the jury's attention. Moving around the courtroom periodically can also be useful. If you look and sound confident, you have a substantially better chance of making the cross-examination effective.

Standing directly before the jury has a second advantage. It allows you to maintain constant eye contact with the witness. In many cases maintaining eye contact gives the witness the impression that you are totally in command and know when the witness is wavering and hedging in his answers. It also forces the witness to either look at you or avoid your gaze by looking down. This keeps the witness from looking at the jury when he answers your questions.

Example:

In the following schematic diagram of a courtroom, you would usually stand near the area marked "X."

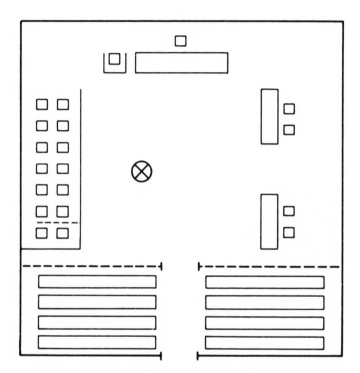

§6.5.   *Eliciting favorable testimony*

The cross-examiner's primary purpose, as mentioned earlier, is to elicit facts from the witness that will support your case in chief and be consistent with your theory of the case. This should be done first, because the witness at the beginning of the cross-examination will be minimally adverse. If you are pleasant and courteous to the witness, your chances of obtaining favorable testimony will be maximized. The witness will relax and be much more likely to cooperate with you in achieving your purposes.

What constitutes favorable testimony? Here a little imagination and ingenuity is useful. You must keep your theory of the case in mind, because the purpose of this phase of the cross-examination is to obtain facts which support your theory or contradict theirs. Consider the following possibilities.

1. Did part of the direct examination help?

Only rarely is an entire direct examination damaging. Usually the witness will testify to a number of facts that are either neutral or are helpful to your position. In those circumstances, it is useful to have the witness repeat the favorable parts of the testimony, because the jury is much more likely to retain the information when you draw it out during the cross-examination.

Example:

In a criminal case where the issue is identification, the victim has testified he was robbed at midnight in an alley and has identified the defendant as the robber. The cross-examination can emphasize that it was nighttime and the crime occurred in poor lighting.

2. Can the witness corroborate your case?

Often it is advantageous to determine if the witness can corroborate aspects of your case, even if those aspects were not directly covered during the direct examination. Review the central parts of your case and determine if the witness can testify to any facts that support it. Such admissions are always more impressive when obtained through the other side's witnesses.

Example:

An effective cross-examination procedure is to use the other side's witnesses to establish the foundations, in whole or part, of your exhibits, even though you won't offer them in evidence until your case in chief. (This can be done unless their subject matter is beyond the scope of the direct.) During closing arguments you can point out that the exhibits must be credible because the other side established their foundations.

3. What must the witness admit?

Review what the witness' prior statements are, as well as statements of your opponent's other witness. Where these prior statements contain favorable information, it is safe to ask the witness about the information. If the witness contradicts his own prior statement, he can be effectively impeached. If he contradicts another of your opponent's witnesses, you have established a contradiction in your opponent's case. The same procedure can be used with exhibits you know your opponent intends to introduce or has introduced at trial.

4. What should the witness admit?

While this category is obviously less safe than the previous one, nevertheless it should always be considered. What the witness should admit can be gauged by common sense, logic, probabilities, and by what your other witnesses will say. If the witness does not admit what you believe he should, the testimony will probably not be accepted by the jury either.

Example:

In a personal injury case, you can probably get the driver of a car involved in a collision to admit that he was not anticipating an accident and wasn't driving any differently than he normally does. If the witness disagrees and claims that he was particularly careful that day, the jury probably will not believe him.

Example:

In a criminal case, the victim was robbed at gunpoint. You can probably get the victim to admit that he was frightened, afraid he was going to be shot, and was staring at the gun pointed at him. If he does not, the witness will have contradicted common sense and logic, and the jury will probably disbelieve that part of his testimony.

§6.6. *Discrediting unfavorable testimony*

Discrediting cross-examinations, regardless of the witness involved, have one fundamental purpose: to demonstrate or suggest that the testimony is less probably true than appeared at the end of the direct examination. This is sometimes called "increasing the improbabilities." Whether your approach is to obtain unlikely explanations, retractions, contradictions, inconsistencies, or implausibilities, the effect is the same.

The emphasis in a discrediting cross-examination is *not* on "destroying the witness." This almost never occurs in actual trials. Rarely will you cross-examine a perjurer and be able to demonstrate that he has totally fabricated his testimony. Most witnesses, much like any other person telling a story, inject their own attitudes, perspectives, and selective recall into their testimony. It is this coloring, usually unintentional and often subconscious, that can realistically be developed and exposed.

There are two basic methods by which cross-examination can increase the improbabilities: discredit his testimony, and discredit his conduct.

1. Discredit the testimony

The most common type of cross-examination, particularly in cases involving occurrence testimony, is one that challenges the reliability of the testimony. Experience tells us that, although most witnesses are honest, attempt to be objective, and try to present an accurate narrative of an event, often just the opposite results. The witness himself is usually not aware of this. Witnesses often see only parts of an event, and "fill in" the gaps of their observations by what they think are the logical facts. After a while they honestly believe that they actually observed the filled-in facts, since their memory has blurred the distinction between actual observation and the filled-in facts. Consequently, the cross-examination cannot be a direct assault on the witness' integrity, because the jury will resent and reject this tactic.

The sounder approach is to accept the witness' honesty and integrity, but have your cross-examination suggest that certain factors adversely affect his testimony and undermine its impact. The basic methods are to discredit the witness' perception, memory, and ability to communicate.

a. Perception

A common challenge to occurrence testimony centers on the witness' ability and opportunity to observe the event involved. Usually this will involve showing that an event occurred quickly and unexpectedly, and that the witness was frightened or surprised. When this is done effectively, the jury will realize that the circumstances under which the witness made the observations were not conducive to accuracy.

Example:

A witness has testified to driving down a street and observing a collision between two other cars. The cross-examination will show that the collision occurred quickly and unexpectedly, and that the witness was too far away to accurately observe what really happened.

Q. Ms. Jones, Maple Avenue is a north-south street and Elm Street runs east-west, correct?
A. Yes.
Q. The accident you say you observed was at that intersection, correct?
A. Yes.
Q. When the accident happened, you were driving toward the intersection on Elm Street, correct?
A. Yes.

Q. You were about one-half block from the corner when it happened, isn't that so?

A. Yes.

Q. It's fair to say that you weren't expecting an accident that day, isn't it?

A. Yes.

Q. So you were driving the way you usually would just before the accident, weren't you?

A. Yes.

Q. You had a passenger in the car, correct?

A. Yes.

Q. You were talking with him while driving, weren't you?

A. Yes.

Q. Ms. Jones, each block in this city is one-eighth of a mile long, isn't it?

A. I think so.

Q. So each block is about 600 feet long, isn't it?

A. That sounds about right.

Q. This means that you were about 300 feet from the corner when the accident happened, weren't you?

A. I guess so.

Q. 300 feet is the length of a football field, isn't it?

A. Yes.

Q. Both Maple and Elm have buildings on both sides of the street, don't they?

A. Yes.

Q. As you were driving toward the corner, you couldn't see traffic on Maple other than at the intersection, could you?

A. No.

Q. That's because the buildings were blocking your view, weren't they?

A. Yes.

Q. So you couldn't see the two cars involved in the accident until they were actually in the intersection, could you?

A. No.

Q. Ms. Jones, there was other traffic on Elm Street as well as Maple that morning, wasn't there?

A. Yes.

Q. I'm sure you were watching that other traffic as you were driving, weren't you?

A. Yes.

Q. Elm Street has a good amount of traffic during the rush hour, doesn't it?

A. Yes.

Q. There were probably cars going in both directions on Elm Street, weren't there?

A. Probably.

Q. Some of those cars were in your lane, while others were in the opposite lane, weren't they?

A. That's possible.
Q. And some of the cars were in front of you, while others were behind you, weren't they?
A. That's possible, but I'm not sure.

Through this cross-examination you have demonstrated that the witness was a good distance from the accident, could not see the cars involved until they were in the intersection, and probably had traffic blocking her view at the critical moments. In short, her observations are not as reliable as they first appeared to be.

b. Memory

The witness' ability to remember details of an event, and his efforts to record or otherwise preserve these details, are often important considerations. Even where the witness had an excellent opportunity to make accurate observations of an event, the time between an event and the witness' testimony in court may be substantial. When this happens, cross-examinations often point out that the witness has forgotten details, has made no effort to record them, or cannot really separate this event from other similar ones.

Example:

A police officer has testified that he arrested the defendant in a hotel room and took a statement from him. The cross-examination will show that the officer did not put the statement in his report and, because of the intervening time and the number of arrests he has made during that time, cannot possibly remember what the defendant said.

Q. Officer Jones, this arrest you made took place over a year ago, didn't it?
A. Yes.
Q. One of a police officer's duties is to make arrests, isn't it?
A. Yes.
Q. How many arrests would you estimate you make each week?
A. Oh, perhaps two or three, on the average.
Q. This means that in the year since this arrest, you've arrested as many as 150 persons, haven't you?
A. It's possible. I can't really say how many.
Q. It's impossible to remember all the details of every one of those arrests, isn't it?
A. I suppose so.
Q. Because of this, you prepare police reports, don't you?
A. Yes.
Q. The reports are made to refresh your memory about the details of every arrest, aren't they?
A. Yes.

Q. You write the report to include everything you think could be important, don't you?

A. I try to.

Q. The report you made in this case, previously marked Defendant's Exhibit #1 for identification, included those things you thought were important, didn't they?

A. Yes.

Q. But your report doesn't say anything about a statement other than the notation, "Defendant made statement," does it?

A. No.

Q. Your report says nothing about what the defendant actually said, does it?

A. No.

Example:

Plaintiff's secretary has testified that she mailed to the defendant a letter that accepted a previous offer the defendant made to the plaintiff. The defendant has denied receiving plaintiff's letter. The cross-examination will demonstrate that, because the secretary types and processes so many letters, she cannot possibly remember how this particular letter was handled.

Q. Ms. Jones, you've been Mr. Doe's secretary for some five years now, haven't you?

A. Yes.

Q. The events to which you just testified took place almost three years ago, didn't they?

A. Yes.

Q. How many letters, on the average, do you type during a working day?

A. It varies, of course, but it's probably around 5 a day.

Q. So you would type approximately 25 letters a week, right?

A. Approximately.

Q. That would make about 100 each month?

A. Approximately.

Q. And over 1,000 each year?

A. I guess so.

Q. This means that you've probably typed over 5,000 letters for Mr. Doe since you started working for him, correct?

A. Probably.

Q. Ms. Jones, now and then Mr. Doe will make changes on a letter you've given him to sign, won't he?

A. Yes.

Q. In those instances you'll type a new draft of the letter, won't you?

A. Yes.

Q. How often does that happen?

A. Oh, perhaps once or twice a week.

Q. Now and then Mr. Doe will decide not to send a letter you've typed at all, won't he?

A. Yes.

Q. How often does that happen?

A. Oh, maybe a couple of times a month.

Q. Every now and then Mr. Doe will keep a letter on his desk that you've typed, won't he?

A. Yes.

Q. Every now and then you've probably had to remind him to send a letter out, haven't you?

A. Yes.

Q. Ms. Jones, as you sit here now, you can't remember which letters over the past five years you've retyped, can you?

A. No.

Q. Or which letters Mr. Doe decided not to mail?

A. No.

Q. Or which letters you had to remind him to put in the mail?

A. No.

Q. It's simply a case of too many years and too many letters, isn't it?

A. Yes.

   c. Communication

Another method of discrediting testimony is to examine the witness' ability to communicate. What good does it do for a witness to have observed an event, remember what happened, yet be unable to describe the event logically and accurately to the jury? The observations are only as good as is the witness' ability to tell what actually happened. A common cross-examination technique is to test the witness' ability to describe details and directions and to estimate distances and time, to demonstrate that the witness cannot accurately recreate a picture of what actually happened for the jury. Another technique is to review the witness' observations in great detail, injecting as much technical information as possible, so that the witness' testimony becomes unclear or confusing, and its purpose is lost on the jury.

Example:

A witness has testified to the details of a collision and the times and distances involved. The cross-examination will demonstrate that the descriptions, times, and distances are inaccurate and unreliable.

Q. Mr. Jones, you were sitting on the porch of your house when the accident happened, correct?

A. Yes.

Q. From your porch you could see both cars involved in the accident, is that right?

A. Yes.

Q. The impact between the two cars happened right in front of your house, correct?

A. Yes.

Q. The defendant was pulling out of his driveway across the street from you, right?

A. Yes.

Q. How long is that driveway?

A. Well, it's a long driveway, so it's maybe 100 feet.

Q. How long did you estimate it took for the car to go the length of the driveway?

A. Maybe four seconds or so.

Q. The plaintiff's car on the street going toward you was moving at about 40 mph, is that your estimation?

A. Yes.

Q. How far away from you was the plaintiff's car when you first saw it?

A. Oh, maybe 500 feet away.

Q. And how long did it take the plaintiff's car to travel 500 feet?

A. Oh, maybe 20 seconds or so.

Q. Mr. Jones, I'd like you to estimate 20 seconds for me. I'm going to clap my hands once, and when you think 20 seconds have passed, please tell me. (Clap hands.)

A. Now. (The jurors, of course, have been looking at their watches and timing it.)

Q. Your Honor, may the record reflect that, according to my watch, 25 seconds actually passed.

Court: It may — that's what I timed it at.

Q. Mr. Jones, could you estimate the distance from the witness stand to the doors at the back of the courtroom?

A. Well, that's about 25 feet.

Q. Your Honor, may the record reflect the distance is actually 38 feet?

Court: It may — we've measured that before.

You now have, partly by indirection, generated ammunition that you can use in closing arguments to demonstrate that this witness is an unreliable source of information, because he is not capable of accurately estimating distances and times. The second part of the cross-examination demonstrated this. When you can get a witness to make significantly inaccurate estimates of distances and time, it undermines the credibility of his entire observations. However, this approach should be used only in circumstances when you have a realistic possibility of success. It works best with children or persons who do not deal with technical information on a daily basis.

The first part of the cross-examination can also be used fruitfully in closing arguments. Every lawyer handling automobile cases soon learns that 15 mph = 22 ft./sec. The witness said the defendant's car traveled 100 feet in four seconds, or over 15 mph. As plaintiff, you can argue that this was an excessive rate of speed for a driveway. The witness also stated that the plaintiff's car traveled 500 feet in twenty seconds, or less than 20 mph. As plaintiff, you can easily argue that this was a safe speed to be traveling on a residential street. This type of cross-examination, pinning the witness down to specific estimates of distances, time, and speed, is a common technique in accident cases and often reveals internal inconsistencies.

2.   Discredit the conduct

A witness will sometimes testify in a seemingly reasonable manner, yet have acted inconsistently with the testimony. In these instances, the cross-examination should emphasize the inconsistency between the testimony and the conduct. This is based on the established principle that actions speak louder than words. Since this is so, the inconsistent conduct will usually nullify the testimony.

Example:

The defendant in an automobile collision case has testified that he was not negligent in the operation of his car. The cross-examination will develop that he left the scene of the collision without calling the police, never told his wife about it, and never reported it to either the police or anyone else.

Q.   Mr. Jones, this collision happened about 7:30 at night, correct?
A.   Yes.
Q.   There are gas stations at that corner, aren't there?
A.   Yes.
Q.   They were open when the collision occurred, weren't they?
A.   Yes.
Q.   You only remained at the scene of the collision for approximately 15 minutes, didn't you?
A.   Yes.
Q.   You were not injured during the collision, were you?
A.   No.
Q.   At no time following the collision while you were at the corner did you call the police, correct?
A.   No.
Q.   You never attempted to flag down any police cars, did you?
A.   No.
Q.   When you drove away from that corner, you didn't drive to the police station, did you?
A.   No.
Q.   You drove straight home, didn't you?
A.   Yes.

Q. When you got home your wife and family were home, weren't they?

A. Yes.

Q. You didn't tell your wife or children that you had just been involved in a collision, did you?

A. No.

Q. At no time that evening did you call the police to report that fact, did you?

A. No.

Q. In fact, you never reported this collision to the police at any time, did you?

A. No.

Q. And you never reported this collision to anyone else, did you?

A. No.

Example:

The defendant in a criminal case is charged with raping Ms. Smith. On direct examination he denied the charge. His defense is consent. The cross-examination will show his consciousness of guilt by his actions following the incident.

Q. Mr. Jones, on December 13, 1984, you were working at the XYZ Company, weren't you?

A. Yes.

Q. That date was a Tuesday, wasn't it?

A. Yes.

Q. You were living at 1420 Maple Street, weren't you?

A. Yes.

Q. You were with Ms. Smith during the evening of December 13 until about 11:00 P.M., weren't you?

A. Yes.

Q. You then left?

A. Yes.

Q. You didn't go back to your apartment that night, did you?

A. No.

Q. You didn't go to work the next day, did you?

A. No.

Q. You weren't sick though, were you?

A. No.

Q. You didn't go home either, did you?

A. No.

Q. You didn't tell anyone at work where you were, did you?

A. No.

Q. You didn't tell any friends or family where you were, did you?

A. No.

Q. In fact, you were staying at a friend's house, weren't you?

A. Yes.

Q. That's where you stayed for the next three days, isn't it?

A. Yes.

Q. During those three days, you never went to work, did you?

A. No.

Q. You never returned home, did you?

A. No.

Q. And the only person who saw you at your friend's house was your friend, isn't that so?

A. Yes.

§6.7. *Impeachment*

Impeachment is the most dramatic trial technique in the lawyer's arsenal. Selectively used and effectively employed, it can have a devastating effect at trial. Jurors appreciate effective impeachment. They enjoy seeing a witness get "caught" changing his story. Impeachment, however, should be selectively used because, like any dramatic weapon, its impact is diluted with overuse. Impeachment must be effectively employed because it must be dramatically executed using a persuasive technique. Consequently, learning when and how to use impeachment is an essential skill for any trial lawyer.

Impeachment is a cross-examination technique that discredits the witness. Its purpose is simple: show the jury that this witness cannot be believed. Many lawyers mistakenly attempt the same thing through the refreshing recollection technique. Remember that refreshing recollection is a direct examination technique that steers a favorable but forgetful witness back on the beaten path. It is an accrediting technique and should usually not be used during cross-examination.

Impeachment is governed by a series of technical rules from the Federal Rules of Evidence, case law, and custom. Under FRE 607 any party can impeach any witness. This permits a party to "volunteer" impeaching facts on direct examination, an approach usually called "drawing the sting."

There are seven basic impeachment techniques:

a. bias and interest
b. prior convictions
c. prior bad acts
d. prior inconsistent statements
e. contradictory facts
f. bad reputation or opinion for truthfulness
g. treatises

Each of these will be discussed later in detail.

1. Impeachment requirements

Impeachment procedures are governed by statutes, case law, local custom, and rules of persuasion. These rules for the most part apply regardless of the particular impeachment technique used.

a. Must have good faith

Central to impeachment is the requirement of good faith. You must have a good faith basis for believing that the impeaching fact you are disclosing is in fact true. Unless you have such a good faith belief, you cannot inquire into it. The judge may require you to disclose to him your good faith basis for going into a particular matter. In addition, case law ordinarily requires that you can prove up in good faith an impeaching matter if the witness denies its existence. If you cannot prove up something that you may be required to, you cannot ask about it. This requirement protects a witness from being attacked with unsupportable impeachment.

b. Must raise on cross-examination

If you intend to raise an impeaching matter, you must do so during cross-examination. The reasons are fairness and judicial economy. Fairness requires that a witness be asked about an impeaching fact, so that he can admit, deny, or explain it. Judicial economy requires that an impeaching fact be brought out on cross because if the witness admits the impeachment, there is no need to prove it up with extrinsic evidence. In addition, an impeached witness can explain away, or reduce the effect of, impeachment on redirect examination, an efficient way of dealing with this situation.

c. Must prove up if required

Whether you must prove up an impeaching matter depends on two questions. First, did the witness admit the impeachment? If the witness unequivocally admits the impeachment, there is nothing left to do. If the witness denies or equivocates, however, you may need to prove up the impeaching matter. Equivocations such as "I'm not sure," "I don't remember," or "I might have" are treated like denials.

Second, whether the impeaching matter is "collateral" or "noncollateral" determines whether you will be required to prove up a denial or equivocation. The reason is again based on judicial economy. Only noncollateral matters that are denied must be proved up with extrinsic evidence. If a collateral matter is denied, you must "take the witness' answer" and cannot prove up a denial. Whether a matter is noncollateral is really a practical question addressed to the judge's discretion. Is the matter that was denied by the witness important enough, given the issues of the case and significance of the witness, that we should use court time to prove up the denied matter with extrinsic evidence? If the answer is yes, it is noncollateral. For instance, if a witness says he was 20 feet away when he saw an accident, and denies saying previously that he was 200 feet away, this fact is obviously noncollateral. Some categories of impeachment are viewed as always noncollateral, others are always collateral, while some may fall in either category.

d. When to prove up

If a witness denies or equivocates on a noncollateral matter, you must "prove up the denial" when you next have the opportunity to call witnesses. For example, if a defense witness denies a noncollateral matter during cross-examination, plaintiff's attorney must wait until the defense rests and it is plaintiff's turn to call rebuttal witnesses. Only then can plaintiff call a prove-up witness. How this is done is discussed later in this section.

Once the basic procedure regulating impeachment is understood, the persuasive impeachment techniques can be learned. The techniques depend in large part on the particular impeachment method being used.

2. Bias, interest, and motive

This category includes bias, prejudice, interest, and motive. While there is no federal rule on this category, bias and interest are always considered noncollateral. If the witness does anything other than admit the matter, you must prove it up with extrinsic evidence.

Regardless of the particular area, the approach is the same. Your cross-examination must, bit by bit, carefully suggest the impartiality, then stop. An overly zealous cross-examination runs the considerable danger of offending the jury. Accordingly, subtlety is essential. The jury will respect your good taste and reach the proper conclusion on its own.

a. Bias and prejudice

Bias and prejudice are particular tendencies or inclinations that a person has that prevent him from being impartial. A person is biased in favor of, or prejudiced against, some person or position. This usually involves exposing a family or employment relationship that renders the witness incapable of being impartial and objective.

Example:

The defense in a criminal case is alibi. The defendant's mother has testified that the defendant was at home when the crime was committed. The cross-examination will develop the mother's obvious bias for her son.

> Q. Mrs. Jones, your son was living with you on the date this robbery was committed, wasn't he?
> A. Yes.

Q. In fact, he's still living with you now, isn't he?
A. Yes.
Q. So you see him just about every day?
A. Yes.
Q. Do you talk to him?
A. Yes.
Q. He talks to you when he has problems, doesn't he?
A. Yes.
Q. Mrs. Jones, you've probably talked with your son about this case many times, haven't you?
A. Yes.
Q. Would it be fair to say you talk about it with him almost every day?
A. Probably.
Q. You weren't subpoenaed to come to court today, were you?
A. No.
Q. Didn't your son and his lawyer ask you to come?
A. Yes.

Notice that the cross-examination was fairly gentle. In such a situation the jury can easily sympathize with the poor woman whose son obviously put her up to testifying for him. In this kind of cross-examination, being gentle and brief is being safe.

Demonstrating bias is often an effective technique when cross-examining expert witnesses. Such witnesses, particularly if consulting experts, are often "professional witnesses" for one side and have an obvious institutional bias and interest. Consequently, demonstrating that the witness invariably testifies for the plaintiff or defendant, or for this lawyer in particular at an expensive hourly rate, can often significantly diminish the impact of the testimony.

Example:

Q. Dr. Smith, you've previously testified as an expert in cases where Mr. Jones was the lawyer for one side, haven't you?
A. Yes.
Q. Over the past five years, how many times would you say you've done that?
A. Oh, perhaps seven or eight times.
Q. Each of those seven or eight times, you were called as a witness by Mr. Jones, isn't that so?
A. Yes.
Q. You've also testified in cases where other lawyers from Mr. Jones' law firm were involved, haven't you?
A. Yes.
Q. Over the past five years, how many times?
A. Oh, I'd say maybe 10 to 15 times.

Q. In those cases, you were called as a witness by Mr. Jones' partners, weren't you?

A. Yes.

Q. Dr. Smith, have you ever testified as a consulting doctor in a case for one side, when the *other* side was represented by anyone from Mr. Jones' firm?

A. Well — I can't recall any.

Q. In each of those 10 to 15 times you've testified as a consultant for someone from Mr. Jones' firm, you've charged $100 per hour for your time, haven't you?

A. Yes.

Q. And how much was your fee in this case?

A. Approximately $900.

The jury will quickly understand that this doctor is little more than a repeated "hired gun" for the same side.

b. Interest

Interest refers to the witness' possible benefit in, or detriment from, the outcome of a particular case. Most commonly, though not always, the witness' interest is financial. Since human greed is one of the most common instincts, demonstrating it can a powerful adverse effect on the witness' credibility.

Example:

In a will contest suit, the heirs at law who were excluded by the will have challenged the testator's mental capacity to execute the will. The witness is an heir who would receive part of the estate under intestacy should the will be barred.

Q. Mr. Jones, you are one of the late William Jones' children, aren't you?

A. Yes.

Q. You're one of three surviving children?

A. Yes.

Q. You knew your father had substantial property and other assets, didn't you?

A. Yes.

Q. When you learned that his estate was valued at over $200,000, that didn't surprise you, did it?

A. No.

Q. But when you learned that he had willed his entire estate to three different charities, that did surprise you, didn't it?

A. Yes.

Q. You knew that this meant that the three charities would get all your father's money, right?

A. Yes.

Q. Shortly after you learned the contents of your father's will, you consulted a lawyer, didn't you?

A. Yes.

Q. You learned that if the will were invalid, the state laws of intestacy would apply, correct?

A. Yes.

Q. Those laws would provide that you, as one of three surviving children, would get one-third of his estate, correct?

A. Yes.

Q. So, you knew that if the will were declared invalid, you would get about $70,000 from the estate, isn't that so?

A. Yes.

Q. But you also knew that if the will were upheld, you wouldn't get one dime, isn't that also true?

A. Yes.

c. Motive

Motive is the urge that prompts a person to think and act in a certain way. Common examples are greed, love, hate, and revenge. Each, in the right circumstances, can be a compelling emotion. Where such a motive can be effectively suggested, it is a powerful weapon because, like bias and interest, it personally taints the credibility of the witness, regardless of how plausible his testimony might appear to be.

Example:

Defendant is charged in a criminal case with forging endorsements on stolen checks and then cashing them. The cross-examination is designed to show his financial plight and obvious need for money as the motive for committing the crime.

Q. Mr. Jones, over the past two years you've invested in the stock market, haven't you?

A. Yes.

Q. You bought over $100,000 worth of commodities stock, didn't you?

A. Yes.

Q. Commodities are high-risk investments, aren't they?

A. Yes.

Q. It would then be fair to say you were speculating in the commodities market, wouldn't it?

A. I suppose so.

Q. You bought the stock on a 10 percent margin, correct?

A. Yes.

Q. This meant you only had to put up 10 percent, or $10,000, of your own money to buy all the stock, isn't that true?

A. Yes.

Q. However, because of this, if the market value dropped by 10 percent, you'd lose your entire investment unless you put up more money, isn't that also true?

A. Yes.

Q. That's what's known as a margin call, isn't it?

A. Yes.

Q. On December 13, 1984, you got a margin call from your brokerage firm, didn't you?

A. Yes.

Q. And it was the day after the margin call that you deposited these checks in your savings account, wasn't it?

A. Yes.

Q. The same day you used that money to meet the margin call, didn't you?

A. Yes.

3. Prior convictions

Prior convictions are governed by FRE 609, which has two basic provisions. First, any felony conviction, and any misdemeanor conviction involving dishonesty or false statements, can be used to impeach the credibility of any witness who has testified. However, the conviction, or release from confinement, must have been within 10 years of the present date. Second, a balancing test is applied in two situations: where the witness is a defendant in a criminal case, and where the conviction is more than 10 years old. In these situations the court must determine whether the probative value of the conviction outweighs its prejudicial effect. If so, the conviction can be used to impeach.

Prior convictions must be raised on cross, unless the witness has already "volunteered" it on direct examination, a situation that frequently occurs. If a witness denies or equivocates about the prior conviction, you must be prepared to prove it up with extrinsic evidence, since prior convictions are always considered noncollateral.

It is always a good idea to raise the question of prior convictions before trial to get a ruling on precisely what convictions can be used to impeach. In recent years courts have frequently used the balancing test required when the witness is a criminal defendant to permit the fact of the conviction to be raised, but bar any reference to the actual crime. For instance, the court might rule that the defendant can be shown to have a "felony conviction," but not that the conviction was for armed robbery, in order to reduce the prejudicial effect of the conviction. This is sometimes done when the prior conviction is for the same or similar crime as the one for which the defendant is currently on trial.

When cross-examining a witness, the usual rule is that any fact appearing on the judgment order, or record of conviction, can be raised. This usually includes the jurisdiction, presiding judge, dates of conviction and sentencing, the crimes the witness was found guilty of, and the sentence imposed. If the witness has volunteered only part of this information on direct, the cross-examiner may still develop the remainder.

Example:

> Q. Mr. Doe, you told us that in 1984 you were convicted of income tax evasion, right?
> A. Yes.
> Q. In fact, you were convicted on June 30, 1984, on three counts of that charge, weren't you?
> A. Yes.
> Q. That was before Judge Smith in the U.S. District Court for the Northern District of Indiana, wasn't it?
> A. Yes, it was.
> Q. Judge Smith sentenced you to six months imprisonment and five years probation on all three counts, didn't he?
> A. Yes, he did.
> Q. And you are still on probation for that crime today, aren't you?
> A. Yes.

Impeachment with a prior conviction is a technical area, and the rules governing it may vary substantially in those jurisdictions not following FRE 609. Consequently, you must do two things whenever you plan to use prior convictions at trial. First, make sure you know the applicable law. Second, raise impeachment matters before trial, since improperly impeaching with a prior conviction can easily result in a mistrial.

4. Prior bad acts

Prior bad acts are admissible under FRE 608(b) if the acts are "probative of truthfulness." This is a change from previous law, and today many jurisdictions that have not adopted the Federal Rules of Evidence do not permit this type of impeachment. Hence, research is required in these jurisdictions to determine the status of prior bad acts. Bad acts that are probative of truthfulness commonly include submitting false loan applications or inaccurate employment applications.

Prior bad acts are viewed as collateral. The cross-examiner must "take the witness' answer," and the bad act cannot be proved up extrinsically. This being the case, the cross-examiner should pursue the cross-examination to get the witness to admit the bad act, or show that a denial is not believable.

Example:

> Q. Mrs. Johnson, didn't you fill out a false employment application at Sears last year?
> A. I don't think so.

Q. Well, you applied there for a job, didn't you?
A. Yes.
Q. You filled out an application form, right?
A. Yes.
Q. You submitted it on March 31 of last year, correct?
A. Around then.
Q. And you signed it, didn't you?
A. I think so.
Q. Mrs. Johnson, on the line asking for the extent of your education, didn't you write down "received a B.A. degree in economics from U.C.L.A. in 1981"?
A. Yes.
Q. In fact, Mrs. Johnson, you haven't received a B.A. degree from U.C.L.A. or any other college, have you?
A. No.

As a matter of technique, you should ask about the bad act by revealing enough detail that lets the witness and jury know that you have done your homework on this subject. The witness is then more likely to admit it, or the jury is unlikely to believe a denial.

5. Prior inconsistent statements

Raising prior inconsistent statements is the most frequently used impeachment method at trial. More than any other impeachment method, however, impeaching with prior inconsistent statements requires a precise technique to be effective before the jury.

FRE 613 expressly requires that the witness have an opportunity to admit, deny, or explain making the inconsistent statement. Hence, you should raise it on cross. Prior inconsistent statements can be either collateral or noncollateral. If it is noncollateral, and the witness does not admit making it, you must prove it up later with extrinsic evidence.

a. Techniques

The impeachment technique must be both structured and simple. The basic structure involves three steps — recommit, build up, and contrast. First, recommit the witness to the fact he asserted on direct, the one you plan to impeach. Try to do this in a matter-of-fact way that does not arouse the witness' suspicions. Use the witness' actual answer on direct when you recommit him, since he is most likely to agree with the actual answer, rather than a paraphrasing. It is also usually effective to ask the witness to admit the facts he stated in the prior inconsistent statement, and get a denial of them.

Second, build up the importance of the impeaching statement. Direct the witness to the date, time, place, and circumstances of the prior inconsistent statement, whether oral or written. Under FRE 613(a), you no longer need to show an impeaching writing to the witness before using it, although you must show it to the opposing counsel on request. However, it is usually more effective to show the witness his prior written statement and make him admit having made or signed it. Building up the impeaching statement also involves showing that the statement was made when the witness' memory was fresher, and under circumstances showing that the statement was seriously made.

Third, read the prior inconsistent statement to the witness and ask him to admit having made it. Use the actual words of the impeaching statement. If you are using a lengthy statement such as a deposition, tell opposing counsel the page you are reading from. You can also have the witness read the impeaching statement, but this usually is not as effective, since the witness will not be as forceful in reading the impeaching section.

Example:

Q. Mr. Jones, you say you were about 50 feet from the accident when it happened?

A. Yes.

Q. There's no doubt in your mind about that, is there?

A. No.

Q. Weren't you actually *over 100 feet* away?

A. No.

Q. Mr. Jones, you talked to a police officer right at the scene a few minutes after the accident, didn't you?

A. Yes.

Q. Since you talked to him right after the accident, everything was still fresh in your mind, right?

A. Yes.

Q. You knew the police officer was investigating the accident, didn't you?

A. Yes.

Q. And you knew it was important to tell the facts as accurately as possible?

A. Yes.

Q. Mr. Jones, you told that police officer, right after the accident, that you were *over 100 feet away* when the accident happened, didn't you?

A. Yes.

Here the basic technique — recommit, build up, and contrast — was executed cleanly and simply. A simple fact — 50 feet — was singled out for impeachment, then contrasted cleanly with the contradictory earlier oral statement — 100 feet.

Simplicity is essential for the jury to understand the contrast, but is often difficult to achieve. Three problems frequently arise. First, you cannot effectively impeach long statements, paragraphs, or even lengthy sentences. These have to be reduced to a critical fact or essential few words that can be effectively contrasted with a prior statement. Second, you cannot effectively impeach several facts at one time. To make the inconsistencies clear and understandable, each fact you intend to impeach should be brought up separately and contradicted separately. This keeps things clear, and clarity is essential.

Example:

> Q. Mr. Jones, you said you were about 50 feet away when you saw the accident, right?
> A. That's right.

Build up the impeaching statement, in this case an oral statement to a police officer shortly after the accident, then:

> Q. You told Officer Adams that you were *over 100 feet* away, didn't you?
> A. Yes.
> Q. Mr. Jones, today you told us that you'd been at that corner for 30 minutes, correct?
> A. Yes.
> Q. But you told Officer Adams that you'd gotten there *only moments earlier*, isn't that right?
> A. Yes.
> Q. Mr. Jones, you claim today that you had a clear view of the accident, correct?
> A. Yes, that's correct.
> Q. However, you told Officer Adams, a few minutes after the accident, that you were looking away and only saw the crash *after* it happened, isn't that right?
> A. Yes.

This basic technique, impeaching one simple fact at a time, is applicable to every type of prior inconsistent statement.

Third, you cannot effectively impeach unless you recommit the witness to facts that clearly contradict the impeaching statement. If the contradiction is not obvious, you must first convert the fact asserted on direct examination to a fact that is clearly contradicted by the impeaching statement.

Example:

The witness on direct stated that "the northbound car ran the red light." In an oral statement to an investigator he said that "the plaintiff ran the red light."

> Q. Mr. Smith, you say that the northbound car ran the red light, right?
> A. Yes.

Q. The northbound car was driven by Jones, wasn't it?
A. Yes.
Q. Jones is the defendant here, isn't he?
A. Yes.
Q. So you're saying that the *defendant* ran the red light, correct?
A. That's right.
   (After building up the impeaching statement:)
Q. Mr. Smith, didn't you tell that investigator that the *plaintiff* ran the red light?
A. Yes.

Finally, the basic three steps approach — recommit, build up, and contrast — can be varied to make the contrast sharper. It is often more effective to build up the impeaching statement *first*, then recommit and contrast.

Example:

Q. Mr. Jones, you talked to a police officer at the scene a few minutes after the crash happened, didn't you?
A. Yes.
Q. Everything was fresh in your mind then?
A. Sure.
Q. You knew it was important to tell the investigating officer everything you knew, as accurately as possible, right?
A. Yes.
Q. Mr. Jones, you say today that you were about *50 feet* from the accident when it happened, correct?
A. Yes.
Q. But you told that police officer, right after the accident, that you were *over 100 feet away* when the accident happened, didn't you?
A. Yes.

These impeachment examples have all assumed that your purpose is to attack the witness' credibility by forcefully exposing the changed testimony. If your approach is that the witness is mistaken or forgetful and may freely change his testimony, it is probably more effective not to recommit the witness to his direct examination. Instead, simply bring out the prior statement and have the witness agree that it is true and accurate.

b. *Prior testimony*

Prior testimony includes any testimony given under oath, such as depositions, former trials, evidentiary hearings such as preliminary hearings and grand jury proceedings, and hearings before governmental bodies such as inquests. Because prior testimony is under oath — subject to perjury penalties — made at a formal proceeding, its impeachment value is high, and it is particularly important to build up the prior testimony.

Example:

Witness testifies in a personal injury case that he saw the cars involved before the collision. At his deposition he testified that he saw the cars only after hearing the crash.

> Q. Mr. Jones, you saw the two cars before they actually collided, is that right?
> A. Yes, I did.
> Q. There's no question in your mind that you saw them before the collision, is there?
> A. No, sir.
> Q. Mr. Jones, you gave a deposition in this case last year, didn't you?
> A. I think so.
> Q. Well, you remember you were in my offices on March 15, 1984, don't you?
> A. Yes, it was about then.
> Q. Before the deposition, you met with Mr. Franklin, the other lawyer, didn't you?
> A. Yes.
> Q. So you knew the things you would be asked about, right?
> A. Yes.
> Q. And at that deposition, Mr. Franklin, a court reporter, you, and I were all present, isn't that right?
> A. Yes.
> Q. Both Mr. Franklin and I asked you questions about the collision, didn't we?
> A. Yes.
> Q. Before you answered those questions you were sworn by the court reporter to tell the truth, weren't you?
> A. Yes.
> Q. That's the same oath you took today, right?
> A. Yes.
> Q. You did tell the truth, didn't you?
> A. Of course.
> Q. After you finished testifying you had a chance to read your testimony to make sure it was accurate, didn't you?
> A. Yes.
> Q. After reading it to make sure it was correct, you signed it, didn't you?
> A. Yes.
> Q. You gave that deposition just four months after the collision, right?
> A. Yes.
> Q. So what you saw that day was still pretty fresh in your mind, wasn't it?
> A. I guess so.

Q. Mr. Jones, during that deposition — page 18, counsel — you were asked the following questions and you gave the following answers, didn't you?
(Reading transcript):

Q. What's the first thing that drew your attention to the collision?
A. Well, I guess when I heard a loud crash.
Q. What did you do then?
A. I looked over and saw that two cars had just collided.
Q. Was that the first time you actually saw the cars?
A. Yes.

A. That's what I said.
Q. You were also asked this question and gave this answer, didn't you? — page 33, counsel.
(Reading transcript):

Q. Did you see the cars before the collision?
A. No, I didn't really notice them then.

A. Yes.

When impeaching from a transcript, read the questions and answers verbatim. It is improper to summarize or paraphrase the testimony. When impeaching with any kind of writing or recorded statement, make sure that it is materially and fairly impeaching. Avoid using statements that only marginally impeach. Not only is it questionably admissible, it is ineffective as a technique. Avoid asking "do you remember" questions, since they allow a witness to avoid the substance of the question. The "did you" question form is stronger. Most of all, avoid impeaching with statements taken out of context. Under FRE 106, your opponent can require you to read the entire relevant portion of the statement.

c. Written statements

Written statements include statements in either narrative or question-and-answer form, and are written by the witness or signed by him. Although written statements are usually statements given to investigators or police officers, they can include any other writings such as letters and records.

Example:

Witness testifies in a criminal case that the person who robbed him was about 24 years old and 5 feet 11 inches tall. In a signed written statement to a police detective, he stated the robber was about 18 years old and 5 feet 7 inches tall.

Q. Mr. Doe, you now say that the man who robbed you was about 24 years old and about 5 feet 11 inches tall, isn't that so?

A. Yes.

Q. You were face to face with him for perhaps two minutes, weren't you?

A. Yes.

Q. There was plenty of light, wasn't there?

A. Yes.

Q. So you had an opportunity to see his face and gauge his height, didn't you?

A. Yes.

Q. How tall are you, Mr. Doe?

A. I'm 5 feet 8 inches.

Q. So the robber was about 3 inches taller than you?

A. Yes.

Q. And he was about 24 years old?

A. Yes, about that.

Q. Your estimate of his age at 24 and his height at 5 feet 11 inches was based on your two-minute face-to-face confrontation, is that correct?

A. Yes.

Q. Mr. Doe, you made a written statement the same day of the robbery, didn't you?

A. Yes.

Q. That was made to Detective Smith?

A. Yes.

Q. After he typed the statement he gave it to you, didn't he?

A. Yes.

Q. He asked you to read it and make any corrections necessary, didn't he?

A. Yes.

Q. You did that, didn't you?

A. Yes.

Q. You wanted to be sure that your statement was accurate, didn't you?

A. Yes.

Q. After making sure it was accurate, you signed the statement, isn't that right?

A. Yes.

Q. (Have the statement marked as an exhibit, show it to opposing counsel, then to the witness.) Mr. Doe, I'm showing you a two-page document marked Defendant's Exhibit #1. That's your signature at the bottom, isn't it?

A. Yes.

Q. This is the signed statement you made for Detective Smith, isn't it?

A. Yes.

Q. In that written statement, didn't you say — page 1, counsel — "The man looked about 18 years old. He was approximately 5 feet 7 inches tall"?

A. Yes.

Make sure your reading of the written statement is verbatim, not a summarization. As noted above, FRE 613 now gives you the option of not showing the prior inconsistent statement to the witness before impeaching him with it. However, most lawyers prefer to use the traditional method demonstrated in the example, on the theory that it is a more persuasive technique.

d. Oral statements

Oral statements most commonly are made to police officers or private investigators. However, any statement made by the witness to any person can be used to impeach if it is inconsistent with the in-court testimony on an important fact.

Example:

Same fact situation as above, except that the statement to the police detective is oral. The detective summarized the oral statement in his report. Use the same approach as above to lock the witness into his direct examination testimony that the robber was 24 years old and 5 feet 11 inches tall. Then proceed in the following manner.

> *Q.* Mr. Doe, you talked to Detective Smith a couple of hours after the robbery, didn't you?
> *A.* I think so.
> *Q.* That was in an interview room at the police station, correct?
> *A.* That's right.
> *Q.* Detective Smith's partner was also in the room?
> *A.* Yes.
> *Q.* Detective Smith asked you all about the robbery, didn't he?
> *A.* Yes.
> *Q.* And you told him everything you could remember, isn't that so?
> *A.* Yes.
> *Q.* You told him everything as accurately as you could?
> *A.* Yes.
> *Q.* You wanted to make sure that the right person was arrested, didn't you?
> *A.* Yes.
> *Q.* Detective Smith and his partner were taking notes during your conversation, weren't they?
> *A.* I think so.
> *Q.* Mr. Doe, didn't you tell Detective Smith, in the presence of his partner, that the robber was 24 years old?
> *A.* Yes.
> *Q.* Didn't you also tell him that the robber was approximately 5 feet 7 inches tall?
> *A.* Yes, I think that's what I said.

When impeaching with an oral statement that was noted in someone else's report, you cannot impeach the witness with the report itself, because the witness did not write the report. Hence, in the above example it would be improper to ask: "Didn't you say in Officer Smith's report that. . . ." The report is Officer Smith's, not the witness', and it is unfair to cross the witness using someone else's report. This is a frequent mistake when impeaching with oral statements.

e. Pleadings

Any court document that is signed by the witness, such as an answer to the complaint or answers to interrogatories, may be used to impeach. Technically, of course, statements in such documents are admissions by parties. It can happen, however, that a party forgets what was stated in a pleading or other court document and testifies inconsistently. In those situations, the document can be used to impeach.

Example:

Defendant in a contract action is testifying, and has stated on direct, that he cannot remember if he received the contract. In his answer to the complaint he admitted receiving the contract in the mail.

Q. Mr. Doe, you're telling us that you can't remember if you received the contract, is that correct?
A. That's right.
Q. This contract, Plaintiff's Exhibit #1 in evidence — did you ever see it or a copy of it before?
A. I'm not sure.
Q. Mr. Doe, when you were sued you received a copy of our complaint, didn't you?
A. Yes.
Q. You then hired a lawyer to represent you, isn't that correct?
A. Yes.
Q. You read the complaint?
A. Yes.
Q. So you know you were being sued on the contract, didn't you?
A. Yes.
Q. You discussed the complaint and the allegations in the complaint with your lawyer, didn't you?
A. Yes.
Q. A short time later your lawyer filed an answer to our complaint, isn't that right?
A. Yes.
Q. You discussed that answer with him, didn't you?
A. Yes.
Q. After making sure it was correct you signed it, didn't you?
A. Yes.

Q. Mr. Doe, I am handing you the complaint, previously marked Plaintiff's Exhibit #1 for identification, and the answer, marked Plaintiff's Exhibit #2 for identification. That's the complaint and your signed answer, isn't it?

A. Yes.

Q. Mr. Doe, Paragraph 5 of the complaint says: (Reading) "On or about December 13, 1985, defendant Doe received the contract in the U.S. mails." Isn't that correct?

A. Yes.

Q. Paragraph 5 of your signed answer says: (Reading) "Defendant admits the allegations contained in paragraph 5 of the complaint." Isn't that correct?

A. Yes.

f. Omissions

Impeachment by omission is a common trial technique whenever a witness testifies who previously prepared a written report of his activities. Police officers and other investigators commonly fall into this category. Whenever such a witness testifies to any important fact that he failed to include in his report, he can be impeached by the omission of this fact from his report. The technique is the same as for impeachment with a prior written statement, only that the prior statement is nonexistent. The purpose is obvious: If what he is saying now was so significant, why didn't he put it in his report?

The buildup is critical. You must establish that the witness knows how to prepare good reports, because he knows when information is important enough that it would always be included. Once this has been driven home, force the witness to admit that the omitted fact is an important one that should always be included in a report. With this established, the conclusion is obvious: The claimed fact never actually occurred.

Example:

A police officer has testified that immediately after arresting the defendant, the defendant said, "I don't know what got into me. It just happened." That statement is not in his written report.

Q. Officer Doe, right after you arrested Bobby you claim he said, "I don't know what got into me. It just happened." Is that what you're telling us?

A. Yes, sir.

Q. You're sure that's what he said?

A. Yes.

Q. Officer Doe, you prepared a written report of this incident, didn't you?

A. Yes.

Q. You received training on how to prepare such written reports at the police academy, didn't you?

A. Yes.

Q. You were taught to prepare complete and accurate reports, right?

A. Yes.

Q. You were also taught to include everything about the incident that was important, right?

A. Yes.

Q. That's because you, your commanding officer, and the county attorney all rely on that report to evaluate the case, don't they?

A. Yes.

Q. One of the most important things to write down is what any person arrested says about the incident, right?

A. Yes.

Q. In fact, you're taught to write down the actual words a defendant uses, aren't you?

A. Yes.

Q. (Have the officer's report marked as an exhibit, show it to opposing counsel, then to the witness.) I show you what has been marked Defendant's Exhibit #1. That's your written report, isn't it?

A. Yes.

Q. Your narrative of the incident covers the entire back side of the form, and is in single spaced type, isn't it?

A. Yes.

Q. After typing it you read it over?

A. Yes.

Q. You wanted to make sure it was complete and accurate, didn't you?

A. Yes.

Q. And that it included everything that was important, right?

A. Yes.

Q. After making sure it was complete and accurate, you signed that report, correct?

A. Yes.

Q. The purpose of the report is to have an accurate record of what you saw, heard, and did, correct?

A. Yes.

Q. You also use such a report to refresh your memory before testifying about the incident, isn't that also correct?

A. Yes.

Q. That's important, because everyone's memory fades with time, doesn't it?

A. Yes.

Q. In fact, you read this report today before testifying here, didn't you?

A. Yes.

Q. That was important, because you'd probably forgotten some of the details of the case, isn't that so?

A. I suppose so.
Q. Officer Doe, nowhere in this report that you prepared did you state Bobby said, "I don't know what got into me. It just happened." Isn't that so?
A. That's not in the report.
Q. In fact, your report says absolutely nothing about any statement, does it?
A. No.

While this is an effective approach, there are more persuasive techniques to expose an important omission. One way is to have the witness look over his report and attempt to find the absent information. Another is to give the witness a pen and ask him to circle the absent information. The witness' obvious inability to do this effectively exposes the omission.

Example:

Q. Officer Doe, show me where in your report you state Bobby said, "It's all my fault. I just lost my head."
A. (Looks at report) It's not there.
Q. Show me where your report contains anything at all about anything Bobby said.
A. There's nothing in my report.

Example:

Q. Officer Doe, please take this red felt pen and circle on your report where it states Bobby said, "It's all my fault. I just lost my head." (Give pen to witness)
Q. Officer, you haven't circled anything with the pen. Is there a problem?
A. It's not in my report.

6. Contradictory facts

A cross-examiner may wish to show that certain facts are different from what the witness claims. This is usually called impeachment by contradiction. How the fact is asserted on cross-examination determines whether you are under an obligation to prove up the asserted fact if the witness denies it.

Example:

Q. Did you drink any alcoholic beverages that day before the accident?
A. No.

> Q. Didn't you have three double martinis at O'Malley's Pub one hour before the accident?
>
> A. No.

The first question, because of its form, does not directly assert a fact, and the denial ends the matter. In the second question, however, its form directly suggests that the drinking in fact occurred, and if the witness denies it, you may be required to prove it up. As always, you cannot ask such an impeaching question unless you have a good faith basis to believe that the facts you are suggesting as true are in fact true.

If the witness denies the contradictory facts suggested by the cross-examination, whether you are required to prove it up with extrinsic evidence depends on whether the contradictory facts are collateral or noncollateral. This is the same distinction used for prior inconsistent statements. If it is noncollateral, you must prove it up.

Example:

The witness in an automobile negligence action testifies he was wearing a green tie and was 10 feet from the accident when it happened. On cross the witness is asked: "weren't you wearing a red tie?" and "weren't you really 100 feet from the accident?," and he denies both facts.

In this example the cross-examiner has directly suggested that both contradictory facts are true. However, only the denial of the 100 feet distance is important, and the cross-examiner must prove it up. The denial that his tie was red is collateral and cannot be proved up.

7. Bad reputation or opinion for truthfulness

Whenever any witness testifies at trial, his credibility is in issue. Hence, the witness' character trait of truthfulness is relevant to his credibility and under certain circumstances may be introduced at trial.

The procedural requirements must be kept clear. A witness must have his character for truthfulness attacked before it can be supported. This is because witnesses are presumed to be truthful and must be discredited before they can be accredited. Hence, the opponent must first call a witness to testify that the earlier witness' truthfulness is bad. This is proper, under FRE 608(a), through either reputation or personal opinion. Once attacked, the proponent of the earlier witness can present supporting reputation or personal opinion evidence. Remember that the reputation or opinion witness must be properly qualified by showing the basis for the reputation or opinion, before he can testify what it is.

Example:

Plaintiff calls Smith as a witness. After plaintiff rests, defendant calls Johnson to testify that Smith has a bad reputation for truthfulness. After defendant rests, plaintiff calls Edwards to testify that Smith has a good reputation for truthfulness.

Keep in mind that calling a reputation witness has a built-in risk. The reputation witness can be asked on cross-examination if he knows, or has heard, anything that is inconsistent with the claimed reputation. This may open the door to specific acts of misconduct that might not otherwise come out at trial.

Example:

The defendant in a criminal case testifies. The prosecution later calls Jones, who says that the defendant has a bad reputation for truthfulness. The defense counters this evidence by calling Johnson, who says the defendant has a good reputation for truthfulness. On cross-examination of Johnson the prosecutor may ask, 'Didn't you hear that the defendant was arrested for credit card fraud last year?" This is a proper test of Johnson's knowledge, even though it raises the defendant's arrest, which would otherwise be inadmissible in the trial.

8. Treatises

Expert witnesses can be cross-examined and impeached by using treatises, periodicals, and pamphlets. Keep in mind, however, that under FRE 803(18) the treatise must be established as being a reliable authority in the field through the testimony of the witness, another expert witness, or by judicial notice. When its authoritative nature has been established, the appropriate impeaching part of the treatise can be read into evidence, although the treatise itself is not admitted as an exhibit.

The impeaching technique is the same. Recommit the expert to his statement or position, reducing it to its simplest terms. Have the expert define, in simple lay terms, any technical terms used in the treatise excerpt. Then use the treatise, reading from the appropriate section, to show that the treatise differs from the expert's testimony. Read as little from the treatise as possible without reading out of context. As always, keep the impeachment as simple and clear as possible.

Example:

Q. Dr. Smith, you say that (repeat the doctor's statement made during his direct testimony that you want to contradict), is that correct?
A. Yes, it is.

Q. Dr. Smith, Anthony's Textbook of Anatomy and Physiology has been an accepted authoritative treatise on human anatomy for many years, hasn't it?

A. Yes.

Q. You consider its most recent edition as authoritative today, don't you?

A. Yes.

(If witness denies it, ask the court to take judicial notice of the treatise's authoritativeness or represent that you will call a witness to establish it.)

Q. Dr. Smith, you agree with the following statement, which appears on page 283 of Anthony's textbook, don't you? (Then read the impeaching section to the witness and jury.)

A. In general, I do.

or

Q. Dr. Smith, I'm going to read to you a section from page 283 of Anthony's textbook. Afterward I'm going to ask you if you agree or disagree with it. The section states the following: (then read the impeaching section to the witness and jury). Doctor, do you agree with that paragraph?

A. Yes.

Since the witness did not make the impeaching statement, there is nothing for him to admit or deny making, and never any impeachment to complete.

Treatises are usually written to deal with the common situations and standard procedures that deal with those situations. An expert who has been impeached with a treatise will often try to avoid the impeachment by stating that the treatise section read in court deals with the ordinary situation, while the actual situation was not ordinary. To prevent this type of escape, it is often a useful approach to get the expert to agree that the actual situation the expert was involved in was a routine, or ordinary, one before you impeach with the treatise.

9.   Completing the impeachment

Whether you will be required to prove up an impeaching fact with extrinsic evidence depends on two things. First, did the witness unequivocally admit the impeachment? If the witness either denied or hedged with responses, such as "I don't remember," "I may have," or "I'm not sure," you may be required to prove up. Second, was the impeachment noncollateral? For trial efficiency reasons, proving up is permitted and required only for noncollateral matters, those matters that are important enough, in the overall context of the trial, to use court time to prove up. Some impeachment methods are always considered noncollateral: bias and interest, and prior convictions. Another method is always considered collateral: prior bad acts. Still others can be either collateral or noncollateral:

prior inconsistent statements and contradictory facts. This dichotomy does not apply to bad reputation for truthfulness or to treatises.

In short, you must have both noncollateral impeachment and something short of an unequivocal admission by the witness before you are permitted and required to prove up the impeachment with extrinsic evidence. How you do this persuasively depends on the particular type of impeachment involved.

You prove up impeachment the next time it is your turn to call witnesses. For example, if you have impeached a plaintiff's witness during the plaintiff's case in chief, you can prove up the impeachment only after the plaintiff has rested and it is the defense's turn to call witnesses. You should then call a witness who can testify to the impeaching fact.

a. Bias and interest

Where a witness on cross-examination has not admitted a fact showing bias or interest, you must prove up that fact, since bias and interest are always noncollateral. You must call a witness or present evidence that demonstrates that the fact showing bias or interest actually is true. For instance, if a witness has denied being financially indebted to a party, call a witness who has personal knowledge of the indebtedness, or present documentary proof of it.

b. Prior convictions

To prove up a prior conviction, simply obtain a certified copy of the witness' record of conviction. The certified copy is self-authenticating and is admissible without further foundation. Simply offer the certified copy as an exhibit at your next opportunity to present evidence, and ask the court for permission to read or show the record to the jury.

Where the name of the witness is the same as the name on the record, this usually creates a presumption that the witness is the same person as named on the record. Where the names are different (and changing names is not uncommon) or the witness denies he is the person named on the record, you must be prepared to prove the identity of the witness. Usually the underlying prison record, which includes fingerprints, photographs, and signatures, will be adequate to demonstrate that the convict is the same person as the witness in court.

c. Prior inconsistent statements

These are the most common impeachment sources that may require proving up, particularly oral inconsistent statements, which are the type most frequently denied during cross-examination.

When proving up, call the prove-up witness, establish his familiarity with the inconsistent statement, lead the witness to the actual inconsistency, and establish that it was in fact made. A common error is to have the prove up witness testify to the entire statement, not just the inconsistent part of it.

i. Prior testimony. To prove up statements made under oath during a deposition or other judicial proceeding, you must call as a witness the court reporter who made the verbatim stenographic notes of the testimony. Establish that the court reporter is a certified shorthand reporter, that he was present at the proceeding, had sworn the witnesses to tell the truth, and prepared verbatim stenographic notes of all questions and answers. Have the reporter identify as an exhibit his stenographic notes (not his transcript — that is not the original record of the testimony). Establish that the exhibit includes the testimony of the witness involved. Finally, have the witness read from the notes the exact questions and answers that prove up the impeachment. (Have the reporter go through his notes in advance and mark the part that contains the impeaching questions and answers).

In practice this is frequently handled by a stipulation that states that if the court reporter were called as a witness, he would testify that the transcript is accurate and verbatim. You would then read the appropriate transcript section to the jury.

ii. Written or signed statements. To prove up statements that are written or signed, simply call any witnesses who can identify the writing or signature or who saw the person write or sign the statement. Have the witness establish his presence at the writing or signing of the statement (if he was in fact present), show the statement to the witness (have it marked as an exhibit), and have the witness either identify the handwriting or signature as that of the person or describe having seen the person write or sign the statement. Finally, have the witness read from the written statement the part that proves up the impeachment.

Make sure your witness reads fairly, so that the impeaching words are not taken out of context. When impeaching with a writing, FRE 106 permits the adverse party to require that you read or introduce any other parts of the writing or statement which in fairness should be included. The purpose of the rule is to prevent impeachment by using statements taken out of context. Requiring that all relevant parts of the statement be introduced prevents this unfairness.

iii. Oral statements. To prove up oral statements, simply call any witness who was present when the person made the prior inconsistent statement. Establish the usual foundation questions for oral conversations, then bring out the specific inconsistent statements. Since this type of statement is the one most likely to be denied on cross-examination, take the time to develop the background of the impeachment witness and the circumstances under which the statement was made, because this will build up the credibility of the impeachment.

Example:

Jones on cross-examination has denied telling a police officer at the scene of an automobile accident that he only saw the cars involved after hearing them collide. To prove that Jones made that statement, you must later call the police officer as a prove-up witness. Establish the police officer's background, how he came to the accident scene, and what he did after he arrived. Then proceed as in the following manner.

> Q. Officer Martin, while you were at the scene of the accident, did you talk to any witnesses?
> A. Yes.
> Q. Was one of them a Mr. Roger Jones?
> A. Yes.
> Q. Did you tell Mr. Jones why you needed to talk to him?
> A. Yes, I told him I needed to find out exactly what everyone saw so I could prepare a report about the accident.
> Q. Did you ask Mr. Jones what he had seen and heard?
> A. Yes.
> Q. What was the first thing he said he noticed?
> A. He said he was walking down the street, heard a crash, looked up, and saw that two cars had collided in the intersection.
> Q. Did Mr. Jones ever tell you he had seen those two cars *before* the crash?
> A. No. He specifically told me he first saw them after hearing the crash.

iv. Pleadings. It is highly uncommon for a witness to deny signing a pleading that contains an inconsistent statement. Showing the pleading to the witness and drawing his attention to his signature on it will invariably draw out the admission. If this does not happen you must prove that the signature on the pleading was the witness', then ask the court for permission to read the appropriate parts of the pleading to the jury.

Since an attorney is an agent of the party, pleadings signed and filed by the attorney will be binding on the party as admissions. However, since the party did not sign the pleading, it probably cannot be used to impeach unless you can establish that the party read the pleading and approved it before it was filed.

v. Omissions. It is also unlikely that a witness, after being shown his previous statement, will deny that what he testified to in court is not in the statement. If anything, the witness will claim that what he said is implicitly stated in the statement.

To prove that a prior written statement does not contain facts or statements that the person testified about at trial, you must put in evidence the entire statement to show that the facts and statements are omitted from the written statement. Use the same method as used to prove up a prior inconsistent written statement. Since the witness will in all likelihood admit having made the prior written statement, the statement need only be shown to the jury to demonstrate the omission.

d. Contradictory facts

Contradictory facts, like prior inconsistent statements, can be collateral or noncollateral. If it is noncollateral, you must prove up the fact with extrinsic evidence.

Example:

On direct examination a plaintiff witness says she was 20 feet from an intersection when she saw the accident. On cross-examination she denies being 200 feet away. Since this denied fact is noncollateral, the defendant during the defense case in chief must call a witness who will testify that the plaintiff's witness was in fact 200 feet away when the crash occurred.

e. *Failure to prove up*

What happens if the cross-examiner fails to prove up an impeaching fact that he is obligated to prove up? There are two basic approaches to the problem.

First, make a motion to strike the cross-examiner's question and the answer, and ask the judge to instruct the jury to disregard them. Obviously the jury cannot "unremember" the unproved fact, particularly if the judge just reminded them of it. However, it does alert the jury to the fact that the cross-examiner failed to prove the fact he suggested was true during his cross-examination and, since the witness denied it, it must be considered untrue. Ask the judge to tell this to the jury expressly, rather than casually admonishing the jury to "disregard it." Making the motion is of course necessary to preserve error on appeal. If the violation is serious enough, move for a mistrial.

Second, consider *not* making the motion for tactical reasons. If the cross-examiner's failure to prove up is not important, then failing to preserve error for appeal is also unimportant; consider not making the motion to strike so you can comment on it during closing arguments. If the cross-examiner had no affirmative evidence to present, and only attacked your witnesses, commenting on the opponent's tactics and showing that his insinuations were never proved can be an effective approach during closing arguments.

10. Impeaching out-of-court declarants

Statements of an out-of-court declarant are frequently admissible since they often qualify for admission as hearsay exceptions. The most common example is a transcript qualified as former testimony. The opponent may wish to attack the credibility of the out-of-court declarant using one of the permitted impeachment methods.

This situation is governed by FRE 806. Since the declarant is not in court, it is impossible to ask him the questions normally required on cross-examination. However, the opponent can introduce extrinsic evidence to impeach the out-of-court declarant whenever the impeachment is noncollateral.

Example:

In an automobile negligence action, plaintiff introduces the deposition of Jones, who has recently died. Since Jones is unavailable, his deposition transcript qualifies as former testimony under FRE 804(b)(1). In the defense case the defendant can introduce the fact that Jones was convicted of perjury five years ago, since this prior conviction is admissible to attack Jones' credibility under FRE 609. This would be done by introducing a certified copy of Jones' record of conviction.

§6.8. Special problems

Cross-examiners commonly must deal with certain recurring tactics that witnesses employ to frustrate or defeat the purposes of the cross-examination. These include the following.

1. Evasive witnesses

Often a witness who had no difficulty testifying on direct examination will become evasive the moment you begin your cross-examination. The evasion can take several forms. The witness' tone and demeanor change. He constantly repeats your question or asks that you repeat the question. He is slow in answering. He constantly answers, "I don't know," "I don't remember," "I can't recall," "I'm not sure," "I might," "I could," or avoids answering directly.

The key to cross-examining such a witness is to keep in mind that all this evasive activity is making a horrible impression on the jury, an impression that can spill over on the other parts of your opponent's case. Accordingly, you should not attempt to squeeze better answers out of him. Instead, continue in the same vein. Extract as many "I can't remember" responses as possible. Ask the witness if he has difficulty hearing or understanding your questions. Try to get evasive responses to some of the same questions that the witness had no difficulty answering during the direct examination. The jury will quickly recognize what the witness is doing and treat his testimony appropriately.

2. Argumentative witnesses

The explaining or arguing witness presents the opposite cross-examination problems from those of the evasive witness. This witness wants to expound on everything. He wants to answer your question with one of his own. He wants to argue over everything. The key to such a witness is control. When the witness answers a question and keeps on talking, cut him off by asking your next question. If the witness insists on running on, ask that the court strike the unresponsive part of the answer. If the witness continues this tack, ask the court to admonish the witness only to answer the question actually asked.

Where the witness argues with you or answers your question with a question, make your questions particularly short and clear, and the only possible answer obvious. Repeat the question and insist on a responsive answer. Ask the court's assistance if appropriate. If the witness continues in the same vein, the jury will again quickly comprehend what is going on.

Another approach is to make a "contract" with the witness.

Example:

Q. Mr. Franklin, before I begin my cross-examination, I'd like to agree with you on how to go about it. I'm going to ask you questions as clearly as I can. If it's not clear, let me know, all right?
A. Okay.
Q. If my questions are clear, you'll answer them simply and clearly, all right?
A. Yes.
Q. Can we agree on this?
A. Yes.
Q. That's fair, isn't it?
A. Yes.

It's hard for a witness not to agree to such an arrangement. Then, if the witness is evasive or argues with you, the jury will view the witness as violating a fair arrangement he himself agreed on.

3. Memorized or identical stories

While not a common phenomenon, sometimes a witness on direct examination will give clues that his testimony, at least in critical parts, is memorized, or is so similar in certain respects to another witness' testimony that it suggests they got together and planned identical stories. The clues may be words and phrases that are not natural for the witness. They may be that the witness has testified to details that normally would not be remembered, or has omitted facts that would ordinarily be recalled. A clue may be in the deliberateness of the testimony or some other unusual delivery. Whatever the clue, the approach is the same. These witnesses can be asked to violate one of the cardinal rules of cross-examination: Never repeat the direct examination. Witnesses who have memorized parts of their testimony, particularly children who have been coached, will usually repeat the testimony essentially verbatim, using the same words, phrases, and details as before. These witnesses will often claim to remember details you would not expect them to, or fail to remember facts that they normally would remember. They will sometimes use a vocabulary that is not natural for them. The jury will usually pick up on the striking similarity between the two narrations, or the peculiar recall of the witnesses, or an odd word choice. Once this has been demonstrated, you should inquire whom the witness talked to before testifying, to uncover the origins of the memorization.

4. "Apparent" cross-examinations

While cross-examinations are not required, under most circumstances the jury will expect some type of cross. This is particularly so when the witness is a significant one for your opponent. In such a case some sort of cross-examination is obligatory, and you should always consider using any of the standard techniques discussed in this chapter.

Sometimes, however, you will have neither a realistic expectation of eliciting favorable admissions nor any real ammunition for conducting an effective, discrediting cross-examination. In short, you have nothing that has a chance of succeeding, yet the jury will expect some kind of cross-examination. In these situations your best approach may be to conduct an "apparent" cross-examination. Consider examining the witness on the following collateral points:

a. Who asked him to be a witness?
b. Was he subpoenaed?
c. Who has he talked to about the case?
d. Discussed testimony with lawyer?
e. Attend any meetings with other witnesses present?
f. Read other materials to prepare his testimony?
g. Make any notes on the incident?
h. Read depositions and prior statements?
i. Any financial or business interest in outcome of case?
j. Any personal interest in outcome of case?
k. Know any of the parties or witnesses?
l. Compensation as a witness?

None of these topics directly attempts to attack the testimony. However, pursuing the appropriate ones can plant a seed of doubt in the jury's mind so that it will at least think about the testimony rather than blindly accept it.

Another technique that can sometimes be effectively used when you have no ammunition for cross-examination, is to use the cross-examination to get *your* version of the facts before the jury, even though the witness will deny it. At least it tells the jury that there is a second side to the lawsuit they will hear. This technique can work well for the defendant, since he presents his evidence second, and suggests to the jury that it should keep an open mind and hear all the evidence before deciding who is right. Keep in mind, however, that using this technique will probably obligate you to actually produce evidence of your version during your case in chief.

5. Opposing counsel

Although regrettable, it is nonetheless a fact of life that some lawyers will step beyond the bounds of proper evidentiary objections and make objections solely to help or coach a witness who is being cross-examined. While it is always proper to make any objection whenever a good faith basis for the objection exists, it is improper to make an objection solely to warn or coach the witness so that he gives a safer or better answer. There are three basic problems.

First, lawyers will constantly interject "if he knows" objections after a proper question has been posed. Invariably the witness will then answer the question: "I don't know." This kind of interjection is improper and is an obvious attempt to coach the witness in answering the question. You should object forcefully if your opponent constantly resorts to such tactics and, if necessary, ask the court to direct your opponent to desist. Regardless of what the court does, the jury will quickly realize what the lawyer is doing.

Another tactic is the "clarification" request. When the witness has given an answer on cross that the lawyer does not like, he will interrupt your examination and say, "Your Honor, could the witness tell what he means by the term 'transfer'? I'm not sure that was clear to the jury," or some similar interjection. The effect, of course, is to interrupt the flow of your cross-examination and, at the same time, cue the witness that the last answer was not very good. When this happens, you should again object to the lawyer's conduct and point out that these "clarifications" can properly be made during the redirect examination.

Probably the most common problem the cross-examiner faces is the lawyer who constantly makes speeches in conjunction with the objections. (E.g., "Objection, your Honor, I don't see how the witness can possibly answer the question in light of the other evidence which has clearly shown that. . . .") Objections, of course, should only state the legal basis for the objection. Any argument should be out of the jury's hearing. The lawyer who constantly objects is trying to disrupt your examination and make periodic summations to the jury. Pointing this out to the judge promptly and forcefully will usually cure the problem.

§6.9. *Special witnesses*

This chapter has emphasized developing a methodology that will systematically allow you to identify and achieve realistically attainable objectives during cross-examinations. If the methodology is learned and followed, you should be able to cross-examine any witness in a competent way — not just occurrence witnesses.

Certain special types of witnesses, however, do appear with some frequency at trials, and it is useful to analyze the additional methods of cross-examinations that can be effective with them.

1. The expert witness

The expert witness can for purposes of cross-examination be treated like any other witness. The usual sequence — obtaining favorable admissions, discrediting unfavorable testimony, and impeachment — still applies. However, the expert witness requires additional preparation and involves other cross-examination and impeachment methods.

a. Additional preparation

Preparation for the cross-examination of an expert witness should include the following additional matters:

1. Your pretrial discovery should elicit the witness' professional qualifications and relevant experience, his expert opinion, a detailed basis and explanation of that opinion, all materials and sources he used in forming that opinion, reasons for the opinion, and his previous publications.

2. Read the expert literature on the particular field and area of expertise involved. This is essential, not only to educate yourself but also to develop potential impeachment materials. Pertinent sections of texts, articles, and other publications should be copied for possible use at trial.

3. Consult your own experts about your opponent's possible weaknesses, including his professional qualifications, expert opinion, and reasoning in forming that opinion. Your own experts are usually essential in preparing the cross-examination of your opponent's experts.

b. Cross-examination techniques

In addition to the cross-examination techniques applicable to all witnesses, certain specific techniques are particularly applicable to expert witnesses:

1. Inquire into professional fees charged and whether they have already been paid, the frequency with which the expert testifies, which side most frequently calls him as a witness, and whether he has previously done consulting work and has testified for the same lawyer. This type of collateral attack is sometimes used where the witness' opinions and reasoning cannot be directly challenged. Keep in mind, however, that trials are a two-way street. Your opponent can do to you what you contemplate doing to him. Before pursuing this approach, make sure your own experts are less vulnerable than your opponent's.

2. Narrow the witness' apparent expertise. Often an expert will appear to be highly qualified, yet his actual expertise and experience are in areas different from those directly involved in the case. The cross-examination technique is to build up the witness' real expertise, then show that

this particular expertise is not directly applicable to the type of case on trial.

This is not a direct challenge to the witness' qualifications as an expert. The cross-examiner normally has the right to cross-examine the witness on his qualifications *before* he can testify on the substantive areas. This opportunity is rarely used because by today's liberal qualifications standards, a witness rarely fails to qualify as an expert. Consequently, narrowing his expertise on cross is usually the better approach.

3. Inquire into the witness' basis for his opinion, then ask him if his opinion would be different if other facts were relied on as true (e.g., "If ____ were the true facts, Dr. Doe, would those facts change or modify your opinion?"). This is called varying the hypothetical. If the witness admits his opinion would change, in closing arguments you can argue that your facts are the true facts, and that even your opponent's expert agrees with you. If his opinion would never be different, you can argue that the witness is not credible because he has a fixed opinion that nothing could ever change.

4. It is sometimes useful to cross-examine an expert to establish your own expertise in the subject. You can do this by defining technical terms or describing technical procedures and having the expert agree that you have defined or described them correctly. Use a treatise to obtain accurate definitions and descriptions. If this expert disagrees, you can impeach him with the treatises. Doing this will show the jury that you are also knowledgeable about this subject. This enhances your credibility, which will be particularly useful during closing arguments when you discuss the subject again.

5. Review the standard treatises on the subject and have the text available in court to use for impeachment if necessary. The technique for impeachment with treatises is discussed in §6.7.

6. Instead of attacking your opponent's expert, use him to agree with and corroborate many of the propositions that make up the basis for your own expert's opinion and reasons.

7. Force the witness to define technical terms and phrases and use common language. Although experts often have difficulty doing this, it is your technique for removing the mystery and aura of self-importance surrounding experts. It is effective when the opinion does not make common sense to the jury, or the opinion simply "dresses up" something insignificant or commonplace.

8. Have the witness spell and define technical terms and phrases. This sometimes embarrasses an expert who has trouble with it, although it can easily backfire on you.

9. Use the witness to criticize his own party's conduct in select areas. Sometimes a party will have done something in a way that the expert will state is not the easiest, safest, or most reliable way to perform that particular function.

10. Force the witness to agree that in his field of expertise, legitimate differences of opinion between qualified experts can exist and often do occur. This works well in interpretive fields such as medicine and psychiatry and shows that the expert's opinion is only an opinion and noth-

ing more. Show that at different times in his career he's had differences of opinion with other consulting experts and that sometimes he's been proven right, but sometimes he was just wrong.

11. Demonstrate that the witness has no firsthand knowledge of the topic on which he is testifying. Have him admit that it is always advantageous and preferable to conduct examinations and tests yourself. This approach can work well where the witness being cross-examined has testified to a hypothetical and never had any direct contact with the facts or events involved.

12. Point out that the witness' opinion is based solely on an unreliable patient. This technique can be effective for psychiatrists and psychologists whose opinions are based mainly on interviews with a patient who may or may not be truthful during the interview, since the patient may have a vested interest in a certain result.

13. Demonstrate that the witness did not do all the things a thorough, careful expert should have done. Demonstrate that a variety of tests could and should have been performed to arrive at a reliable opinion in this case. Where appropriate, contrast the thoroughness of this expert and the time he spent on his examinations and evaluations against those of your experts.

2. The records witness

The records witness has one principal function at trial: to qualify records and other documentary evidence for admission in evidence. Since the records witness is neither an occurrence nor an expert witness and will only rarely have made prior statements of any kind, many of the usual cross-examination techniques will be ineffective. Although records witnesses are frequently not cross-examined at all, you should always consider the alternative approaches that are possible with such a witness.

With a records witness your first cross-examination approach is to attempt to keep the records from being admitted in evidence. The usual bases for attacking the records are the grounds of relevance, foundation, or multiple hearsay. However, if you have been unsuccessful in keeping the records from being admitted in evidence, or you have decided as a matter of trial strategy not to object to their admission, you should then consider the following additional approaches.

a. Look for favorable material in the records and have the witness point it out.

b. Look for inconsistencies, errors, and incompleteness in the records and have the witness point them out.

c. Point out that the witness is merely the custodian of the records, has no firsthand knowledge of the underlying facts, and has made no attempt to verify the accuracy of those facts. An alternative approach is to get the witness to repeatedly assert the records' accuracy despite having no firsthand knowledge that the facts are accurate.

d. Stress that no one is infallible, that mistakes can be and sometimes are made, and that the witness has no way of knowing if they occurred here. Point out that the business generating the records has no independent verification system or internal audit controls that would discover and correct any mistakes.

Note that your first purpose is, as always, to use the witness to point out evidence in the records favorable to your side. If none exists, your secondary purpose must be to minimize the significance and impact of the records themselves. Remember, however, that records witnesses are often clerical personnel who, although able to provide the necessary foundation for the records admission, are not experts on complicated company procedure. Accordingly, do not attack the witness for something he is not. Save your challenges for the records themselves.

3. The reputation witness

A witness who testifies about another's reputation, whether for truth and veracity or for a specific character trait, can be cross-examined much like any other witness. Such a witness may be asked with whom, where, and when he actually discussed the reputation. He may be questioned about the nature and extent of his relationship with the person about whom he is testifying. He may be examined regarding any bias, prejudice, or interest in the outcome of the case.

In addition, in federal and most state courts other matters can be probed. (See FRE 608.) The cross-examiner may expose relevant specific instances of conduct, regardless of the type of reputation evidence involved. This is allowed, not as proof of prior misconduct, but as a legitimate inquiry into the knowledge and credibility of the witness. Accordingly, the cross-examiner may ask about reports of prior acts, conduct, offenses, and arrests of the person relevant to and inconsistent with the articulated reputation, if such reports arose in the time period relevant to the type of reputation evidence involved. However, the witness may not be used to establish the truth of such reports, nor may the cross-examiner by the manner of his questioning directly suggest that the reports or rumors are true. The traditional proper form for cross-examination questions is: "Have you heard . . .". "Do you know" is improperly suggestive. This has been the approach adhered to in most jurisdictions, including the federal courts. Since FRE 608 now allows character trait evidence based on personal opinion, the "do you know" form is now proper when cross-examining such a witness.

The cross-examiner, faced with a reputation witness, should consider the following approaches:

First, as in any trial where the witness has been unconvincing or his testimony ineffectively presented, no cross-examination at all might well be the safest approach. However, a single question emphasizing that the witness was not present during the event involved may be appropriate.

Example:

> Q. You weren't in Joe's Tavern on April 1, 1985, between 8:00 P.M. and 10:00 P.M., were you?
>
> A. No.

When the witness has personal or business ties to the person in question, a cross-examination designed to emphasize his apparent bias and interest may be effective.

A common approach on cross-examination is to show that the witness has only limited knowledge on which he bases his testimony. This is usually done by demonstrating that the witness has talked to few people, on infrequent occasions, and that his conclusion is no more than one man's opinion. This works best on a witness who has been inadequately prepared.

Example:

> Q. Whom have you talked to about John Doe?
>
> A. I've talked to Fred Smith, a neighbor.
>
> Q. When was that?
>
> A. I can't really remember the times.
>
> Q. Whom else have you talked to?
>
> A. I have talked to Jack Jones.
>
> Q. Where was that?
>
> A. I can't recall.
>
> Q. Other than Fred Smith and Jack Jones, whom else can you remember specifically talking to about John Doe?
>
> A. I can't remember the names right now.
>
> Q. Where did you talk about John Doe with these other people whose names you can't remember?
>
> A. I can't remember.

Finally, the witness may be cross-examined in most jurisdictions on specific rumors and reports about the person in question inconsistent with the reputation expressed, provided a good-faith bias for asking the questions exists.

Example:

> Q. Have you heard that John Doe was arrested for battery and disorderly conduct on April 1, 1985?
>
> A. No.
>
> Q. Have you heard that John Doe was involved in a fight in the Blarney Tavern on January 30, 1986?
>
> A. No, I didn't hear about that.

§6.10. *Summary checklist*

The above sections have discussed the various approaches and techniques of cross-examinations and the sequence under which they should be employed. Before you conduct any cross-examinations, always ask yourself the following questions, which are organized in the way you should approach each cross-examination of any witness that has testified for the other side:

1. *Must I cross-examine this witness?*
   a. Has the witness hurt my case?
   b. Is the witness important?
   c. What are my reasonable expectations?
   d. What risks do I need to take?
2. *What favorable testimony can I elicit?*
   a. What parts of the direct helped me?
   b. What parts of my case can he corroborate?
   c. What must the witness admit?
   d. What should the witness admit?
3. *What discrediting cross-examination can I conduct?*
   a. Can I discredit the testimony? (perception, memory, communication)
   b. Can I discredit the witness' conduct?
4. *What impeachment can I use?*
   a. Can I show bias and interest?
   b. Can I use prior convictions?
   c. Can I use prior bad acts?
   d. Can I use prior inconsistent statements?
   e. Can I show contradictory facts?
   f. Can I show bad reputation or opinion for truthfulness?
   g. Can I use treatises?
   h. How will I prove up the impeachment if necessary?

VII

CLOSING ARGUMENTS

§7.1. Introduction

Closing arguments are the chronological and psychological culmination of a jury trial. They are the last opportunity to communicate directly with the jury. For that reason, it is imperative that the arguments logically and forcefully present your side's position on the contested issues and the reasons you are entitled to prevail.

As with all other phases of the trial, the arguments must be organized and planned in advance of trial. They should be constructed to parallel both your opening statement and your case in chief. This parallel construction can be achieved only where each phase of the trial is planned as an integral part of the overall trial strategy. Preparing for closings after the evidence is in should then be limited to reviewing the specific evidence you will mention in your argument that supports your points, and deciding how, if you are the party with the burden of proof, you will divide the available material between your closing and rebuttal arguments.

This chapter will discuss the elements and structure of effective closing arguments and present illustrative closing arguments in representative civil and criminal cases.

§7.2. Elements

Effective closing arguments invariably have two characteristics: they must be simple, yet respect the jury's intelligence. The arguments must be simple, because the jury has a limited capacity to absorb and retain aural information. They must also respect the jury's intelligence by avoiding arguments that, while superficially appealing, cannot survive closer scrutiny.

Experienced trial lawyers know that effective closing arguments invariably have, in addition to the above, certain characteristics and techniques that account in large part for the argument's effectiveness. Among these are the following.

271

1. Have a logical structure

The closing arguments must be structured in a way that will argue the facts in a logically progressive manner that the jury can understand and retain. How this is done will be discussed in detail in the next section.

2. Argue the theory of the case

Previous chapters have repeatedly emphasized that you must develop a theory of the case in advance of trial and stick with it throughout the trial. Your closing arguments should present your theory of the case explicitly to the jury, and demonstrate why your theory most logically incorporates and explains both the contested and undisputed facts admitted at trial.

3. Argue the facts and avoid personal opinions

We no longer live in an age where dazzling oratory consistently wins trials. Jurors are too well informed and perceptive to be easily spellbound. They usually follow the court's instructions and decide the case on the evidence. This means that today's jurors are persuaded by facts. The closing arguments that have staying power, that jurors remember during deliberations, are those that argue the facts.

Arguing facts involves more than a simple recitation of the testimony. It involves analysis. Juries decide cases on the basis of impressions—what they think the truth is—based on the way the parties have presented the evidence. Effective trial lawyers selectively pick and emphasize those parts of, and inferences from, the evidence that, when presented as an integrated whole, create an impression that convinces the jury that their side should win.

Refer to specific witnesses and their testimony when arguing the facts. A "fact" becomes a fact only when a jury accepts it as true. Hence, you must tell the jury why something is a true fact by reminding them what witness or witnesses said it, how it was said, and why it makes sense.

Example:

Keep in mind that the defendant was going 40 mph in a 30 mph zone. How do we know this? Well, both Mrs. Phillips and Mr. Jackson told you so. Remember where they were standing? Both were standing right on the corner and saw the defendant's car go by. They were in a perfect position to see how fast he was going. That's why we know he was going 40 mph.

It is improper for a lawyer to directly state his personal beliefs and opinions about the credibility of witnesses or the quality of the evidence presented during the trial. Statements like "I think that" or "I believe that" are objectionable. These phrases are both improper and unpersuasive and are best eliminated entirely from your trial vocabulary.

4. Use exhibits

Successful courtroom techniques maximize the use of exhibits and other demonstrative aids. Chapter V reviewed how to use exhibits in your case in chief. Do not forget these techniques now. Closing arguments should use at the appropriate places those exhibits admitted in evidence that corroborate and highlight the main points of your argument.

Exhibits do more than augment the closing arguments. They also provide refreshing breaks. Psychological studies have shown that the average person is able to devote his uninterrupted attention to one topic for only a few minutes. Accordingly, any argument that drones on for 10 or 15 minutes on any one point, regardless of how effective its content is, will lose the jury. Exhibits, in addition to their obvious value as a tool of persuasion, can provide that refreshing change of pace that recaptures the jury's attention.

In closing arguments, however, exhibits are the same double-edged sword they are during witness examinations: They both attract and distract. Accordingly, keep the exhibits you intend to use during closings out of sight until you need them, and after showing them to the jury put them out of sight. Doing this will make the exhibits supplement your argument, rather than distract and detract from it.

5. Weave instructions into the argument

Closing arguments that selectively utilize instructions have a greater impact on the jury. By suggesting that the court's instructions of law as well as the facts support your side, a doubly effective argument can be fashioned. If, for example, you are arguing that a witness should not be believed because he was impeached, tell the jury that the court will instruct them that a prior inconsistent statement can properly be considered in determining a witness' credibility. Argue your facts, then argue that the law permits or even approves your interpretation of those facts. The key to utilizing this technique is to follow your factual argument immediately with the corresponding instruction, so that the association is firmly fixed in the jury's mind.

The jury instruction conference is usually held after both sides have rested and before closing arguments. Even though each side may have submitted its proposed instruction early — at the pretrial conference — the judge will not usually decide which instructions to give until the instruction conference, since this decision depends on the evidence presented at trial.

How the jury is actually instructed and how the lawyers can use the instructions vary widely. Some judges only read the instructions; others both read and give them to the jury. Some judges require that lawyers quote verbatim from any instructions they use, while other judges disapprove of direct quotes and require that instructions be paraphrased. Learn what your judge's practices are.

Instructions frequently woven into the closing arguments include those covering the elements of claims and defenses, burdens of proof, credibility of witnesses, and definitions of critical legal terms.

6. Use themes

A theme, periodically woven into your argument, can be an effective way to capsulize your theory of the case so that the jury will remember it.

Example:

As the plaintiff in a personal injury case in which plaintiff's damages are primarily pain and suffering, you might argue that *"The only companion Louise Burch has today is her pain."* You can then remind the jury periodically, as you discuss the effect of plaintiff's injuries, that her only companion now is pain, your theme for the damages argument.

Example:

As the defendant in a criminal case, you might argue that *"The real victim in this case is Bobby Smith. He is the victim of an unreliable identification and the victim of a shoddy police investigation."* You can then remind the jury, after each of your major points, that each contributed to this miscarriage of justice.

7. Use rhetorical questions

Since the jury cannot ask questions during the trial, having unanswered questions can be a very frustrating experience. Experienced lawyers recognize this and try to anticipate those questions the jurors would probably ask if they could.

Example:

As plaintiff in a personal injury case, you might argue: *"You're probably saying to yourself: Mr. Jones, that's a lot of money you're asking for. Why should we award him $300,000? You're right, of course. That is a substantial sum of money. But in this case Jane Smith's injuries have been devastating."* Then argue that the amount requested is the bare minimum necessary to adequately compensate the plaintiff for his injuries.

Rhetorical questions can also be used effectively to challenge your opponent with difficult or unanswerable questions. If he fails to answer these questions, the jury will undoubtedly remember it.

Example:

As the prosecutor in a criminal case, you might argue: *"In this case, the evidence showed that the defendant just happened to be one block from where the robbery occurred moments earlier, just happened to have a nickel-plated revolver on him, just happened to have $47.00 in his pocket, and just happened to be wearing a red velour shirt. If he's so innocent, I'm sure his lawyer will have a great explanation for how all these things just happened at the same time when he argues to you."*

8. Use analogies and stories

Analogies and stories, if short and pertinent, can be effective in defining and crystalizing an idea in the jury's mind. They must be short, because the time for arguing is limited, and pertinent, because a story told for its own sake, without making a point, is counterproductive.

Example:

In a case where the evidence is largely circumstantial you might make the following argument: *"Exactly what is circumstantial evidence? Imagine you're looking out your living room window before going to bed. You can see the grass on your lawn. The next morning you look out and see that the lawn is covered by snow. You conclude, of course, that it snowed during the night. You didn't actually see it snow, but there's absolutely no doubt that it did. You're positive, although the evidence that snow fell is completely circumstantial."* Then argue that the evidence in the case, while circumstantial, compels only one conclusion in your favor.

9. Make your opening and closing points without notes

Experienced trial lawyers minimize their use of written notes. They know that jurors react negatively to closing arguments that appear to be read, and only professional actors can make a prepared text sound spontaneous.

Nowhere are these concepts more important than at the beginning and end of your closing argument. The introductory phase, as well as the concluding comments, should be made without any notes so that you can maintain eye contact with the jurors. Jurors remember best what they hear and see first and last, and the impression you convey during those times will be a lasting one. Prepare your opening and closing comments, know what you want to say, then stand in front of the jury, look the jurors in the eye, and tell them what you have decided on.

10. Use understatement as well as overstatement

Since closing arguments are the last opportunity to address the jury, state your side's positions as forcefully as the evidence reasonably permits. The usual method is to use overstatement and normal exaggeration.

Understatement, however, particularly if intermingled with overstatement, can be a powerful argumentative tool. Jurors tire of constant overstatement. Understatement, on the other hand, can be a refreshing change of pace and enhances your personal credibility as an advocate. Studies have shown that jurors are more likely to accept a conclusion if they make it themselves, with the lawyer merely suggesting it. Understatement can effectively utilize this fact by hinting and suggesting answers as an alternative to always pounding them home.

11. Argue strengths

Argue your strengths, not your opponent's weaknesses. Successful arguments are those that have a positive approach and concentrate on the evidence produced at trial that affirmatively demonstrates your party should prevail. Jurors soon realize that arguing extensively your opponent's weaknesses occurs only when you have little good to say about your own case. Negative arguments often create negative impressions and should be avoided.

12. Volunteer weaknesses

While your closing argument should positively argue your strengths, this does not mean that you should entirely avoid weaknesses. Every trial will have some weaknesses. If it did not, the case would have been settled before trial.

Confronting weaknesses has two advantages. First, your weaknesses are your opponent's strengths. By addressing them first, you can in part deflate his later argument so that the jury does not hear those points for the first time from your opponent, the way he wants them argued. Take the wind out of his sails by raising his points first, and they will sound hollow and tired when he argues them. Second, the jury will respect your honesty and candor when openly and candidly discussing those weaknesses. Since your credibility as an advocate is critically important, this consideration should not be downplayed. Remember that jurors, like everyone else, are influenced by whom they like. Make sure that's you and your party.

Example:

Folks, I have a problem here. You're undoubtedly going to say: "Mr. Jones, you're asking us to give your client $150,000. Isn't that an awful lot of money?"

You're right, of course. That is a great deal of money to ask. But this is the kind of case where that kind of verdict is both reasonable and necessary. I propose that we review each element of damages and see why this is the minimum amount Frank Johnson is entitled to.

13. Force your opponent to argue his weaknesses

For the same reasons that you want to concentrate on your strengths, force your opponent to argue his weaknesses. The standard method is to ask a series of rhetorical questions during your argument that challenge your opponent to explain his weaknesses.

Example:

If, as the defense has been claiming all along, the collision happened the way the defendant said it did, why isn't there any corroboration? Wouldn't you expect that of all the people who witnessed the collision, they could find one person who would back them up? I'm sure Mr. Smith, when he argues, will answer this question that we've all been asking and wondering about.

When it is your opponent's turn to argue, he may take the bait and attempt to answer the question, thereby arguing a weakness and creating a negative impression. A few well-selected questions can often produce this desired effect.

14. Collect exceptional arguments

Every trial lawyer collects memorable approaches, excerpts, analogies, and techniques he has heard other lawyers use during closing arguments, adapts them to suit his own style, and adds them to his repertory for appropriate use in later trials. Note the emphasis on adaptation. All lawyers borrow from each other. However, any analogy, story, theme, or other type of argument that is borrowed and used verbatim will sound artificial and contrived. Borrowings must be put in your own language and style to be an effective persuasive tool.

15. Length of the argument

The trial judge, if he chooses to exercise his discretion, can set time limitations on the closing arguments. Many judges do set specific limits. Where, however, the judge does not, the only limitations are those imposed by the jury. Jurors, like other people, have a limited capacity to listen and absorb. Trials can be boring. Closing arguments, coming at the end of the trial, reach the jurors when their patience and attention are lowest.

A closing argument should therefore take the *minimum* time necessary to adequately summarize and analyze the evidence received at trial. A reasonable rule of thumb is for each side to use approximately 10 minutes of argument for every full day of evidence. A typical five-day jury trial would then give each side approximately 40 minutes for closing arguments. While these are only guidelines and should be varied by the number of witnesses and exhibits and the complexity of the case, it is clear that a closing argument that "runs on" loses the jury's attention and even incurs the danger of generating resentment.

16.   Splitting the plaintiff's closing and rebuttal arguments

Plaintiff, having the burden of proof, has the right to argue twice; that is, the right to argue first and, after the defense has argued, to make a rebuttal argument. How does plaintiff best utilize this advantage? Two considerations are involved. First, to what extent should plaintiff apportion his ammunition between his closing and rebuttal? Second, how should plaintiff apportion his time between the two arguments?

Plaintiff should fully cover all the points he intends to argue in the closing argument and resist the temptation to save the best arguments for rebuttal. Doing this has two dangers. The defendant, sensing that plaintiff has "sandbagged" during his closing argument, can waive his closing argument and prevent the plaintiff from arguing again. He can also make a restricted closing argument that will argue only one or two issues and prevent the plaintiff from arguing the unmentioned issues during his rebuttal. Knowing how strictly the court will sustain scope objections to far-ranging rebuttal arguments is of course critical here. Apportioning the time between the opening and rebuttal arguments rests in the sound discretion of the court. Some judges set specific time limitations on the arguments and hold counsel to them. Others may set no limits at all. Absent court requirements, plaintiff should split his time and use at least twice as much on the closing as on the rebuttal argument. This will allow a full closing argument, yet reserve enough time to make a complete rebuttal.

17.   Presentation style

Closing arguments are usually made directly in front of the jury box, approximately halfway from either end. You should stand close enough to maintain eye contact with each of the jurors, yet not so close that they feel uncomfortable. You should ordinarily stay seven or eight feet from the first row of jurors, so that those wearing bifocal glasses have no difficulty seeing you, moving closer only when necessary to show exhibits to them. Many courtrooms have lecterns, and some judges require you to make your arguments from the lectern. If you wish, or are required, to use it, make sure that the judge will allow you to move it to the location you want. However, don't use the lectern unless required, because it places a barrier between you and the jury.

Example:

In the following schematic diagram of a courtroom, you would normally make your closing arguments near the area marked "X."

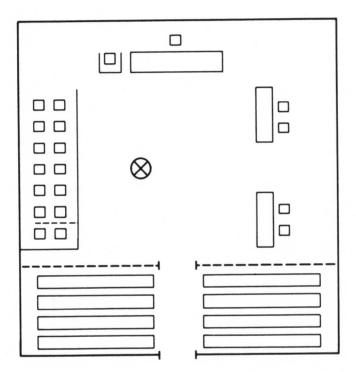

Presenting an effective closing argument involves both a physical and verbal style. They must be harmoniously combined to continuously project the belief that your side, based on the evidence, is entitled to win.

Your physical, or nonverbal, style must support your verbal presentation. First, maintain periodic eye contact with each juror, but neither single out any one juror or ignore others. This is most effectively done by directing an idea, in one or two sentences, to a specific juror, then directing your next point to another juror. Maintain eye contact with the juror you are talking to. Doing this will make each juror feel that you are individually talking to him.

Second, control your body movement so it reinforces your speech. Stand straight, with your feet planted firmly, and lean forward slightly. This stance is positive and authoritative. Avoid wandering around constantly, since this merely serves as a distraction. However, changing your position from time to time can effectively signal that you have completed one topic and are moving to another.

Third, use gestures that reinforce your points. Such gestures are those that draw jurors' attention to your face, since this is where the words are coming from. Accordingly, the gestures must be from the upper body, which include facial expressions, head and shoulder movement, and hand gestures that are above waist level. Avoid tapping feet, moving legs, slouching, playing with objects in your pockets, or using your hands while they are down at your sides, since these are all lower-body movements that distract jurors from concentrating on your speech.

Your verbal style must also be appropriate for persuasive speech. A closing argument is not an opening statement, which is basically informational speech. A closing argument must be forceful and persuasive. It recites evidence, but should also include inferences from the evidence, instructions, appeals to fairness and common sense, analogies and other persuasive techniques. Perhaps the safest approach is to view a closing argument as a discussion with the jury, in the same manner you would present your views on an important issue to a gathering of neighbors at someone's house.

Use plain, forceful, and active language, avoiding either slang or formal, stilted language. Jurors expect lawyers to use good English. Keep your sentences short and your structure simple, since this is much easier to follow and understand.

Also, vary your verbal style to support your arguments and maintain juror interest. Good, persuasive speakers have learned to control and use the variables that make up speech. These include loudness, pitch, speech rate and rhythm, pauses, silence, articulation and pronunciation. Each of these can and should be used and modulated to keep your speech patterns forceful and interesting.

Making effective closing arguments is an acquired skill. There is no such thing as the right way to make a closing argument. Every trial lawyer through experience learns what kind of presentation he is comfortable with, that seems natural for his personality and style, and that appears to work for him. Accordingly, do not try to copy or imitate another lawyer's style. That style will only work for him. Learning from others is important, but always adapt what you learn to your own individual style. Only the delivery style that you feel comfortable with will be effective with a jury.

§7.3. Structure

Closing arguments, like any other phase of the trial, should be prepared in advance and should usually follow a structure that parallels the opening statements and your case in chief. This procedure has two advantages. First, if the opening statement and case in chief were logically organized and effectively presented, your closing argument will be as well. Second, the parallel construction reinforces the earlier impressions.

Accordingly, the closing arguments should be a logical continuation and conclusion to your entire trial presentation.

The arguments, whether by plaintiff or defendant, are frequently patterned on the structural outline that follows. There is nothing mandatory about the outline. Your approach to closing arguments must necessarily be flexible to adapt to different types of cases and the unique characteristics of each case. Experienced, effective trial lawyers all argue cases differently by adding their own organization, perspective, and routines to the arguments. For the inexperienced, however, this structural outline is a useful guide on which to organize your closings.

1. Introduction
2. Parties
3. Scene
4. Instrumentalities
5. Weather and lighting
6. Damages (def.)
7. Issue
8. What happened
9. Basis of liability/nonliability or guilt/innocence
10. Corroboration
11. Other side and refutation
12. Instructions
13. Damages (pl.)
14. Conclusion

Notice that this structure divides the closing argument into two basic components. The first part, which essentially parallels the opening statement, simply reviews the evidence, using a narrative approach. The second part selectively takes the important evidence, witness by witness, exhibit by exhibit, and uses it to support your position on the issues in the case. The first part is a basic, logically organized review of the facts; the second part is essentially argument, using only those witnesses, exhibits, inferences, and techniques that will persuade the jury to resolve the disputed issues in your favor.

The following sections will analyze each of the components of this closing argument structure. To see how these components fit together to create an integrated closing argument, see the examples in §7.5 below.

1. Introduction

In the traditional introduction to the closing arguments the attorney usually thanks the jurors for their attention in fulfilling their duty to our system of jury trials, tells the jurors that the parties are allowed to review the evidence already presented, and leads into the discussion of the evidence. It should be short, smooth, and in good taste. The first few lines should be positive and get the jury's attention.

Example (plaintiff):

May it please the court (look at the judge) . . . *counsel* (look at opposing counsel) . . . *members of the jury* (direct and continue eye contact with the jury): *On behalf of my client, Frank Smith, and everyone else connected with this trial, we thank you for your attention to our case. Being jurors is a difficult duty, and six days is a long time to listen to evidence. Every case, however, is an important case, not only to the parties, but to our jury system. For carrying out your duties as jurors, we all thank you.*

In my opening statement I said we expected the evidence to show certain facts. I think we have kept our promise to you.

Example (defendant):

May it please the court . . . counsel . . . and members of the jury: We also wish to express an appreciation on behalf of the Court, the lawyers, the parties, and everyone connected with this case for the attention and consideration you have given us throughout this trial.

I have said many times that there are always two sides to a lawsuit, just as there are two sides to every argument or controversy. What has the evidence shown our side of this case to be?

Most lawyers today avoid thanking the jury for its attention, and other introductory remarks, and get directly to the facts. They believe that any such remarks can be interpreted the wrong way by the jury and use up time that could be better spent arguing the facts.

Example (plaintiff — civil):

May it please the court, counsel, members of the jury: On June 15, 1983, Joan Carter's life ended when the defendant, drunk and speeding, crashed into her car and crushed the life out of her body. Her family is here today asking that you do her, and them, justice.

Example (defendant-criminal):

Your Honor, counsel: This case has shown how, when the police fail to do their job, when they fail to do a thorough investigation, the wrong person can be accused of a crime. It's a nightmare that happened to Bill Johnson, and it all started on May 15, 1985.

These modern types of openings are effective because they immediately grab jurors' attention and let them know that you are worth listening to. Such openings are also consistent with modern psychology and speech research, which show that listeners give speakers a very short time to impress them before tuning out. Accordingly, the quick, forceful introduction is becoming the standard way in which effective trial lawyers begin their closing arguments.

In the next sections, from parties to what happened, highlight the most significant and favorable aspects of the evidence. As previously noted, these other introductory sections should not be a detailed review. The jurors heard the evidence. Unless the trial was unusually long or complicated, they will collectively remember everything that was put in evidence during the trial. Your job is to refresh their recollection of what you consider important to convince them that you are entitled to win.

Lead into sections under the assumption, however, that the jurors have remembered everything. Collectively, the chances are overwhelming that they have. Not acting under this assumption creates the substantial risk that you will sound condescending. This is always fatal to your credibility.

Examples:

> *As you remember....*
>
> *You will recall that....*
>
> *This intersection, as we now know....*
>
> *As we heard during the trial....*

The significance of these sections is that the pertinent background will be created for the closing argument's critical latter sections. When this is effectively done, you will have created a mental picture of the parties, scene, weather, and other elements that the jury will use as a framework against which it can understand and evaluate the rest of your argument.

Reviewing these preliminary matters should not be too argumentative. It's a good place to reinforce your credibility as a fair and accurate reporter of the evidence, credibility you can advantageously use later.

The defense, of course, argues second. It should not repeat the same evidence. Its role is to supplement the plaintiff's argument and fill in what is important to its side of the case.

2. Parties

In this section you should briefly survey the important witnesses and remind the jury of certain background facts that bear directly on the witness' credibility.

Example (pl.):

> While the parties are now known to you, there are a few things in Mr. Smith's background that are important to keep in mind as you consider the evidence. As you know, Mr. Smith is a. . . .

Example (def.):

> Counsel for the plaintiff has mentioned certain things about the parties here. He forgot, however, to mention certain facts and they are important to keep in mind as you decide this case. My client, Mr. Jones, has been employed by the XYZ Company for thirty years. He. . . .

3. Scene

If the scene of an event is important, or is in dispute, you should again describe it, stressing the important aspects.

Example (pl.):

> This robbery, as we know, occurred in a tavern at the corner of North Avenue and Clark Street. This tavern itself was. . . .

Example (def.):

> There are certain things about this tavern that are important. First, like any tavern, it was dimly lighted. It was crowded. It. . . .

4. Instrumentalities

In many cases, particularly in accident and products liability cases, a vehicle, a piece of machinery, or other objects play important roles, so they should be reviewed in appropriate detail.

Example (pl.):

> The car Mr. Smith was driving was a Ford sedan. It was only one year old and had only 6,000 miles on it. The car had passed the city vehicle inspection and had recently been tuned up and checked by the dealership. That car was in excellent mechanical condition.

Example (def.):

> This insurance policy, it's true, had a double indemnity clause, which provided for payment of twice the policy amount in the event of accidental death. It

also had what is commonly known as a suicide clause. This clause, which the insured agreed to, provided that. . . .

5. Weather and lighting

Weather and lighting are important considerations whenever eyewitness testimony is involved, since they bear so heavily on a witness' ability to observe accurately.

Example (pl.):

What was the weather like that day? It was clear and dry. It had rained earlier in the day, but when this collision occurred, the streets had already dried.

Example (def.):

We have no issue about the weather. It was sunny, clear, and dry.

Example (pl.):

That tavern was well lighted. There were lights over the bar, lights over the front entrance, lights in the street that shined through the front windows, and lights from the jukebox. There was more than enough light for the patrons to observe accurately and identify the robbers.

Example (def.):

That tavern wasn't well lighted. It was pretty much like any other tavern you've ever seen. Successful taverns create moods, in large part through dim lighting. This tavern was no exception. It had only a few small shaded lights spread throughout the tavern. This is hardly the kind of lighting you would want to have when correctly identifying the robbers is critically important.

6. Damages (defendant)

In civil cases where both liability and damages are in issue, the usual order for the defendant is to argue damages first, then liability. The damages can be most easily and credibly discussed before the discussion of the issues. Under this order you can review the damages and conclude that if the plaintiff has in fact been damaged, his demands are unreasonable and he is certainly not entitled to the amounts he is demanding. Immediately afterwards you can state that the real issue is liability, and spend the remainder of your argument on that issue. This order gives the defendant's argument a positive tone. Revising the order, arguing damages last, makes you end the argument on a negative tone and usually gives the impression that the defendant is really conceding liability in the case.

Even when the defense is defending principally on liability, the only safe approach is still to discuss damages to reduce them as much as possible. If you fail to discuss damages at all, and the jury finds for the plaintiff on the issue of liability, it will have only the benefit of plaintiff's damages analysis when deciding on the amount of damages to award.

Example:

Plaintiff has asked for $220,000. It is clear in this case that Mr. Jones does not owe anything since he is not liable. However, since it relates to another issue, we would like to discuss these claimed damages now, and see how well they hold up.

Defendant should then go into the permissible elements of damages, particularly the intangible ones, and show that plaintiff has inflated the reasonable damages to get a windfall recovery. You are then in a good position to go into the real issue in the case.

Example:

It is unreasonable for the plaintiff to claim he has actually been damaged in the amount of $220,000, but, as I mentioned before, that is not even the issue here. The real issue that you have to decide is: was the plaintiff contributorily negligent? The answer is obvious: yes, he was. Whatever damages he may have sustained, they were at least in part the result of the plaintiff's own negligence.

7. Issue

Selecting and stating the issue is critically important. The issue should obviously be your strongest point, the one you can win on. Just as important, you must state the issue as simply as possible, in a way that the jury will remember. The issue should be phrased in such a way that a favorable answer will be obvious. After stating the issue you should emphatically answer the issue in your favor. In civil cases, this is also a convenient time to review, or even read from, the pleadings in the case.

Remember that stating the issue is a contest to determine which side can force the jury to recognize and evaluate the issue from its perspective. If you can get the jury to see the issue your way, the jury is much more likely to evaluate the evidence favorably as well.

As plaintiff, the issue can also be effectively stated *after* the narration of events and the basis of liability, just before beginning the corroboration argument. As defendant, however, you normally want to get your version of the issues before the jurors as soon as possible.

Example (pl.):

What is the question you are to decide in this case, or, as the lawyer put it, what's the issue in this case? There is only one issue. It is simply this: Was the defendant negligent in driving his car so that he caused the collision which injured Mr. Smith? The evidence in this case clearly *shows that the defendant was the sole cause of Mr. Smith's injuries, and that the defendant most certainly was negligent.*

Example (def.):

Counsel for the plaintiff has said that the only issue is whether the defendant was negligent in driving his car. That's not really the issue here. The real *issue is: Was the plaintiff contributorily negligent? Are his injuries the result of his own negligence? The evidence here clearly shows that the plaintiff was injured through his own fault.*

Example (pl.):

What, then, is this case all about? The issue, simply put, is: Did we prove, as required by law, that the defendant intentionally and without provocation shot and killed Bobby Jackson? The evidence in this case has obviously shown that the defendant did precisely that, and is therefore guilty of murder.

Example (def.):

The prosecutor would like *you to believe that the issue here is whether my client, John Franklin, intentionally shot the deceased. But that's not the issue here. That's not it at all! What you've really got to decide here is: Did the prosecution* disprove, *beyond a reasonable doubt, that John Franklin was entitled to defend himself against Johnson's assault? The answer is obvious. The prosecution hasn't disproved it, because it's perfectly clear here that John Franklin shot Jackson because Jackson was about to attack him with a weapon, and defending yourself under those circumstances simply is not a crime. That's justified self-defense.*

8. What happened

Your description of what happened should parallel your opening statement and be in the same narrative form that you have utilized up to this point.

The picture of an event, whether a collision or some other action, should be done *toward* the jurors so that you are facing them, and should be from your party's perspective. Have the jury assume that they are facing a certain direction, so that streets and buildings will be in their most advantageous position. Plan the picture so that the critical action goes toward them. The picture should be done through the eyes of *your* party or an important favorable witness, so *your* version becomes clear.

In personal injury cases the plaintiff's picture should stop at the point where the accident and injury occurred. Save what happened to the plaintiff afterwards for the damages arguments.

Example (pl.):

What happened at the intersection of Elm Avenue and Clark Street the afternoon of December 13, 1984? John Smith was driving south on Clark Street. He. . . .

Example (def.):

December 13, 1984, started out as an ordinary day for Bob Jones. He was driving on Elm Avenue, eastbound, on his way home. Up ahead he could see the intersection of Clark Street. He. . . .

Notice that both plaintiff's and defendant's narration of the accident is from each one's own perspective. The picture is done as though the jury is sitting in the car, traveling toward the intersection where the collision occurred. This technique works equally well in criminal cases and any other cases involving action. The reason for this technique is simple: Get the jury to accept your picture of the event involved, and you are well on the way to a favorable verdict.

9. Basis of liability/nonliability or guilt/innocence

This section should be the emotional culmination of your picture narrative. It should sum up the facts that you have just reviewed in legal terms so that the jury clearly understands that what happened necessarily leads to the legal conclusion that requires a verdict in your favor.

Example (pl.):

What did the defendant do that was negligent here? He failed to keep a proper lookout. He failed to yield the right of way. He failed to maintain a proper speed under the circumstances involved. All of this was contrary to law. From the evidence you have heard here the defendant was clearly the direct and sole cause of this collision.

Example (def.):

Ladies and gentlemen of the jury, the plaintiff did not look to see if any cars were coming. He did not come to a complete stop before entering the intersection. He failed to drive his car with the due care and caution required. It is obvious that the plaintiff was contributorily negligent and that his own negligence caused this unfortunate accident.

10. Corroboration

The narrative portion of the closing argument is now over. From this point on, your review of the evidence should be through the testimony of individual witnesses and exhibits admitted in evidence. This allows you to repeat the critical testimony that supports your side without really appearing to do so, thus avoiding boring the jury.

At this point selectivity becomes important. Skip neutral facts. Pick the significant parts of the important testimony and exhibits that are the heart of your case and argue them emphatically. This should be done in some detail, since the corroboration part of your argument will normally be the lengthiest segment.

Consider the following types of corroboration that you can argue:

1. Client's testimony
2. Other witnesses' testimony
3. Exhibits in evidence
4. Other physical facts
5. Common sense
6. Human nature
7. Probabilities and improbabilities
8. Particular cautionary instructions
9. Pleadings
10. Discovery answers

When you are arguing corroboration based on a particular witness, identify that witness to the jury.

Example:

You remember Mr. Doe. He was the man standing on the southwest corner of the intersection and saw the whole thing happen.

After identifying the witness, build him up before you review what the witness' critical testimony was.

Example:

Mr. Doe has been employed at XYZ Corporation for 18 years. He has no interest in the outcome of the case. He does not know the parties.

Argue that your witnesses are the best and most reliable ones available.

Example:

Isn't this the way it really happened? Who was in a better position to see what really happened? Who was the only witness who was looking at the intersection before the crash occurred? Who was the only person who saw this entire collision from the beginning to the end?

If a witness is an expert or has special qualifications, build those up before reviewing his testimony.

Example:

You recall Dr. Good. He was the distinguished-looking gentleman in the gray suit who had the silver hair. What are his qualifications? He is a board-certified orthopedist, the chief resident in orthopedics at Rush Hospital. He has treated hundreds of leg fractures just like the one involved here.

When you get into the witness' testimony itself, drag out the significant testimony slowly, bit by bit. The question and answer method is a useful one to accomplish this.

Examples:

Remember when I asked Dr. Good how, based on his experience, he believed this injury could have occurred, and he said: "In my opinion this injury was caused when the left leg was struck by a sharp, heavy object"?

Remember when I asked Dr. Good if . . . ? And remember his answer? He said: ". . ." What else did Dr. Good say? ". . ." Remember my last question to Dr. Good? ". . ." Remember his answer to that question? ". . ."

Exhibits and statements of other physical facts can be effective corroborative elements. Like witness testimony, these should be drawn out bit by bit. Show or read the exhibit to the jury, but put it away when done.

Example:

How else do we know this is true? Remember plaintiff's Exhibit #1, the insurance policy? It is in evidence and you will be able to take it to the jury room. Look particularly closely at page 2 of the policy. It says there that. . . .

Common sense, human nature, and probabilities and improbabilities can be argued in the same way.

Example:

Does it make sense that a 68-year-old woman would get on a bus that way? Wouldn't she be extremely careful every time she entered a bus and went up the steps?

Example:

> *Does it square with your common sense and ordinary human nature that Mr.*
> *Smith would. . . . This simply does not make any sense, yet that is what the other*
> *side would have you believe here.*

11. Other side and refutation

It is generally advisable as plaintiff to mention at least what the defense's
likely contentions are and refute them. In this way, the jury will not hear
the defense's arguments for the first time from that side. By stating their
arguments first, you can phrase them in a favorable way and more easily
refute them with evidence produced during the trial. Psychology research
has shown that persons are more resistant to counterarguments if they
have been given reasons to resist them beforehand.

Example (pl.):

> *What does the defendant contend here? He would have you believe that he*
> *was driving in a safe and diligent manner. He contends that. . . . He claims*
> *that. . . .*

After stating each significant claim that the other side has or will
make, refute it with any available evidence. The refutation is done in the
same manner as the corroboration of your side. Pick the important testimony, exhibits, and other corroborative elements and demonstrate to the
jury that this evidence contradicts the other side's contentions. Argue that
the reasonable and sensible result of that evidence is that the other side's
contentions cannot be accepted.

A key element of refutation is to minimize and belittle the unfavorable testimony in the case. You can challenge the witness' background
and qualifications, his recollection, or knowledge of facts. This is a good
place to work in the cautionary instructions relating to the credibility of
witnesses and factors the jury can consider that reflect adversely on a
witness, such as bias, interest, and prejudice.

The defendant, of course, arguing second and not having a rebuttal
argument, must spend more time on the plaintiff's contentions and their
refutation.

Example (def.):

> *What does the other side claim happened? They would have you believe that*
> *the plaintiff was exercising due care for his safety and others', and that he was*
> *acting as the ordinary prudent man would act in every respect. Well, let's go back*
> *to Clark Street and get into that car with the plaintiff. What did the plaintiff do?*
> *He. . . . You remember Mr. Doe. He testified that. . . . He also told you that. . . .*
> *Isn't that what the plaintiff really did here? On the other hand, what would an*

ordinary prudent man do under these identical circumstances? Wouldn't he ...? Isn't that what you would expect a safe and cautious driver to have done?

12. Instructions

The key instructions that the court will submit to the jury should be summarized and related to the evidence. Since the instruction conference will usually occur at the close of all the evidence, you will know exactly what instructions the court will give when you present your closing argument. Instructions that are commonly used are:

a. credibility of witnesses
b. using common sense and experience in life
c. sympathy cannot be considered
d. burden of proof
e. elements of your causes of action
f. elements of damages
g. elements of the defense
h. definitions of important legal terms

These instructions need not be argued at this point. Although the elements instructions are often discussed here, the other instructions involving credibility of witnesses, common sense, and sympathy are more appropriately used when discussing the corroboration of your case or the refutation of theirs.

Arguing instructions involves both favorable and unfavorable instructions. You should argue not only the key instructions that favor you, but must also meet the unfavorable instructions and supply the jury with answers to them. As defendant you should usually emphasize that the jury must follow, as they previously promised, the law as the court gives it, whether or not they agree with it.

Some jurisdictions require that you read instructions verbatim when referring to them. Other jurisdictions do not allow you to read instructions verbatim but require you to paraphrase the essence of the instructions when discussing them.

Example:

I would like for a moment to discuss with you the instructions which I believe the court will give you at the conclusion of your case. I believe the court will instruct you that.... The court will also tell you that.... And what has the evidence shown here? It clearly shows that....

Example:

The court will instruct you, I believe, that you are entitled to use your common sense and experiences in the affairs of life when you deliberate on your verdict. The court will also tell you that. . . . The evidence in this case clearly shows that plain-tiff did not. . . . I also believe the court will instruct you that if you find that we were not guilty of negligence, or if you find that plaintiff was at fault in any way for his own injuries, then you are not to consider damages at all because there will be no reason to do so. What has this case shown? The evidence shows clearly that you need not consider damages here at all because the plaintiff was the cause of his own injuries.

13. Damages (plaintiff)

Damages in civil cases, as previously noted, should be argued by plaintiff and defendant at different times. Plaintiff should use the damages argu-ment as the last part of his closing argument. In personal injury cases the injuries to plaintiff are the emotional highlight of his case and the one that he wants to leave as the last impression on the jury. Many plaintiff's attorneys merely ask for a certain sum in their closing argument, saving the detailed support for their rebuttal argument, when the defense can no longer respond to it.

Plaintiff should argue all the facts in the damages argument from the point of the collision on, since this is where his picture ended. After summarizing what happened to the plaintiff, he should then review each permissible element of damages.

Example:

Before this collision Mr. Smith was a healthy man. He was a successful busi-nessman moving up in his company. He enjoyed outdoor sports and a wide variety of recreational activities. He was active with his children and took care of his home and property. What happened to Mr. Smith after the collision occurred?

(Symptoms) You will recall that Bob Smith was struck on his side by the car and thrown down. He felt a sharp pain in his lower right leg. Finally, someone helped him into the ambulance that arrived and took him to Rush Hospital. . . .

(Diagnosis) Dr. Good arrived at the hospital a short while later. He saw Bob Smith in the emergency room. Dr. Good ordered X rays and examined Mr. Smith. . . .

(Treatment) Bob Smith was in the hospital for 23 days. His cast was not removed until four months later. During that entire period of time, he could not move his leg or exercise in any way. After the cast was removed, the doctors told him he should try to exercise his leg. Mr. Smith began a program of exercise. . . .

(Prognosis) Members of the jury, that is the way Mr. Smith remains to this day. What is his present condition? What can he do with that leg? He can't. . . . He can't. . . .

Members of the jury, if a man is injured because of the negligence of another, the law allows him compensation for those injuries which are known as damages. You will be instructed, I believe, that if you find by the greater weight of the evidence that the defendant caused and was responsible for Mr. Smith's injuries, then you may award damages to Mr. Smith and against the defendant.

In considering the damages, there are numerous elements you may and should properly consider. You will be instructed that one of the proper elements is. . . . The next element of damages is. . . . There is one final element of damages which is very important, and that is. . . .

The following are the usual permissible elements of damages:

a. nature and extent of injuries
b. physical disability
c. loss of earnings
d. loss of future earnings
e. medical expenses
f. future medical expenses
g. disfigurement
h. mental anguish
i. pain and suffering
j. future pain and suffering

It is usually preferable to state what the amount of damages you are asking for is, and then justify it by discussing each permissible and relevant element. Jurors may resent your withholding the final figure by discussing the elements first, particularly where the amount is large or composed mainly of general damages. This can sound a good deal like a salesperson's pitch, discussing the merits of the product before disclosing its price. In arguing the elements themselves, it is best to argue them in the same order in which they will be read to the jurors when the judge instructs them on damages.

As plaintiff, compute each element of the damages precisely. It is usually effective to use a chart and compute the damages before the jury. This tells the jury you are careful, have thought about each element of damages, and are not inclined to casually throw out the figures and expect the jury to accept them. In addition, show how the damages will actually help the plaintiff, rather than merely argue he's entitled to them. Jurors will be much more receptive to awarding large verdicts if they can visualize how the money will help restore what the plaintiff lost.

Example:

Why is the sum of $43,000 the minimum that is necessary to cover Mr. Smith's future medical expenses? You heard how he will need to use a wheelchair for the rest of his life. You have heard how a wheelchair today costs $700 and lasts at best five years. Mr. Smith's life expectancy is 30 years. This means that he will have to spend $4,200 solely to have a decent wheelchair throughout his life. But that's only the beginning. He will need regular physical therapy treatment for the next 30 years. This will cost $700 each year. In addition. . . .

A more difficult question is whether to argue the concrete elements (specials) or the intangibles (general damages) first. It is easier, of course, to prove the concrete elements. On the other hand, the jury may be startled by the amounts you are asking for the intangibles, where the concrete damages are low. Trial lawyers differ in their approach to this problem. Regardless of your order, after stating the total figure, you should use a blackboard or poster board and review the elements of damages one by one.

Example:

The first element of damages you should consider is the nature and extent of the injuries. In a land of normal people, what is it worth to be able to walk, stand, and lead a normal active life like everyone else? May I suggest the sum of $40,000 as a fair figure? If you think this figure is too high, it is your duty to determine what is fair. If you believe the figure is too low, it is your duty to raise it. We leave that figure to your sound judgment. If counsel thinks $40,000 is too high to adequately compensate Mr. Smith for the injury to his leg, which he lives with every day, and will continue to live with every day of his life, let the defense tell you why it is too large.

Each permissible element of damages should be reviewed in the same fashion, to justify the total figure you have asked.

14. Conclusion

Your conclusion should smoothly and efficiently sum up your position and request a proper verdict. The conclusion is a proper place to give the jurors a tastefully stated emotional request for a favorable verdict.

Example (pl.):

Above all, please remember this. This is Bob Smith's only day in court. This is the only time he can come before the jury and present his evidence and obtain justice under the law. This is the only time that he can receive in a court of law lawful compensation and an adequate award for the serious injuries he has suffered.

Based on the evidence and under the instructions of the court, we ask you to return the only verdict you can reasonably return, a verdict in favor of Mr. Smith for $220,000, the only sum sufficient to lawfully compensate him for the injuries and losses he sustained through the negligence of the defendant.

As defendant you must mention that you do not have a rebuttal argument as the plaintiff does, so you will not have a second opportunity to address the jury.

Example (def.):

> *This is my last chance to tell you our side of this case. I don't have a second chance, as they do, to address you again. I have tried to anticipate everything they say, but I can only ask you to remember to search through the evidence because all the answers to what they will say will be there.*
>
> *It is unfortunate, members of the jury, that the plaintiff was injured. I know you feel just as we do on that subject, and that is only natural, but at the beginning of the case each of you told me that sympathy was not going to govern you in making your decision here. You told me that you would decide this case solely from the evidence and from the instructions which you would receive from the court.*
>
> *We ask you, therefore, that under this evidence and under these instructions, you return the only verdict justice calls for, a verdict in favor of my client, Frank Jones.*

§7.4. *Rebuttal*

Plaintiff, having the burden of proof, is allotted a last time at bat during closing arguments: rebuttal. Everyone likes to have the last word, and trial lawyers are no exception. Hence, they view the rebuttal argument as a valuable trial weapon, one that can sometimes mean the difference between victory and defeat.

The rebuttal argument, like all parts of the trial, should be planned in advance. Here coordination between the opening argument and the rebuttal is essential. While the opening should not "sandbag" and leave everything important to the rebuttal, neither should it steal the rebuttal's thunder. What is required is an intelligent apportionment between the two. Decide what aspects of the case should be emphasized in each argument. What stories, analogies, or other routines will each argument use? Make sure that neither the opening nor rebuttal argument steps on the other's toes. This can only be accomplished where both arguments are viewed as integral halves of a single process. For example, in personal injury cases plaintiff's attorneys often save their details of the damages argument for rebuttal.

Just as there is no single "right way" to organize and deliver a closing argument, the same holds true for rebuttal. Experienced trial lawyers vary greatly in their content and delivery of rebuttal arguments. However, it is useful to structure your rebuttal argument along the following lines:

a. introduction
b. your strongest points
c. other side's contentions
d. refutation with other strong points
e. conclusion

Notice the emphasis on *your* strong points. Many trial lawyers, even experienced ones, make a major conceptual mistake during rebuttal: they merely respond to questions raised during the defense's closing argument. This is a serious mistake, because it is a negative, passive posture. That's exactly what the defense wants you to do. A clever defense lawyer will, during his argument, throw out a series of questions and challenge you to answer each and every one of them during your rebuttal. Resist the temptation. Use the rebuttal to hit hard with your strongest points. Drive home your theory of the case. Keep the argument active. Use it to pose obvious questions that the defense has not answered yet (and now can not). Periodically weave in some of the defense's contentions when your refutation fits in logically with the preconceived structure of your rebuttal. Above all, keep the rebuttal active and positive, stressing the major points that will convince the jury to return a favorable verdict.

§7.5 Examples of closing arguments

The following closing arguments are from the same cases as the opening statements examples in Chapter III.

1. Criminal case (murder): *People v. Sylvester Strong*

(The defendant, Sylvester Strong, has been charged with murdering Shelley Williams on April 25, 1985. The prosecution claims that the shooting was in retaliation for a prior incident. The defense claims the shooting was justifiable self-defense.)

Closing argument — prosecution

May it please the court, counsel, ladies and gentlemen of the jury. On behalf of my client, the People of the State of Illinois, we thank you for your attention to this case. Being jurors, as I'm sure you've come to appreciate, is a difficult duty. This case, like every other case, is important, not only to the people directly involved in it, but also to our country's system of justice, which is the jury trial system. For carrying out your duty, all of us thank you.

At the beginning of the case, during the opening statements, we said that the evidence you would hear in this case would show that this defendant, Sylvester Strong, is guilty of the

(Introduction)

The introduction here is done simply. The prosecutor should generally avoid extended "thanking the jury" statements.

crime of murder. What has that evidence turned out to be?

We now know that the defendant, Sylvester Strong, shot and killed the victim, Shelley Williams, on the 2300 block of Bloomingdale Avenue on April 25, 1985. We know that the victim was completely unarmed when he was shot, and we know that he was shot two times in the back, the second shot coming when he was lying face down on the sidewalk, helpless and unprotected. In short, we have shown, and the defense concedes, that Sylvester Strong killed Shelley Williams; and the only remaining question is whether that killing is a murder as well!

How did Shelley Williams come to die so tragically? As we now know, Shelley, his mother, Rosie Garrett, and various other family members and friends were in two cars, returning from the north side of Chicago. As the cars turned from Winnebago on to Bloomingdale, the first car, driven by Shelley, stopped. He saw the defendant, Sylvester Strong, riding down Bloomingdale on a bicycle. Shelley got out of his car and walked over to where the defendant had stopped and started talking to him. Shelley stopped and talked to the defendant because he had heard that the defendant had sworn at his mother at a party the previous day. Shelley motioned to his mother, who had parked at the corner, to get out and come over. This she did. Shelley then asked her: "Is this the boy that cussed you out?" She answered, "Yes, it is." Shelley told him to apologize directly to his mother.

Suddenly, George Howard, the defendant's brother-in-law, ran up to them, with a handgun. He fired two shots in the air. The defendant then grabbed the gun from Howard, saying: "Give me the gun — you're not trying to shoot him." The defendant then pointed the gun at Shelley, who said: "I don't want to fight," while waving his arms. Shelley backed up, and the defendant fired the first shot, hitting him in the arm. Shelley turned to run, and the defendant fired the second shot, hitting

(Parties, scene, instrumentalities, weather and lighting)

Since none of these is really in issue, they are skipped over.

(Issue)

The issue is stated as positively as possible.

(What happened)

Notice that the narrative of the occurrence closely parallels the prosecution's opening statement. This always reinforces the impression that you have delivered on the representations you made during the opening statement.

Note also that the narrative is done in an active, "you are there" style.

him in the back. Shelley fell, face down, on the sidewalk, next to a fire hydrant by the corner of Bloomingdale and Winnebago. That's when the defendant walked over and fired the third shot into the back of a helpless and unarmed victim.

The defendant then ran westbound on Bloomingdale. Rosie yelled for someone to stop him. Clarence Williams, the victim's brother, jumped into the victim's car and drove down Bloomingdale to cut the defendant off and keep him from escaping. Clarence jumped out of the car, and kicked the defendant in the head to keep him from running away.

Other people, including the defendant's wife, who was armed with a baseball bat, came to the scene. Rosie took the bat away from her, then started beating the defendant with it. We don't deny that one bit. She kept on hitting the defendant, who had just shot her son to death, until the police arrived.

Not contesting that the defendant was beaten is probably the better approach, since it prevents the defense from making a big issue out of it.

Shelley Williams, the victim, was taken to a nearby hospital, but it was too late. The three gunshots had done their job. Shelley Williams was dead by the time he reached the hospital. The autopsy later showed that the fatal shot entered Shelley's lower back, traveled in an upward direction, piercing the lungs so that they filled up with blood, and pierced his heart as well.

That, in a nutshell, is what our evidence has proved here. That evidence has proved, beyond a reasonable doubt, that on April 25, 1985, the defendant, Sylvester Strong, intentionally shot and killed the victim, Shelley Williams, with a handgun, and that there was absolutely no justification for the shooting. That is why this evidence has proved that the defendant is guilty of murder.

(Basis of guilt)

This summary closely parallels the elements of murder.

How do we know it really happened this way? Remember when Rosie Garrett testified? What did she tell you? She told you she'd been following her son's car to Bloomingdale Avenue, when she saw her son Shelley stop

(Corroboration)

The corroboration takes the essential parts of the important

his car, get out and walk over to the defendant, who'd been riding down the street on a bicycle. She saw them talking, then Shelley motioned for her to join them. When Shelley asked her if this was the man who had previously insulted her and cussed her, she said, "Yes." Shelley then demanded that the defendant apologize directly to her. What else did Rosie Garrett tell you? Suddenly George Howard appeared and fired a gun two times into the air. The defendant then grabbed the gun from him, yelling: "You're not trying to shoot him — give me the gun!" Rosie Garrett then stood there as the defendant, methodically and deliberately, fired three shots into her son, killing him on the spot. What did Rosie do next? Realizing that the gun was now empty, she grabbed a baseball bat from Sylvester's wife and, seeing the defendant trying to escape, did what any reasonable person would have done under the same circumstances. She ran to where the defendant was and started hitting him with the bat to keep him from getting away, until the police arrived a couple of minutes later.

witnesses and repeats the testimony. This should be done by referring directly to the heart of the witness' testimony.

Who else told you it happened this way? Clarence Williams, the victim's brother, who graduated from high school, enlisted and served in the Army in Vietnam, and, since his return, has been working as a master mechanic for General Motors, also testified. Everything he saw and heard corroborated Rosie Garrett. Of course, since he remained by his car, he couldn't hear all of the conversation between Shelley, his mother, and the defendant. However, he could see that Shelley did nothing to provoke the defendant, and could see that neither Shelley nor his mother were armed in any way. What he told you he saw next was that George Howard came up, fired a handgun into the air, the defendant grabbed it and emptied the gun into his brother's back. Seeing the defendant running away, he jumped into the car, chased the defendant, and cut him off a short distance away. He then kicked the defendant to keep him from getting away until the police came. Ladies and gentlemen of the jury, everything Clarence Williams told you

Using rhetorical questions is often an effective way of introducing a new topic.

about that day supports, is consistent with, and corroborates, Rosie Garrett's testimony.

Who else testified? Remember Willie Williams? He was only an acquaintance of the victim, not a family member, who happened to be with them that afternoon. He doesn't have any ax to grind here. He's not biased in favor of any side here. He simply told you what he saw that day to the best of his memory. What did he see? Since he had run a short distance away when the first shots rang out, he was a little further away than the others, but he did turn to see the defendant pull the trigger of the gun three times, shooting the victim three times, the last time when he was lying helpless on the sidewalk.

What about the other witnesses? All of them — the police officers who arrived at the scene, the ballistics expert who confirmed that this handgun matched the bullets removed from the victim's body, and the pathologist who performed the autopsy and learned that the fatal shot pierced the victim's lungs and heart — as well as the exhibits admitted in evidence, all of these are consistent with the eyewitness. In short, all of the evidence, bar none, corroborates the eyewitnesses.

> Corroboration by exhibits, physical evidence, and expert testimony should always be mentioned.

Now, you're probably going to ask yourself, why did this shooting happen? What motive was there? It's apparent that the defendant shot and killed Shelley Williams because he got angry when forced to apologize to Rosie Garrett and, as so often happens, a gun was nearby. Please keep in mind, however, that we are not required to prove a motive for the shooting. The Court will instruct you on this point later. All we are required to prove, and we have proved, is that the defendant shot and killed Shelley Williams, he intended to do it, and was not justified in doing it.

> A weakness in the case is that there is no apparent motive in the case sufficient to cause a murder. The best the prosecution can do is to suggest one, then remind the jury that the law does not make motive a required element of murder.

What would the defense have you believe? The defendant testified, and claims that on the day before, April 24, there was a party where he and Rosie Garrett had words. He, however, would have you believe that Rosie Garrett, not

> **(Other side and refutation)**
>
> Note that the other side's contentions are

he, was using all the foul and insulting language. He claims that after the police arrived and broke up the argument, Rosie and some others said they would come back tomorrow and finish it. What does he say about the 25th? The defendant would have you believe that he was merely riding his bicycle down the street when he was confronted by Shelley, who immediately started swearing at him. He claims that George Howard came by, and suddenly everyone was getting out of the two cars with baseball bats and two-by-fours. They surrounded him, and for no apparent reason, started beating him. He claims he was already bloodied and couldn't really see because of all the blood in his face, when he heard the gunshots and somehow got the handgun from George Howard. He then claims that he fired blindly, solely to get this armed mob off him.

They also called Ada May, the defendant's mother-in-law. Her recollection, to no one's surprise, was exactly consistent with the defendant's when it came to the argument the day before. As far as the 25th is concerned, she really couldn't remember any details, although she was sure, again to no one's surprise, that she saw Rosie Garrett beating the defendant with a baseball bat.

We have, then, a classic case of testimony that, as far as what happened on April 25 is concerned, is contradictory, and it's your duty as the finder of fact to decide where the truth lies. In other words, you've got to decide which witnesses are telling the truth. When you decide on the credibility of the witnesses, the court, I believe, will tell you that you should consider their demeanor while testifying, gauge it against other testimony, measure it against your common sense and experiences in life, and see if the witnesses have any bias, interest, or motive that could affect their testimony.

Remember the witnesses we called in our case? They were all hardworking, decent people who told you what happened. Their testimony was consistent on every important fact. They all said that the victim was completely unarmed when

stated to make clear that you don't believe they are true. Using the "he claims that" types of predicates clearly establishes that.

Credibility of witnesses, where you have two diametrically opposed versions of the facts, must be argued. It's always effective to refer to the credibility instruction the court will give.

Common sense should always be argued, since this is probably the single most important basis for the

he was shot. They were not contradicted in any way during the cross-examinations. Finally, doesn't what they say make sense? Doesn't it square with your experiences in life? The *only way* the victim could have been shot the way he was — once in the arm, and twice in the back — is if it happened the way our witnesses say it did. It is totally impossible for the defendant, shooting "blindly" as he would have you believe, to just happen to shoot *only* the victim, and just happen to shoot him twice in the back. Not only does the physical and medical evidence contradict the defense, but the only witness who testified directly to this version of the events was the defendant himself. When you consider the credibility of his testimony, keep in mind that, of all the witnesses here, he's the most obviously biased and interested one. If ever a man had a motive to distort the truth and fabricate a story, it's got to be the defendant in a criminal case charged with murder.

Finally, there's one witness the defense simply can't get around, and that's Arthur Anderson. Mr. Anderson, you'll remember, is a friend of the *defendant*. If his testimony was going to be slanted toward anyone, it would be toward the defendant. Yet, what did he testify to? He told you he was on the street and saw the defendant with some other people, then saw George Howard run by with a gun and fire it. What did he see next? He saw the defendant grab the gun and say: "Give me the gun — you're not trying to hit him," then aim the gun at Shelley Williams and pull the trigger. He saw Shelley backing up, waving his arms and turning, and the gun went off a second time. He then saw the defendant walk over to where Shelley had fallen and put the third shot in his back. Immediately afterwards he saw the defendant run past him, and noticed that *at that time* there was absolutely no blood on his head, face, or clothes.

So there you have it. When the defendant's own friend comes into court and, under oath, tells you what he saw, and his testimony totally contradicts the defense, you know for certain which side has been telling the truth here.

jury's decision on who is telling the truth.

Where the defendant testifies, his obvious bias should be pointed out.

Showing that a witness who would be expected to testify favorably to the defense actually supported the prosecution's version of the facts is usually very persuasive. When this happens, the element of support in the testimony must be driven home.

The court will, I believe, instruct you that, under our law, a man commits the crime of murder when he: first, performs an act or acts which cause the death of another; second, he intended to kill or do great bodily harm to another; and third, he was not justified in killing the other person under the circumstances.

(Instructions)

The prosecution should usually tell the jury what the elements of the offense are, and argue that he's met each of the requirements.

We have demonstrated, with convincing, credible, and consistent witnesses, that the defendant, Sylvester Strong, killed the victim, Shelley Williams, that he did so intentionally, and that by no stretch of the imagination was this a legitimate self-defense situation. These witnesses have demonstrated each of these propositions beyond a reasonable doubt. Accordingly, we ask that you return the only verdict that this evidence supports and fairness demands, a verdict finding the defendant, Sylvester Strong, guilty of the crime of murder. Thank you.

(Conclusion)

Closing argument — defense

May it please the court, Ms. Berry, Mr. Sklarsky, Mr. Cole, ladies and gentlemen of the jury, good morning.

(Introduction)

Before I make any comment to you about the evidence in this case, Sylvester Strong, Mr. Cole, and myself would like to thank you for being attentive jurors in this case. We realize you have made a sacrifice in your businesses, you have left your homes and loved ones, and you left your other obligations, but we realize the reason you are doing this is not only because it's your recognition of civic duty, but because you want to make sure that justice is properly administered in our courtroom. Because of this, ladies and gentlemen, we would like to thank you for serving as jurors in this case.

The defense's introductory remarks are often much longer than the prosecution's. The defense usually stresses that each juror promised to follow the law when the jurors were selected, and calls upon them to adhere to their promises.

Folks, at the beginning of this case, when his Honor, Judge Cousins, was questioning you with respect to your qualifications to serve as jurors, he asked you whether or not you would follow the law, whether or not you would be fair, and whether or not you would hold the prosecutors to their burden of proving Sylvester Strong guilty beyond a reasonable doubt. There was a lot of talk about that and each of you indicated and promised that you would hold the prosecutors to their burden. His Honor, Judge Cousins, when you were being selected as jurors, also asked you whether or not you would presume Sylvester innocent throughout this entire trial and through your deliberations and presume him so unless the State was able to prove him guilty beyond a reasonable doubt. All of you indicated that you presumed him innocent. Additionally, ladies and gentlemen, you were asked to use your common sense and experiences in life in evaluating the testimony of the witnesses. Based upon your responses: "Yes, I can follow the law," "Yes, I will hold the prosecutors to their burden of proof beyond a reasonable doubt," "Yes, I will presume the defendant innocent unless he is proven guilty beyond a reasonable doubt," you were selected as jurors in this case. We are calling upon you now, ladies and gentlemen, to abide by those promises that you made.

Let's now look at the evidence and see why the prosecutors failed to prove Sylvester Strong guilty beyond a reasonable doubt. As Mr. Cole told you at the beginning of this case, we do not contest the fact that Shelley Williams was shot and killed, an unfortunate thing that has happened, and nothing that I can say, nothing that anyone in this courtroom can do can change this. That fact, however, is not the issue in this case. The issue here is: was Sylvester Strong justified in defending himself under the circumstances that existed on that day? Our answer, ladies and gentlemen, is that the evidence indeed shows that the State failed to prove Sylvester Strong guilty beyond a reasonable doubt, because they did *not* prove, beyond a reasonable doubt, that when he shot Shelley Williams he did *not* reasonably believe that it was a necessity to defend himself against death or great bodily harm.

(Parties, scene, instrumentalities, weather and lighting)

Since these are not in issue, and the defendant probably does *not* have an admirable background, they are skipped.

(Issue)

The defense should put the issue in terms of the prosecutor's burden of proof, since this is the easiest statement of the issue to answer.

The answer should emphatically and immediately follow the statement of the issue.

Now why do I say this? Ladies and gentlemen, basically it comes down to whose account of the incident you believe. Do you believe the version provided by Rosie Garrett, Willie Williams, Clarence Williams, or Arthur Anderson on that stand, or do you believe the defendant, Sylvester Strong, and Ada May Howard? We have diametrically opposed versions in this case as to what happened.

The four occurrence witnesses — we call them occurrence witnesses because they are supposed to have been on the scene and observed the occurrence — were Rosie Garrett, Willie Williams, Clarence Williams, and Arthur Anderson. They would each have you believe that before April 25th, the date of the shooting, there had been absolutely no threats, no threatening gestures made by members of the Williams family directed to members of Sylvester's family.

Rosie Garrett, the first occurrence witness, testified that on April 25, at the corner of Bloomingdale and Winnebago, she observed her son Shelley talking with Sylvester Strong. She claimed that the only thing that happened before the shooting was that Shelley asked her if Sylvester was the person who cursed her. She said Shelley got out of the car and told Sylvester, "I want you to apologize." So Sylvester apologized. Shelley then said, "No, don't apologize to me, apologize to my mother." As Sylvester was turning to apologize to his mother, according to Rosie Garrett's testimony, that is when George Howard came running down the street and shot in the air. She then claims that Sylvester ran over to George Howard, grabbed the gun, saying, "You are not trying to hit him," and started shooting. Rosie Garrett claims that just before the shooting there was no fighting, no cursing, no argument, everything was peaceful, low tones of voice, not yelling; just a quiet, peaceful conversation.

Clarence Williams also got on the stand. He said the same thing, nothing happening, no argument — in fact, he couldn't hear what was

(Other side and refutation)

Since the prosecution has the burden of proof, the argument addresses the prosecution's witnesses *before* arguing the defense version of what happened.

being said because the tape deck in the car was playing. He also claims that, for no apparent reason, George Howard ran down the street firing the gun. He claims that Sylvester then, again for no apparent reason, grabbed the gun and started shooting. And he claims that only after the shooting stopped did anybody on the street lay a hand on Sylvester Strong, and that was when Clarence caught him down here by the end of the street with the car and kicked him in the face.

Now, ladies and gentlemen, if you believe the version of what occurred on the day of April 25 given by Rosie Garrett, given by Willie Williams, given by Clarence Williams, given by Arthur Anderson, you would have to believe the following: That when George Howard ran down the street and fired the shots, he was firing them because he was berserk, because there was absolutely no reason at all to fire.

Their witnesses would have you believe there was only peaceful conversation, no fighting, no hitting; not a darn thing happening to Sylvester when, for no apparent reason George Howard went berserk, and then Sylvester went berserk as well. We then got two berserk individuals in the street, just shooting up everybody for no reason at all. If you believe that, I say convict the man of murder. This simply defies common sense, and everybody in this courtroom knows it.

Let's look at some of the other things, ladies and gentlemen: You remember when we went through the addresses of all of the individuals? Did you notice how they all *just happen* to be from outside of this neighborhood? Doesn't it seem just a little suspicious that all these friends of Shelley Williams decided to be on Bloomingdale at the same time? Incidentally, they *just happened* to catch Sylvester out there in the street around the time Ada May said Shelley Williams would come over there to finish the mess that occurred the night before. Don't these coincidences alone create a reason-

Arguing that the prosecution's witnesses are incredible because their testimony is illogical and does not provide a common-sense explanation of the subsequent shooting is an effective approach.

able doubt in your mind about whether their witnesses are telling the truth?

When you get in the jury room, ladies and gentlemen, take a look at the photographs of this street. The officer said that the distance between where the shots were fired, and where he saw Sylvester being beaten, was only around 100 feet. Other testimony showed there was nothing wrong with his legs and feet. The testimony also was that Clarence got into the car, drove down the street, and cut Sylvester off. If that's all true, then why couldn't he get more than a hundred feet away? There had to be something wrong with him or he would have gotten much further. Doesn't this prove that Sylvester was attacked *before* the shots were fired? Isn't the fact that he managed to get only one hundred feet explained *only* by the fact that he was already injured, and couldn't run very well?

Just as the prosecution used the available physical evidence, presenting the same evidence to contradict the prosecution is always a good tactic.

The issue in this case is *why* Sylvester Strong shot that gun. That is the *only* issue; and the *only* one that can tell you the reason for the shooting — why he shot — is this man, Sylvester Strong. He is the only one that can tell you what was going through his mind. The issue, stated in legal terms, is whether or not he reasonably believed, under the circumstances that existed at the time of the shooting, he would sustain great bodily harm or death to himself if he didn't defend himself. Shelley Williams can't testify to that, Clarence Williams can't testify to that, and Arthur Anderson can't testify to that. Only Sylvester can, and you heard him tell you what he felt when he fired those shots.

Since the prosecution had more occurrence witnesses, pointing out that only the defendant can testify directly on the issue of intent is an effective argument.

How many shots did he fire? He testified that he just kept on shooting. *Why did you shoot? Because they were trying to kill me. When did you shoot? When they were coming at me, trying to get me.* The only person who could testify as to his intent is Sylvester himself.

I have only a few moments left, so we must go on. The prosecutor talked a lot about the entrance of the bullets, and said that two of the bullets entered Shelley Williams' back. He wants you to believe that Sylvester Strong should be convicted simply because two shots entered Williams' back. Well, it's not as simple as that.

Just for a moment, put anyone else in that same situation. A mob has surrounded you. They are armed with bats and two-by-fours. You instinctively fire your gun. Do you stop to see whether or not the first shot hits anyone? Do you stop to see if anyone is turning while you shoot? *Of course not!* You would fire that gun as fast and as often as you could. Isn't that exactly what a reasonable person would have done under these circumstances? Well, that is exactly what happened, and only what happened, here. The question is whether or not, when the first shot was fired, Sylvester Strong reasonably believed that he was justified in defending himself. If so, it does not make any difference where that first shot or, for that matter, any other shots actually struck.

(What happened)

Having refuted the prosecution witnesses, the argument now gives the defense version of what happened.

I believe Judge Cousins will instruct you that a person is justified in using deadly force when that person reasonably believes that such force is necessary to prevent imminent death or great bodily harm to himself. Isn't that what really happened here? Isn't that what Sylvester Strong must have been thinking when he fired that gun? Under these circumstances, surrounded by an angry mob, isn't what Sylvester Strong did exactly what any other reasonable person would have done if faced with the same situation? *Of course it is!* Because what he did was reasonable, Sylvester is simply not guilty of any crime.

(Instructions)

The defense will naturally stress the self-defense instructions, particularly the burden of proof's being on the prosecution.

The court will also instruct you that the prosecution has the burden of proof in this case, and that this burden of proof never shifts to the defendant. Although we presented evidence in this case, we are not required to prove anything. *We* do not have to prove that Sylvester Strong was justified in defending himself as he did. It is the *prosecution* that is required to *disprove* this proposition, and they have to *disprove* it beyond a reasonable doubt.

Who among you can't say that you have a reasonable doubt whether or not Sylvester reasonably defended himself here? Of course you have doubts! You have got to have doubts about that. If nothing else, the evidence you heard here is filled with doubt.

This case will be over soon. I have tried my best to show you what really happened on Bloomingdale Avenue during the afternoon of April 25, 1985. I have tried my best, but my job is done. This case now rests in your hands. When this case is over, you, I, and probably some others, will from time to time think back and reflect on this case. It may be in the morning during a spare moment. This case may suddenly come back to you at night when you are trying to fall asleep. Wherever you think of this case, you are probably going to ask one thing: Did I do this defendant, Sylvester Strong, justice? If you have doubts about this case, have them now. For him there is no tomorrow, no second chance. Ask yourself those hard questions now, because for him tomorrow is too late. If during your deliberations you keep that in mind, we are sure that you will return a verdict of not guilty.

Now, ladies and gentlemen, I only have this one chance to talk with you. When I am finished, the prosecutor will have a second chance to get up and make what is known as a rebuttal argument. I don't have a chance to talk to you after him and rebut anything he might tell you. I am confident, however, that since you heard the evidence, you will be able to come up with an answer for anything he might tell you. When he gets up, ladies and gentlemen, ask him to explain to you how it was so unreasonable for Sylvester to defend himself under these circumstances. Have him explain to you why, when surrounded by an armed, angry mob, Sylvester was not entitled to protect himself and save his own life. Have him tell you what would have been more reasonable here. If you have a doubt as to what the right thing to do would have been, then you can't say that what Sylvester did was not reasonable.

(Conclusion)

There is nothing wrong in having an emotional conclusion to your argument, if it is appropriate to the case and is done in good taste.

Challenging the prosecutor to answer a difficult issue can be an effective approach. However, make sure the prosecutor does not have an obvious good answer he can use.

Ladies and gentlemen of the jury, I say again that the prosecution has not proved beyond a reasonable doubt that when Sylvester fired that first shot, he did not reasonably believe it was necessary to do so to defend himself. The posecution has utterly failed to prove that issue beyond a reasonable doubt. Because of their failure, we ask you to return the only verdict this evidence demands. Let him go free. Let him return to his job, his family, and his friends. Find him not guilty.

Rebuttal argument — prosecution

Your Honor, ladies and gentlemen of the jury.

Before I deal with the evidence you heard and what it adds up to, I want to spend a moment on the State's burden of proof. We are required, as has been said many times, to prove the defendant guilty beyond a reasonable doubt. It does *not* require us to prove him guilty beyond *all* doubt, just reasonable doubt. We ask you to keep that in mind as you review the evidence and decide on the proper verdict.

About what happened on Bloomingdale Avenue during the afternoon of April 25, 1985, there can be no doubt. We presented four credible, consistent eyewitnesses, all of whom told you the same thing. I'm not going to review their testimony again. Suffice it to say that all of them told you Shelley Williams was merely insisting that the defendant apologize to his mother for swearing at her; George Howard arrived and fired two shots in the air; the defendant grabbed the gun, saying, "Give me the gun — you're not trying to shoot him"; he aimed the gun and fired the first shot, hitting Shelley in the arm; as Shelley turned and ran, the defendant shot him in the back; Shelley fell face down, and took the third shot in his back, too. That, in a nutshell, is what four decent persons told you, under oath, happened.

(Introduction)

Where the defense has hit hard on the burden of proof, it is often useful to remind the jury that that burden is not an impossible one to meet.

(In some jurisdictions the jury is not given a definition of reasonable doubt in the instructions.)

(Your strongest points)

The rebuttal cannot be negative in tone. Accordingly, get right into your strongest ammunition and hit hard.

Mr. Hill makes much of the fact that there were inconsistencies in their testimony. Of course there were! There always are minor inconsistencies. That's because every witness to an event sees it from his own vantage point, remembers it with different degrees of recall, and testifies about it, using his own verbal style and expressions. You ought to be suspicious of testimony that is perfectly identical because it usually means that the testimony is rehearsed. That obviously didn't occur here, because each eyewitness simply told you what he saw, in his own unique way.

(Other side's contentions)

Note that the defense's arguments are woven into the middle of the rebuttal. This keeps your refutation from creating a negative atmosphere.

What Mr. Hill *didn't* talk about is more revealing. He spent almost no time talking about the testimony of the four witnesses to this crime that we presented. Instead, he spent most of his argument talking about the defendant. Why do you suppose he decided to do that? Could it be that he wants you to forget that four persons saw the defendant shoot an unarmed, defenseless man three times, twice in the back? Could it be that by constantly talking about the defendant he's trying to appeal to your emotions and get you to ignore the evidence? I leave it to your collective intelligence and experience to draw the proper conclusions.

(Refutation and other strong points)

In the same vein, use your refutation to again raise the strongest parts of your proof.

Mr. Hill also chose not to talk about the significant corroboration of these witnesses. Remember Dr. Ibram, the pathologist, who told you about the autopsy he performed on the body of Shelley Williams? He told you that he found three bullet wounds in the body. One was in the arm, and two were in the back. Aren't his findings completely consistent with and corroborative of the eyewitnesses, all of whom told you they saw Shelley Williams raise his hands to protect himself when the first shot was fired, saw him turn and run when the second shot was fired, and saw him fall, after which the defendant deliberately put the third shot into his back?

Since shooting a man in the back is such a repulsive fact, cutting against the defendant, you can hardly mention it too much!

There's something about physical evidence that's impossible to ignore. It never lies, never forgets, and never disappears. It simply always is there, to prove which side is telling the truth.

In this case, what does the physical evidence, the location of the bullet wounds, show? It conclusively proves that the way the four eyewitnesses told you this crime happened is true.

What about the defense they presented here? There's an old saying: "The defense doesn't have to prove anything, but if they decide to call witnesses, they'd better make sense and wash with the other evidence." That, needless to say, is hardly what happened here. The defendant's testimony made no sense, and it was flatly contradicted by the four eyewitnesses.

The defendant, you'll remember, claimed he was surrounded by an angry, armed mob that beat him with baseball bats and two-by-fours simply because he didn't apologize to Rosie Garrett. Does that make any sense? Your common sense and experience in how life works tells you it didn't happen that way. The defendant claims that he somehow managed to grab George Howard's gun and fired it blindly to get the mob off him. If that's so, isn't it simply amazing how all three bullets ended up in only one person, and two of the shots ended up in his back? Now that's truly amazing! Finally, the defendant tells you that he was bleeding profusely from the face and head, fell down repeatedly, and staggered the one hundred feet to where he was when the police arrived. If that's so, wouldn't you expect to see blood spots and blood smudges all along the path he took down Bloomingdale? Of course you would — if his story is in fact true. But what did Officer Genowski tell you? When he arrived at the scene, he saw the defendant on the ground, and there was blood at that spot. He then walked over to where Shelley Williams was lying, and saw blood there as well. He then checked the sidewalk and street between those two places, and did not see any blood anywhere else. That's absolutely positive proof that the defendant's story is not true. Again, it's the physical evidence that conclusively proves who's telling the truth here.

What this case comes down to, then, is who you decide to believe. Are you going to believe Ro-

There's nothing wrong with employing sarcasm and showing disbelief in appropriate situations.

Note that the prosecutor, through the use of sarcasm, leaves little doubt that he thinks the defendant is lying, but he never says it directly. Instead, he lets the jurors reach this conclusion on their own. This is the better approach.

(Conclusion)

sie Garrett, Clarence Williams, Willie Williams, Arthur Anderson, and the physical evidence as presented through Dr. Ibram and Officer Genowski? Or are you going to believe the defendant's story? There's no middle ground in this case.

Since you have four eyewitnesses to the defense's one, this should be repeatedly stressed.

Mr. Hill in his closing argument asked the prosecutor to tell you what would have been the reasonable thing to do. I'll do that. The reasonable thing for the defendant to do would have been simply to say, "I'm sorry," apologize to Rosie Garrett and walk away. That's what a reasonable person would have done. But not Sylvester Strong. That's not the way he does things, and that's why he's in this courtroom today.

Since the defense made the argument, you're entitled to respond to it directly, under the "invited reply" doctrine.

We are sure that after you have reviewed the testimony of the witnesses, and have reviewed the physical evidence, in the light of your experiences in life and plain old common sense, you're going to arrive at only one possible conclusion. We proved that the defendant shot and killed Shelley Williams, that he fired that gun intending to kill or cause bodily harm to Shelley Williams, that the defendant was in no way justified in doing what he did; and we proved it beyond a reasonable doubt. In short, ladies and gentlemen, what the defendant did on the afternoon of April 25, 1985, is what the crime of murder is all about. Thank you.

2. Civil case (products liability): *Hi-Temp, Inc. v. Lindberg Furnace Company*

(Hi-Temp, a company that treats metal products in furnaces, purchased an industrial vacuum furnace in September, 1983, from the defendant manufacturer. On December 31, 1984, the furnace exploded. Hi-Temp had the furnace repaired. Hi-Temp claims that a design defect in the furnace, particularly in a valve, was the cause of the explosion. Lindberg maintains that the furnace was safely designed and manufactured.)

Closing argument — plaintiff

Ladies and gentlemen of the jury, I would like to begin my closing argument by thanking you for listening these five days to all of the evi-

(Introduction)

dence presented by Mr. Quade and myself. Throughout most of this trial the evidence was highly scientific and extremely technical. We all had to deal with a field of knowledge that we don't come into every day in order to settle disputes. I hope the evidence you heard was probative and revealing.

During my opening statement I told you what I expected the evidence to prove. I feel that the evidence has borne me out.

You heard Mr. Don Lyons, the general vice-president of engineering for Hi-Temp, testify that in early 1983, Hi-Temp had entered into negotiations with Lindberg for purchase of a vacuum furnace. Mr. Lyons told you that during these negotiations, Hi-Temp told Lindberg they needed a furnace that could go at least as high as 2150 degrees and would operate around the clock, seven days a week.

Based on these requirements, Lindberg designed and manufactured a furnace which they said had an Inconel shield good to 2300 degrees, which they sold to Hi-Temp without any reservation whatsoever for $103,000. The furnace was put into service in September of 1983.

You heard testimony from Mr. Dan Waller, the maintenance foreman from Hi-Temp, that for the next 15 months, until December 31, 1984, he was the person primarily responsible for maintaining that furnace. His duties included cleaning the Poppet valve, cleaning O-rings, replacing worn parts, and maintaining and cleaning all water lines of calcium and lime deposits. Whenever he had to, he would contact Gerald Scott of Lindberg and consult with him.

You also heard from Mr. Vern Molitar, the plant foreman. He testified that he was working the evening of December 31, 1983. That night the furnace had steel-plated turbine parts being processed for a customer.

Mr. Molitar told you that when he came to the plant, he was told that there was no vacuum in

(Review of testimony)

The opening argument uses the witness-by-witness method of reviewing the evidence. This technique is useful if your witnesses were credible and convincing and you want to remind the jury of this. Its drawback is that where many witnesses are involved, the technique can become boring to the jury.

It's always a good idea to briefly remind the jury who the witness was before summarizing his testimony.

the furnace, that there was atmospheric pressure in the furnace, and it was supposed to be pumping down to a vacuum.

Mr. Molitar checked the entire unit. He told you that he examined the gauge settings and they were proper. He examined the pumps and they appeared proper. He examined the oil levels and they were proper. He examined the charts and he told you that when he examined the charts, he noted that on the previous cycle, the load in the furnace had achieved a temperature of 1970 degrees and it also achieved vacuum. After Mr. Molitar's examination of this entire unit on the night of December 31, 1984, what he described as an explosion occurred.

He described this explosion as a tremendous shock wave, which felt like wind pushing at him. It was accompanied by a loud noise, something like an artillery gun. He also told you that he saw black sooty smoke coming out of the unit. He told you that he did not see any flame, flash, spark, or fire, but as soon as the explosion was over and he looked into the unit, he saw that the load inside the chamber was pushed to one side.

After the explosion, other employees from Hi-Temp had a chance to examine the wreckage. You heard from several of them. All noticed that the load in the chamber had been pushed aside and that the pump and related parts had been damaged.

Immediately after the explosion, Hi-Temp hired Mr. J. K. Davis to determine the cause of the explosion. Mr. Davis has a master's degree in mechanical engineering. He is a licensed professional engineer in several states. He is the president of an engineering firm and he has extensive experience in the laws of thermodynamics. For 11 years he has designed control systems for vacuum furnaces.

During Mr. Davis' initial visit to the plant, he examined the entire furnace wreckage. He ex-

(What happened)

Throughout the argument, plaintiff refers to the "explosion." This is a much stronger term than "event," "incident" or "occurrence." Choosing your basic descriptive terms can have a significant impact on the jury's perception of what really happened.

Since Davis is plaintiff's only expert, and the outcome of the case depends in large part on the jury's accepting his explanations, his testimony must be covered in detail.

His background credentials should also be reviewed in some detail, since they will have a significant impact on his credibility.

Since the jury has heard the testimony

amined the diagrams. He examined the charts and spoke to the witnesses. Based upon that initial visit, Mr. Davis was not able to come to a conclusion as to what occurred. The reason was that this pump had been crated along with the foreline valve and sent to Massachusetts, and he did not have an opportunity to inspect the pump on that occasion. He reported on his first inspection that he could not come to a conclusion.

Mr. Davis then went to Massachusetts, where this pump had been sent, and he inspected it. He found the drift eliminator, the small metal guides on the foreline valve, had been bent around the foreline valve and rammed into the skirt of the adjacent pump.

Based upon his inspection of the wrecked furnace, the pump, the foreline valve, and the drift eliminator, Mr. Davis concluded that this explosion was the result of a design defect in the furnace.

Specifically, Mr. Davis said the defect in the furnace was that there was no absolute locking device on the foreline valve when it was in the manual mode. This foreline valve could open when you had atmospheric pressure on top of it and a vacuum beneath it.

Mr. Davis further testified that a proper design of this furnace would have had an absolute locking device so that in no case could the foreline valve accidentally open when the vacuum furnace was in operation.

Mr. Davis' conclusions were based upon the following physical findings:

First, this drift eliminator was found bent around the valve and rammed into the skirt of the pump. Second, there were signs of a destructive push this way, in *toward* the chamber. Third, there was damage *inside* the chamber

and seen the exhibits, they will already be familiar with the technical terms used. Nevertheless, the summary should still be as simple as possible, using few technical terms. Here plaintiff has managed to reduce a difficult technical case to three basic parts — pump, foreline valve, and drift eliminator.

(Basis of liability)

Here the attorney is using a diagram of the furnace and referring to the important parts, which are la-

and a shifted load. Finally, the pump was in a shifted position.

Based upon these physical findings, it was Mr. Davis' conclusion that this damage that resulted could only be accounted for by a force that came from *above* the foreline valve. That's the only way he could account for the destruction which rammed the drift eliminator around the valve, into the pump, and created the damage inside the furnace.

He concluded the damage could *not* have originated from inside the furnace because if it had, all the damage would have been in an *outward* direction, yet there was none. All the forces went inward. Furthermore, the *only* force that could have caused the damage was a high-pressure force coming from the pressurized side of the foreline valve into the vacuum chamber.

He explained that when you have atmosphere on one side of the foreline valve and a vacuum on the other side, if that foreline valve opens, the air pressure charges into the vacuum at something like twice the speed of sound. This speed easily accounts for the resulting damages in the vacuum chamber and is entirely consistent with what Mr. Molitar described as a shock wave pushing at him.

Mr. Davis further told you that a simple and feasible design system could have prevented what had occurred. He told you that all that would have been required was an automatic locking device on the foreline valve in the manual mode to prevent it from opening at a time when there was atmospheric pressure on one side and a vacuum on the other.

You also heard testimony regarding the damages in this case. Mr. Lyons, the plant manager, told you that immediately after the occurrence, he contacted the pump manufacturer in Massachusetts, who told him to ship the pump to them. Once the pump was

beled. The diagram, of course, was previously admitted as an exhibit.

It is always important to explain *why* the expert's opinions and conclusions are reasonable and are supported by the facts.

(Anticipating defenses)

In the same vein, you should argue that the other side's position is illogical or not supported by the facts.

It is always effective to show that favorable witnesses corroborate each other.

(Damages)

Notice how the elements of damages are reviewed in detail, down to the precise

shipped to Massachusetts, Hi-Temp learned that the pump was not repairable.

Mr. Lyons also ordered replacement parts for the furnace. You heard him read the invoices. There were 17 separate orders from Lindberg, totaling $30,575.01. There were 23 separate orders from other suppliers, totaling $8,231.83. These are parts that were necessary to put the equipment back into serviceable operation.

Mr. Lyons told you that it took a total of 10 weeks, from January 1 to March 10, 1985, to ascertain the damage, make the orders, receive the shipments of the supplies necessary to put the unit back together, and install them.

Mr. Baker, the certified public accountant, determined what the lost gross earnings for Hi-Temp were during those 10 weeks. Mr. Baker examined all the books and records and, using what he termed the general trend method, he ascertained the loss to be $34,265.

He also determined that the labor cost to Hi-Temp for paying company employees to do the 560 hours of repair work came to $3,773.

When you total all the damages that have been before you, you get a number in excess of $55,000, the amount we are asking. You have a business interruption loss in excess of $34,000. You have a labor charge of $3,700. You have the parts ordered from Lindberg for $30,500, and you have the parts ordered from other suppliers for $8,200. That totals to $76,400. However, some of the replacement items that were ordered by Hi-Temp admittedly were more costly than the items that were in there prior to the explosion.

The molybdenum shield for the furnace, and some of the other parts were more expensive than the parts they replaced. In addition, the damaged parts had been used for 15 months, and were no longer new. It would not be fair to treat the damaged parts as new. Therefore,

amounts involved. It is dangerous to be sloppy in your damages argument. The jury may well interpret sloppiness or generalizations as an attempt to inflate the damages.

This is also a good time to put each element of damages on a poster board, so that the elements can be emphasized and a total reached before the jury.

(Anticipating defenses)

This is an effective argument to refute what will certainly be argued by the defense.

we are reducing the damages from $76,400 to the sum of $55,000 to fully adjust for these changes.

It shows the jury how fair and reasonable plaintiff's damages request is.

The $55,000 amount is what fairly and exactly reflects the damages as a result of that explosion of December 31, 1984. When you have reviewed the evidence, ladies and gentlemen, a fair examination of all the evidence in this case clearly supports a verdict of $55,000 in favor of Hi-Temp and against the defendant.

(Conclusion)

Closing argument — defendant

May it please the Court, Mr. Kaplan, ladies and gentlemen of the jury.

Notice how the defendant has chosen not to do the standard "thanking the jury" routine.

The issue in this case is quite simple. They claim that the vacuum furnace is designed with a foreline valve that's unreasonably dangerous and that this claimed condition caused $55,000 worth of damage. That's the whole dispute.

(Issue)

Now, I am going to talk for a moment about damages. I'd be derelict in my duty to my client if I didn't, but I don't want you to think we owe the plaintiff money. However, plaintiff spent time on this issue, and I feel there are some things we should answer.

(Damages)

The defendant will usually argue damages before liability, since you cannot credibly argue the liability issue if you end up arguing damages.

Are we really talking about damage as a result of an occurrence, or are we talking about routine maintenance and upgrading? We know that the pump oils and gaskets have to be changed yearly. When were they changed last? We know that there was thermal insulation on the furnace when it was originally sold, and now they submit bills for graphite felt at a much higher price with a much higher service life.

We know there was an Inconel lining inside the furnace, and we know they ordered a new one. They started getting quotes in May of '83, and ordered a replacement lining in September on a "rush basis." That was three months before this so-called explosion. Again, they're moving up to a longer service life and a more expensive material for a higher temperature rating. Ken Taylor told you that the only thing wrong with the pump was that a bent baffle had to be straightened out. This would take only about $100 worth of labor and materials, yet they want us to buy them a whole new pump at a cost of $6,400. Are they really repairing damages, or are they doing routine maintenance and upgrading of the furnace? How much life was left in the old materials? Obviously it couldn't have been much, since they were already replacing them.

Now, you heard Ken Taylor, the expert from Lindberg, testify that he could have repaired the furnace in two weeks. However, Lindberg was not asked to repair the furnace. Lindberg was not asked to quote a price on repairing the furnace. Lindberg was not asked to tell them how soon they could repair the furnace. Was Hi-Temp aggressively pursuing the repair of that furnace? Did they order any repair materials on a special or rush basis? The answer is obviously no. They dragged it out for ten weeks, a job that could be done in two.

Ten weeks of business interruption they are claiming for $34,000. If it really is business interruption, and the furnace can be repaired in two weeks, and the furnace is needed that badly, two weeks would amount to $7,300.

I am suggesting to you that we may not be talking about damage as a result of an occurrence but mostly routine maintenance and upgrading in this case.

Now, the court will instruct you that the plaintiff in this case, Hi-Temp, had a duty to minimize its damages. They had a duty to aggressively pursue the repair of the furnace if it would save them money, and to the extent they failed to do that, they should not collect for the excess over what an agressive pursuit of a repair would be.

Weaving the appropriate instructions into the argument is always an effective technique, since it puts a judicial stamp of approval on the argument.

Now, let me tell you why Lindberg is not liable to Hi-Temp in this case. You're going to say: "Quade, you've got a tough job. Your client made the furnace and you can't explain how it happened." Let me suggest some reasons why we can't tell you what happened, and why that's not our obligation.

(Basis of nonliability)

The rhetorical question is a good way to squarely confront a difficult problem.

Who loaded the furnace? Did the person that loaded the furnace testify? No. What was in the furnace besides the turbine blades? Did anybody come in and tell what they saw in that furnace when they loaded it? No. Who programmed the furnace? What program was it set for? We don't know.

The rhetorical question is also a useful device to raise questions your opponent should have answered but didn't.

What were the control switch settings? We don't know that either. And why is it a secret? I suggest that the reason we don't know what happened is that these persons never came forward.

Now, there is another missing piece of information that would be very important to all of us in determining what happened. The evidence shows that Abel Navaret was the operator of the furnace, and had no other duties. Navaret still works for Hi-Temp. Where was he? What does he know about this? Why didn't they bring him in?

The court is going to instruct you that if a witness is under a party's control and not equally available to the other parties, and he doesn't come in to testify and no reasonable excuse is made for his not testifying, it is presumed that his testimony will be adverse to their side of the case. Their plant is only perhaps 20 miles from here. That's where Navaret is. They chose not to bring him in and they know what the law is.

Here again the relevant instruction is discussed and used to reinforce the argument.

The court is also going to instruct you on what the plaintiff has to prove in this case. The plaintiff has to prove five things, two of which we take no issue with. We intentionally made the furnace without an interlock on the fore-line valve, and that condition existed when we

(Instructions)

turned over the furnace to Hi-Temp. There's no dispute about that.

The plaintiff will have to prove *all five* things, and the plaintiff has trouble with the other three. First, does the design of the furnace without a locking device on the foreline valve constitute an unreasonably dangerous condition? The answer is no. That's one element of the remaining three that they are going to have a problem with.

You heard three experts, Carl Seelandt, Ken Taylor, and Cris Dobrowalski testify that it does not constitute an unreasonably dangerous condition. It's a necessary condition for servicing. You can't run the furnace, conduct an ordinary leak check, or do routine maintenance without it.

The defendant can use the elements instruction to his advantage, particularly if there are several essential elements and the defense is based on more than one, since the plaintiff should lose on the liability issue if it fails to prove each element by a preponderance of the evidence.

On that point, I'd like to review a few things Mr. Dobrowalski has covered. He was our outside expert. He has no ax to grind, yet he corroborated our own people. He says the foreline valve mechanism is very reputable. He is ashamed to say he doesn't do so well at his company in the design of their products.

Showing that the "outside" expert corroborates the employee experts necessarily enhances the credibility of them all.

You need the manual operation of the furnace to disconnect the pump. You need the manual mode so that an operator can use his brains and do the testing, checking, and maintenance such a furnace requires. Does this sound unreasonably dangerous? Of course not! Mr. Dobrowalski's opinion was that that design of the foreline valve without an interlock in the manual mode does not constitute an unreasonably dangerous condition. So here we are, years later, and normally the industry progresses and you learn new things on the way, but we haven't invented anything better than the design that was used on this furnace.

So much for the proposition that the condition was an unreasonably dangerous one. The evidence shows that the plaintiff has not sustained its burden in that regard.

The second proposition that the plaintiff has not met its burden on is proximate cause. The condition which it claims renders the furnace unreasonably dangerous must be the condition that causes the damage in the furnace.

We have had three experts who have made their life's work vacuum engineering testify they don't know what caused the damage. As I told you before, if you don't have any of the facts about what's in the furnace, how it's loaded, what the control settings are on, and who operated the furnace, you just can't determine it. But we also know that the condition in the product which they claim is unreasonably dangerous, didn't cause it. Simply opening the foreline valve, according to Carl Seelandt, Chris Dobrowalski, and Ken Taylor, could not have created the kind of damage that occurred. Three experts said this could not be the cause of the damage. We submit that the plaintiff has failed to prove by a preponderance of the evidence that the damage was proximately caused by any unreasonably dangerous condition.

Since the defense has three experts to the plaintiff's one, this advantage should be repeatedly stressed.

The third proposition that the plaintiff has failed to meet its burden on is damages, and I have already talked about that.

Now, a few words about Mr. Davis, the plaintiff's witness and only person who condemns the design. The case involves vacuum engineering, doesn't it? Has Mr. Davis ever built one? No. Ever designed one? No. Has he ever run one? No. Has he ever leak-checked one? No. Has he ever read any of the literature on it? No. Has he ever run any experiments on it? No. Has he run any kind of tests? No.

(Their side and refutation)

The safest way to attack an expert is to challenge his professional expertise, since this is not an attack on the expert himself, which always runs the risk of offending the jury.

Is this the kind of expertise you want to rely on to determine whether this furnace system is unreasonably dangerous? I think not. You have to determine the credibility of the witnesses and the weight to be given to their testimony, and you should consider Mr. Davis' qualifications in deciding whether his testimony can be accepted. When you look at his background, and particularly when you compare it to the expertise and experience of the three experts we presented, you can only reach one conclusion: Mr. Davis' opinion simply cannot be accepted.

The court will instruct you not to speculate or enter into conjecture. If you have to speculate on liability or damages, I suggest that the plaintiff has failed to meet his burden on both issues.

In short, the evidence here has failed to show that the furnace and foreline valve were unreasonably dangerous. Lindberg purposely designed the valve to allow the operator to select between manual and automatic modes. The operator must be somebody who knows what he is doing when he operates a sophisticated machine. Lindberg gave its sophisticated industrial customers credit for having brains. Don't hold it against them.

This type of ending can have a much greater impact than the standard "request for a favorable verdict" ending.

Rebuttal argument — plaintiff

Ladies and gentlemen, I hate to get into arguments over witness' qualifications, but since Mr. Quade raised this issue I'm going to respond to it. He told you Mr. Davis was not qualified. Why? Simply because he hasn't spent his life in the vacuum furnace industry. They'd conveniently like you to forget that Mr. Davis is a mechanical engineer who has worked 11 years for a company that designs the control systems for vacuum furnaces.

If you want to argue about qualifications of experts, however, let's look at the witnesses that the defense provided for you. First of all, he brings in Mr. Seelandt, who was an employee of Lindberg at the time of the occurrence. That's hardly the kind of neutral, unbiased expert you'd want to rely on. When was he first contacted and given sufficient facts upon which to testify? Friday of last week, when the trial was about to begin.

Notice how little time is spent defending the qualifications of plaintiff's expert before the argument shifts to attacking the bias of defendant's experts. This converts a defensive response into an aggressive, affirmative argument.

How about Mr. Dobrowalski, the man who came here from Boston? What did he tell you? Well, I am not so much bothered by the fact that Mr. Dobrowalski is not a licensed professional engineer, as is Mr. Davis. I am not even bothered by the fact that Mr. Dobrowalski has only a bachelor's degree, in electric engineering. What bothers me about Mr. Dobrowalski is this: He was first contacted only weeks ago by the defendant, and he told you that even at that time he was not provided sufficient facts upon which to base his opinion.

When did he first get those facts? After he flew to Chicago Monday night to testify Tuesday morning to you. In other words, he came to Chicago to testify the very next day without even knowing the facts upon which he was going to testify. Doesn't that bother you a little bit?

Finally, they called Mr. Taylor, who they claim was so neutral and objective. Did he ever see the furnace? No. Did he ever examine the wreckage? No. Did he ever talk to any of the witnesses? No. But whom does he work for? Kinney Vacuum Company. And what do they manufacture? Vacuum pumps. And who buys their vacuum pumps? The defendant, Lindberg, of course.

I suggest to you, ladies and gentlemen, that they had every reason in the world to come here and testify on behalf of Lindberg, to come here even before they knew the facts upon which they were going to testify.

Let's go back to damages for a second. Mr. Quade tells you that the damages were not quite as bad as what we told you. Obviously when you repair a unit with new parts, it is more valuable than it was before the occurrence. That's why we tell you that although the

---

There's nothing wrong with using a little sarcasm in appropriate situations.

Notice that this is a fairly strong attack on these defense experts, yet it does not go overboard. The plaintiff never *directly* argues that these experts were bought and paid for; instead, the jury is allowed to reach this conclusion on its own.

(Damages)

The weakest part of the defense argument was on the ten weeks repair time. Consequently, this is the

repair costs were $75,000, we are asking only for the sum of $55,000.

Mr. Quade told you we could have put the thing back together in two weeks. Two weeks? What did the evidence show you? On January 5, Hi-Temp ordered a series of parts from Lindberg. Half the parts didn't get from Lindberg to Hi-Temp until January 30. The other parts didn't arrive until February 16 and 18. They knew that the unit was down. If anybody could have accelerated the delivery, you would have thought it would have been the defendant, Lindberg. It took them seven weeks just to get the parts to Hi-Temp, and yet they tell you they could have put the unit back together in two weeks. Their claim is simply preposterous.

Next, Mr. Quade complains that there are certain witnesses to the explosion that we haven't seen. However, Mr. Molitar testified he was on duty at the time. He examined all of the instruments, all of the pumps, all of the oil levels prior to the explosion. He knew what was in the furnace at the time. Rather than challenge what Mr. Molitar told you, Mr. Quade instead says: "Where is Abel Navaret? Why haven't we heard from him?"

However, remember what Mr. Taylor told you? Lindberg performed an investigation immediately after this thing. They had men in there immediately and, based upon what they learned in their investigation, if they for one moment thought Abel Navaret could help their case and hurt mine, they could have and would have subpoenaed him into court. They have the same power to subpoena as I do. He's still up in Northlake. They knew that. Mr. Navaret could have been subpoenaed and been examined by Mr. Quade as well as myself — if he for a moment thought Mr. Navaret would have helped the defense.

Ladies and gentlemen, Mr. Quade's argument works both ways. You heard Mr. Taylor testify that Lindberg had many people investigate this

point the plaintiff jumps on and argues the most.

This is the standard reply to the "missing witness" argument.

Turning an argument around and using it against the other side

loss. Where are they? Why does Lindberg rely on experts that they contacted the week of trial rather than their own people that initially investigated this occurrence? If you want to interpret a witness' absence against the party who didn't bring them, then take a hard look at them.

Finally, it's important in this case to realize that Lindberg has not given you one plausible explanation of a force which could cause the extensive damage you saw, not one theory in all their investigations.

Instead, what do they tell you? They tell you Mr. Davis' theory isn't plausible. What did Mr. Seelandt say? He said it couldn't happen the way Mr. Davis explained it. He claimed that air rushing into the vacuum chamber couldn't produce such damage. Yet the damage was obviously there; and Mr. Seelandt, their own expert, couldn't explain it.

What did Mr. Dobrowalski tell you? He's simply a carbon copy of Mr. Seelandt. He's also quick to tell you that Mr. Davis is wrong, yet he can't explain it either.

What about having a locking safety system on the foreline valve of the furnace? That would have prevented the explosion from happening. That obviously could have and should have been included in its design and manufacture. The only reason you have been given for not having interlock protection is that then you would not be able to detect leaks. That's been the only reason that Lindberg has given.

Yet their own expert, Mr. Seelandt, admitted on cross-examination that you would *not* have to open the foreline valve to check for leaks in the system. He admitted that even if the foreline valve had a locking device, that would not prevent you from testing for leaks. Their own expert refutes their main argument.

Ladies and gentlemen, the evidence in this case has shown that in 1983, Hi-Temp purchased a furnace from Lindberg for $103,000. After

is always effective (and something to consider before making an argument that can later be used against you).

this explosion, Hi-Temp spent $34,000 to repair it, and incurred other costs and damages. Lindberg has denied responsibility for this occurrence for years. They have had Mr. Davis' report on the explosion at least since last year. Doesn't it seem strange they would deny responsibility all this time but wait until during the week of the trial to contact two of their experts, who didn't even know the facts of the case until they got here to testify for them?

Lindberg's defense, at best, is that although they designed and manufactured the furnace, they can't explain how what wasn't supposed to occur, in fact, did occur. It's their furnace, they designed it, they made it, yet they can't explain it.

Of all the experts you have heard, Mr. Davis was by far the most persuasive. Mr. Davis is the only expert witness in this case who took the trouble to go to the plant, see the unit, inspect the wreckage, talk to the witnesses, examine the charts, and go to Massachusetts to examine the pump.

Based on that extensive study of the facts, Mr. Davis concluded that the explosion was caused when the foreline valve opened, allowing atmospheric pressure to rush into the vacuum chamber of the furnace. The foreline valve did not have a locking safety system which would have prevented the valve from improperly opening. This failure made the furnace unreasonably dangerous, and this failure was the defect which was the direct cause of the explosion.

Accordingly, we ask that you return the only verdict this evidence warrants, a verdict in the amount of $55,000 in favor of Hi-Temp and against the defendant.

Notice how many times plaintiff has argued that the defendant's experts are "recent arrivals." This is probably plaintiff's best point to rebut the fact that the defense has three experts to plaintiff's one.

Immediately afterwards, plaintiff builds up, and contrasts, its sole expert, so that the jury's last thought is on that expert.

VIII
OBJECTIONS

§8.1. Introduction

In many ways making proper, timely objections is the most difficult skill for the inexperienced trial lawyer to master. This is difficult for two reasons. First, evidence is usually taught in law schools at a theoretical level, which, while important, has little to do with the contexts in which evidentiary and procedural problems routinely arise during trials. Trial lawyers learn to associate "buzz words" with appropriate objections until the association is automatic. A buzz word is simply a word or phrase that an experienced trial lawyer is conditioned to know is objectionable. For instance, when a lawyer starts a question with "Isn't it conceivable that . . . ," a trial lawyer will instantly react because the question necessarily calls for a speculative answer. Second, timeliness is essential when making objections, since making a late objection is often worse than not objecting at all.

The difficulty in mastering objections is that recognizing the buzz words and reacting to them in timely fashion can only be developed thoroughly through trial experience. They are difficult if not impossible to master in a textbook environment.

Despite these problems, objections in a trial context can and should be studied to develop a methodology that, when joined with some actual experience, will result in ultimate mastery of this essential trial skill. This chapter will discuss when to make objections, how to make them, how to make offers of proof, and the types of evidentiary objections commonly encountered at trial.

§8.2. When to make objections

Every trial involves numerous situations in which objections can properly be made. When to make objections, however, involves more than simply having proper situations in which to make them. It also involves almost instantaneous decisions on whether to make the objections at all. The following should always be considered.

1. Jurors dislike objections

Jurors see lawyers who make constant objections as lawyers who are try-ing to keep the real truth from them. Since your credibility as a lawyer has a substantial influence on the outcome of the trial, minimize your interference while evidence is being introduced before the jury. Antici-pate evidentiary problems. Your trial preparations will usually show what the significant evidentiary issues at trial will be, so these should be raised through pretrial motions, at the pretrial conference, or through motions in limine. During trial, try to make your objections out of the jury's pres-ence, during recesses, motions in limine, and side-bar conferences. On the other hand, don't be afraid to make objections. Jurors have all seen enough television to know and expect that some objections will be made.

2. Will the answer hurt your case?

Unless you are reasonably sure that the answer to a question will hurt your case, it is usually better not to object. If you make the objection and the court sustains it, the jury will naturally wonder what the answer would have been, had the witness only been allowed to answer. What the jury thinks the answer would have been is often far worse than the actual answer. Save your objections for what you are reasonably certain will be damaging.

On the other hand, you must keep the judge in mind. Repeatedly failing to make a proper objection (because the answer won't hurt your case) can result later on in the judge overruling a proper objection (where the answer will hurt your case), since you have through your con-duct conditioned the judge to assume that what was repeatedly asked ear-lier was proper. Object enough to let the judge know that you know when to make proper objections.

3. Does your objection have a solid legal basis?

If you do make an objection, be reasonably sure you will be sustained. Have authority ready to support the major objections you anticipate mak-ing during the trial. Making an objection and having it overruled is often worse than not making it at all, since the objection merely draws the ju-rors' attention to the question and eventual answer.

4. Protect the record

Evidentiary objections must be made with two purposes in mind. First, to keep the jury from hearing improper evidence; second, to preserve any error on appeal.

You must make and protect your record. Errors in admitting evi-dence at trial are usually waived on appeal unless a proper, timely objec-tion was made during the trial. There may be times when you must object to protect the record even though the particular question or answer was not damaging.

5. Can you use an objection as a tactical device?

Making an objection necessarily has the effect of breaking the flow and pace of the opponent's examination or argument. While it is unethical to make an unfounded objection solely to disrupt your opponent, it is proper to make an objection whenever there is a legitimate evidentiary basis for it, even if the inevitable effect is to disrupt your opponent's presentation.

§8.3. How to make objections

1. Timeliness

Evidentiary objections must be timely. If a question is improper, an objection must be made before an answer to the question is given. Ordinarily, you should object to a question only when it is completed. However, if the question itself is directly prejudicial as well as improper, you must object promptly when this first becomes apparent.

If an answer is improper, an objection must be made as soon as that fact becomes apparent. Although it is entirely proper (and necessary in order to protect the record) to object to a completed answer and, if sustained, ask that the answer be struck and the jury instructed to disregard it, this is obviously an unsatisfactory solution. You can't "unring the bell," nor will the jury be able to, although the instruction to disregard alerts jurors to the improper evidence so that they will not be likely to discuss it during deliberations.

Tell the court that you are making an objection. All too often lawyers begin to state the reasons for the objections without ever announcing that they are objecting.

Example:

> *Counsel:* Your Honor, it seems to me that what counsel is trying to do here is to delve into the . . .
>
> *Court:* Are you making a speech or do you have an objection in mind?

Tell the court you are making an objection before stating anything else.

Examples:

> *Objection, your Honor. . . .*
>
> *Your Honor, we object. . . .*

Some courts require that objections be made while standing. Be sure you know what the practice in your court is.

2. Legal basis

Objections should state the legal basis for the objection. This should be done succinctly, without excessive argument.

Examples:

> *Objection, your Honor. The question calls for a hearsay answer.*
>
> *We object to the answer. It's unresponsive.*

If you wish to argue the matter, or your opponent attempts to make a long-winded, argumentative speech before the jury, ask for a side-bar conference. In that way the arguments on the objections can, as they should, be made without the jury hearing them.

Insist on a ruling. The objecting party is entitled to obtain a ruling on every objection made. Failure to obtain a ruling usually results in waiving any error on appeal.

Example:

> *Your Honor, may we have a ruling on our objection?*

Sometimes opposing counsel will withdraw the question being objected to before the court rules on the objection. When this is done, make sure that the next question is not essentially the same as the last. If it is, renew the objection.

Where, to preserve the record, you must have an answer struck and the jury instructed to disregard it, do so promptly and in a way that lets the jury know why it is being instructed.

Example:

> *Counsel:* Objection, your Honor, to the hearsay answer.
> *Court:* Objection sustained.
> *Counsel:* Your Honor, may we have the answer stricken and the jury instructed to disregard the improper answer?
> *Court:* Very well. The answer is stricken, the jury is instructed to disregard the answer.

Make sure that your objections, as well as any arguments for the objection, are directed to the judge. Don't argue directly with the opposing lawyer or try to interrupt him. The judge will usually let both sides argue on the objection at a side-bar conference, the usual procedure being to let the objector argue first and then have the other side respond before ruling on the objection. Be professional, make a legal argument based on the evidentiary rules, and make it to the judge.

Finally, if an objection is sustained against you, think about how you can overcome the objection. Was the objection based on a significant rule of evidence, such as hearsay or privilege, or was it based on an improper form of questioning? If the former, you should always see if you can get the same, or nearly the same, evidence properly admitted. If the latter, simply rephrasing the question will usually get around the objection.

Inexperienced lawyers are usually intimidated by objections, and frequently abandon an important point or line of questioning when an objection is sustained. As the direct examiner, you should always ask: If the point is important, how can I overcome the objection and get the evidence properly admitted?

3. Procedure

The safest procedure is to make the objection, then hesitate a moment before stating a legal basis for the objection. If the basis for the objection is obvious, the court will ordinarily sustain the objection without requiring you to state the legal basis. This is the best of all possible worlds, because the court's ruling is proper if there is *any* proper basis for the ruling. By momentarily hesitating, you give the court a chance to sustain your objection without having to state a basis for it. Under FRE 103, stating a specific ground for your objection is necessary only if it is not apparent from the context of the question or answer. If you state a specific ground for an objection, but it's not a proper one, the court can overrule your objection, even if there is another proper legal basis for objecting.

Always be prepared, of course, to state the legal basis for any objection you make. If the court overruled your objection, you preserve error only if you state a proper legal basis.

Learn what your judge's practices are. Some judges always want you to state the basis for any objection. Others will only ask for a basis when the reason is not apparent from the question or answer.

Finally, always remember that in many situations more than one legal ground may exist for excluding testimony or exhibits. For instance, a witness' testimony could violate the hearsay and privilege rules. A record, even where a proper business-records foundation was established, could still violate hearsay rules. A photograph could both lack a proper foundation and be unduly prejudicial. Accordingly, don't hang your hat on just one reason for excluding evidence. Where the evidence is damaging, develop alternative grounds why the evidence should be excluded.

§8.4. *Offers of proof*

When your opponent's objection has succeeded in excluding important evidence, you must make an offer of proof. The offer is necessary for two reasons. First, it may convince the trial judge to reverse his ruling. Second, the offer will create a record so that the reviewing court will know what the excluded evidence was and be able to determine if the exclusion was improper, and, if so, whether the improper exclusion constituted reversible error. An offer of proof is required under FRE 103 whenever it is not apparent from the context what the excluded evidence is.

There are two principal ways to make an offer of proof. Under the first method the lawyer simply tells the court what the proposed testimony would be, either in a narrative or question-and-answer format. This must be done out of the jury's presence. Tell the court you would like to make an offer of proof and ask for a side-bar conference, or, if your offer of proof will be lengthy, ask that the jury be excused for a few minutes.

Example:

> *Counsel:* Your Honor, if we were allowed to pursue this line of questioning, the witness would testify that one week after the robbery, the defendant tried to sell her a watch taken during the robbery.

Example:

> *Counsel:* Your Honor, if allowed to answer the question objected to, the witness would testify as follows:
>
> *Q.* What did he tell you at that time?
> *A.* He said: "I think I'm going home. I've got to pay the plumbing contractor for the work he did."

The second method involves using the witness himself. Again out of the jury's presence, continue the examination of the witness, using the same questions to which objections had been sustained. In this way the reviewing court will have a verbatim transcript of the testimony the trial court excluded. Under FRE 103(b) the trial court can require an offer of proof in question-and-answer form.

The first method has the advantage of efficiency, the second, the advantage of completeness. Although the second is preferable because it creates a clear record, it is time-consuming and impractical. Repeatedly asking that the jury be excused so you can make an offer of proof will incur both the court's and jury's disapproval. Save this for the critical parts of your case.

The offer should conform to the usual rules of evidence, since there is no error when the trial court excludes evidence that, as disclosed by the offer of proof, is objectionable for any reason, even if the objections could be cured. The opposing counsel can make any appropriate objections during the offer of proof.

Where the evidence successfully objected to is an exhibit, it must be made part of the record so the appellate court can review it, if its exclusion is raised as error on appeal. At the end of the trial the clerk will usually collect all exhibits. Make sure he receives all the exhibits you have offered in evidence.

§8.5. *Evidentiary objections*

Any law student who has taken a course in evidence can define the basic evidentiary objections. Trial lawyers, however, do not react to evidence in terms of those definitions. By the time they could determine whether a given question or answer falls within an evidentiary definition, the objection would hardly be timely. Trial lawyers shorten this thought process by learning and reacting to "buzz words," those forms that objectionable questions and answers commonly take in an actual trial.

The following evidentiary objections are commonly encountered at trial. Note that the objections can be classified into two broad categories, objections directed to form and those directed to substantive evidence. Objections to form can usually be cured by rephrasing the question or answer. On the other hand, objections to substantive evidence, if sustained, will actually result in excluding evidence.

Example (form):

> Q. Mr. Jones, is it possible that the driver of the other car didn't come to a complete stop at the stop sign?
> Counsel: Objection, your Honor. Counsel is asking the witness to speculate.
> Court: Sustained.
> Q. Mr. Jones, did you see the other car as it approached the sign?
> A. Yes.
> Q. Describe what the car did.
> A. It came to the corner, slowed down to around 10 mph, then kept going through the intersection without ever stopping.

In this example, the examining lawyer overcame the objection simply by rephrasing his questions in proper form to elicit the desired information. The objection only forced the examining lawyer to ask better phrased questions and ultimately obtain a better answer than he would probably have gotten to his original question. For this reason, it is often better not to object to questions that are improper in form only.

Example (substance):

> Q. Mr. Jones, tell the jury what you heard the bystander, Shirley Smith, say about how this accident happened.
> Counsel: Objection, hearsay.
> Court: Sustained.

In this example, the objection has succeeded in excluding from evidence any statements by Shirley Smith. Since there are no applicable exceptions to the hearsay rule, the statement simply cannot get into evidence, unless the proponent calls Shirley Smith as a witness to describe what she personally saw. If the proponent believes that a hearsay exception such as present sense impression or excited utterance applies, he should ask for permission to make an offer of proof out of the jury's presence.

The following objections are commonly encountered at trial:

Objections to questions
a. calls for irrelevant answer
b. calls for immaterial answer
c. witness is incompetent
d. violates the best evidence rule
e. calls for a privileged communication
f. calls for a conclusion
g. calls for an opinion (by an incompetent witness)
h. calls for a narrative answer
i. calls for a hearsay answer
j. leading
k. repetitive (asked and answered)
l. beyond the scope (of the direct, cross, or redirect)
m. assumes facts not in evidence
n. confusing/misleading/ambiguous/vague/unintelligible
o. speculative
p. compound question
q. argumentative
r. improper characterization
s. mistakes evidence/misquotes the witness
t. cumulative
u. improper impeachment

Objections to answers
a. irrelevant
b. immaterial
c. privileged
d. conclusion
e. opinion
f. hearsay
g. narrative
h. improper characterization
i. violates parol evidence rule
j. unresponsive/volunteered

Objections to exhibits
a. irrelevant
b. immaterial
c. no foundation

d. no authentication
e. contains hearsay
f. prejudice outweighs its probative value
g. contains inadmissible matter (mentions insurance, prior convictions, etc.)

1. Relevance (FRE 401 et seq.)

a. Definition

Relevant evidence under FRE 401 is evidence that has "any tendency to make the existence of any fact that is of consequence to the determination of the action more probable than it would be without the evidence." This definition incorporates both traditional relevance and materiality concepts. Relevance issues are directed to the sound discretion of the court.

In dealing with relevancy issues, it is useful to break the topic into sequential stages.

(1) Is it generally relevant (FRE 401-402)?
(2) Do FRE 403 considerations prevent admission?

Under FRE 403, relevant evidence may be excluded if its probative value is "substantially outweighed" by considerations such as unfair prejudice, confusion, delay, or waste of time. This balancing test is intentionally tipped in favor of admissibility.

If evidence is generally admissible under the FRE 401-403 balancing test, special relevance rules may nevertheless exclude the offered evidence.

(3) Do character trait rules apply (FRE 404, 405)?
(4) Do other acts rules apply (FRE 404(b))?
(5) Do habit rules apply (FRE 406)?
(6) Do policy exclusion rules apply (FRE 407-412)?

Basic relevance objections are important and can usually be anticipated in advance of trial. Hence, the safest procedure is to raise likely issues through pretrial motions and motions in limine.

b. Objection

Your Honor, we object. The question calls for an irrelevant answer.

Objection, your Honor. The witness' answer is going into irrelevant matter.

Objection. The exhibit is irrelevant.

c. Examples

Relevancy objections during trial usually arise where circumstantial evidence is offered, because the probative value of the proffered evidence may not be readily apparent. These circumstantial evidence issues usually are based on one of the special relevancy rules such as other acts or habit evidence.

Since relevancy issues can be complex and may involve substantial areas of additional testimony, as the opponent you should usually insist on an offer of proof. Do not be satisfied by a conclusory assertion from opposing counsel that the proffered evidence is relevant or will be "connected up." Do not tolerate a long-winded narrative by opposing counsel before the jury, explaining why the proffered testimony is relevant. Ask for a side bar and request a full offer of proof. At the conclusion of the offer of proof, make any relevancy or other objections that are appropriate.

Consider the following example of permissible other acts evidence. In a burglary case, the prosecutor can prove that the defendant obtained a copy of the building's floor plan several weeks before the burglary. This is circumstantial evidence of a plan or opportunity, and is admissible under FRE 404(b) as a permissible use of other acts evidence.

2. Materiality

a. Definition

Evidence is material if it has some logical bearing on an issue in the case. What is at issue is determined by the elements of the claims and defenses and by the pleadings. Each allegation not admitted is in issue.

The Federal Rules of Evidence have abandoned the term "materiality," which is now incorporated in the broad definition of relevancy contained in FRE 401. However, many state jurisdictions still differentiate between relevancy and materiality.

b. Objection

Objection, your Honor. This evidence is immaterial.

c. Examples

In the standard automobile case, the plaintiff must prove negligence, causation, and damages. Hence, proffered evidence that the defendant was insured is immaterial to the issues in the case.

In a worker's compensation case, where contributory negligence is not a defense, proof that the worker was negligent is immaterial.

3. Incompetent (FRE 601-606)

a. Definition

Incompetency refers to witnesses. A witness is incompetent if he suffers from a statutory disqualification that prevents him from testifying. The federal competency rules are in FRE 601-606. The only requirements are that a witness take an oath to testify truthfully and that he have personal knowledge about the matter he is testifying on. However, FRE 601 defers to state competency rules in civil diversity cases. Hence, you must also know the applicable state competency rules. Many states still have competency rules such as age, sound mind requirements, and Dead Man's Acts.

b. Objection

I object, your Honor. The witness is attempting to testify to a business transaction in violation of the Arizona Dead Man's Act.

c. Examples

Witness competency issues can usually be anticipated in advance, since discovery rules in civil cases, and in some criminal cases, require disclosure of witness lists. Today, however, incompetency disqualifications are uncommon and are usually limited to young age, infirm mind, and Dead Man's Acts. Dead Man's Act issues can be complex and should always be researched thoroughly whenever the lawsuit is by or against the estate of a deceased.

4. Privileged communication (FRE 501)

a. Definition

Communications made in confidence between parties having certain relationships are, upon objection, barred from disclosure. FRE 501 leaves unchanged the prior law on privilege. The privileges are based on the policy that it is preferable to foster open, frank communications between persons having certain relationships by protecting these communications from disclosure at trial. The most common privileges are attorney-client, physician-patient, priest-penitent, and husband-wife.

FRE 501 defers to state privilege rules in civil diversity cases. Hence, you must know the estate privilege rules as well. The state rules are frequently different from the federal ones, particularly in the marital privileges area, and the jurisdictions vary considerably regarding what relationships are protected by privilege rules.

b. Objection

I object. The question calls for a privileged communication between attorney and client. I claim the privilege for my client.

c. Examples

Problems in the privilege areas commonly center on whether the matter discussed is subject to a privilege, whether the communication was made under confidential circumstances, and whether a waiver of the privilege has occurred.

Privilege issues can frequently be anticipated. These issues are usually complex and must be thoroughly researched in advance of trial. If you anticipate a privilege problem, the best procedure is to raise it with a pretrial motion — as part of a pretrial conference hearing — or in a motion in limine, so that the issues can be resolved before trial if possible. If the problem suddenly arises during trial, the best practice is to object and ask for a side-bar conference so that you can adequately argue the objection.

Consider the following example of an exchange where a privileged issue has been raised by the opposing counsel:

Q. Mr. Smith, what did you tell your lawyer about what happened at the intersection?

Counsel: Objection, your Honor. That is a privileged communication. I claim the privilege for my client. May I be heard at side bar?

5. Best evidence rule (FRE 1001 et seq.)

a. Definition

The best evidence rule is more accurately called the original documents rule, since it applies principally to writings. The federal rule, contained in FRE 1001-1008, makes substantial changes from previous law.

The federal rule applies to any writing, recording, or photograph if it is "closely related to a controlling issue." If it applies, the general rule is that a "duplicate," such as a carbon copy or photocopy, is generally admissible to the same extent as the "original." However, if there is a genuine dispute over the writing's authenticity, such as a claim that the signature is forged or the contents have been altered, the original must be produced. Finally, in these situations the production of the original is excused if it is unavailable because, in good faith, it was lost or destroyed, it cannot be obtained by legal process, or the opponent has the original and refuses to produce it after being served with a notice to produce. The contents of the writing can then be proved by "other evidence," which includes duplicates as well as any other proof, such as oral testimony.

Keep in mind that some states still follow the traditional original documents rule, which usually requires production of the original.

b. Objection

Objection, your Honor. This evidence is not the best evidence of the contract.

Your Honor, we object to this exhibit on grounds of the best evidence rule.

c. Examples

Best evidence objections arise less frequently because the federal rule generally permits the admission of duplicates. However, if the original is still required, three things must usually be proved. First, the nonproduction of the original must be accounted for before other evidence of its contents is admissible. Second, a duplicate must be shown to be accurate before it can be admitted (see §5.3.15). Third, there must be proof that the original was in fact signed by the parties, if the writing is a legal document, such as a contract or promissory note.

Perhaps the most common example involves contracts. Consider the following:

Smith executes a contract with Jones. The original, bearing both Smith's and Jones' signatures, is placed in a file drawer in Smith's office. Copies of the contract are made and kept by both Smith and Jones. Two years later, Smith sues Jones for breach of contract. However, Smith cannot find the original of the contract. It's no longer in the file drawer. Smith and his office staff look everywhere for the original, without success. Just before trial they search again, without success. Under these circumstances, a copy of the contract, if properly authenticated, will be admissible at trial.

6. Parol evidence rule

a. Definition

The parol evidence rule bars from admission in evidence extrinsic oral evidence that modifies or contradicts a contractual instrument, freely entered into by competent parties, complete and clear on its face. Its purpose is to prevent a written agreement from being attacked and contradicted by oral testimony.

b. Objection

Objection, your Honor. The question calls for an answer which violates the parol evidence rule.

c. Examples

Violations of the parol evidence rule most frequently occur in contract cases when testimony relating to the execution of the contract is elicited. While it is proper (and necessary) to present evidence showing that the contract was signed by the parties, it is usually improper to elicit testimony between the parties as to what they intended the contract to do or what the terms of the contract mean to them.

Most problems involving the parol evidence rule concern the exceptions and whether they apply in a given situation. Exceptions include mistakes, incompleteness, ambiguities, and other uncertainties on the contract. Since the application of an exception will allow into evidence an entire additional line of inquiry, a prompt objection and insistence on an offer of proof is essential. Parol evidence objections can raise complex issues and should always be researched and raised in advance of trial, through pretrial motions or motions in limine, whenever possible.

7. No foundation

a. Definition

All exhibits must have the necessary foundations established before they can properly be admitted in evidence. The objection should be made when the exhibit is offered in evidence. It is always preferable for the proponent of the exhibit to offer it when the witness is still on the stand. If an objection is sustained, the witness is still there to supply any missing foundation elements.

b. Objection

Objection, your Honor. There is no proper foundation for the exhibit.

We object. There has been no showing that the photograph accurately portrays the intersection as it existed on the date of the accident.

c. Examples

A difficult decision involving exhibits is whether or not to object on foundation grounds. If the foundation problem can easily be solved, an objection may only force the other party to establish the missing element, at the same time enhancing the credibility and impact of the exhibit. Sometimes the better approach in these situations is not to object at all, then mention the missing element in closing arguments (e.g., "Of course it's a picture of the intersection, but is it worth anything? No one ever said that's the way the intersection looked on the date of the accident.").

Where you definitely want to keep the exhibit from being admitted and there is a substantial likelihood that a proper foundation cannot be established, a timely objection is essential.

8.   No authentication (FRE 901 et seq.)

a.   *Definition*

Writings and conversations must be authenticated to be admissible at trial. Signed writings such as contracts and notes must be shown to have been executed by a party or agent. This is true even if the signed writing can be qualified as a business record, since the business records exception solves only the hearsay problems, not the authentication requirement. (e.g., Smith signs a promissory note of the XYZ Company. The original is retained in the company's files. In a lawsuit on the unpaid note, the note can be qualified as a business record. However, the signature of Smith on the note must be proved before the note can be admissible against Smith.). Where conversations are involved, the identity of the parties to the conversation must be demonstrated.

b.   *Objection*

We object. This exhibit has not been authenticated.

Objection, your Honor. There has been no proof of who executed this document.

We object. There's no evidence that the witness knew who the person on the other end of the telephone was.

c.   *Examples*

The same considerations involving foundation objections apply equally to authentication objections.

9.   Hearsay (FRE 801 et seq.)

a.   *Definition*

Hearsay is a statement, other than one made by the declarant while testifying at the trial or hearing, offered in evidence to prove the truth of the matter asserted. The statement may be oral, written, or nonverbal conduct intended as an assertion. The federal rule essentially follows the classic definition of hearsay. However, it treats certain categories of statements as nonhearsay.

b.   *Objection*

Objection, your Honor, the question calls for a hearsay answer.

Objection, hearsay.

c. Examples

The most obvious and recurring hearsay problems arise when a question calls for, or a witness testifies to, out-of-court statements made by another person.

Q. What did Mr. Doe tell you about the accident?

Q. What did he say to you at that time?

These questions are objectionable if no exceptions to the hearsay rule, such as admission by parties, exist.

Hearsay problems can be more subtle, as when the form of the question does not obviously call for hearsay, yet the answer necessarily incorporates hearsay information.

Q. What did you learn from them?

Q. What did your investigation disclose?

Q. Did Dr. Johnson agree with you?

Q. What did your committee conclude?

Q. Was he a witness to the crash?

Answers to these questions will probably include facts obtained from other persons and, if in issue, will be hearsay and inadmissible unless an exception or a nonhearsay rationale exists.

Witnesses' answers often spontaneously fall into hearsay when the witness goes beyond the intended bounds of the question.

Q. Who was present at the meeting?
A. The eight people I mentioned previously.
Q. Did all of them talk during the meeting?
A. Yes. Mr. Jones, for instance, kept saying that. . . .
Counsel: Objection, your Honor, hearsay.

Hearsay objections are very common at trial and can be made in a variety of ways. Two frequently heard objections, however, should *not* be made. One is that the evidence is "self-serving." This objection is poorly stated, since all evidence tends to serve its proponent. The real objection is that evidence is hearsay and no exception applies. The other objection is that "the statement was made out of the presence of the defendant" in a criminal case. This objection has no basis, since the presence or absence of a defendant, or any other party, has nothing to do with its hearsay analysis. Don't make this objection! It is probably derived from an inaccurate and misplaced extension of the admission-by-silence concept.

10.   Leading (FRE 611)

a.   Definition

A leading question suggests the desired answer to the witness. This is generally improper during direct examination. Qualifiers such as "if anything" and "did you or did you not" do not make a question proper where the rest of the question is leading. Under certain circumstances, such as preliminary questions, child witnesses, and questioning hostile or adverse witnesses, the leading form is permissible.

b.   Objection

I object, your Honor. The question is leading.

Objection, your Honor. Counsel is leading the witness.

c.   Examples

Q.   Immediately after the robbery, did the victim scream? (A nonleading form is: Did the victim do anything after the robbery?)

Q.   Did he or did he not look both ways before stepping off the curb into the intersection? (A nonleading form is: Did he do anything before stepping off the curb?)

Note that either question can be asked and a responsive answer obtained in a nonleading way. Since the questioner can cure the objection, it is sometimes better not to object unless this happens repeatedly, since the leading questions usually detract from the impact of the answer.

11.   Narrative (FRE 611)

a.   Definition

A long narrative answer is objectionable because it allows a witness to inject inadmissible evidence into the trial without giving opposing counsel a reasonable opportunity to make a timely objection. By requiring the direct examiner to ask a series of specific questions to which the witness can give reasonably succinct answers, opposing counsel will have a reasonable opportunity to object. FRE 611(a) gives the court broad discretion to control the mode of interrogating witnesses.

b.   Objection

Objection, your Honor, the question calls for a narrative answer.

Objection, your Honor, the witness is giving a narrative answer.

c. Examples

Q. Tell the jury what happened that day.

Q. Please describe exactly how this collision occurred.

Q. Tell us what you know about the plaintiff.

Each of these questions potentially calls for a long narrative answer. A timely objection will force the proponent to ask specific questions that will break the narrative into manageable segments.

Sometimes witnesses will "take off" on an otherwise proper question and go way beyond what the answer reasonably calls for. The moment you detect this happening, object. One or two objections that are sustained will usually train the witness not to give narrative answers.

On the other hand, narrative objections should not automatically be made whenever an appropriate situation arises. Often narrative answers are an ineffective way of presenting a direct examination. If the witness' answers ramble or appear disorganized, making a narrative objection will only help the direct examiner regain control over his witness.

12. Conclusions (FRE 701)

a. Definition

A conclusion is a deduction drawn from a fact or series of facts. In general, witnesses can only testify to facts. Conclusions, based on those facts, are for the jury to draw as it sees fit. FRE 701 has expanded the permissible extent of lay witness conclusions by permitting the witness to testify to inferences from facts actually perceived by the witness under certain circumstances.

b. Objection

Objection, your Honor. The question calls for a conclusion.

We object. The witness is attempting to give his conclusion on a matter in issue.

c. Examples (questions)

Q. Was he driving the car recklessly?

Q. You got there as fast as possible, didn't you?

Q. Didn't the defendant intend to kill the victim?

d. Examples (answers)

Q. Describe what he looked like.
A. He was drunk as a skunk.

Q.   What's the next thing he did?
A.   He just quit trying, that's what.

Q.   Describe the work the repairman did.
A.   He didn't do any of the repairs competently.

13.   Opinions (FRE 701 et seq.)

a.   Definition

Opinions are generally proper only in those areas in which special-ized knowledge will assist the trier of fact and the witness has been prop-erly qualified as an expert (FRE 702). Lay witnesses can give opinions and inferences only where the opinion is based on the witness' perception of an event and is helpful to the jury in understanding the facts. (FRE 701) Common examples are speed, time, distance, and sobriety.

b.   Objection

Objection, your Honor. The question calls for an improper opinion.

Objection. The witness has not been sufficiently qualified as an expert.

We object. This matter is not a proper subject for expert opinion.

c.   Examples

The most common problems in this area involve issues of whether the subject matter is a proper one for opinion testimony, particularly when a lay witness is on the stand.

Q.   (To lay witness) Was the design of the automatic clutch pedal of this forklift truck unreasonably dangerous?

Unless the lay witness has some special knowledge in this area, such as a forklift truck operator would have, asking his opinion on a technical sub-ject is objectionable. Answers that are objectionable as conclusions often run afoul of the opinion rule as well.

Although FRE 704 permits opinions on "ultimate issues," this does not permit all opinions, since the opinion must be helpful to the jury in understanding the evidence or resolving issues. A legal opinion is proper only if the jury cannot reach it on its own.

Consider the following testimony in a civil commitment proceeding:

Q.   What was your psychiatric diagnosis?
A.   (Psychiatrist) The defendant is a paranoid schizophrenic.
Q.   Is he a danger to himself or others?
A.   Yes.

Here the clinical diagnosis cannot be used by the jury to determine if the defendant was legally incompetent, so asking for an opinion on the ultimate legal issue is proper. (However, note the restrictions in FRE 704(b) governing sanity issues in criminal cases.)

Consider the following testimony in a personal injury case:

Q. What did you conclude from your investigation?
A. (Accident-reconstruction expert) The defendant crossed the center lane just before the impact.
Q. Was the defendant negligent?
Counsel: Objection, your Honor.
Court: Sustained.

Here the expert's opinion on negligence is improper, since the jury can use his investigation results to reach a legal conclusion, and the expert's opinion on negligence does not help the jury understand the facts or resolve issues.

14.   Repetitive (asked and answered) (FRE 611)

a.   *Definition*

Questions and answers previously elicited and made by the same party should not be constantly repeated. The reasons are twofold: First, having the same questions and answers repeated wastes time. Second, it places undue emphasis on those questions and answers repeated. This rule applies equally to direct and cross-examinations. While the federal rules have no specific rule against repetitive questions and answers, FRE 611(a) gives the court discretion in controlling examinations of witnesses to "avoid needless consumption of time." (The cross-examiner, of course, may ask the same questions previously asked during the direct examination.)

b.   *Objection*

Your Honor, we object. The question is repetitive.

Objection, your Honor. That question has already been asked and answered.

c.   *Examples*

The most common problems arise when a lawyer attempts to repeat the substance of the previous question (that elicited a particularly favorable answer), but phrases it in a slightly different way. The significant determination is not whether the new question is identical to a previous question, but whether the new question reasonably calls for the same answer that has previously been given. If it does, and the lawyer constantly is using this method to repeat and emphasize what he considers important testimony, make the objection.

15. Assuming facts not in evidence

a. Definition

This objection often occurs during examinations, particularly cross-examinations, when the introductory part of the question assumes a fact that is not in evidence and the existence of which is in dispute.

b. Objection

Your Honor, we object. The question assumes a fact not in evidence.

Objection, your Honor. There's no evidence that. . . .

c. Examples

With lay witnesses, the objection most commonly arises on cross-examination where the question includes as a fact something that has not been shown to exist.

Q. You were over 50 feet from the skid marks, weren't you?

Q. After you ran from the scene, you never looked back, did you?

If there has been no evidence of any skid marks, or that the witness ran from the scene, these questions are improper.

16. Misstates evidence/misquotes witnesses

a. Definition

A question that misstates and distorts evidence or misquotes a witness is improper, whether this is done during the examination of witnesses or during closing arguments.

b. Objection

Objection, your Honor. Counsel is misstating the evidence.

Objection, your Honor. There's no evidence that. . . .

c. Examples

Misstatements and misquotes usually occur in two types of situations. First, a lawyer in a question refers to evidence produced earlier during the trial, but does so inaccurately. Second, some lawyers habitually repeat a witness' last answer as part of the next question, but again, do so inaccurately. The inaccuracy is usually, but not always, innocently done.

Q. You hit the man, didn't you?

A. Yes.

Q. After attacking him, what happened?

Where inaccurate repetition occurs, a prompt objection is essential.

17. Confusing/misleading/ambiguous/vague/unintelligible

a. Definition

A question must be posed in a reasonably clear and specific manner so that the witness can reasonably know what information the examiner is eliciting.

b. Objection

Objection, your Honor. The question is confusing and ambiguous.

Objection. The question is too vague.

c. Examples

Confusing, ambiguous, and vague questions usually arise where the evidence has involved many occurrences, witnesses, and conversations. The examiner will ask a question about an event or conversation without stating, or it being apparent, which happening the question is directed to.

Q. Who was present at *that* meeting?

Q. What did *he* say during the March 13 meeting?

In both examples the question is unclear if there was more than one meeting or many persons present. Object, and force the examiner to state which meeting or which person he is referring to.

18. Speculative

a. Definition

Any question that asks the witness to speculate or guess is improper. This is because cases should be decided on facts, and guesswork from a witness on what might be the facts or what possibly could have happened is irrelevant. On the other hand, witnesses are permitted to give estimates and approximations, most commonly of distance, time, speed, and age. In addition, greater latitude is given during the examination of expert witnesses, and questions that are essentially speculative in nature will sometimes be permitted.

b. Objection

Your Honor, we object. The question is speculative.

Objection. Counsel is asking the witness to guess.

c. Examples

Q. Isn't it possible that. . . .

Q. It's conceivable that . . . , isn't it?

Q. If the car had been farther away you would have been able to avoid hitting him, wouldn't you?

19. Compound

a. Definition

A compound question is one that brings up two separate facts within a single question. It is objectionable because any simple answer to the question will be unclear.

b. Objection

Objection, Your Honor, to the compound question.

We object, your Honor, to the double question.

c. Examples

Q. Did you go to Smith's Tavern on the 13th and to Frank's Tavern two days later?

Q. Did you go to Smith's store on the 13th and if so, did you buy anything?

If only one of the two facts in each question is true, neither a "yes" nor a "no" response will be accurate. The real danger of the compound question is that the witness will give a simple, innocent answer that is only partially correct. Opposing counsel will then attempt to use the well-intentioned but inaccurate answer during closing arguments. The objectionable question can, of course, be easily divided into two or more separate questions.

20. Argumentative

a. Definition

Any question that is essentially an argument to the jury is improper. Such a question elicits no new information. It simply states a conclusion and asks the witness to agree with it. These "questions" should be saved for closing arguments.

b. *Objection*

Objection, your Honor. The question is argumentative.

We object. Counsel is arguing with the witness.

c. *Examples*

Q. Since you were 80 feet away, it was raining and dark, and the whole robbery took only a few seconds, you couldn't have had a good opportunity to see the robber's face, could you?

21. Improper characterization

a. *Definition*

A close relative of the argumentative and conclusory question, improper characterizations in both questions and answers are really argumentative and conclusory in nature. Since characterization is something that the jury, not the lawyer or witness, should infer, if appropriate, the question is improper.

b. *Objection*

Your Honor, we object to counsel's characterization.

Objection, your Honor. The witness' characterization is improper.

c. *Examples*

Q. He was attacking you like a frenzied dog, wasn't he?

Q. How much money did you lend to this financial wizard?

A. He was acting like a spoiled brat who had his favorite toy taken away.

22. Unresponsive/volunteered

a. *Definition*

An answer that does not directly respond to a question is objectionable as unresponsive. Where the answer goes beyond what is necessary to answer the question, that surplusage of the answer is objectionable as volunteered. Only the party calling the witness can make the objection. This is because if the answer is properly admissible, there is no point in striking the answer as unresponsive. If the answer is objectionable for another reason, the objector need only object on the proper evidentiary grounds.

b. Objection

Objection, your Honor. The answer is not responsive to my question. I ask that the answer be stricken.

I object to the volunteered portion of the answer and ask that everything after . . . be stricken.

c. Examples

Most problems occur when a witness is so eager to tell his story that he uses each question as a springboard for a long narrative answer. Adequate pretrial preparation of witnesses should prevent this problem before it occurs. When it does occur, however, you should promptly reestablish your control over the witness.

Q. Mr. Smith, please listen to my question and answer only that question.

Keep in mind that unresponsive answers can damage both sides. When you are the direct examiner, such answers ruin your pace and logical presentation of your evidence. For the cross-examiner, the danger always exists that the witness will say something prejudicial that is inadmissible.

23. Prejudice outweighs probativeness (FRE 403)

a. Definition

This objection is principally directed to exhibits, although it can also apply to testimony. Merely because an exhibit has probative value does not guarantee that the exhibit will be admissible. Exhibits, although probative, may be extremely prejudicial. Where the prejudicial impact is substantial, and its probative value slight, the court can exercise its discretion and exclude the exhibit.

b. Objection

Objection, your Honor. The exhibit's prejudicial impact exceeds its probative value.

c. Examples

This objection is most commonly made against photographs, usually in color, of the deceased in homicide cases. It is also sometimes raised where personal injury plaintiffs are asked to display their injuries to the jury.

Often the exhibit has been, or can be, duplicated by other less inflammatory evidence. In those situations the exhibit can be challenged not only as being prejudicial, but cumulative as well.

Whenever such a situation arises, a prompt objection or a motion in limine is essential. An inflammatory exhibit, once before the jury, can hardly be retracted. The objection should be anticipated and made out of the jury's hearing whenever possible.

24. Cumulative (FRE 611)

a. Definition

The court has discretion to control repetitive evidence introduced during trials. When one witness after another parades into court reinforcing the previous witness while adding nothing new, or a series of exhibits all demonstrate the same things, the witnesses and exhibits are unnecessarily cumulative and are therefore objectionable.

b. Objection

Objection, your Honor. This evidence is entirely cumulative.

We object to this evidence. It's already been covered by four other witnesses.

c. Examples

Cumulative witnesses are commonly incurred where reputation evidence is involved. A party may choreograph a parade of witnesses, all attesting to the good reputation of a particular person. The time to object is when the jury or judge appears to become restless or bored.

Cumulative exhibits are most commonly photographs. Where each additional photograph adds nothing of consequence to exhibits already in evidence, an objection may be appropriate.

25. Beyond the scope (FRE 611)

a. Definition

Under FRE 611(b), cross-examinations should be "limited to the subject matter of the direct examination and matters affecting the credibility of the witness." Redirect examinations, in turn, should be limited to matters raised during the cross-examination. This controls the efficient and orderly presentation of evidence in each party's case in chief. Where the cross or redirect examination attempts to pursue matters not covered by the preceding examination, an objection is proper.

This objection may also be raised during rebuttal testimony and re-buttal closing arguments. Rebuttal testimony is proper only when it contradicts substantial evidence previously presented by your opponent. In the same vein, the plaintiff's rebuttal argument is proper only when it responds to matters raised during the defendant's closing argument.

b. Objection

Objection. This is beyond the scope of the direct.

We object, your Honor. This matter wasn't mentioned during the direct examination.

We object to this testimony, your Honor. It's improper rebuttal.

c. Examples

Scope objections are most commonly encountered during witness examinations when the cross-examiner attempts to elicit facts from the witness in areas not previously covered during the direct examination. Where the witness can give favorable testimony in new areas to the cross-examiner, he must usually call the witness as his own, in his case in chief, and elicit the testimony at that time. Note, however, that under FRE 611(b) the court in its discretion may permit the cross-examiner to inquire into new matters during the direct examination, provided that the inquiry is done in a nonleading way. Whether the court will permit you to do this will depend largely on how substantial the new matters are and how lengthy the additional examination will be. (Most state jurisdictions follow the federal scope-of-cross rules. A few, however, follow the English, or "wide open" rule, which usually permits cross-examination on any relevant matter, regardless of whether it was previously mentioned on direct.)

On redirect examination the problem usually arises when the examiner realizes he has forgotten to ask a certain line of questions or establish the foundation for an exhibit, and attempts to do so after the cross-examination. If this happens, ask the court to permit you to reopen the direct examination for this limited purpose.

Scope objections to rebuttal testimony or rebuttal closing arguments are proper in similar situations. When the rebuttal testimony attempts to present entirely new evidence, or a rebuttal closing argument ventures substantially beyond the matters covered by the defendant's argument, an objection should be sustained.

26. Improper impeachment (FRE 613)

a. Definition

Impeachment rules are technical and have several requirements. The cross-examiner must have a good faith basis for raising the impeaching matter; the matter must in fact be impeaching; it must be raised on cross; and the witness must be given a reasonable opportunity to admit, deny, or explain the impeaching matter. If the witness denies or equivocates, the matter must be proved up with extrinsic evidence if it is noncollateral. (See §6.7 for a detailed discussion of the various impeachment methods and requirements.)

Under FRE 613(a), a witness can be cross-examined with a prior inconsistent written statement without the cross-examiner first showing it to the witness. Under FRE 607, any party can impeach any witness, including its own.

b. Objection

We object, your Honor. This is improper impeachment.

c. Examples

Problems with impeachment are usually found in four areas. First, the cross-examiner may attempt to use a prior statement that is not materially inconsistent. Second, the cross-examiner may not read verbatim the impeaching statement when he asks the witness to admit it. Where a report, written statement, or transcript is involved, it must be read verbatim. Paraphrasing or summarizing is improper. In addition, the impeaching statement cannot be taken out of context. Under FRE 106, you can require your opponent to read the entire relevant portion of the impeaching statement. Third, the cross-examiner may attempt to introduce in evidence at a later time an impeaching statement without ever having given the witness an opportunity to admit or deny the statement during the cross-examination. Fourth, the cross-examiner may fail to prove up the impeachment where required.

In each case, the remedy is the same: Object promptly to prevent the improper impeachment from getting before the jury. If the cross-examiner failed to prove up where required, you must move to strike and ask that the jury disregard it to preserve error.

§8.6. Other objections

In addition to objections made during the presentation of evidence, numerous other objections can be made during the course of the trial. This section will review the more common objections that can be made during jury selection, opening statements, and closing arguments.

1. Jury selection

Objections commonly made during the jury selection process include the following.

a.   Mentioning insurance

Under FRE 411 and parallel state evidentiary rules, it is improper to mention to the jury that any person involved in the case was or was not covered by liability insurance. This necessarily follows since the existence of insurance is irrelevant to the issue of negligence, while its disclosure is inevitably prejudicial.

However, lawyers conducting the voir dire examination of the jurors in personal injury and other tort cases, particularly plaintiff's attorneys, are vitally interested in knowing whether any of the prospective jurors have ever worked for insurance companies or related enterprises. Accordingly, many jurisdictions permit the lawyers during the voir dire examination to inquire on this subject indirectly. Asking, "Have you ever worked for the claims department of any company," or similar questions is often permitted, since such a question does not directly suggest that a party to the suit was insured. You must, of course, determine in advance whether and how your judge will permit this topic to be raised.

b.   Arguing law

It is usually improper for counsel to discuss in detail the law applicable to the case on trial, or to ask jurors whether they agree or disagree with the law. Advising the jury of the applicable law is a judicial function. The only appropriate consideration is whether the juror will commit himself to follow the law as the judge gives it. However, some judges will permit discussing the applicable law in general terms. Determine what your judge's attitude is in advance of trial.

c.   Arguing facts

It is also generally improper to tell the jury the details of the case it will hear. Attorneys often attempt to determine what jurors' reactions to the evidence will be by revealing portions of it during the voir dire, then challenging those jurors who had negative reactions to it. That this is commonly done accounts in large part for the recent trend of having the voir dire conducted by the court, with the lawyers' participation limited to asking questions solely about jurors' backgrounds.

2.   Opening statements

Objections commonly made during the opening statements include the following.

a.   Arguing the law or the instructions

Opening statements permit the lawyers to tell the jury what they anticipate the evidence at trial will be. Accordingly, it is usually objectionable to review or discuss in detail the law or instructions applicable to the case. Courts, however, differ widely on how strictly they require counsel to adhere to this rule.

b. Argumentative

The opening statements should be a synopsis of the anticipated facts that will be presented during the trial. Accordingly, it is improper to make the opening statement argumentative, such as arguing the credibility of witnesses and other evidence the jury will hear, or arguing inferences and deductions from that evidence. These are appropriate only during closing arguments. Again, judges differ widely in how strictly this rule is enforced.

c. Mentioning inadmissible evidence

It is always improper to bring before the jury, during opening statements or at any time, evidence that is inadmissible. Common forms of inadmissible evidence are:

1. evidence that has been suppressed by pretrial motions
2. privileged matters, such as attorney-client or husband-wife conversations
3. evidence of settlement negotiations in civil cases and plea negotiations in criminal cases are inadmissible at any time under FRE 408 and 410
4. subsequent repairs, made after an event, are inadmissible to prove negligence in connection with that event under FRE 407
5. evidence of payment of, or promise to pay, medical and related expenses resulting from injury is inadmissible to prove liability under FRE 409

d. Mentioning unprovable evidence

It is improper to mention evidence that, although true, is incapable of being proved at trial. Where a witness has died or cannot be found for trial, it is improper to state what that witness' testimony would be. Where exhibits have been lost or destroyed, it is improper to tell the jury what such exhibits contain. The test here is good faith. A lawyer can include in his opening statements only evidence that he in good faith believes is both available and admissible at trial.

e. Giving personal opinions

It is improper to tell the jury your personal opinion on any evidentiary matter. Such personal opinions are not proper because they directly inject the credibility of the trial lawyer into the trial. Accordingly, phrases such as *I think* or *I believe* are best left out of your trial vocabulary.

f. Discussing the other side's evidence

It is improper to tell the jury during opening statements what you expect the other side to present as evidence during the trial, since the other side is not obligated to present evidence and can elect to present whatever it chooses. This is a problem usually limited to criminal cases, where it is highly prejudicial for the prosecutor to suggest what the defense will prove, since the defendant is never required to prove anything.

3. Closing arguments

Objections commonly made during closing arguments include the following.

a. Misstating evidence

It is improper to misstate evidence or misquote testimony admitted during the trial. However, it is proper to argue any reasonable inferences and deductions from such evidence. Trial judges are usually reluctant to sustain such objections absent a clear violation, since what the evidence actually admitted at trial was involves memory and recollection, which can and do often differ. Accordingly, judges often overrule such objections, but remind the jurors that they heard the evidence and should rely on their recollections in determining whether counsel's statements of the evidence are accurate. This objection is best saved for obvious gross misrepresentations and misstatements.

b. Misstating law and quoting instructions

It is improper in some jurisdictions to read the court's instructions verbatim to the jury during closing arguments. This is the court's function. However, it is usually permissible in those jurisdictions to refer to the instructions the court will actually give and paraphrase their contents to the jury. When this is done, the paraphrasing or other reference to the instructions must be fair and accurate.

Other jurisdictions take the opposite approach and require that any instructions used during arguments be read verbatim, so that inaccurate paraphrasing is impossible. You must learn what the practice is in your jurisdiction.

c. Using the impermissible per diem damages argument

In many jurisdictions it is improper when arguing damages in personal injury cases to ask for a specific cash amount on any element of damages on a per diem basis and then multiply that figure by the actual life expectancy of the injured party. This usually leads to astronomical figures (e.g., asking only for $25 per day for pain and suffering will yield $365,000 over a 40-year life expectancy). Many jurisdictions permit the damages argument to ask for only one lump-sum figure for each proper element of damages. As always, make sure you know what the permissible methods of arguing damages are in your jurisdiction.

d. Giving personal opinions

It is improper for counsel to inject his personal opinions, beliefs, and attitudes into the case at any time. Therefore, such comments as *I think* and *I believe*, unless clearly and directly linked to the evidence, are improper. Since these phrases often draw objections when used, they are best excised from your trial vocabulary.

e. Appealing to jury's bias, prejudice, and pecuniary interest

Our jury trial system requires the jury to reach a verdict without resorting to bias or prejudice. That verdict should be based solely on the evidence admitted during the trial and the court's instructions on the applicable law. Accordingly, suggesting to the jury that they may be personally affected by a given verdict is improper, even if done indirectly.

f. Personal attacks on parties and counsel

It is always improper to engage in personal attacks on opposing counsel or the other parties in the trial. This should never be done, for both legal and persuasive reasons. Nothing can diminish your credibility before the jury faster than resorting to this type of argument. Never let things get personal, either at this or any other stage of the trial. Commenting on a party's race, religion, national origin, political affiliations, or other personal characteristics is in most instances highly improper.

g. Prejudicial arguments

A large number of arguments are improper because they are prejudicial comments having little or nothing to do with the evidence. Each substantive area of trial work has developed substantial case law on improper arguments. For instance, in personal injury cases it is improper to argue the wealth or poverty of the parties, the effect of income taxes on a money judgment (in most jurisdictions), or the effect of a judgment on insurance rates and other indirect costs of living. It is usually improper to ask the jury to put itself in the shoes of any of the parties, since this is really a direct appeal to the juror's emotions (e.g., in a paraplegic case, you cannot argue, "If someone came to you and said, 'I'll give you $1,000,000, but you'll have to spend the rest of your life lying on your back,' would you take it?"). In criminal cases it is improper to argue that the defendant will commit more crimes if released, that the jury has a moral obligation to protect society from the defendant, or that the defendant may attempt to retaliate personally against the jury hearing the case.

From a tactical point of view, your approach to making objections during these phases of the trial is essentially identical to the evidentiary phases. Always remember that jurors dislike objections that appear to keep interesting information from them. Where you can anticipate problems, you should raise them out of the jury's hearing whenever possible. Maximize your use of pretrial motions, motions in limine, and sidebar conferences. Where you cannot resolve problems in advance, use your objections sparingly. Consistent with protecting your client's interests and making a good record, save your objections for important situations, when you are reasonably certain that the court will sustain your objections. Utilizing such an approach usually develops a favorable impression on the jury, an impression that can pay dividends when the jury is deliberating on the verdict.

FEDERAL RULES OF EVIDENCE

(as amended through October 1, 1987)

ARTICLE I. GENERAL PROVISIONS

ARTICLE II. JUDICIAL NOTICE

ARTICLE III. PRESUMPTIONS IN CIVIL ACTIONS AND PROCEEDINGS

ARTICLE IV. RELEVANCY AND ITS LIMITS

ARTICLE V. PRIVILEGES

ARTICLE VI. WITNESSES

ARTICLE XI. MISCELLANEOUS RULES

RULES OF EVIDENCE FOR UNITED STATES COURTS AND MAGISTRATES

ARTICLE I. GENERAL PROVISIONS

Rule 101. Scope

These rules govern proceedings in the courts of the United States and before United States bankruptcy judges and United States magistrates, to the extent and with the exceptions stated in rule 1101.

Rule 102. Purpose and construction

These rules shall be construed to secure fairness in administration, elimination of unjustifiable expense and delay, and promotion of growth and development of the law of evidence to the end that the truth may be ascertained and proceedings justly determined.

Rule 103.   Rulings on evidence

(a) **Effect of erroneous ruling.**   Error may not be predicated upon a ruling which admits or excludes evidence unless a substantial right of the party is affected, and

(1) **Objection.**   In case the ruling is one admitting evidence, a timely objection or motion to strike appears of record, stating the specific ground of objection, if the specific ground was not apparent from the context; or

(2) **Offer of proof.**   In case the ruling is one excluding evidence, the substance of the evidence was made known to the court by offer or was apparent from the context within which questions were asked.

(b) **Record of offer and ruling.**   The court may add any other or further statement which shows the character of the evidence, the form in which it was offered, the objection made, and the ruling thereon. It may direct the making of an offer in question and answer form.

(c) **Hearing of jury.**   In jury cases, proceedings shall be conducted, to the extent practicable, so as to prevent inadmissible evidence from being suggested to the jury by any means, such as making statements or offers of proof or asking questions in the hearing of the jury.

(d) **Plain error.**   Nothing in this rule precludes taking notice of plain errors affecting substantial rights although they were not brought to the attention of the court.

Rule 104.   Preliminary questions

(a) **Questions of admissibility generally.**   Preliminary questions concerning the qualification of a person to be a witness, the existence of a privilege, or the admissibility of evidence shall be determined by the court, subject to the provisions of subdivision (b). In making its determination it is not bound by the rules of evidence except those with respect to privileges.

(b) **Relevancy conditioned on fact.**   When the relevancy of evidence depends upon the fulfillment of a condition of fact, the court shall admit it upon, or subject to, the introduction of evidence sufficient to support a finding of the fulfillment of the condition.

(c) **Hearing of jury.**   Hearings on the admissibility of confessions shall in all cases be conducted out of the hearing of the jury. Hearings on other preliminary matters shall be so conducted when the interests of justice require or when an accused is a witness and so requests.

(d) **Testimony by accused.**   The accused does not, by testifying upon a preliminary matter, become subject to cross-examination as to other issues in the case.

(e) Weight and credibility. This rule does not limit the right of a party to introduce before the jury evidence relevant to weight or credibility.

Rule 105. Limited admissibility

When evidence which is admissible as to one party or for one purpose but not admissible as to another party or for another purpose is admitted, the court, upon request, shall restrict the evidence to its proper scope and instruct the jury accordingly.

Rule 106. Remainder of or related writings or recorded statements

When a writing or recorded statement or part thereof is introduced by a party, an adverse party may require the introduction at that time of any other part or any other writing or recorded statement which ought in fairness to be considered contemporaneously with it.

ARTICLE II. JUDICIAL NOTICE

Rule 201. Judicial notice of adjudicative facts

(a) Scope of rule. This rule governs only judicial notice of adjudicative facts.

(b) Kinds of facts. A judicially noticed fact must be one not subject to reasonable dispute in that it is either (1) generally known within the territorial jurisdiction of the trial court or (2) capable of accurate and ready determination by resort to sources whose accuracy cannot reasonably be questioned.

(c) When discretionary. A court may take judicial notice, whether requested or not.

(d) When mandatory. A court shall take judicial notice if requested by a party and supplied with the necessary information.

(e) Opportunity to be heard. A party is entitled upon timely request to an opportunity to be heard as to the propriety of taking judicial notice and the tenor of the matter noticed. In the absence of prior notification, the request may be made after judicial notice has been taken.

(f) Time of taking notice. Judicial notice may be taken at any stage of the proceeding.

(g) Instructing jury. In a civil action or proceeding, the court shall instruct the jury to accept as conclusive any fact judicially noticed. In a criminal case, the court shall instruct the jury that it may, but is not required to, accept as conclusive any fact judicially noticed.

ARTICLE III.   PRESUMPTIONS IN CIVIL ACTIONS AND PROCEEDINGS

Rule 301.   Presumptions in general civil actions and proceedings

In all civil actions and proceedings, not otherwise provided for by Act of Congress or by these rules, a presumption imposes on the party against whom it is directed the burden of going forward with evidence to rebut or meet the presumption, but does not shift to such party the burden of proof in the sense of the risk of nonpersuasion, which remains throughout the trial upon the party on whom it was originally cast.

Rule 302.   Applicability of state law in civil actions and proceedings

In civil actions and proceedings, the effect of a presumption respecting a fact which is an element of a claim or defense as to which State law supplies the rule of decision is determined in accordance with State law.

ARTICLE IV.   RELEVANCY AND ITS LIMITS

Rule 401.   Definition of "relevant evidence"

"Relevant evidence" means evidence having any tendency to make the existence of any fact that is of consequence to the determination of the action more probable or less probable than it would be without the evidence.

Rule 402.   Relevant evidence generally admissible; irrelevant evidence inadmissible

All relevant evidence is admissible, except as otherwise provided by the Constitution of the United States, by Act of Congress, by these rules, or by other rules prescribed by the Supreme Court pursuant to statutory authority. Evidence which is not relevant is not admissible.

Rule 403.   Exclusion of relevant evidence on grounds of prejudice, confusion, or waste of time

Although relevant, evidence may be excluded if its probative value is substantially outweighed by the danger of unfair prejudice, confusion of the issues, or misleading the jury, or by considerations of undue delay, waste of time, or needless presentation of cumulative evidence.

Rule 404. Character evidence not admissible to prove conduct; exceptions; other crimes

(a) **Character evidence generally.** Evidence of a person's character or a trait of character is not admissible for the purpose of proving action in conformity therewith on a particular occasion, except:

    (1) **Character of accused.** Evidence of a pertinent trait of character offered by an accused, or by the prosecution to rebut the same;

    (2) **Character of victim.** Evidence of a pertinent trait of character of the victim of the crime offered by an accused, or by the prosecution to rebut the same, or evidence of a character trait of peacefulness of the victim offered by the prosecution in a homicide case to rebut evidence that the victim was the first aggressor;

    (3) **Character of witness.** Evidence of the character of a witness, as provided in rules 607, 608, and 609.

(b) **Other crimes, wrongs, or acts.** Evidence of other crimes, wrongs, or acts is not admissible to prove the character of a person in order to show action in conformity therewith. It may, however, be admissible for other purposes, such as proof of motive, opportunity, intent, preparation, plan, knowledge, identity, or absence of mistake or accident.

Rule 405. Methods of proving character

(a) **Reputation or opinion.** In all cases in which evidence of character or a trait of character of a person is admissible, proof may be made by testimony as to reputation or by testimony in the form of an opinion. On cross-examination, inquiry is allowable into relevant specific instances of conduct.

(b) **Specific instances of conduct.** In cases in which character or a trait of character of a person is an essential element of a charge, claim, or defense, proof may also be made of specific instances of that person's conduct.

Rule 406. Habit; routine practice

Evidence of the habit of a person or of the routine practice of an organization, whether corroborated or not and regardless of the presence of eyewitnesses, is relevant to prove that the conduct of the person or organization on a particular occasion was in conformity with the habit or routine practice.

Rule 407. Subsequent remedial measures

When, after an event, measures are taken which, if taken previously, would have made the event less likely to occur, evidence of the subsequent measures is not admissible to prove negligence or culpable conduct in connection with the event. This rule does not require the exclusion of evidence of subsequent measures when offered for another purpose, such as proving ownership, control, or feasibility of precautionary measures, if controverted, or impeachment.

Rule 408.   Compromise and offers to compromise

Evidence of (1) furnishing or offering or promising to furnish, or (2) accepting or offering or promising to accept, a valuable consideration in compromising or attempting to compromise a claim which was disputed as to either validity or amount, is not admissible to prove liability for or invalidity of the claim or its amount. Evidence of conduct or statements made in compromise negotiations is likewise not admissible. This rule does not require the exclusion of any evidence otherwise discoverable merely because it is presented in the course of compromise negotiations. This rule also does not require exclusion when the evidence is offered for another purpose, such as proving bias or prejudice of a witness, negativing a contention of undue delay, or proving an effort to obstruct a criminal investigation or prosecution.

Rule 409.   Payment of medical and similar expenses

Evidence of furnishing or offering or promising to pay medical, hospital, or similar expenses occasioned by an injury is not admissible to prove liability for the injury.

Rule 410.   Inadmissibility of pleas, offers of pleas, and related statements

Except as otherwise provided in this rule, evidence of a plea of guilty, later withdrawn, or a plea of nolo contendere, or of an offer to plead guilty or nolo contendere to the crime charged or any other crime, or of statements made in connection with, and relevant to, any of the foregoing pleas or offers, is not admissible in any civil or criminal proceeding against the person who made the plea or offer. However, evidence of a statement made in connection with, and relevant to, a plea of guilty, later withdrawn, a plea of nolo contendere, or an offer to plead guilty or nolo contendere to the crime charged or any other crime, is admissible in a criminal proceeding for perjury or false statement if the statement was made by the defendant under oath, on the record, and in the presence of counsel.

Rule 411.   Liability insurance

Evidence that a person was or was not insured against liability is not admissible upon the issue whether the person acted negligently or otherwise wrongfully. This rule does not require the exclusion of evidence of insurance against liability when offered for another purpose, such as proof of agency, ownership, or control, or bias or prejudice of a witness.

Rule 412.   Rape cases; relevance of victim's past behavior

(a) Notwithstanding any other provision of law, in a criminal case in which a person is accused of rape or of assault with intent to commit rape, reputation or opinion evidence of the past sexual behavior of an alleged victim of such rape or assault is not admissible.

(b) Notwithstanding any other provision of law, in a criminal case in which a person is accused of rape or of assault with intent to commit rape, evidence of a victim's past sexual behavior other than reputation or opinion is also not admissible, unless such evidence other than reputation or opinion evidence is —

(1) admitted in accordance with subdivisions (c)(1) and (c)(2) and is constitutionally required to be admitted; or

(2) admitted in accordance with subdivision (c) and is evidence of —

(A) past sexual behavior with persons other than the accused, offered by the accused upon the issue of whether the accused was or was not, with respect to the alleged victim, the source of semen or injury; or

(B) past sexual behavior with the accused and is offered by the accused upon the issue of whether the alleged victim consented to the sexual behavior with respect to which rape or assault is alleged.

(c)(1) If the person accused of committing rape or assault with intent to commit rape intends to offer under subdivision (b) evidence of specific instances of the alleged victim's past sexual behavior, the accused shall make a written motion to offer such evidence not later than fifteen days before the date on which the trial in which such evidence is to be offered is scheduled to begin, except that the court may allow the motion to be made at a later date, including during trial, if the court determines either that the evidence is newly discovered and could not have been obtained earlier through the exercise of due diligence or that the issue to which such evidence relates has newly arisen in the case. Any motion made under this paragraph shall be served on all other parties and on the alleged victim.

(2) The motion described in paragraph (1) shall be accompanied by a written offer of proof. If the court determines that the offer of proof contains evidence described in subdivision (b), the court shall order a hearing in chambers to determine if such evidence is admissible. At such hearing the parties may call witnesses, including the alleged victim, and offer relevant evidence. Notwithstanding subdivision (b) of rule 104, if the relevancy of the evidence which the accused seeks to offer in the trial depends upon the fulfillment of a condition of fact, the court, at the hearing in chambers or at a subsequent hearing in chambers scheduled for such purpose, shall accept evidence on the is-

sue of whether such condition of fact is fulfilled and shall determine such issue.

(3) If the court determines on the basis of the hearing described in paragraph (2) that the evidence which the accused seeks to offer is relevant and that the probative value of such evidence outweighs the danger of unfair prejudice, such evidence shall be admissible in the trial to the extent an order made by the court specifies evidence which may be offered and areas with respect to which the alleged victim may be examined or cross-examined.

(d) For purposes of this rule, the term "past sexual behavior" means sexual behavior other than the sexual behavior with respect to which rape or assault with intent to commit rape is alleged.

ARTICLE V.   PRIVILEGES

Rule 501.   General rule

Except as otherwise required by the Constitution of the United States or provided by Act of Congress or in rules prescribed by the Supreme Court pursuant to statutory authority, the privilege of a witness, person, government, State, or political subdivision thereof shall be governed by the principles of the common law as they may be interpreted by the courts of the United States in the light of reason and experience. However, in civil actions and proceedings, with respect to an element of a claim or defense as to which State law supplies the rule of decision, the privilege of a witness, person, government, State, or political subdivision thereof shall be determined in accordance with State law.

ARTICLE VI.   WITNESSES

Rule 601.   General rule of competency

Every person is competent to be a witness except as otherwise provided in these rules. However, in civil actions and proceedings, with respect to an element of a claim or defense as to which State law supplies the rule of decision, the competency of a witness shall be determined in accordance with State law.

Rule 602.   Lack of personal knowledge

A witness may not testify to a matter unless evidence is introduced sufficient to support a finding that the witness has personal knowledge of the matter. Evidence to prove personal knowledge may, but need not, consist of the witness' own testimony. This rule is subject to the provisions of rule 703, relating to opinion testimony by expert witnesses.

Rule 603.   Oath or affirmation

Before testifying, every witness shall be required to declare that the witness will testify truthfully, by oath or affirmation administered in a form calculated to awaken the witness' conscience and impress the witness' mind with the duty to do so.

Rule 604.   Interpreters

An interpreter is subject to the provisions of these rules relating to qualification as an expert and the administration of an oath or affirmation to make a true translation.

Rule 605.   Competency of judge as witness

The judge presiding at the trial may not testify in that trial as a witness. No objection need be made in order to preserve the point.

Rule 606.   Competency of juror as witness

(a) At the trial.   A member of the jury may not testify as a witness before that jury in the trial of the case in which the juror is sitting. If the juror is called so to testify, the opposing party shall be afforded an opportunity to object out of the presence of the jury.

(b) Inquiry into validity of verdict or indictment.   Upon an inquiry into the validity of a verdict or indictment, a juror may not testify as to any matter or statement occurring during the course of the jury's deliberations or to the effect of anything upon that or any other juror's mind or emotions as influencing the juror to assent to or dissent from the verdict or indictment or concerning the juror's mental processes in connection therewith, except that a juror may testify on the question whether extraneous prejudicial information was improperly brought to the jury's attention or whether any outside influence was improperly brought to bear upon any juror. Nor may a juror's affidavit or evidence of any statement by the juror concerning a matter about which the juror would be precluded from testifying be received for these purposes.

Rule 607.   Who may impeach

The credibility of a witness may be attacked by any party, including the party calling the witness.

Rule 608.   Evidence of character and conduct of
witness

(a) **Opinion and reputation evidence of character.**   The credibility of a witness may be attacked or supported by evidence in the form of opinion or reputation, but subject to these limitations: (1) the evidence may refer only to character for truthfulness or untruthfulness, and (2) evidence of truthful character is admissible only after the character of the witness for truthfulness has been attacked by opinion or reputation evidence or otherwise.

(b) **Specific instances of conduct.**   Specific instances of the conduct of a witness, for the purpose of attacking or supporting the witness' credibility, other than conviction of crime as provided in rule 609, may not be proved by extrinsic evidence. They may, however, in the discretion of the court, if probative of truthfulness or untruthfulness, be inquired into on cross-examination of the witness (1) concerning the witness' character for truthfulness or untruthfulness, or (2) concerning the character for truthfulness or untruthfulness of another witness as to which character the witness being cross-examined has testified.

The giving of testimony, whether by an accused or by any other witness, does not operate as a waiver of the accused's or the witness' privilege against self-incrimination when examined with respect to matters which relate only to credibility.

Rule 609.   Impeachment by evidence of conviction of
crime

(a) **General rule.**   For the purpose of attacking the credibility of a witness, evidence that the witness has been convicted of a crime shall be admitted if elicited from the witness or established by public record during cross-examination but only if the crime (1) was punishable by death or imprisonment in excess of one year under the law under which the witness was convicted, and the court determines that the probative value of admitting this evidence outweighs its prejudicial effect to the defendant, or (2) involved dishonesty or false statement, regardless of the punishment.

(b) **Time limit.**   Evidence of a conviction under this rule is not admissible if a period of more than ten years has elapsed since the date of the conviction or of the release of the witness from the confinement imposed for that conviction, whichever is the later date, unless the court determines, in the interests of justice, that the probative value of the conviction supported by specific facts and circumstances substantially outweighs its prejudicial effect. However, evidence of a conviction more than 10 years old as calculated herein, is not admissible unless the proponent gives to the adverse party sufficient advance written notice of intent to use such evidence to provide the adverse party with a fair opportunity to contest the use of such evidence.

(c) Effect of pardon, annulment, or certificate of rehabilitation. Evidence of a conviction is not admissible under this rule if (1) the conviction has been the subject of a pardon, annulment, certificate of rehabilitation, or other equivalent procedure based on a finding of the rehabilitation of the person convicted, and that person has not been convicted of a subsequent crime which was punishable by death or imprisonment in excess of one year, or (2) the conviction has been the subject of a pardon, annulment, or other equivalent procedure based on a finding of innocence.

(d) Juvenile adjudications. Evidence of juvenile adjudications is generally not admissible under this rule. The court may, however, in a criminal case allow evidence of a juvenile adjudication of a witness other than the accused if conviction of the offense would be admissible to attack the credibility of an adult and the court is satisfied that admission in evidence is necessary for a fair determination of the issue of guilt or innocence.

(e) Pendency of appeal. The pendency of an appeal therefrom does not render evidence of a conviction inadmissible. Evidence of the pendency of an appeal is admissible.

Rule 610.   Religious beliefs or opinions

Evidence of the beliefs or opinions of a witness on matters of religion is not admissible for the purpose of showing that by reason of their nature the witness' credibility is impaired or enhanced.

Rule 611.   Mode and order of interrogation and presentation

(a) Control by court. The court shall exercise reasonable control over the mode and order of interrogating witnesses and presenting evidence so as to (1) make the interrogation and presentation effective for the ascertainment of the truth, (2) avoid needless consumption of time, and (3) protect witnesses from harassment or undue embarrassment.

(b) Scope of cross-examination. Cross-examination should be limited to the subject matter of the direct examination and matters affecting the credibility of the witness. The court may, in the exercise of discretion, permit inquiry into additional matters as if on direct examination.

(c) Leading questions. Leading questions should not be used on the direct examination of a witness except as may be necessary to develop the witness' testimony. Ordinarily leading questions should be permitted on cross-examination. When a party calls a hostile witness, an adverse party, or a witness identified with an adverse party, interrogation may be by leading questions.

Rule 612. Writing used to refresh memory

Except as otherwise provided in criminal proceedings by section 3500 of title 18, United States Code, if a witness uses a writing to refresh memory for the purpose of testifying, either —
    (1) while testifying, or
    (2) before testifying, if the court in its discretion determines it is necessary in the interests of justice,
an adverse party is entitled to have the writing produced at the hearing, to inspect it, to cross-examine the witness thereon, and to introduce in evidence those portions which relate to the testimony of the witness. If it is claimed that the writing contains matters not related to the subject matter of the testimony the court shall examine the writing in camera, excise any portions not so related, and order delivery of the remainder to the party entitled thereto. Any portion withheld over objections shall be preserved and made available to the appellate court in the event of an appeal. If a writing is not produced or delivered pursuant to order under this rule, the court shall make any order justice requires, except that in criminal cases when the prosecution elects not to comply, the order shall be one striking the testimony or, if the court in its discretion determines that the interests of justice so require, declaring a mistrial.

Rule 613. Prior statements of witnesses

(a) **Examining witness concerning prior statement.** In examining a witness concerning a prior statement made by the witness, whether written or not, the statement need not be shown nor its contents disclosed to the witness at that time, but on request the same shall be shown or disclosed to opposing counsel.

(b) **Extrinsic evidence of prior inconsistent statement of witness.** Extrinsic evidence of a prior inconsistent statement by a witness is not admissible unless the witness is afforded an opportunity to explain or deny the same and the opposite party is afforded an opportunity to interrogate the witness thereon, or the interests of justice otherwise require. This provision does not apply to admissions of a party-opponent as defined in rule 801(d)(2).

Rule 614. Calling and interrogation of witnesses by court

(a) **Calling by court.** The court may, on its own motion or at the suggestion of a party, call witnesses, and all parties are entitled to cross-examine witnesses thus called.

(b) **Interrogation by court.** The court may interrogate witnesses, whether called by itself or by a party.

(c) **Objections.** Objections to the calling of witnesses by the court or to interrogation by it may be made at the time or at the next available opportunity when the jury is not present.

Rule 615.   Exclusion of witnesses

At the request of a party the court shall order witnesses excluded so that they cannot hear the testimony of other witnesses, and it may make the order of its own motion. This rule does not authorize exclusion of (1) a party who is a natural person, or (2) an officer or employee of a party which is not a natural person designated as its representative by its attorney, or (3) a person whose presence is shown by a party to be essential to the presentation of the party's cause.

ARTICLE VII.   OPINIONS AND EXPERT TESTIMONY

Rule 701.   Opinion testimony by lay witnesses

If the witness is not testifying as an expert, the witness' testimony in the form of opinions or inferences is limited to those opinions or inferences which are (a) rationally based on the perception of the witness and (b) helpful to a clear understanding of the witness' testimony or the determination of a fact in issue.

Rule 702.   Testimony by experts

If scientific, technical, or other specialized knowledge will assist the trier of fact to understand the evidence or to determine a fact in issue, a witness qualified as an expert by knowledge, skill, experience, training, or education, may testify thereto in the form of an opinion or otherwise.

Rule 703.   Bases of opinion testimony by experts

The facts or data in the particular case upon which an expert bases an opinion or inference may be those perceived by or made known to the expert at or before the hearing. If of a type reasonably relied upon by experts in the particular field in forming opinions or inferences upon the subject, the facts or data need not be admissible in evidence.

Rule 704.   Opinion on ultimate issue

(a) Except as provided in subdivision (b), testimony in the form of an opinion or inference otherwise admissible is not objectionable because it embraces an ultimate issue to be decided by the trier of fact.

(b) No expert witness testifying with respect to the mental state or condition of a defendant in a criminal case may state an opinion or inference as to whether the defendant did or did not have the mental state or condition constituting an element of the crime charged or of a defense thereto. Such ultimate issues are matters for the trier of fact alone.

Rule 705.   Disclosure of facts or data underlying expert opinion

The expert may testify in terms of opinion or inference and give reasons therefor without prior disclosure of the underlying facts or data, unless the court requires otherwise. The expert may in any event be required to disclose the underlying facts or data on cross-examination.

Rule 706.   Court appointed experts

(a) Appointment.   The court may on its own motion or on the motion of any party enter an order to show cause why expert witnesses should not be appointed, and may request the parties to submit nominations. The court may appoint any expert witnesses agreed upon by the parties, and may appoint expert witnesses of its own selection. An expert witness shall not be appointed by the court unless the witness consents to act. A witness so appointed shall be informed of the witness' duties by the court in writing, a copy of which shall be filed with the clerk, or at a conference in which the parties shall have opportunity to participate. A witness so appointed shall advise the parties of the witness' findings, if any; the witness' deposition may be taken by any party; and the witness may be called to testify by the court or any party. The witness shall be subject to cross-examination by each party, including a party calling the witness.

(b) Compensation.   Expert witnesses so appointed are entitled to reasonable compensation in whatever sum the court may allow. The compensation thus fixed is payable from funds which may be provided by law in criminal cases and civil actions and proceedings involving just compensation under the fifth amendment. In other civil actions and proceedings the compensation shall be paid by the parties in such proportion and at such time as the court directs, and thereafter charged in like manner as other costs.

(c) Disclosure of appointment.   In the exercise of its discretion, the court may authorize disclosure to the jury of the fact that the court appointed the expert witness.

(d) Parties' experts of own selection.   Nothing in this rule limits the parties in calling expert witnesses of their own selection.

ARTICLE VIII.   HEARSAY

Rule 801.   Definitions

The following definitions apply under this article:

(a) Statement.   A "statement" is (1) an oral or written assertion or (2) nonverbal conduct of a person, if it is intended by the person as an assertion.

(b) Declarant.   A "declarant" is a person who makes a statement.

(c) Hearsay. "Hearsay" is a statement, other than one made by the declarant while testifying at the trial or hearing, offered in evidence to prove the truth of the matter asserted.

(d) Statements which are not hearsay. A statement is not hearsay if —

(1) Prior statement by witness. The declarant testifies at the trial or hearing and is subject to cross-examination concerning the statement, and the statement is (A) inconsistent with the declarant's testimony, and was given under oath subject to the penalty of perjury at a trial, hearing, or other proceeding, or in a deposition, or (B) consistent with the declarant's testimony and is offered to rebut an express or implied charge against the declarant of recent fabrication or improper influence or motive, or (C) one of identification of a person after perceiving the person; or

(2) Admission by party-opponent. The statement is offered against a party and is (A) the party's own statement, in either an individual or a representative capacity, or (B) a statement of which the party has manifested an adoption or belief in its truth, or (C) a statement by a person authorized by the party to make a statement concerning the subject, or (D) a statement by the party's agent or servant concerning a matter within the scope of the agency or employment, made during the existence of the relationship, or (E) a statement by a coconspirator of a party during the course and in furtherance of the conspiracy.

Rule 802. Hearsay rule

Hearsay is not admissible except as provided by these rules or by other rules prescribed by the Supreme Court pursuant to statutory authority or by Act of Congress.

Rule 803. Hearsay exceptions; availability of declarant immaterial

The following are not excluded by the hearsay rule, even though the declarant is available as a witness:

(1) Present sense impression. A statement describing or explaining an event or condition made while the declarant was perceiving the event or condition, or immediately thereafter.

(2) Excited utterance. A statement relating to a startling event or condition made while the declarant was under the stress of excitement caused by the event or condition.

(3) Then existing mental, emotional, or physical condition. A statement of the declarant's then existing state of mind, emotion, sensation, or physical condition (such as intent, plan, motive, design, mental feeling, pain, and bodily health), but not including a statement of memory or belief to prove the fact remembered or believed unless it relates to the execution, revocation, identification, or terms of declarant's will.

(4) Statements for purposes of medical diagnosis or treatment. Statements made for purposes of medical diagnosis or treatment and describing medical history, or past or present symptoms, pain, or sensations, or the inception or general character of the cause or external source thereof insofar as reasonably pertinent to diagnosis or treatment.

(5) Recorded recollection. A memorandum or record concerning a matter about which a witness once had knowledge but now has insufficient recollection to enable the witness to testify fully and accurately, shown to have been made or adopted by the witness when the matter was fresh in the witness' memory and to reflect that knowledge correctly. If admitted, the memorandum or record may be read into evidence but may not itself be received as an exhibit unless offered by an adverse party.

(6) Records of regularly conducted activity. A memorandum, report, record, or data compilation, in any form, of acts, events, conditions, opinions, or diagnoses, made at or near the time by, or from information transmitted by, a person with knowledge, if kept in the course of a regularly conducted business activity, and if it was the regular practice of that business activity to make the memorandum, report, record, or data compilation, all as shown by the testimony of the custodian or other qualified witness, unless the source of information or the method or circumstances of preparation indicate lack of trustworthiness. The term "business" as used in this paragraph includes business, institution, association, profession, occupation, and calling of every kind, whether or not conducted for profit.

(7) Absence of entry in records kept in accordance with the provisions of paragraph (6). Evidence that a matter is not included in the memoranda reports, records, or data compilations, in any form, kept in accordance with the provisions of paragraph (6), to prove the nonoccurrence or nonexistence of the matter, if the matter was of a kind of which a memorandum, report, record, or data compilation was regularly made and preserved, unless the sources of information or other circumstances indicate lack of trustworthiness.

(8) Public records and reports. Records, reports, statements, or data compilations, in any form, of public offices or agencies, setting forth (A) the activities of the office or agency, or (B) matters observed pursuant to duty imposed by law as to which matters there was a duty to report, excluding, however, in criminal cases matters observed by police officers and other law enforcement personnel, or (C) in civil actions and proceedings and against the Government in criminal cases, factual findings resulting from an investigation made pursuant to authority granted by law, unless the sources of information or other circumstances indicate lack of trustworthiness.

(9) Records of vital statistics. Records or data compilations, in any form, of births, fetal deaths, deaths, or marriages, if the report thereof was made to a public office pursuant to requirements of law.

(10) Absence of public record or entry. To prove the absence of a record, report, statement, or data compilation, in any form, or the nonoccurrence or nonexistence of a matter of which a record, report, statement, or data compilation, in any form, was regularly made and preserved by a public office or agency, evidence in the form of a certification in accordance with rule 902, or testimony, that diligent search failed to disclose the record, report, statement, or data compilation, or entry.

(11) Records of religious organizations. Statements of births, marriages, divorces, deaths, legitimacy, ancestry, relationship by blood or marriage, or other similar facts of personal or family history, contained in a regularly kept record of a religious organization.

(12) Marriage, baptismal, and similar certificates. Statements of fact contained in a certificate that the maker performed a marriage or other ceremony or administered a sacrament, made by a clergyman, public official, or other person authorized by the rules or practices of a religious organization or by law to perform the act certified, and purporting to have been issued at the time of the act or within a reasonable time thereafter.

(13) Family records. Statements of fact concerning personal or family history contained in family Bibles, genealogies, charts, engravings on rings, inscriptions on family portraits, engravings on urns, crypts, or tombstones, or the like.

(14) Records of documents affecting an interest in property. The record of a document purporting to establish or affect an interest in property, as proof of the content of the original recorded document and its execution and delivery by each person by whom it purports to have been executed, if the record is a record of a public office and an applicable statute authorizes the recording of documents of that kind in that office.

(15) Statements in documents affecting an interest in property. A statement contained in a document purporting to establish or affect an interest in property if the matter stated was relevant to the purpose of the document, unless dealings with the property since the document was made have been inconsistent with the truth of the statement or the purport of the document.

(16) Statements in ancient documents. Statements in a document in existence twenty years or more the authenticity of which is established.

(17) Market reports, commercial publications. Market quotations, tabulations, lists, directories, or other published compilations, generally used and relied upon by the public or by persons in particular occupations.

(18) Learned treatises. To the extent called to the attention of an expert witness upon cross-examination or relied upon by the expert witness in direct examination, statements contained in published treatises, periodicals, or pamphlets on a subject of history, medicine, or other science or art, established as a reliable authority by the testimony or admission of the witness or by other expert testimony or by judicial notice. If admitted, the statements may be read into evidence but may not be received as exhibits.

(19) Reputation concerning personal or family history. Reputation among members of a person's family by blood, adoption, or marriage, or among a person's associates, or in the community, concerning a person's birth, adoption, marriage, divorce, death, legitimacy, relationship by blood, adoption, or marriage, ancestry, or other similar fact of his personal or family history.

(20) Reputation concerning boundaries or general history. Reputation in a community, arising before the controversy, as to boundaries of or customs affecting lands in the community, and reputation as to events of general history important to the community or State or nation in which located.

(21) Reputation as to character. Reputation of a person's character among associates or in the community.

(22) Judgment of previous conviction. Evidence of a final judgment, entered after a trial or upon a plea of guilty (but not upon a plea of nolo contendere), adjudging a person guilty of a crime punishable by death or imprisonment in excess of one year, to prove any fact essential to sustain the judgment, but not including, when offered by the Government in a criminal prosecution for purposes other than impeachment, judgments against persons other than the accused. The pendency of an appeal may be shown but does not affect admissibility.

(23) Judgment as to personal, family, or general history, or boundaries. Judgments as proof of matters of personal, family or general history, or boundaries, essential to the judgment, if the same would be provable by evidence of reputation.

(24) Other exceptions. A statement not specifically covered by any of the foregoing exceptions but having equivalent circumstantial guarantees of trustworthiness, if the court determines that (A) the statement is offered as evidence of a material fact; (B) the statement is more probative on the point for which it is offered than any other evidence which the proponent can procure through reasonable efforts; and (C) the general purposes of these rules and the interests of justice will best be served by admission of the statement into evidence. However, a statement may not be admitted under this exception unless the proponent of it makes known to the adverse party sufficiently in advance of the trial or hearing to provide the adverse party with a fair opportunity to prepare to meet it, the proponent's intention to offer the statement and the particulars of it, including the name and address of the declarant.

Rule 804. Hearsay exceptions; declarant unavailable

(a) Definition of unavailability. "Unavailability as a witness" includes situations in which the declarant —

(1) is exempted by ruling of the court on the ground of privilege from testifying concerning the subject matter of the declarant's statement or

(2) persists in refusing to testify concerning the subject matter of the declarant's statement despite an order of the court to do so; or

(3) testifies to a lack of memory of the subject matter of the declarant's statement; or

(4) is unable to be present or to testify at the hearing because of death or then existing physical or mental illness or infirmity; or

(5) is absent from the hearing and the proponent of a statement has been unable to procure the declarant's attendance (or in the case of a hearsay exception under subdivision (b)(2), (3), or (4), the declarant's attendance or testimony) by process or other reasonable means.

A declarant is not unavailable as a witness if exemption, refusal, claim of lack of memory, inability, or absence is due to the procurement or wrongdoing of the proponent of a statement for the purpose of preventing the witness from attending or testifying.

(b) Hearsay exceptions. The following are not excluded by the hearsay rule if the declarant is unavailable as a witness:

(1) Former testimony. Testimony given as a witness at another hearing of the same or a different proceeding, or in a deposition taken in compliance with law in the course of the same or another proceeding, if the party against whom the testimony is now offered, or, in a civil action or proceeding, a predecessor in interest, had an opportunity and similar motive to develop the testimony by direct, cross, or redirect examination.

(2) Statement under belief of impending death. In a prosecution for homicide or in a civil action or proceeding, a statement made by a declarant while believing that the declarant's death was imminent, concering the cause or circumstances of what the declarant believed to be impending death.

(3) Statement against interest. A statement which was at the time of its making so far contrary to the declarant's pecuniary to proprietary interest, or so far tended to subject the declarant to civil or criminal liability, or to render invalid a claim by the declarant against another, that a reasonable person in the declarant's position would not have made the statement unless believing it to be true. A statement tending to expose the declarant to criminal liability and offered to exculpate the accused is not admissible unless corroborating circumstances clearly indicate the trustworthiness of the statement.

(4) Statement of personal or family history. (A) A statement concerning the declarant's own birth, adoption, marriage, divorce, legitimacy, relationship by blood, adoption, or marriage, ancestry, or other similar fact of personal or family history, even though declarant had no means of acquiring personal knowledge of the matter stated; or (B) a statement concerning the foregoing matters, and death also, of another person, if the declarant was related to the other by blood, adoption, or marriage or was so intimately associated with the other's family as to be likely to have accurate information concerning the matter declared.

(5) Other exceptions. A statement not specifically covered by any of the foregoing exceptions but having equivalent circumstantial guarantees of trustworthiness, if the court determines that (A) the statement is offered as evidence of a material fact; (B) the statement is more probative on the point for which it is offered than any other evidence which the proponent can procure through reasonable efforts; and (C) the general purposes of these rules and the interests of justice will best be served by admission of the statement into evidence. However, a statement may not be admitted under this exception unless the proponent of it makes known to the adverse party sufficiently in advance of the trial or hearing to provide the adverse party with a fair opportunity to prepare to meet it, the proponent's intention to offer the statement and the particulars of it, including the name and address of the declarant.

Rule 805. Hearsay within hearsay

Hearsay included within hearsay is not excluded under the hearsay rule if each part of the combined statements conforms with an exception to the hearsay rule provided in these rules.

Rule 806. Attacking and supporting credibility of declarant

When a hearsay statement, or a statement defined in Rule 801(d)(2), (C), (D), or (E), has been admitted in evidence, the credibility of the declarant may be attacked, and if attacked may be supported, by any evidence which would be admissible for those purposes if declarant had testified as a witness. Evidence of a statement or conduct by the declarant at any time, inconsistent with the declarant's hearsay statement, is not subject to any requirement that the declarant may have been afforded an opportunity to deny or explain. If the party against whom a hearsay statement has been admitted calls the declarant as a witness, the party is entitled to examine the declarant on the statement as if under cross-examination.

ARTICLE IX. AUTHENTICATION AND IDENTIFICATION

Rule 901. Requirement of authentication or identification

(a) General provision. The requirement of authentication or identification as a condition precedent to admissibility is satisifed by evidence sufficient to support a finding that the matter in question is what its proponent claims.

(b) Illustrations. By way of illustration only, and not by way of limitation, the following are examples of authentication or identification conforming with the requirements of this rule:

(1) **Testimony of witness with knowledge.** Testimony that a matter is what it is claimed to be.

(2) Nonexpert opinion on handwriting. Nonexpert opinion as to the genuineness of handwriting, based upon familiarity not acquired for purposes of the litigation.

(3) Comparison by trier or expert witness. Comparison by the trier of fact or by expert witnesses with specimens which have been authenticated.

(4) Distinctive characteristics and the like. Appearance, contents, substance, internal patterns, or other distinctive characteristics, taken in conjunction with circumstances.

(5) Voice identification. Identification of a voice, whether heard firsthand or through mechanical or electronic transmission or recording, by opinion based upon hearing the voice at any time under circumstances connecting it with the alleged speaker.

(6) Telephone conversations. Telephone conversations, by evidence that a call was made to the number assigned at the time by the telephone company to a particular person or business, if (A) in the case of a person, circumstances, including self-identification, show the person answering to be the one called, or (B) in the case of a business, the call was made to a place of business and the conversation related to business reasonably transacted over the telephone.

(7) Public records or reports. Evidence that a writing authorized by law to be recorded or filed and in fact recorded or filed in a public office, or a purported public record, report, statement, or data compilation, in any form, is from the public office where items of this nature are kept.

(8) Ancient documents or data compilation. Evidence that a document or data compilation, in any form, (A) is in such condition as to create no suspicion concerning its authenticity, (B) was in a place where it, if authentic, would likely be, and (C) has been in existence 20 years or more at the time it is offered.

(9) Process or system. Evidence describing a process or system used to produce a result and showing that the process or system produces an accurate result.

(10) Methods provided by statute or rule. Any method of authentication or identification provided by Act of Congress or by other rules prescribed by the Supreme Court pursuant to statutory authority.

Rule 902. Self-authentication

Extrinsic evidence of authenticity as a condition precedent to admissibility is not required with respect to the following:

(1) Domestic public documents under seal. A document bearing a seal purporting to be that of the United States, or of any State, district, Commonwealth, territory, or insular possession thereof, or the Panama Canal Zone, or the Trust Territory of the Pacific Islands, or of a political subdivision, department, officer, or agency thereof, and a signature purporting to be an attestation or execution.

(2) Domestic public documents not under seal.   A document purporting to bear the signature in the official capacity of an officer or employee of any entity included in paragraph (1) hereof, having no seal, if a public officer having a seal and having official duties in the district or political subdivision of the officer or employee certifies under seal that the signer has the official capacity and that the signature is genuine.

(3) Foreign public documents.   A document purporting to be executed or attested in an official capacity by a person authorized by the laws of a foreign country to make the execution or attestation, and accompanied by a final certification as to the genuineness of the signature and official position (A) of the executing or attesting person, or (B) of any foreign official whose certificate of genuineness of signature and official position relates to the execution or attestation or is in a chain of certificates of genuineness of signature and official position relating to the execution or attestation. A final certification may be made by a secretary of embassy or legation, consul general, consul, vice consul, or consular agent of the United States, or a diplomatic or consular official of the foreign country assigned or accredited to the United States. If reasonable opportunity has been given to all parties to investigate the authenticity and accuracy of official documents, the court may, for good cause shown, order that they be treated as presumptively authentic without final certification or permit them to be evidenced by an attested summary with or without final certification.

(4) Certified copies of public records.   A copy of an official record or report or entry therein, or of a document authorized by law to be recorded or filed and actually recorded or filed in a public office, including data compilations in any form, certified as correct by the custodian or other person authorized to make the certification, by certificate complying with paragraph (1), (2), or (3) of this rule or complying with any Act of Congress or rule prescribed by the Supreme Court pursuant to statutory authority.

(5) Official publications.   Books, pamphlets, or other publications purporting to be issued by public authority.

(6) Newspapers and periodicals.   Printed materials purporting to be newspapers or periodicals.

(7) Trade inscriptions and the like.   Inscriptions, signs, tags, or labels purporting to have been affixed in the course of business and indicating ownership, control, or origin.

(8) Acknowledged documents.   Documents accompanied by a certificate of acknowledgment executed in the manner provided by law by a notary public or other officer authorized by law to take acknowledgments.

(9) Commercial paper and related documents.   Commercial paper, signatures thereon, and documents relating thereto to the extent provided by general commercial law.

(10) Presumptions under Acts of Congress.   Any signature, document, or other matter declared by Act of Congress to be presumptively or prima facie genuine or authentic.

Rule 903. Subscribing Witness' Testimony
Unnecessary

The testimony of a subscribing witness is not necessary to authenticate a writing unless required by the laws of the jurisdiction whose laws govern the validity of the writing.

ARTICLE X. CONTENTS OF WRITINGS, RECORDINGS, AND PHOTOGRAPHS

Rule 1001. Definitions

For purposes of this article the following definitions are applicable:

(1) Writings and recordings. "Writings" and "recordings" consist of letters, words, or numbers, or their equivalent, set down by handwriting, typewriting, printing, photostating, photographing, magnetic impulse, mechanical or electronic recording, or other form of data compilation.

(2) Photographs. "Photographs" include still photographs, X-ray films, video tapes, and motion pictures.

(3) Original. An "original" of a writing or recording is the writing or recording itself or any counterpart intended to have the same effect by a person executing or issuing it. An "original" of a photograph includes the negative or any print therefrom. If data are stored in a computer or similar device, any printout or other output readable by sight, shown to reflect the data accurately, is an "original".

(4) Duplicate. A "duplicate" is a counterpart produced by the same impression as the original, or from the same matrix, or by means of photography, including enlargements and miniatures, or by mechanical or electronic re-recording, or by chemical reproduction, or by other equivalent techniques which accurately reproduce the original.

Rule 1002. Requirement of original

To prove the content of a writing, recording, or photograph, the original writing, recording, or photograph is required, except as otherwise provided in these rules or by Act of Congress.

Rule 1003. Admissibility of duplicates

A duplicate is admissible to the same extent as an original unless (1) a genuine question is raised as to the authenticity of the original or (2) in the circumstances it would be unfair to admit the duplicate in lieu of the original.

Rule 1004. Admissibility of other evidence of contents

The original is not required, and other evidence of the contents of a writing, recording, or photograph is admissible if —
   (1) Originals lost or destroyed.   All originals are lost or have been destroyed, unless the proponent lost or destroyed them in bad faith; or
   (2) Original not obtainable.   No original can be obtained by any available judicial process or procedure; or
   (3) Original in possession of opponent.   At a time when an original was under the control of the party against whom offered, that party was put on notice, by the pleadings or otherwise, that the contents would be a subject of proof at the hearing, and that party does not produce the original at the hearing; or
   (4) Collateral matters.   The writing, recording, or photograph is not closely related to a controlling issue.

Rule 1005. Public records

The contents of an official record, or of a document authorized to be recorded or filed and actually recorded or filed, including data compilations in any form, if otherwise admissible, may be proved by copy, certified as correct in accordance with rule 902 or testified to be correct by a witness who has compared it with the original. If a copy which complies with the foregoing cannot be obtained by the exercise of reasonable diligence, then other evidence of the contents may be given.

Rule 1006. Summaries

The contents of voluminous writings, recordings, or photographs which cannot conveniently be examined in court may be presented in the form of a chart, summary, or calculation. The originals, or duplicates, shall be made available for examination or copying, or both, by other parties at reasonable time and place. The court may order that they be produced in court.

Rule 1007. Testimony or written admission of party

Contents of writings, recordings, or photographs may be proved by the testimony or deposition of the party against whom offered or by that party's written admission, without accounting for the nonproduction of the original.

Rule 1008. Functions of court and jury

When the admissibility of other evidence of contents of writings, recordings, or photographs under these rules depends upon the fulfillment of a condition of fact, the question whether the condition has been fulfilled is ordinarily for the court to determine in accordance with the provisions of rule 104. However when an issue is raised (a) whether the asserted writing ever existed, or (b) whether another writing, recording, or photograph produced at the trial is the original, or (c) whether other evidence of contents correctly reflects the contents, the issue is for the trier of fact to determine as in the case of other issues of fact.

ARTICLE XI. MISCELLANEOUS RULES

Rule 1101. Applicability of rules

(a) **Courts and magistrates.** These rules apply to the United States district courts, the District Court of Guam, the District Court of the Virgin Islands, the District Court for the District of the Canal Zone, the United States courts of appeals, the United States Claims Court, and to United States magistrates, in the actions, cases, and proceedings and to the extent hereinafter set forth. The terms "judge" and "court" in these rules include United States magistrates.

(b) **Proceedings generally.** These rules apply generally to civil actions and proceedings, including admiralty and maritime cases, to criminal cases and proceedings, to contempt proceedings except those in which the court may act summarily, and to proceedings and cases under title 11, United States Code.

(c) **Rule of privilege.** The rule with respect to privileges applies at all stages of all actions, cases, and proceedings.

(d) **Rules inapplicable.** The rules (other than with respect to privilege) do not apply in the following situations:

(1) **Preliminary questions of fact.** The determination of questions of fact preliminary to admissibility of evidence when the issue is to be determined by the court under rule 104.

(2) **Grand jury.** Proceedings before grand juries.

(3) **Miscellaneous proceedings.** Proceedings for extradition or rendition; preliminary examinations in criminal cases; sentencing, or granting or revoking probation; issuance of warrants for arrest, criminal summonses, and search warrants; and proceedings with respect to release on bail or otherwise.

(e) **Rules applicable in part.** In the following proceedings these rules apply to the extent that matters of evidence are not provided for in the statutes which govern procedure therein or in other rules prescribed by the Supreme Court pursuant to statutory authority: the trial of minor and petty offenses by United States magistrates; review of agency actions when the facts are subject to trial de novo under section 706(2)(F) of title 5, United States Code; review of orders of the Secretary of Agriculture under section 2 of the Act entitled "An Act to authorize association of producers of agricultural products" approved February 18, 1922 (7 U.S.C. 292), and under sections 6 and 7(c) of the Perishable Agricultural Commodities Act, 1930 (7 U.S.C. 499f, 499g(c)); naturalization and revocation of naturalization under sections 310-318 of the Immigration and Nationality Act (8 U.S.C. 1421-1429); prize proceedings in admiralty under sections 7651-7681 of title 10, United States Code; review of orders of the Secretary of the Interior under section 2 of the Act entitled "An Act authorizing associations of producers of aquatic products" approved June 25, 1934 (15 U.S.C. 522); review of orders of petroleum control boards under section 5 of the Act entitled "An Act to regulate interstate and foreign commerce in petroleum and its products produced by prohibiting the shipment in such commerce of petroleum and its products produced in violation of State law, and for other purposes," approved February 22, 1935 (15 U.S.C. 715d); actions for fines, penalties, or forfeitures under part V of title IV of the Tariff Act of 1930 (19 U.S.C. 1581-1624), or under the Anti-Smuggling Act (19 U.S.C. 1701-1711); criminal libel for condemnation, exclusion of imports, or other proceedings under the Federal Food, Drug, and Cosmetic Act (21 U.S.C. 301-392); disputes between seamen under sections 4079, 4080, and 4081 of the Revised Statutes (22 U.S.C. 256-258); habeas corpus under sections 2241-2254 of title 28, United States Code; motions to vacate, set aside or correct sentence under section 2255 of title 28, United States Code; actions for penalties for refusal to transport destitute seamen under section 4578 of the Revised Statutes (46 U.S.C. 679); actions against the United States under the Act entitled "An Act authorizing suits against the United States in admiralty for damage caused by and salvage service rendered to public vessels belonging to the United States, and for other purposes," approved March 3, 1925 (46 U.S.C. 781-790), as implemented by section 7730 of title 10, United States Code.

Rule 1102. Amendments

Amendments to the Federal Rules of Evidence may be made as provided in section 2076 of title 28 of the United States Code.

Rule 1103. Title

These rules may be known and cited as the Federal Rules of Evidence.

Sec. 2.(a) Title 28 of the United States Code is amended —

(1) by inserting immediately after section 2075 the following new section:

"§2076. Rules of evidence

"The Supreme Court of the United States shall have the power to prescribe amendments to the Federal Rules of Evidence. Such amendments shall not take effect until they have been reported to Congress by the Chief Justice at or after the beginning of a regular session of Congress but not later than the first day of May, and until the expiration of one hundred and eighty days after they have been so reported; but if either House of Congress within that time shall by resolution disapprove any amendment so reported it shall not take effect. The effective date of any amendment so reported may be deferred by either House of Congress to a later date or until approved by Act of Congress. Any rule whether proposed or in force may be amended by Act of Congress. Any provision of law in force at the expiration of such time and in conflict with any such amendment not disapproved shall be of no further force or effect after such amendment has taken effect. Any such amendment creating, abolishing, or modifying a privilege shall have no force or effect unless it shall be approved by Act of Congress"; and

(2) by adding at the end of the table of sections of chapter 131 the following new item:

"2076. Rules of evidence."

(b) Section 1732 of title 28 of the United States Code is amended by striking out subsection (a), and by striking out "(b)".

(c) Section 1733 of title 28 of the United States Code is amended by adding at the end thereof the following new subsection:

"(c) This section does not apply to cases, actions, and proceedings to which the Federal Rules of Evidence apply."

Sec. 3. The Congress expressly approves the amendments to the Federal Rules of Civil Procedure, and the amendments to the Federal Rules of Criminal Procedure, which are embraced by the orders entered by the Supreme Court of the United States on November 20, 1972, and December 18, 1972, and such amendments shall take effect on the one hundred and eightieth day beginning after the date of the enactment of this Act.

Approved January 2, 1975.

INDEX